Communications in Computer and Information Science 1139

Commenced Publication in 2007
Founding and Former Series Editors:
Phoebe Chen, Alfredo Cuzzocrea, Xiaoyong Du, Orhun Kara, Ting Liu,
Krishna M. Sivalingam, Dominik Ślęzak, Takashi Washio, Xiaokang Yang,
and Junsong Yuan

Siddharth Swarup Rautaray · Gerald Eichler ·
Christian Erfurth · Günter Fahrnberger (Eds.)

Innovations for Community Services

20th International Conference, I4CS 2020
Bhubaneswar, India, January 12–14, 2020
Proceedings

 Springer

Editors
Siddharth Swarup Rautaray (iD)
Kalinga Institute of Industrial Technology
Bhubaneswar, India

Christian Erfurth (iD)
University of Applied Sciences Jena
Jena, Germany

Gerald Eichler (iD)
Deutsche Telekom Technology &
Innovation
Darmstadt, Germany

Günter Fahrnberger (iD)
University of Hagen
Hagen, Germany

ISSN 1865-0929   ISSN 1865-0937 (electronic)
Communications in Computer and Information Science
ISBN 978-3-030-37483-9   ISBN 978-3-030-37484-6 (eBook)
https://doi.org/10.1007/978-3-030-37484-6

This Springer imprint is published by the registered company Springer Nature Switzerland AG
The registered company address is: Gewerbestrasse 11, 6330 Cham, Switzerland

Foreword

The International Conference on Innovations for Community Services (I4CS) went eastward, and for the first time to the subcontinent of India, to celebrate its 20th edition in 2020. As an exception, it took place in January rather than in June due to the more convenient climate conditions. Furthermore, an overlap with the 16th International Conference on Distributed Computing and Internet Technology (ICDCIT 2020) was contemplated to allow a fruitful exchange between participants on a joint Sunday excursion day.

In June 2001, Herwig Unger and Thomas Böhme at the Technical University of Ilmenau, Germany, founded the Workshop on Innovative Internet Community Systems (IICS). It continued its success story under its revised name I4CS since 2014. IICS/I2CS published its first proceedings in Springer's *Lecture Notes in Computer Science* series (LNCS) until 2005, followed by Gesellschaft für Informatik (GI), and Verein Deutscher Ingenieure (VDI). I4CS had commenced with the Institute of Electrical and Electronics Engineers (IEEE) before it switched back to Springer's *Communications in Computer and Information Science* (CCIS) in 2016 and created a permanent partnership in 2018. The combination of printed proceedings and the SpringerLink online edition generates a high interest of external readers.

The selection of conference location, alternating foreign and German places, reflects the conference concept: our members of the Program Committee (PC) can offer suitable locations. For 2020, the Steering Committee had the honor to hand over the organization responsibility to Siddharth Swarup Rautaray and, therefore, to determine the city of Bhubaneswar in the state Odisha as the venue. The Kalinga Institute of Industrial Technology (KIIT) perfectly filled the current year's motto: "Technology Unites Cultures."

We are proud to have reached the envisaged number of scientific presentations, combined with invited talks, and a great social conference program to strengthen the cultural community spirit. The proceedings of I4CS 2020 comprise 5 sessions that cover the selection of 16 full papers out of 46 submissions, received from authors of 8 countries, and 2 invited talks. Interdisciplinary thinking is a key success factor for any community. Hence, I4CS 2020 covered the established plurality of scientific, academic, and industrial topics, bundled into three key areas: Technology, Applications, and Socialization.

Technology: Distributed Architectures and Frameworks

- Data architectures and models for community services
- Innovation, rating, and social system's management
- 5G technologies and ad-hoc mobile networks
- Search, information retrieval, and artificial intelligence
- Common data models and big data analytics

Applications: Communities on the Move

- Social networks, news, and open collaboration
- Block chain for business and social life
- Recommender solutions and context awareness
- Augmented reality, robotics, and location-based gaming
- Intelligent transportation, logistics, and connected cars

Socialization: Ambient Work and Living

- eHealth challenges and ambient assisted living
- Smart energy and home control
- Business models and municipal infrastructure
- Digitalization, IoT, and cyber physical systems
- Security, identity, and GDPR privacy protection

Many thanks to the 26 members of the current PC, representing 13 countries worldwide, for their 151 worthwhile reviews, especially to its chair Christian Erfurth and, secondly, to the publication chair Günter Fahrnberger, who challenges a very successful cooperation with the Springer publishing board.

Following the rule, the 21st I4CS will take place in Germany in June 2021. The location has not yet been determined by the Steering Committee. Please check the permanent conference URL regularly http://www.i4cs-conference.org/ for more details! Proposals on emerging topics as well as applications of prospective PC members and potential conference hosts are kindly welcome to request@i4cs-conference.org.

Best regards on behalf of the entire Steering Committee and the Editors' Board.

January 2020   Gerald Eichler

Preface

The 20th International Conference on Innovations for Community Services (I4CS 2020), took place in Bhubaneswar, India, during January 12–14, 2020. It was hosted by the Kalinga Institute of Industrial Technology (KIIT) Deemed to be University.

The I4CS conference series focuses on the emergence of web technologies and rich mobile devices. ICT support for communities is possible on the next quality level. Moreover, different types of applications are using the Internet as a large distributed system. So mobile users and pervasive systems pose new technological and organizational challenges. Trying to achieve this, we challenge new research questions in a wide range of connected fields. In search of innovative solutions, multi-disciplinary collaboration among researchers and industry partners is essential. Hence, the goal of this conference is to bring researchers, experts, and practitioners together from various areas related to novel Internet Community Services.

I4CS 2020 received a total of 46 submissions. Each submission was reviewed by at least three Program Committee members. The committee decided to accept 16 full papers. This volume also includes the two invited talks. Papers were accepted on the basis of technical merit, presentation, and relevance to the conference. I4CS 2020 was enriched by the lectures and insights given by the following two distinguished invited speakers: Wolfgang Halang from the University of Hagen, North Rhine-Westphalia, Germany, and Gerald Eichler from Deutsche Telekom Technology & Innovation Darmstadt, Hesse, Germany. We thank the invited speakers for sharing the enthusiasm for research and accepting our invitation to share their expertise as well as contributing papers for inclusion in the proceedings. I4CS has been able to maintain standards in terms of the quality of papers due to the contribution made by many stakeholders.

We are thankful to the program chair Christian Erfurth, the University of Applied Sciences Jena, Thuringia, Germany, and to the publication chair Günter Fahrnberger, the University of Hagen, North Rhine-Westphalia, Germany, for their guidance and valuable inputs. We are grateful to Achyuta Samanta (Founder of KIIT and KISS) for his support for the I4CS conference. We are thankful to the higher authorities of KIIT, specially Hrushikesha Mohanty, Vice-Chancellor, Sasmita Samanta, Pro-Vice-Chancellor, Jnyana Ranjan Mohanty, Registrar, Samaresh Mishra, Director, and D. N. Dwivedy, Mentor, for providing the infrastructure and resources to organize the conference.

Thanks are due to the Advisory Committee members for their guidance related to the conference. We would also like to thank all the Program Committee chairs of previous editions of the conference for setting a benchmark for the conference. We acknowledge the contribution of EasyChair in enabling an efficient and effective way in the management of paper submissions, reviews, and preparation of proceedings. Finally, we thank all the authors and participants for their enthusiastic support. We sincerely hope that you find the book to be of value in the pursuit of academic and professional excellence.

January 2020   Siddharth Swarup Rautaray

Organization

Program Committee

Biswaranjan Acharya	Kalinga Institute of Industrial Technology Bhubaneswar, India
Amr Azzam	Cairo University, Egypt
Gilbert Babin	HEC Montréal, Canada
Gerald Eichler	Deutsche Telekom Technology & Innovation Darmstadt, Germany
Christian Erfurth	University of Applied Sciences Jena, Germany
Günter Fahrnberger	University of Hagen, Germany
Sapna Gopinathan	Coimbatore Institute of Technology, India
Michal Hodoň	University of Žilina, Slovakia
Kathrin Kirchner	Technical University of Denmark Lyngby, Denmark
Peter Kropf	University of Neuchâtel, Switzerland
Ulrike Lechner	Bundeswehr University Munich, Germany
Andreas Lommatzsch	Technical University of Berlin, Germany
Karl-Heinz Lüke	Ostfalia University of Applied Sciences Wolfsburg, Germany
Hrushikesha Mohanty	Kalinga Institute of Industrial Technology Bhubaneswar, India
Raja Natarajan	Tata Institute of Fundamental Research Mumbai, India
Deveeshree Nayak	University of Washington Tacoma, USA
Dana Petcu	West University of Timisoara, Romania
Frank Phillipson	TNO The Hague, The Netherlands
Srinivan Ramaswamy	Asea Brown Boveri Columbus, USA
Siddharth Rautaray	Kalinga Institute of Industrial Technology Bhubaneswar, India
Jörg Roth	Nuremberg Institute of Technology, Germany
Amardeo Sarma	NEC Laboratories Europe Heidelberg, Germany
Volkmar Schau	Friedrich Schiller University Jena, Germany
Pranav Kumar Singh	Indian Institute of Technology Guwahati and Central Institute of Technology Kokrajhar, India
Julian Szymánski	Gdansk University of Technology, Poland
Leendert W. M. Wienhofen	City of Trondheim, Norway

Additional Reviewer

Priya, Mohana

Contents

Invited Papers

The Telecommunication Data Cockpit – Full Control for the Household Community

Gerald Eichler[1]([✉]) [ID], Claudia Pohlink[2], and Wolfgang Kurz[3]

[1] Product Innovation & Customer Experience,
Deutsche Telekom AG, T-Online Allee 1, 64295 Darmstadt, Germany
gerald.eichler@telekom.de
[2] Telekom Innovation Laboratories,
Winterfeldtstraße 21-27, 10781 Berlin, Germany
claudia.pohlink@telekom.de
[3] Deloitte Consulting GmbH,
Franklinstraße 46-48, 60486 Frankfurt am Main, Germany
wkurz@deloitte.de

Abstract. Consumers of telecommunication services become more and more aware and concerned of how their data is treated by providers. Both, the European General Data Protection Regulation and the versatility of new communication-related data use cases drive this challenge. The Data Cockpit Minimum Viable Product is an important step to generate more transparency for private telco customers. It is part of a new 360-degree customer view, which is generated to emphasize the user position in managing telco services and contracts of an entire household. Extensive user research has identified crucial steps to reach use case acceptance, respectively opt-in, by customers as well as key success factors behind building up users' confidence and giving them more control over their data.

Keywords: CRM telecommunication · GDPR compliance · Data transparency · User data · Customer experience · Customer data dashboard · Household view · Permission management · Contract optimization

1 Telecommunication Customer's Need for Transparency

Customers have been consumers for a long time but in the time of new media, their role is changing towards increased interactivity. Given "General Terms and Conditions" are scrutinized. A clear message is expected, rather than long, incomprehensible fine prints.

1.1 GDPR Governance

A spectre is haunting Europe – the spectre of the EU General Data Protection Regulation (GDPR), effective since May 2018 [1]. It has been a great amplifier for data transparency amongst both, the public and the boardrooms. Although, there are not that many changes of the already existing data protection rules, the public awareness increased significantly. End users start thinking deeply about their personal data and

© Springer Nature Switzerland AG 2020
S. S. Rautaray et al. (Eds.): I4CS 2020, CCIS 1139, pp. 3–22, 2020.
https://doi.org/10.1007/978-3-030-37484-6_1

how companies treat the business-to-consumer (B2C) relationship in practice. Especially, the telecommunication providers are in public focus. Due to the very high potential fines of GDPR, executives also gave more attention to data privacy, in order to control their potential risk exposure. Therefore, GDPR compliance has been seen as an early challenge to be covered by a set of appropriate proactive actions.

Telecommunication providers see themselves as a secured data hub for the digital society. At the Mobile World Congress (MWC) 2019, Deutsche Telekom, Orange and Telefonica issued a white paper under the roof of the GSM Association (GSMA) to prove this position and to transport the key message that data is the fuel for great customer experience and opportunities in the future [2].

1.2 Improvement of the Customer Relationship

The Project Innovation Board of Deutsche Telekom called already early in 2016 for proposals to intensify the dialog with the customer, addressing both, customer data and customer insights. By setting up a project on a 360° Customer Dialogue two main questions were discussed and brought to the following formula:

1. **Trust = Transparency + Benefits**
   How can we get more knowledge about our customers' wishes and reach more opt-ins required to leverage those insights?
2. **Experience = Integration + Relevance**
   How can we integrate customer data across channels to improve customer service and user experience?

While point 2 is treated in the *T-Touch* sub-project, focusing on a cross-channel customer contact history, the contribution of this paper is targeting point 1 by the development of a Minimum Viable Product (MVP) called *Data Cockpit*. The Data Cockpit is a user-friendly interface providing customers with controlled transparency over private data, creating trust and offering attractive benefits in exchange for opt-ins – created in close collaboration with customers.

To generate trust, three protection methods are invented, namely *protection by rules*, *protection by technology*, and *protection by yourself* (user control) [3].

1.3 User Data Categorization

Whenever personal user or user-related data is collected, a clear purpose has to be defined. The storage of data has to be authorized by at least one of the following reasons:

1. **Legal requirements** e.g., person identification for establishing a contract
2. **Business relationship** e.g., service usage metering for billing
3. **Customer permission** e.g., active opt-in for receiving new product offers

Compared to other big new media providers, a high degree of transparency has been identified as a key acceptance enabler in the telecommunication domain. As a proper starting point, the categorization of user data, a telco provider deals with, has been selected.

The most basic data category is personal data. It covers mainly semi-permanent data like name, address, date of birth and a record for proof of legitimation. Further data categories are related to the business relationship of providing and procuring telecommunication services. While the classical business covers fixed and mobile phone usage, by migration towards Voice over IP (VoIP) it moves towards a sub-category of Internet usage. Furthermore, personal TV offers extend the portfolio called Entertain usage. The latest trend covers everything around home control and security, known as Smart Home usage.

Finally, location data is a separate category, which results out of increasing customer mobility and the potential for tracking mobile device locations, which on a technical level is required to register the mobile device at the nearest radio cell and ensure seamless connectivity.

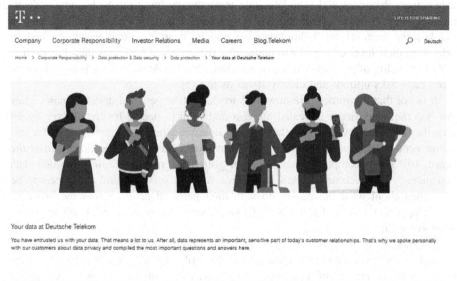

Fig. 1. Information on user data classification at Deutsche Telekom's web pages.

As a first project result, the six identified data categories are described in a more fashionable manner, accompanied by young speech at a dedicated section of the Deutsche Telekom web presentation labelled *Corporate Responsibility* [4], see Fig. 1. To summarize, transparency is achieved as a combination of general information plus individual communication, and personal control, which is an important aspect for the second and third pillars of the Data Cockpit. The message of enhanced data transparency was already transported to visitors at Deutsche Telekom's booth of MWC 2018 [3].

1.4   External Related Work Inspires Internal Research

It is a relatively new possibility for businesses to differentiate themselves from the competition by highlighting data transparency objectives. With an increasing awareness amongst consumers about the value of their data and on the backdrop of numerous data privacy breaches and scandals, data transparency has risen to become a determining factor. A 2016 survey with 2.404 responses found 59% of respondents stating that keeping them informed about data-use policies is an important aspect for them to determine their level of trust for a company. That is just a little less than fair pricing (60%) or quality of products (61%). In addition, 45% would share their personal data if a company asks upfront and clearly states its use [5].

It is not that consumers are unwilling to share their personal data anymore. They just become increasingly educated about it and want to decide for themselves which uses they allow and which one they object. In cases where companies are not transparent enough, such a behaviour quickly generates concern or objection. Across the board, still many companies have not yet gotten the message how important data transparency has become for their customers. Another survey found consumers to be concerned about what businesses do with their personal data - across the board of demographics at a level of about 60%. Covered were 15 countries and 4.368 responses were given [6].

Another survey in eight countries with 8.256 responses shows an even lower degree of trust in companies and institutions. Only 26% of respondents agree that organizations respect the privacy of their personal data, only 20% say they know what happens with their personal data, and only 29% feel in control about it [7]. Since data is also increasingly becoming a key ingredient for targeted marketing activities or even used in products themselves to create better experiences, businesses need to address this general trust issue if they want to benefit from the many use cases that customer data opens for them.

So how go generate trust? It starts with an honest and open communication, of being fully transparent with customers. The top three measures to generate more trust mentioned in our early representative survey with 1.000 interviewees in 256 corporations in Germany [8] are to

- Ensure data is never sold onwards to third parties (73%),
- Clearly communicate the purpose of using data (60%), and
- Provide easy-to-understand and available guidelines about data privacy (54%).

Some of the big tech companies have addressed this issue with customer privacy dashboards, extensive advertising campaigns and related prominently placed information on their websites. Some of them have also been the ones most prominently involved in data scandals, but still, other industries have not really followed the data transparency trend to the same extent. Even though data plays an increasingly important role in value generation across numerous industries.

Inspired by all these external surveys, a customer survey to emphasize the positive impact of transparency with 1.500 German participants was carried out for the project by our partner IPSOS in 2017. Once trust is established, customers indeed would be open to share their data. Asking for telecommunication use cases, 44% would likely share rich information with their telecommunication provider, while another 47% would share some but not all information. This generates a second requirement after transparency and guidelines: Users need to be able to select, which data they are willing to share for what purpose, and which permissions they want to withhold.

2 Data Cockpit Minimum Viable Product

To cover the overall envisaged approach and guided by the research mentioned above, the entire Data Cockpit project has been divided into separate pillars, which add three more directions to the 360-degree customer view (Fig. 2), aside the T-Touch aspect:

1. **Data Transparency:** General provider positioning on data for clear customer information, refer to Sect. 1.3.
2. **Customer Data Cockpit:** Individual and aggregated dashboard for visualization of ongoing communication service consumption, refer to Sect. 2.3.
3. **Household View:** Interactive mobile app component for benefit and contract management, refer to Sect. 3.2.

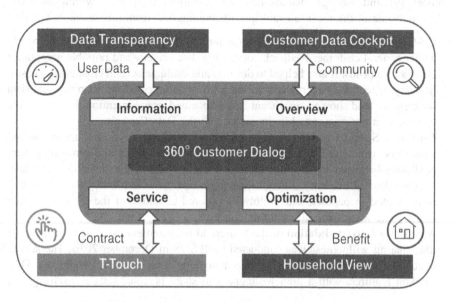

Fig. 2. Pillars and targets of the 360-degree customer dialog.

To support rapid prototyping and evaluate user acceptance, the development result should be an iteratively improved MVP, driven by continuous user feedback loops. Out of the Telekom Innovation Laboratories an adaptive Scrum team was formed, combining enhanced skills in the domains of:

- User-driven design (UX) and innovation,
- Market research and customer interviews,
- Public affairs, legal – especially GDPR – expertise,
- Data models and architectures,
- Software frameworks and operation hosting, and
- Implementation and testing.

Within 31 two-week Sprint cycles, the MVP was designed, implemented, evaluated and transferred to business units by the highly motivated, distributed agile team.

2.1   Research Studies for User Driven Design Methodology

The development of the Data Cockpit has been accompanied by extensive primary research. A large-scale study was conducted to test various Data Cockpit features, especially representative of German population. The "Customer Sprint Club" delivered biweekly customer feedback influencing the development process. The "Innovation Forum" members answered additional quantitative user surveys as online questionnaires. They aimed at testing the latest prototype features and investigated detailed aspects on the respondents' willingness to share data.

From ideation, where potential users were involved in a *Design Thinking* process workshop to end-user interface testing, the whole process was designed around customer needs and expectations. Furthermore, feedback was collected at several conferences [9] and through management and frontline interviews within Deutsche Telekom. Some of the most relevant insights coming out from this research include:

1. **Co-Creation and Ideation Workshops** throughout the project duration helped to gather general customer feedback concerning data privacy and possible acceptance criteria for opt-ins. It also helped to develop and evaluate several concrete use cases. In every aspect, they reemphasized the high importance of transparency and data sovereignty, and showed significant acceptance and usage intention for a proactive approach on personal data like intended with the Data Cockpit.
2. **Customer Sprint Club** designed as qualitative feedback sessions cantered around customers' needs, requirements, insights and ideas. Concept and prototypes were continuously tested in several repeated iterations within the development cycle. This resulted in two very different prototypes for the transparency dashboard that were created in parallel, and prototypes ensured coverage of the whole customer journey and addressing all customer concerns.
3. **A representative validation** of the household management use case as well as the data sharing willingness was conducted by IPSOS in December 2016. The survey concluded that about 75% of the German population like and would use Data Cockpit features, with a high willingness to share personal data in exchange for

using Data Cockpit features. For example, 76% of intended users would share mobile provider data for a feature that gives them a contract and usage overview.

4. **The effect of implemented results** has also been validated besides the concept phase. Regarding the data transparency overview page, a quantitative comparison between the old status quo and the newly implemented information site measured multiple user experience and usability Key Performance Indicators (KPI) in a remote setting. 66% of respondents liked the first impression of the new page, while more specifically significant improvements across all dimensions: comprehension, ease of use, relevance, structure, completeness, and layout have been recorded. This lead to a positive impression on transparency with 74% of survey participants.

As a summary, a broad analysis of existing user research on transparency, own primary research in focus group discussions, and regular Customer Sprint Club consulting during development provided new insights in customer thinking.

2.2 Basic Architecture and Implementation Framework Selection

A robust client-server-architecture has been selected to implement the Data Cockpit MVP. The user client should be a simple web browser, available on all potential customer devices like mobile phone, tablet or laptop. Following user surveys, the MVP followed a *mobile first strategy*. However, the rapid prototyping considered a responsive design, to be adaptive for a wide range of mobile devices using different web browsers.

To reach this aim, two independent components form the server side, named *Household Manager* (frontend) and *Household Controller* (backend). A REST interface for intercommunication allows a flexible distribution of the hardware and software components, see Fig. 3.

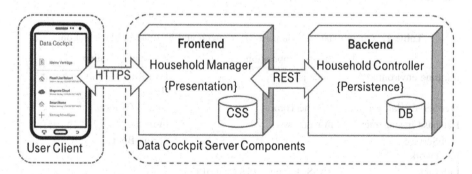

Fig. 3. Client-server-architecture of Data Cockpit MVP.

The architecture is designed to fit with other relevant Telekom apps and customer self-service portals for easy future integration via given Telekom system APIs later on. Clear focus of the MVP is a lean and self-dependent Proof of Concept (PoC) as showcase for necessary alignments.

The project team carefully evaluated different implementation frameworks. To gain creativity in the frontend development for emerging use cases, a key driver was flexibility in graph type selection for data visualization. Node.js® is an open source JavaScript runtime, built on the Chrome V8 JavaScript engine[1]. It operates on a single threaded event based loop to make all executions non-blocking. Developed applications can be easily scaled in horizontal manner by providing additional nodes to the existing system. Rich graphical libraries are available as open source.

Table 1. Development tools for frontend and backend.

	Frontend development tools	Backend development tools
Integrated Development Environment (IDE)	Editor	Eclipse
Programming language	JavaScript, CSS and HTML	Java, Servlets
Source Control Management (SCM)	Git + Tortoise Git, Redmine	Git + Tortoise Git, Redmine
Built tool/documentation	Node.js, NPM	Apache Maven/Swagger
Issue tracker	Atlassian Jira	Atlassian Jira
Knowledge sharing	Atlassian Confluence	Atlassian Confluence

Table 1 summarizes the selection of development tools for the MVP implementation, while Table 2 gives an overview about the operational environments. In-memory databases provide a good performance and can be easily brought back into its initial configuration for comparable user test series.

Table 2. Operational environment for frontend and backend implementation.

	Frontend operation	Backend operation
Runtime environment	Node.js	Java Runtime Environment (JRE)
WebServer/platform	Apache/Tomcat	Apache/Tomcat
Database management	In-memory	In-memory
WebService framework		Spring-Boot
Libraries	SASS, Express, PUG, cujoJS	
Compiler	Node.js	Java
Operating system	Linux 64 bit, MS Windows 64 bit	Linux 64 bit, MS Windows 64 bit

---

[1] URL: https://nodejs.org/en/.

2.3 GUI Development

By means of partner agencies, two different designs were developed and provided as mock up for user surveys.

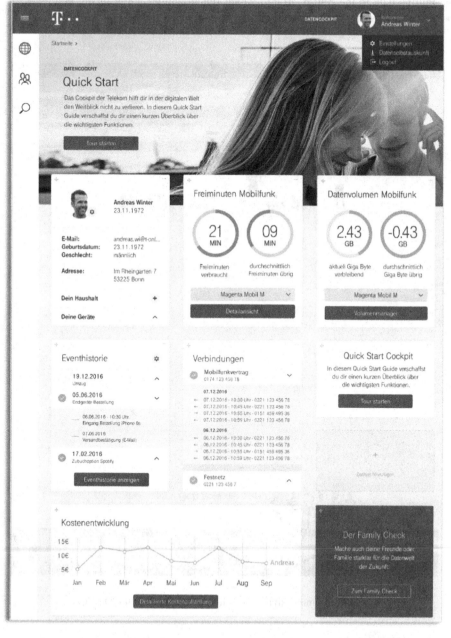

Fig. 4. Full web page design approach for "My Data" in the Data Cockpit.

The prototypes for enhanced personal data display based on user expectations and general market trends. Those were regularly tested with users and challenged in terms of clarity, sequence in the flow and on the page. Consequently, key principles for design were:

- Intuitive design to convey transparency message also with UX design,
- Putting data in the centre, around which functionalities are grouped, and
- Fit with existing Telekom web and mobile app experience

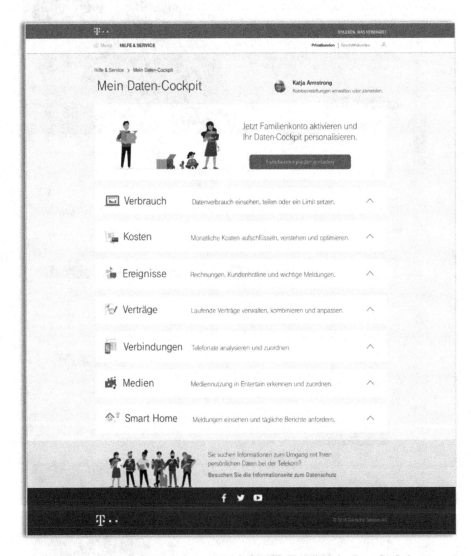

Fig. 5. Single column design approach for "My Data" in the Data Cockpit.

The first approach has a full web page in mind, covering all aspects of user touchpoints, presented in a single screen, as shown in Fig. 4. The second approach was led by mobile consumption, following a single column visualization with extensible sections as depicted in Fig. 5. The applied style follows the one of the data transparency presentation as previously introduced in Fig. 1.

Survey results with 1.500 responses turned out that users have very basic preferences, which can be summarized as need for:

- High intuitivism and simplicity,
- Clear icon and colour speech,
- Logical order and sequence of interaction points, and
- Preferred mobile usage.

3   Community Aspects of Telecommunication Customers

A telecommunication provider's view on customers data comes traditionally from a SIM card view (mobile line unit), has evolved to a contract view (several SIMs) and then customer view (several contracts) slowly with the onset of more holistic Customer Relationship Management (CRM) and customer care services. With the advent of many new services (dual play, triple play, quadruple play) such a combination was more and more necessary, from the customer invoice to handling key customer master data to optimizing the contract bundle as a whole. This already took great effort in consolidating SIM and contract data in the systems to match them to individual customers, especially when coming from previously different business areas like fixed, mobile, internet or TV.

The next step is to view a customer not alone, but in the context of their household (i.e. family). This is the logical level customers themselves apply, when thinking about their contractual obligations, so in most scenarios it makes sense to offer customers to manage all their household contracts together. For telecommunication providers, this information is valuable because up- and cross-sell within a household provide the highest potential – if competitors hold some of the contracts, there is potential for contract changes without cannibalization.

This is why the Data Cockpit takes not only the Telekom contract view, but also includes further external contracts. So for the customer, it is a complete view on all telecommunication services and for Deutsche Telekom it gives the most complete view when considering potential optimization of the contract landscape of a household. Of course, this optimization is only conducted, when the customer approves the respective use of their data.

An additional consideration that complicates this scenario and had to be addressed is the opt-in of other family members for having their contracts managed centrally by one person in the household.

3.1 From Household and Family View Towards a Community Approach

The classical telecommunication business concentrated on access services for fixed line. The Plain Old Telephone System (POTS) got enrichment by digitalization and service integration with the Integrated Services Digital Network (ISDN). In the mid 1990th, Mobile Network Operators (MNO) entered the market. For both, a Fixed Mobile Convergence (FMC) was introduced due to the joint migration based on the Internet Protocol (IP) suite. All-IP networks increase the data overhead but reduce the administrative effort. Therefore, Voice over IP (VoIP) became todays telephone standard.

Looking at the user behaviour over time, contracts belonging to a single person are completed with offers, which address an entire household. The classical communication domain is extended by domains like entertainment and smart home. Complete sets that offer all services to the customer like MagentaEINS dominate the market for households. Products, services, packages and devices are brought together with multiple contracts and a heterogeneous world of identifiers. Figure 6 illustrates this complex view and its dependencies.

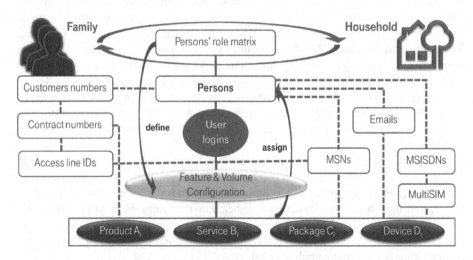

Fig. 6. Object classes for a joint family and household community approach.

In practice, it is difficult to assign specific mobile contracts to a single household. It turned out that typically selected persons of a family are in charge of managing telecommunication and local IT infrastructure. Therefore, a differentiation between household view and family view was introduced.

- A **family** is characterized by one responsible legal person. while service consumption is spread over multiple locations.
- A **household** is characterized by multiple legal persons living at the same physical location.
- A **community** is defined as a manageable conjunction of multiple persons, multiple locations and multiple contracts.

To cover both with a single model, a role management needs to be introduced. The joint family and household view is called the *community* approach.

3.2 Data Model Classes and Functions for the Household View

The implementation relies on object orientation with a community member centric approach. The dependency complexity is modelled as member and contract functions as depicted in Fig. 7. For personal member data, the mandatory set of data is limited to a minimum, following the principle of data sparsity.

The household view (Fig. 8) is designed as add-on part for the Magenta SERVICE App, available for Android and iOS. Following the logical usage, it offers three sections below each other:

- Household member management,
- Contract management, and
- Usage statistics.

For fast user and intuitive interaction, icons guide to the available actions. The user gets the offer to add manually external contracts to gain a complete household cost overview in segments, see Fig. 8. Only Deutsche Telekom contracts can be added automatically after a two-factor authentication.

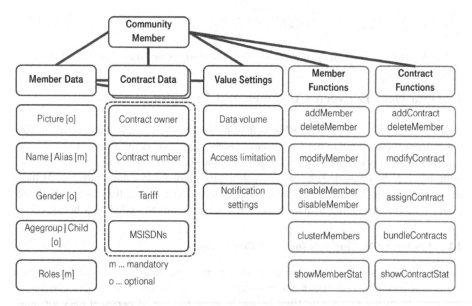

Fig. 7. Initial object-oriented data model for the Data Cockpit.

Step by step, the project owner added additional use cases to the backlog. Accordingly, the data model was extended and new functions were added.

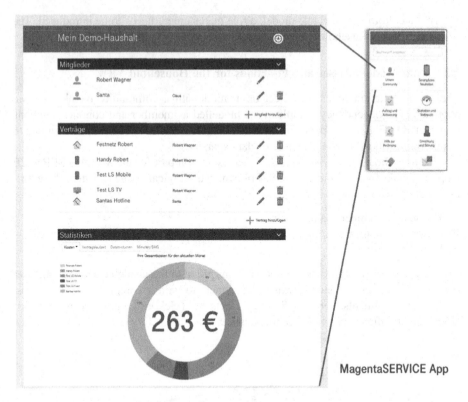

Fig. 8. Mobile screen of "household view" as tile (part) of the MagentaSERVICE App.

4 Data Deal Between Customer and Provider

"Data is the oil of the 21st century" is a citation, which is ascribed to many sources. The big difference compared to natural resources is the data ownership. As soon as personal data is touched, it is rather clear. To get the owner's permission to use it, a win-win setup needs to be created. Telecommunication providers are in a good position, as they are considered to be trusted by many customers. Even more, they are one of the primary candidates acting as data broker in a secure manner, called data hub [2].

4.1 Customer Willingness for Data Provisioning

Looking back, user of a software or service in practise hardly ever read the general terms and conditions, although the installation process or contract signature requires this step. With the given new legal option to deny the use of personal data for non-contractual use [1], many customers at least formally, reject any utilisation. As a logical consequence, two things happened. Firstly, the granularity of any declaration of consent became finer. Secondly, more background information was provided.

It turned out, that customers are generally willing to share their data, but they want clarity over the data that is used as well as the concrete mechanisms and use cases behind, so there are no "creepy" results coming out. However, customers have different standards e.g., their contract data towards providers such as Deutsche Telekom, where they have high awareness, contrasted with the much more sensitive usage and location data that is collected from their smartphone operating systems or smart speakers more or less constantly, where they have much lower awareness and in consequence object much less. With GDPR, transparency, information and other aspects have become much more a hygiene factor that needs to be in place.

4.2   Favourite Use Cases

Most willingness to share data can be achieved, when concrete benefits relate to those and ideally for use cases, where the type of data and the type of benefit have some clear logical associations.

From several data-benefit pairs, the household view has been selected in customer discussions as the best: give access to the telecommunication contracts of the household in return for a clear and informative contract and usage overview plus potential optimization recommendations.

Customer preferences, evaluated by a user survey, led into the primary use case selection. The family check was selected out of options from Table 3. A high acceptance of customers was recognized for this use case:

- 67% of customers were interested in use case,
- 72% of customers would use household view features, and
- 84% of customers would share personal data in exchange for these features.

Table 3. Use case offers for data sharing between provider and customer.

Use case	Customer opt-in	Customer benefit
Household view	Share household info	Get contract optimization
Hotspot access	Share location	Get special hotspot access
Smart home energy	Share smart home usage data	Get rebates and tips
Entertain experience	Share Entertain view history	Customized recommendation
Paperless & eco-friendly	Share e-mail address	Be environmentally friendly
Movement	Share location	Movement history visualization
Meaningful invoices	Share your contacts	More informative invoices
Cloud storage	Share cloud usage	Get additional cloud storage
Browser history	Share browser history	Get rewards and rebates
E-reader experience	Share e-reader data	Customized CX, relevant content

4.3   Evaluation of the Household Data Use Case

Diving deeper into the household view use case, an online survey within the T-Labs Innovation Forum was conducted with 320 participants end of 2016 in order to evaluate different telecommunication services and the customers' willingness to share their personal and household data. The tested detailed services within the use case were:

- Overview of current telecommunication contracts,
- Contract management, and
- Tariff optimizer.

Each service was divided into three abstraction levels, see Table 4. Based on a drawing and a description per service and feature each respondent evaluated nine features concerning liking and usage intention.

Table 4. Use case selection for data sharing to be evaluated.

Service A: Overview of current tele-communication contracts	Service B: Contract management	Service C: Tariff optimizer
A.1 Overview only for me	B.1 Contract management only for me	C.1 Tariff optimizer only for me
A.2 Overview for my household	B.2 Contract management for my household	C.2 Tariff optimizer for my household
A.3 Provider comprehensive overview	B.3 Transfer of budget and data volume	C.3 Additional product & service suggestions

As a reference, the representative social structure of the evaluation group of the 320 responds looked like that:

- Gender: male – 62%, female – 38%
- Age: 18…29 – 14%, 30…38 – 23%, 40–49 – 16%, 50…59 – 22%, 60+ – 28%
- Household size: single – 28%, 2 p. – 49%, 3…4 p. – 19%, 5+ p. – 4%
- Deutsche Telekom customer: fixed – 54%, mobile – 38%, Entertain – 24%

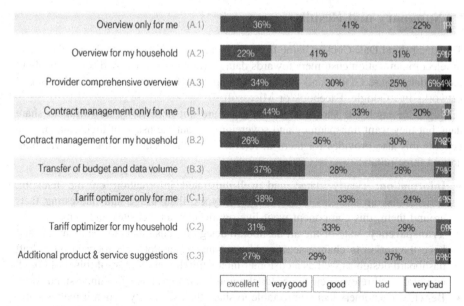

Fig. 9. User survey: spontaneous impression as liking on a five-grade scale.

All three services show a similar high likes, see Fig. 9 and usage intension, see Fig. 10. The three features "only for me" receive a significantly better evaluation than all other features.

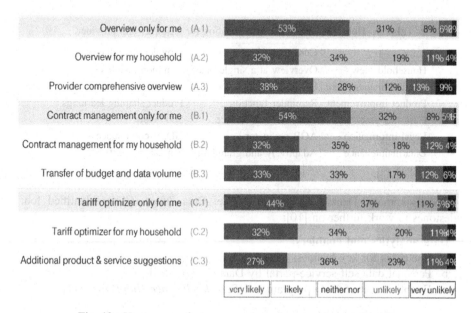

Fig. 10. User survey: feature usage intension on a five-grade scale.

5 Summary and Results

The idea behind Data Cockpit came from the increasingly informed and critical opinion of telecommunication customers towards data privacy, also filled by discussions about recent data leaks, GDPR and respective campaigns by companies enforcing social networks like Google, Facebook or Microsoft.

Initial research has shown that customers are not necessarily unwilling to share data, but they want transparency and sovereignty about the usage of their data and the benefits this also provides for them in return. Thus, the Data Cockpit itself was built around three pillars:

- **Information:** clearly stated and well-illustrated information on the telekom.de/telekom.com sites about different data types, their usage and interesting facts around them; this component went live on all relevant websites and apps.
- **Transparency:** state-of-the-art dashboard design for customers to see their data and have the option to change settings like opt-in; in our PoC, we focused on a draft dashboard design as well as a customer interaction history as part of this dashboard, combining all relevant customer touchpoints/events in an easy-to-understand form.
- **Benefits:** Customers feel comfortable to share their data only, when it makes sense for them and brings benefits. We tested several use cases and for the PoC developed a *household view*, which gives an overview to the customer to all Telekom and external telecommunication contracts and their usage/costs in their family/household, plus the possibility to request offers for optimization.

The household view generates a win-win for both, customer and provider as summarized in Table 5.

Table 5. Household view win-win situation for customer and provider.

	Customer advantages	Provider advantages
Household view	Overview at a single place	Common insights
Contract management	Contract optimization	Targeted advertising
Product improvement	Reminder function	Product shaping learnings
Customer care	Customer self-service	360° view
Legal information	AGB navigator	GDPR compliance
Data maintenance	Adaptively and granularity	Refresh support

As a summary, Deutsche Telekom's Chief Data Office (CDO) identified four milestones to work further on [10]:

1. **Data analytics and enablers:**
   a. Use cases for key business stakeholders,
   b. Personal data self-service-portal by Data Cockpit, and
   c. Establishment of *Halo* program and *Data Intelligence Hub* (DIH) [11].

2. **Data architectures and models:**
   a. Harmonized group-wide *T-Data Model*,
   b. One data lake per National Company (NatCo) strategy, and
   c. Central data virtualization.
3. **Skills and culture:**
   a. DT common use case and asset repository,
   b. Exchange within and across communities, and
   c. Alignment of activities and roadmaps.
4. **Data governance:**
   a. Best practice research and
   b. Data governance with enterprise blueprints.

All phases of the Data Cockpit project have been conducted with focus on the customers and their experience, including various focus group discussions and usability tests. In addition, the use cases are optimized for their business potential together with the Customer Relationship Management department.

The so-called "Customer Acceptance Clause" (Konzerneinwilligungsklausel 4.0) experienced further developments on finer granularity. The MagentaSERVICE App got a new user experience and better feedback channels for the customer in its follow-up version, called *MeinMagenta App* [12], available for free on Android and iOS devices from Google Play Store and Apple App Store, respectively.

References

1. European Union: General Data Protection Regulation GDPR. Regulation EU 2016/679, OJ L 119 cor. OJ L 127, 23.5.2018 (2018)
2. GSMA Europe: Telecoms as the "Secured Data Hub" for the digital society (2019). https://www.gsma.com/gsmaeurope/resources/secured_data_hub/
3. Deutsche Telekom Homepage: Your data at Deutsche Telekom. https://www.telekom.com/en/corporate-responsibility/data-protection-data-security/data-protection/your-data-at-dt/. Accessed 22 Sept 2019
4. Data Cockpit: Turning Data Transparency into Trust and Business Value to Create Customer Experiences. Fact sheet at Mobile World Congress (2018)
5. Cognizant: The business value of trust, Asia-Pacific Region (2016). https://www.cognizant.com/whitepapers/the-business-value-of-trust-codex1951.pdf
6. SAS: Mobility, vulnerability and the state of data privacy (2016). https://www.sas.com/en/whitepapers/mobility-vulnerability-state-of-data-privacy-108097.html. Accessed 7 Oct 2019
7. Vodafone Institute: Big Data – A European survey on the opportunities and risks of data analytics (2016). https://www.vodafone-institut.de/wp-content/uploads/2016/01/VodafoneInstitute-Survey-BigData-en.pdf
8. Deloitte Analytics Institute: Datenland Deutschland – Die Transparenzlücke (2014). https://www2.deloitte.com/de/de/pages/trends/studie-datenland-deutschland.html. Accessed 7 Oct 2019

9. Pohlink, C.: #DataCockpit – Make Data Great Again. At Media Convention Berlin 2017 (2017). https://17.mediaconventionberlin.com/de/session/datacockpit-make-data-great-again
10. Competence Center Corporate Data Quality, CDQ Good Practice Award 2018: Deutsche Telekom Chief Data Office Start-Up Program. https://www.cc-cdq.ch/sites/default/files/cdq_award/CDQ%20Good%20Practice%20Award%202018_Deutsche%20Telekom.pdf. Accessed 20 Oct 2019
11. Deutsche Telekom: Data Intelligence Hub – extract value from your data securely. A business customer collaboration platform. https://dih.telekom.net/en/. Accessed 20 Oct 2019
12. Deutsche Telekom: MeinMagenta App – alle Infos und bester Service für Mobilfunk & Festnetz. https://www.telekom.de/hilfe/meinmagenta-app/. Accessed 20 Oct 2019

A Mobile Recommender System for Location-Aware Telemedical Diagnostics

Maytiyanin Komkhao[1], Sunantha Sodsee[2], and Wolfgang A. Halang[3]([✉])

[1] Faculty of Science and Technology,
Rajamangala University of Technology Phra Nakhon, Bangkok, Thailand
`maytiyanin.k@rmutp.ac.th`
[2] Faculty of Information Technology,
King Mongkut's University of Technology North Bangkok, Bangkok, Thailand
`sunanthas@kmutnb.ac.th`
[3] Chair of Computer Engineering, Fernuniversität in Hagen, Hagen, Germany
`wolfgang.halang@fernuni-hagen.de`

Abstract. As recommender systems have proven their effectiveness in providing personalised recommendations based on previous user preferences in e-commerce, this approach is to be transferred for use in medicine. In particular, the aim is to complement the diagnoses made by physicians in rural hospitals of developing countries, in remote areas or in situations of uncertainty by machine recommendations that draw on large bases of expert knowledge to reduce the risk to patients. To this end, a database of patients' medical history and a cluster model is maintained centrally. The model is constructed incrementally by a combination of collaborative and knowledge-based filtering, employing a weighted similarity distance specifically derived for medical knowledge. In the course of this process, the model permanently widens its base of knowledge on a medical area given. To give a recommendation, the model's cluster best matching the diagnostic pattern of a considered patient is sought. Fuzzy sets are employed to cope with possible confusion in decision making, which may occur when large data sets cause clusters to overlap. The degrees of membership to these fuzzy sets are expressed by the Mahalanobis distance, whose weights are derived from risk factors identified by experts. The therapy actually applied after the recommendation and its subsequently observed consequences are fed back for model updating. Readily available mobile digital accessories can be used for remote data entry and recommendation display as well as for communication with the central site. The approach is validated in the area of obstetrics and gynecology.

Keywords: Medical recommender system · Telemedical diagnostics · Location awareness · Computational intelligence · Incremental collaborative filtering · Knowledge-based filtering · Obstetrics and gynecology

© Springer Nature Switzerland AG 2020
S. S. Rautaray et al. (Eds.): I4CS 2020, CCIS 1139, pp. 23–37, 2020.
https://doi.org/10.1007/978-3-030-37484-6_2

1   Introduction

Diseases are best coped with by detecting their symptoms as early as possible [5]. This is, however, difficult in remote areas, such as the rural regions of Thailand, where medical specialists and facilities are scarce and insufficient. Therefore, to support general practitioners in diagnostics and to reduce the risk of hazardous complications, e.g. cephalopelvic disproportion as considered in this paper, it would be beneficial if physicians could detect diseases before their onset and, then, transfer patients from insufficient hospitals to well-prepared ones [23,24].

Recommender systems have proven to be effective tools for retrieving information from large databases. The most common objective for their use is, however, to make recommendations of yet unrated items to interested users based on their previous preferences [19,26,28]. A recommender system can suggest to its user the item(s) with the highest estimated rating by employing many different methods from machine learning [4] and approximation theory [20] or by various heuristics. So far, particularly for e-commerce, a wide range of recommendation techniques has been developed [19,26,29] and deployed successfully. Hence, it stands to reason to employ recommender systems to solve medical problems as well.

The creation of information systems to predict the risk incurred by individual diseases is a topic of intensive research [5,7,11]. The main goal of such computer-aided methods is to assist physicians in making decisions without consulting specialists directly [1,30]. Recently, there were some studies employing collaborative techniques of recommender systems in medicine [5,11]. Their leitmotif is to advise a consulting patient based on the medical records of patients with similar indications [5,7,11]. Reasons to employ collaborative filtering techniques in searching medical databases are, first, to maximise effectiveness and quality of medical care. Then, prediction should not only be accurate, but a recommender system should also be able to help physicians in defining appropriate treatments [6], and to predict to any patient in a personalised way the risk both with respect to the disease [5] and to undesirable outcomes of possible treatments [10].

In the further course of this paper we shall first take a closer look on collaborative filtering, and sketch the idea of the algorithm, called FB-InCF, to be devised. Then, it will be described how recommender systems based on FB-InCF can be deployed as information systems having a central unit maintaining database and model, and communicating with remote stations where queries are entered and recommendations displayed. For the considered case of medical applications, the remote stations may be mobile digital accessories of any kind connecting to the central site by telecommunication networks. The approach presented will finally be validated empirically by a case study in the area of obstetrics and gynecology using data on cephalopelvic disproportion.

2 Combining Collaborative Filtering with Rule Bases

Collaborative filtering requires user profiles to identify user preferences for making recommendations in e-commerce [29]. To transfer the methodology of recommender systems to medical applications, we draw on the analogy identified in [5,6,10] as follows: (i) patients are identified with users, (ii) feature vectors (called patterns) containing data of medical histories and physical examinations are identified with user profiles, (iii) for both users and patients a notion of similarity is employed, and (iv) patient diagnoses are identified with user ratings. As the geographical distribution of the occurrence probabilities of diseases is uneven, and since there are distinct regions where diseases such as scrub typhus, typhoid, meliodosis or leptospirosis spread, the patterns need to contain geographical data. Thus, by the contents of their databases, medical recommender systems become inherently location-aware.

In [5] a collaborative filtering method combining the memory-based and model-based approaches was presented for personalised diagnosis of diseases. The method aims to predict the diseases a patient may contract in the future based on his or her medical record. To this end, it calculates values of similarity between the patient's data and patterns taken from a medical database employing International Classification of Diseases codes (ICD-9-CM) from [3], and predicts the patient's disease and associated risk as that of the closest match found in the database.

Whereas expert systems require the expert knowledge employed to be available before they can be developed, recommender systems can compile this knowledge in the course of being utilised, in particular when working incrementally. The algorithmic foundation for this will be laid in the next section, where the previously developed algorithm InCF [17] will be generalised into a hybrid combining content-based with collaborative filtering as well as incorporating domain knowledge. The latter is derived by experts, and structured for processing in form of IF-THEN rules. Apart from achieving better results, involving rule bases overcomes the incapacity of purely clustering-based models to provide explanations.

The proposed algorithm operates in three modes, viz.

1. the learning mode, in which a cluster model of a large number of feature vectors extracted from the application domain is constructed incrementally,
2. the recommendation mode, in which a feature vector under consideration is compared with the model to determine the most similar cluster, and
3. the feedback mode, in which for model improvement after any recommendation the consulting recommendees are queried for feedback on what happened after an action was recommended.

Fuzzy sets are employed to cope with possible confusion in decision making caused by overlapping clusters. The degrees of membership to these fuzzy sets are not expressed in terms of an ordinary distance such as the Euclidean one, but by the Mahalanobis distance [21], here based on weights derived from risk factors identified by experts, to improve recommendation accuracy and avoid the scalability problem encountered in the model creation of incremental learning.

Constituting a novel characteristic, the therapy actually applied after a recommendation and its subsequently observed consequences are fed back into the model's learning mode. For this feedback mode, the algorithm is called FB-InCF.

3   Recommender System

Based on the analogy between commercial and medical applications as outlined above, the algorithm to be devised shall create models in form of cluster sets from medical history data (instead as from user-rating matrices in the commercial domain), with each cluster representing a group of similar feature vectors, i.e. diagnostic patterns. Clustering has successfully been used in several exploratory pattern analyses, in data mining, machine learning and in pattern classifications [13]. The effect of clustering is that items are grouped in such a way that the values of item characteristics within the same cluster have high similarity to one another, but are rather dissimilar to the characteristics in other clusters [9].

Various clustering algorithms are employed in model-based collaborative filtering such as K-nearest neighbours (K-NN), hierarchical, density-based and K-Means clustering [4]. In our experimental comparison presented below, K-Means and K-NN are considered for model creations, since they are most widely utilised for pattern classification based on similarity measurement to compute distances between users. It needs to be noted, however, that both K-Means and K-NN require to indicate a priori the number of clusters in a model to be formed. Hence, they lack scalability and do not lend themselves for unattended automatic operation. In contrast, FB-InCF adjusts clusters in a model and their total number dynamically upon arrival of new feature vectors. In other words, the algorithms comprises preclustering as an integral part.

Both in proper clustering and in matching input patterns with the constituents of cluster models for recommendation purposes, the functions employed to measure distance or similarity, respectively, are the decisive elements. It has always to be kept in mind that extreme caution needs to be exercised when combining different and mutually independent quantities with different physical dimensions in a single arithmetic expression finally giving rise to just a single number. Therefore, as stressed in [2] [p. 26], in any application area considered, a suitable distance function must be defined on the basis of domain knowledge:

> It is to be emphasised that no method can a priori be called the "best": the selection of a measure for similarity or distance has always to comply with the requirements of the practical case under consideration and to bear the real semantics of the data in mind.

To keep the description of FB-InCF general, we thus do not specify a certain distance function. We just note that it does not necessarily have to be a metric, i.e. the triangular inequality is not required to hold, and we assume that it is suitably selected for the application area considered.

The incrementally learning algorithm compares an input pattern entered with known clusters. It either associates the pattern with the best matching cluster, called the winning cluster, already existing in the model and updates the cluster's parameters accordingly, or it includes the pattern into the model as a new cluster. Before the algorithm FB-InCF can commence its operation, an initialisation phase needs to be executed. Here, medical history records are preprocessed if they are too complex. Vectors of relevant features are extracted from the medical history to reduce calculation complexity. In this paper we assume that the data set in form of a set of feature vectors ($\mathbf{F}$) was elaborated by experts and does not require preprocessing.

3.1   Learning Mode

Learning from history and knowledge are both represented here when creating a model. This is performed incrementally, processing feature vectors submitted as input one by one in relation to the current version of the model. The learning process of FB-InCF comprises the following steps.

Initialisation: Select an input vector f_1 randomly, and let the cluster $\{f_1\}$ form the model $\mathbf{M}$ initially.
Loop for all further feature vectors $f \in \mathbf{F}$:

1. Calculate the membership of f in all clusters of $\mathbf{M}$.
2. Determine the winning cluster as the one in which f assumes the highest membership value.
3. **If** the value of f's membership in the winning cluster does not exceed a given threshold, **then** merge f with the winning cluster and exit the loop.
4. Evaluate the base of expert rules for f.
5. **If** the rules are fulfilled, **then** extend the model by a new cluster consisting just of f ($\mathbf{M} := \mathbf{M} \cup \{f\}$).

3.2   Recommendation Mode

The recommendation mode of FB-InCF is aimed to classify the characteristics of a consulting recommendee r by associating with him or her the closest cluster in the model resulting from the learning mode. Its steps read:

1. Calculate the membership of r in all clusters of $\mathbf{M}$ generated in the learning mode.
2. Determine the winning cluster as the one in which r assumes the highest membership value.
3. **If** the value of r's membership in the winning cluster does not exceed a given threshold, **then** associate r with the winning cluster and its characteristics.
4. Save this recommendation for the feedback mode.

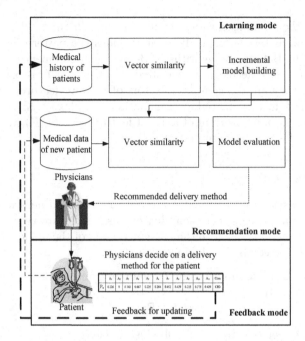

Fig. 1. Using FB-InCF for telemedical recommendation

3.3 Feedback Mode

In order to allow the model to adapt to changes that occurred in the course of its use, and to improve its recommendation quality, the algorithm is designed to obtain feedback on what happened after an action was recommended. Thus, any time a recommendation is given to a consulting recommendee r in the corresponding mode, querying feedback from the recommendee is scheduled for some time later. When results become available, it is carried out as follows (Fig. 1).

1. Query a recommendation's recipient for the action taken and for the results this action gave rise to.
2. Combine the data saved in the recommendation mode and the acquired feedback data into a feature vector.
3. Execute the learning mode's loop body for this feature vector.

Note that the last step may lead to an updating of the model **M**. Thus, it evolves permanently comprising the knowledge contained in both the historical and example cases provided as well as in the experiences obtained by observing the effects of the recommendations it generated.

4 Membership in Clusters

In most cases the Euclidean and Manhattan distances are used as proximity measures for quantitative variables, because they are easy to implement. For many real-world data sets such as the one considered in Sect. 6, however, clusters of data tend to be elongated in certain dimensions and sized differently. Here the Mahalanobis distance [21] turns out to be more suitable than the Euclidean one [25]. The Mahalanobis distance considers the orientation of data in the sample space, and groups them by mean and covariance matrices. The shapes of clusters are hyper-ellipsoidal rather than hyper-spherical, as obtained when working with the Euclidean distance. Accordingly, the Mahalanobis distance is used to determine the membership in and the decision boundaries of clusters.

Between two feature vectors $\mathbf{x}_j$ and $\mathbf{x}_s$ the Mahalanobis distance ($\mathbf{dist}_M$) is defined as

$$\mathbf{dist}_M(j, s) = [(\mathbf{x}_j - \mathbf{x}_s)^T \mathbf{K}^{-1}(\mathbf{x}_j - \mathbf{x}_s)]^{\frac{1}{2}} \tag{1}$$

where the patients' covariance matrix

$$\mathbf{K} = \begin{bmatrix} k_{1,1} & k_{1,2} & \cdots & k_{1,n} \\ k_{2,1} & k_{2,2} & \cdots & k_{2,n} \\ \vdots & \vdots & \ddots & \vdots \\ k_{m,1} & k_{m,2} & \cdots & k_{m,n} \end{bmatrix} \tag{2}$$

is calculated as

$$\mathbf{K} = \frac{1}{N-1} \sum_{j=1}^{N} (\mathbf{x}_j - \bar{\mathbf{x}})^T (\mathbf{x}_j - \bar{\mathbf{x}}). \tag{3}$$

The size and complexity of real-world data sets often leads to overlapping clusters rendering decision making difficult. Therefore, we employ a broader concept of membership in the algorithm FB-InCF. Thus, a feature vector's membership to a cluster may be expressed in terms of its distance to the cluster's centroid but, for instance, also as fuzzy membership with a corresponding function. Here, we utilise the Mahalanobis distance again, because it can take into account different scalings and weights in the component spaces as well as possible correlations between them.

Fuzzy membership is formulated in terms of the Mahalanobis distance as follows. Let p be an input vector and $\mathbf{w}_i$ the centre of the ith cluster in a model $\mathbf{W}$. Then p's degree of membership to the ith cluster $\mathbf{mem}(p, \mathbf{w}_i)$ is calculated with a weighted Mahalanobis distance ($\mathbf{dist}_{M\varphi}$)

$$\mathbf{dist}_{M\varphi} = [\varphi(p - \mathbf{w}_i)^T \mathbf{K}^{-1} \varphi(p - \mathbf{w}_i)]^{\frac{1}{2}}, \tag{4}$$

as:

$$\mathbf{mem}(p, \mathbf{w}_i) = \mathbf{exp}(-\frac{1}{2}\varphi(p - \mathbf{w}_i)^T \mathbf{K}^{-1} \varphi(p - \mathbf{w}_i)). \tag{5}$$

It will be shown in Sect. 6 that the weights (φ) may, for instance, be derived from risk factors.

The comparison given in Table 1 of the techniques employed by the three algorithms considered here shows decisive differences between FB-InCF on one hand and K-Means and K-NN on the other. Clearly, FB-InCF adjusts more specifically to data sets by allowing for a variable number of clusters with variable

Table 1. Comparison of the three algorithms' characteristics

Aspect	K-Means	K-NN	FB-InCF
Number of clusters	Fix	Fix	Variable
Type of learning	Off-line learning	Off-line learning	Off-line learning for model creation, On-line learning for updating models with new patterns
Outliers (Patterns significantly deviating from clusters)	Sensitive to outliers	Sensitive to outliers	Thresholds of clusters identify distance of distinct patterns +threshold of risks
Clustering characteristic	Clustering only	Clustering + neighbourhood	Clustering + membership function + medical knowledge
Decision shape	Spherical	Spherical	Elliptical

shapes. Furthermore, it lends itself to on-line learning right from the start. All three algorithms are sensitive to outliers, but FB-InCF is more specific than the others in also creating new clusters on the basis of risk considerations or discarding patterns from model creation due to their insignificance. Finally, in contrast to K-Means and K-NN, FB-InCF can also accommodate overlapping clusters, because it constructs fuzzy sets employing the Mahalanobis distance.

5   Deployment as a Pervasive Computing System

Considering the above description of the algorithm FB-InCF, it is straightforward how a system consisting of computing devices and telecommunication facilities has to be structured in order to be suitable as an execution platform of a corresponding recommender system for use in a certain application area.

At its centre there needs to be a unit charged with maintaining the—permanently growing—database of feature vectors. For highest comprehensiveness of this database, there ought to be either only one such unit worldwide or the corresponding units ought to synchronise their databases frequently. The central unit's further functions are model updating (i.e. learning) any time a new feature vector arrives, serving requests for recommendations by means of the database and the model, and obtaining feedback on the recommendations provided to extend the database accordingly and to update the model incrementally. Physically, the central unit may just be a mainframe computer or a server equipped with telecommunication facilities to meet these requirements.

In case the recommender system's users are not machines, but humans, it is straightforward to let them communicate with the system via browser-based, possibly mobile web interfaces or by providing smartphone apps. The function of

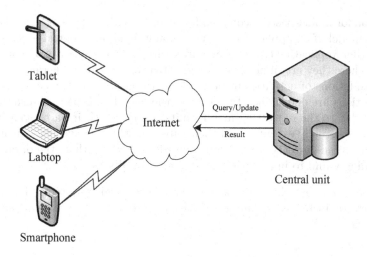

Fig. 2. Configuration of the telemedical ICT system

both is to support data entry, some preprocessing, transmission of recommendation requests to the central unit, which includes visualising the feature vectors'
locations relative to their closest clusters, display of the recommendations given
by and received from the central unit as well as to later query the requester for
the action(s) actually performed and their effects subsequently observed to be
fed back to the central unit for permanent model updating.

For dedicated smartphone apps, the following operating modes can be distinguished (Fig. 2).

On-line Since there is direct connectivity between a requester's smartphone and
the central unit, in addition to the functions mentioned above the latter can
search in the entire database for the feature vectors most similar to the one
provided by the requester, and present the therapies and results achieved in
these cases. Essentially, the cluster model is not needed in this mode, but it
serves well to reduce the computational effort of searching.

Off-line In this mode recommendations are made only on the basis of the model,
because the storage capacity of smartphones or other mobile digital appliances
is too small for holding the entire database. The feature vectors entered as well
as the actions and their effects queried in this mode are saved for execution
of the synchronisation mode.

Synchronisation This mode requires connectivity to the central unit. If data
were saved during off-line operation, they are sent to the central unit for
updating the database and the model. The current model is downloaded to
be used off-line.

The deployment of the algorithm FB-InCF in a recommender system for
telemedical purposes gave rise to a pending patent application [18], whose claim
reads:

Method for model-based recommendation of activities, whereby a database and a model of an application area are maintained on a central unit, data on further application cases are acquired and preprocessed by mobile units, from where they are, if need be, transmitted together with queries for recommendations of activities to be taken to the central unit, where recommendations are determined by means of the model and, then, transmitted for display to the requesting mobile units, which, on their part, query the activities actually executed and their subsequently observed consequences for transmission to the central unit, in order to extend there the database accordingly and to update the model incrementally.

It is emphasised that this claim also covers early-warning systems. The mobile units may, for instance, assume the form of sensors if data are to be acquired automatically.

6   Case Study of a Telemedical Recommender System

During the past two decades, the proportion of child births carried out with Caesarean section continuously increased worldwide [15,31]. According to several studies, the common indications for Caesarean sections are dystocia, fetal distress, breech presentation and repeated Caesarean sections [15,22]. For dystocia it was proposed to restrict Caesarean deliveries to cases of true cephalopelvic disproportion, with symptoms such as advanced cervical dilation and adequate uterine contractions combined with molding and arrest of the fetal head [27]. At Bhumibol Adulyadej Hospital in Thailand, for instance, 30% of the deliveries are by Caesarean section, and indication for it from cephalopelvic disproportion is between 5% and 7% [16,22]. In Sisaket Hospital, the rate of Caesarean sections increased from 32.7% in 2006 to 35.7% in 2010 [31].

According to [15,16,22], Caesarean section due to cephalopelvic disproportion is necessitated by three criteria, viz.

1. cervical dilatation of at least 4 cm and an effacement of at least 80% at the time of diagnosis,
2. regular uterine contractions for at least 2 h before the time of decision making and
3. abnormal partograph such as protraction disorders, arrest disorders or second-stage disorders.

These criteria determine a delivery route in the intrapartum period, i.e. during labour and delivery, but their detection may lead to hazards in Caesarean delivery. Radiographic pelvimetry is, therefore, performed in these cases. Unfortunately, measuring the pelvic dimensions to diagnose cephalopelvic disproportion and predicting labour outcome remains of limited value [8].

This section shows how the algorithm FB-InCF proposed is utilised in a medical recommender system with input patterns defined by medical records of pregnant women. The system aims to estimate in advance the risk incurred by normal childbirth or by delivery with Caesarean section due to cephalopelvic disproportion, instead of determining a delivery route not until or during labour. This approach underlines the key ideas of recommender systems, viz. to advise a consulting patient based on the medical records of similar cases, and of telemedicine, viz. to provide advice swiftly to any location and specific to this location.

6.1   Risk Factors Identified by Experts

The medical data set used in this case study [16] includes attributes from the medical history of patients, and risk factors significantly associated with Caesarean section due to cephalopelvic disproportion when analysed by multivariate logistic regression. These risk factors, viz. Maternal Age, Nulliparous Parity, Maternal Height, Fundal Height, Pre-pregnancy body-mass-index (BMI) and BMI before Delivery, are characterised by odds ratios (OR). Values for the latter were obtained by a case-control study, in which the case group consisted of 401 pregnant women who delivered by Caesarean section due to cephalopelvic disproportion. The control group also comprised 401 pregnant women who delivered normally, and whose members were determined by random sampling from a large database of medical histories. Both groups were compared by using t-test or Chi-square test as appropriate. All 802 deliveries took place in Thai public hospitals between 1 July 2005 and 31 May 2007. These risk factors are applied as weights (φ) in the weighted Mahalanobis distance according to Eqs. (4) and (5).

Experts have condensed their medical knowledge in form of rules to identify and quantify the risks of Caesarean delivery due to cephalopelvic disproportion. Such a rule may say, for instance, that if a pregnant woman's maternal age exceeds 34 years, the odds ratio of her risk is 2.73 when opting for a Caesarean delivery due to cephalopelvic disproportion instead of a normal one. The entire set of rules established in [16] to identify the risks due to cephalopelvic disproportion reads as follows.

1. **IF** Maternal Age ≥ 35 years **THEN** OR $= 2.73$
2. **IF** Nulliparous Parity **THEN** OR $= 6.79$
3. **IF** Maternal Height $\leq 150\,\mathrm{cm}$ **THEN** OR $= 1.9$
4. **IF** Fundal Height $\geq 35\,\mathrm{cm}$ **THEN** OR $= 2.11$
5. **IF** Pre-pregnancy BMI $> 26\,\mathrm{kg/m^2}$ **THEN** OR $= 3.54$
6. **IF** BMI before Delivery $> 26\,\mathrm{kg/m^2}$ **THEN** OR $= 2.5$

Thus, for instance, a patient undergoing Caesarean section due to cephalopelvic disproportion fulfilling just Rule 2 related to nulliparous parity bears a risk for any kind of failure with probability $\frac{6.79}{\text{sum of all risks to cephalopelvic disproportion}} = \frac{6.79}{2.73+6.79+1.90+2.11+3.54+2.50} = 0.3469$. A patient has a risk value of 1 if all odds ratios are present.

6.2   Empirical Evaluation

To demonstrate the FB-InCF algorithm's applicability to real-world data sets, we first compare it with traditional clustering algorithms such as K-Means and

K-NN in recommending delivery alternatives and, then, we investigate the correctness of the recommendations by comparing them with the choices actually made.

There is a vast diversity of metrics that could be used to evaluate the quality of a recommender system [12,28]. Here, the accuracy metric [12]

$$AC = \frac{\text{number of correct recommendations}}{\text{number of recommendations}} \times 100$$

is utilised, i.e. the proportion of the number of correct recommendations (recommendations coinciding with the actual diagnoses) to the total number of recommendations.

In Table 2, a subset of 10 patients selected from the entire data set comprising 802 medical records is shown. The table contains the values of nine attributes from the medical history of patients (Pa), viz. Maternal Age, Nulliparous Parity, Gravidity, Pre-pregnancy Weight, Weight, Maternal Height, Pre-pregnancy BMI, BMI before Delivery and Fundal Height.

Table 2. Example of a medical data set

Pa	A	P	G	PW	W	H	PB	BD	FH
1	21	0	2	48	61.5	1.58	19.22	24.63	33
2	27	1	2	47	66	1.52	20.34	28.56	35
3	33	0	1	98	108	1.65	35.99	39.66	35
4	24	0	1	48	67	1.6	18.75	26.17	40
5	25	2	3	68	75	1.6	26.56	29.29	36
6	15	0	1	50	64	1.55	20.81	26.63	32
7	25	1	2	55	66	1.65	20.20	24.24	32
8	22	1	2	39	53	1.575	15.72	21.36	31
9	27	0	1	48	67	1.57	19.47	27.18	35
10	33	2	3	45	56	1.59	17.79	22.15	33

Due to different ranges of medical data attributes presented in Table 2, such as height represented in meters and weight represented in kilograms, they need to be transformed in order to reduce the variance of data, which is affecting to the quality of recommendations. To increase their quality, the real values of attributes is replaced by values obtained from min-max normalisation calculated as $\frac{value-min}{max-min}$ [14], e.g. with the max-min values from the medical history of the 802 patients represented in the considered data set, the normalised maternal age of patient 1 aged 21 is $\frac{21-14}{45-14} = 0.226$. Thus, all transformed data are within the range [0, 1].

6.3   Experimental Results

Employing the medical data set introduced above, recommendations were simulated to compare the performance of the algorithm FB-InCF proposed with that of K-Means and K-NN clustering. The results indicate that K-Means clustering yields the lowest value of recommendation accuracy (62.84%) in comparison to K-NN (68.32%) and FB-InCF (69%). This relates also to the number of correct estimations of the risk incurred to patients: with 277 correct risk estimations FB-InCF outperforms K-Means (252) and K-NN (274).

7   Conclusion and Future Work

A knowledge-based incrementally working collaborative filtering algorithm was proposed. In order to allow the models maintained to adapt to changes brought about by its use, and to improve its recommendation quality, the algorithm is designed to obtain feedback on what happened after an action was recommended. Thus, the models evolve permanently comprising the knowledge contained in both the historical and example cases provided as well as in the experiences obtained by observing the effects of the recommendations generated. Moreover, the algorithm is to be used in (tele)medical recommender systems.

In a case study, the algorithm was employed here to assist physicians in—at least approximately—predicting to pregnant women the risk of childbirth with or without Caesarian section before delivery actually takes place, in order to replace the current practice of detecting and assessing criteria during labour and delivery. The approach is expected to be helpful in improving the quality of medical services in remote areas with insufficient infrastructure, such as rural regions of developing countries. The recommendation quality of FB-InCF was evaluated and compared with that of conventional techniques with respect to various criteria. In summary, the algorithm was shown to yield more accurate recommendations than existing model-based collaborative filtering algorithms, since it employs a similarity measure adequately devised by experts from knowledge on medical risk factors, and it adjusts more specifically to data sets by allowing for a variable number of clusters with varying shapes. Thus, it lends itself to on-line learning right from the start. To show the algorithm's effectiveness, experiments were carried out utilising a medical data set on the need for Caesarean sections due to cephalopelvic disproportion obtained from public hospitals in Thailand.

The objective of future work is to improve the algorithm's accuracy even further. To this end, the usage of rule bases derived from expert knowledge will be extended, and the clustering will be refined, e.g. by removing outliers and by allowing for irregular shapes of clusters.

Acknowledgement. We gratefully acknowledge the contributions of Aunsumalin Komkhao, M.D., specialist in obstetrics and gynecology, who provided medical knowledge.

References

1. Adlassnig, K.-P.: Fuzzy set theory in medical diagnostics. IEEE Trans. Syst. Man Cybern. **16**(2), 260–265 (1986)
2. Bock, H.H.: Automatische Klassifkation. Vandenhoeck & Ruprecht, Göttingen (1974)
3. CDC Website. https://www.cdc.gov/nchs/icd/icd9cm.htm. Accessed 6 Sept 2019
4. Da Silva, E.Q., Camilo-Junior, C.G., Pascoal, L.M.L., Rosa, T.C.: An evolutionary approach for combining results of recommender systems techniques based on collaborative filtering. Expert Syst. Appl. **53**, 204–218 (2016)
5. Davis, D.A., Chawla, N.V., Christakis, N.A., Barabási, A.L.: Time to CARE: a collaborative engine for practical disease prediction. Data Min. Knowl. Disc. **20**, 388–415 (2010)
6. Duan, L., Street, W.N., Xu, E.: Healthcare information systems: data mining methods in the creation of a clinical recommender system. Enterp. Inf. Syst. **5**(2), 169–181 (2011)
7. Folino, F., Pizzuti, C.: Comorbidity-based recommendation engine for disease prediction. In: Proceedings of the 23rd IEEE International Symposium on Computer-Based Medical Systems, pp. 6–12. IEEE, Perth (2010)
8. Gong, S.: A collaborative filtering recommendation algorithm based on user clustering and item clustering. J. Softw. **5**(7), 745–752 (2010)
9. Han, J., Kamber, M.: Data Mining: Concepts and Techniques, 2nd edn. Morgan Kaufmann Publishers, San Francisco (2006)
10. Hassan, S., Syed, Z.: From netflix to heart attacks: collaborative filtering in medical datasets. In: Proceedings of the 1st ACM International Health Informatics Symposium, pp. 128–134. ACM, New York (2010)
11. Heckerman, D., Horvitz, E., Nathwani, B.: Towards normative expert systems: Part I, the pathfinder project. Methods Inf. Med. **31**(2), 90–105 (1992)
12. Hernández-del-Olmo, F., Gaudioso, E.: Evaluation of recommender systems: a new approach. Expert Syst. Appl. **35**(3), 790–804 (2008)
13. Jain, A.K., Murty, M.N., Flynn, P.J.: Data clustering: a review. ACM Comput. Surv. **31**(3), 264–323 (1999)
14. Jain, A.K., Nandakumar, K., Ross, A.: Score normalization in multimodal biometric systems. Pattern Recogn. **38**(12), 2270–2285 (2005)
15. Khunpradit, S., Patumanond, J., Tawichasri, C.: Risk indicators for Caesarean section due to cephalopelvic disproportion in Lamphun Hospital. J. Med. Assoc. Thail. **88**(2), 63–68 (2005)
16. Komkhao, A.: Delivery due to cephalopelvic disproportion in Bhumibol Adulyadej Hospital Thailand. R. Thai Air Force Med. Gaz. **54**(70), 54–70 (2008)
17. Komkhao, M., Li, Z., Halang, W.A., Lu, J.: An incremental collaborative filtering algorithm for recommender systems. In: Kahraman, C., Kerre, E.E., Bozbura, F.T. (eds.) Uncertainty Modeling in Knowledge Engineering and Decision Making 2012, pp. 327–332. World Scientific, Singapore (2012). https://doi.org/10.1142/9789814417747_0052
18. Komkhao, M., Sodsee, S., Halang, W.A.: Method and apparatus for model-based recommendation of activities. Thai Patent Registration 1301002291 (2013)
19. Lu, J., Shambour, Q., Xu, Y., Lin, Q., Zhang, G.: BizSeeker: a hybrid semantic recommendation system for personalized government-to-business e-service. Internet Res. **20**(3), 342–365 (2010)

20. Luo, M., Zhao, R.: A distance measure between intuitionistic fuzzy sets and its application in medical diagnosis. Artif. Intell. Med. **89**, 34–39 (2018)
21. Mahalanobis, P.C.: On the generalised distance in statistics. In: Proceedings of the National Institute of Science of India, pp. 49–55 (1936)
22. Moryadee, S., Smanchat, B., Rueangchainikhom, W., Phommart, S.: Risk score for prediction of Caesarean delivery due to cephalopelvic disproportion in Bhumibol Adulyadej Hospital. R. Thai Air Force Med. Gaz. **56**(1), 20–29 (2010)
23. O'Driscoll, K., Jackson, R.J.A., Gallagher, J.T.: Active management of labour and cephalopelvic disproportion. J. Obstet. Gynaecol. Br. Commonw. **77**(5), 385–389 (1970)
24. Papungkorn, S., Wiboolphan, T.: Risk factors of Caesarean section due to cephalopelvic disproportion. J. Med. Assoc. Thai. **89**(4), 105–111 (2006)
25. Schwenker, F., Kestler, H.A., Palm, G.: Three learning phases for radial-basis-function networks. Neural Netw. **14**(4–5), 439–458 (2001)
26. Shambour, Q., Lu, J.: A hybrid trust-enhanced collaborative filtering recommendation approach for personalized government-to-business-services. Int. J. Intell. Syst. **26**(9), 814–843 (2011)
27. Spörri, S.: MR imaging pelvimetry: a useful adjunct in the treatment of women at risk for dystocia? Am. J. Roentgenol. **179**(1), 137–144 (2002)
28. Su, X., Khoshgoftaar, T.M.: A survey of collaborative filtering techniques. Adv. Artif. Intell. **2009**, 1–20 (2009)
29. Wang, J., Huang, P., Zhao, H., Zhang, Z., Zhao, B., Lee, D.: Billion-scale commodity embedding for e-commerce recommendation in Alibaba. In: Proceedings of the 24th ACM SIGKDD International Conference on Knowledge Discovery & Data Mining, pp. 839–848. ACM (2018)
30. Weiss, S.M., Kulikowski, C.A., Amarel, S., Safir, A.: Model-based method for computer-aided medical decision-making. Artif. Intell. **11**(1–2), 145–172 (1978)
31. Wianwiset, W.: Risk factors of Caesarean delivery due to cephalopelvic disproportion in nulliparous women at Sisaket Hospital. Thai J. Obstet. Gynaecol. **19**, 158–164 (2011)

Communities and Social Networks

NewYouthHack: Using Design Thinking to Reimagine Settlement Services for New Canadians

Christopher Schankula[1], Emily Ham[1], Jessica Schultz[1], Yumna Irfan[1],
Nhan Thai[1], Lucas Dutton[1], Padma Pasupathi[1], Chinmay Sheth[1],
Taranum Khan[1,2], Salima Tejani[2], Dima Amad[2], Robert Fleisig[1],
and Christopher Kumar Anand[1](✉)

[1] McMaster University, Hamilton, Canada
{schankuc,irfany1,anandc}@mcmaster.ca
[2] Brampton Multicultural Centre, Brampton, Canada
Salima.Tejani@bmccentre.org,
http://outreach.mcmaster.ca/
http://bmccentre.org/

Abstract. In 2018–2019 we applied Design Thinking (DT) to reimagining settlement services for refugee and immigrant youth in Canada. DT continues to gain followers as a practical approach to incorporating human factors into the design process. One insight motivating DT is that design is a series of experiments in which we learn about our users. Iterative prototyping and user feedback are paramount. But we also wanted to expose them to career pathways related to software design and development. In this paper we report on (1) the NewYouthHack process, (2) the resulting app and central role played by social interactions, and (3) the framework we developed to support this work.

We launched with a two-day designathon with 12 identified problems and proposed solutions. Social interaction and community supported by software were threaded through almost all of the solutions. This presented two new challenges: securing iteratively developed network software for vulnerable users, and meaningfully engaging the youth in necessarily complex software. Previously we had developed an outreach curriculum with tool support based on a library in Elm for stand-alone graphical web apps. We taught interaction using state diagrams. In Petri App Land (PAL), we generalized this, with tokens representing users visiting places within the app. Transitions now capture user interactions. To facilitate significant changes from iteration to iteration, much of the code is (re)generated based on a PAL spec.

Keywords: Design Thinking · Petri net · Collaborative platform · Mentorship · Social network · Immigration · Refugees

Supported by Immigration, Refugees and Citizenship Canada.

S. S. Rautaray et al. (Eds.): I4CS 2020, CCIS 1139, pp. 41–62, 2020.
https://doi.org/10.1007/978-3-030-37484-6_3

1   Introduction

The goal of the paper is twofold: (1) to describe a new model-driven web framework and (2) to describe its use in NewYouthHack, a project to reimagine youth settlement services in Canada. In Sect. 1 we provide context for this project in a larger body of similar research. In Sect. 2 we provide essential background information on several relevant topics, including Design Thinking, our outreach program, our partner in this project, the Elm language, and Petri nets. In Sect. 3, we describe the design of this project and its progression throughout. In the Sects. 4 and 5, we introduce our new platform for multi-user interaction, with an example application in Sect. 6. Finally, we conclude with results in Sect. 7 and ongoing and future work in Sect. 8.

1.1   Related Work

The advantages of Human-Centred Design and Design Thinking in designing networked services has been established. Natvig et al. used observations, interviews, innovation games and paper prototyping to develop enhanced support for collaboration in the transport sector [11]. Like our case, they needed to understand the problem from the points of view of multiple stakeholders. Design Thinking has also been successfully taught to children, including by Stanford researchers who enabled the children to redesign systems at their school [2].

Tech4SocialChange is a platform to connect universities, and especially undergraduates, with social problems [16]. The developers identified undergraduates' need for relevant real-world problems matching numerous unmet needs in the community. This differentiates their platform from HeroX and OpenIDEO which also match developers and community needs, but are not specifically geared to students. SOCRATIC is both an online platform and a step-by-step process for identifying problems, forming teams to solve them, and iterating prototypes [19]. It includes analytics to measure typical Design Thinking processes, like number of ideas generated, and it has been designed based on an analysis of several previous initiatives, with the explicit goal to be able to produce scalable solutions to large scale challenges such as migration [5]. The Experts in Teamwork project addresses the same problems, but their focus is on equipping potential social innovators with the skills they need [14]. This Stanford study concluded that Design Thinking "fosters the ability to imagine without boundaries and constraints", which is instrumental in developing children's creative confidence and that "design thinking may help students become empowered agents in their own learning who possess both the tools and the confidence to change the world" [2]. Since the youth involved were mostly high school students, we get this secondary benefit that they can apply DT to their own learning. This mirrors the emphasis that we placed on Design Thinking training for all of the participants, not just the McMaster University students involved in the project.

What distinguishes our approach to NewYouthHack, is the attempt to build a technology platform which supports iterative development and the integration of novice programmers. It is too early to say that this platform will lead to more sustainable solutions, but we are fairly certain that software developers will remain in high demand in the next decades, so these features are important.

One valuable service which other groups have been able to develop, but we have not considered in this project are services to support on-line design communities [1, 7].

2   Background

2.1   Design Thinking

Design Thinking (DT) is a human-centred methodology that focuses on the end-user and iterates rapidly through conceptual prototyping to produce innovative and creative solutions to complex problems [15]. The DT process is designed to avoid the creation of technically perfect but unwanted or incomprehensible products by focusing on the end-user while creating the product, while considering three dimensions: technical feasibility, economic viability, and desirability to the user [15]. Many people contributed to the development of DT, starting with Cross's study of designers in several fields and identification with Simon's *Sciences of the Artificial*[1], and Norman's definition of human-centred design.

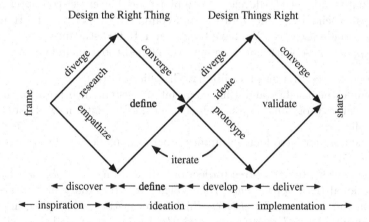

Fig. 1. This modified Double Diamond shows the key processes in Design Thinking, blending elements of the *British Design Council* and Standford's *d.school.*

DT assumes that the end-user is complex and that an understanding of their needs requires experiment and inquiry. Working with end-users is not a validation process. It is a discovery process. Hypotheses are not formulated as precisely, and are not about natural phenomena, but about the user's needs and experience.

There are multiple models and ways of thinking about DT. One of them includes three phases: inspiration, ideation, and implementation. Inspiration

---

[1] See [6] for a discussion focused on software.

is where the designer empathizes with the end-user, understands their hopes and desires, and uses this to understand the depth of the challenge. Ideation involves making sense of the research, generating ideas, identifying opportunities for design then testing and refining the solutions. Implementation is bringing the solution to life, as well as figuring out how to market it while maximizing its impact on the world [8].

Another view into DT is the double diamond process model developed at the British Design Council in 2005, see Fig. 1. There are divergent thinking stages followed by convergent stages where ideas are narrowed down towards the best one [18]. When designing, some people ignore the left side of the diamond, which leads them to focus on solving the wrong problem. This is why, in DT, *discovering* the problem through empathizing and research, as well as *defining* the right problem, are integral to the process. The *develop* stage involves developing prototype, testing, and iterating. Finally, the *deliver* stage is when the product is finalized, produced, and launched [18].

2.2 Software: Tool for Change Program

The McMaster University Outreach Program *"Software: Tool For Change"* has been operating for the past decade. It consists mainly of volunteer undergraduate and graduate students who develop lesson plans and deliver free computer science workshops to schools, public libraries, and community centres in the Hamilton, Ontario, Canada area [12]. We have taught over 15,000 students.

To support these workshops, we have developed tools, including:

1. An open-source Elm graphics library, GraphicSVG [17].
2. An online mentorship and Elm compilation system incorporating massive collaborative programming tasks, including the Wordathon[2] and comic book storytelling[3].
3. A curriculum for introducing graphics programming designed to prepare children for algebra [4].
4. A type- and syntax-error-free projectional iPad Elm editor, *ElmJr* [13].
5. Educational iPad apps, *Image2Bits* which supports binary image encoding, sharing and decoding; *TouchMRI* which mixes instruction about spin physics with an interactive k-space game; and *MacVenture* a tap-and-type editor for text-and-picture adventure games.

2.3 Brampton Multicultural Community Centre

BMC is a nonprofit organization with a mandate to

1. To enhance the capacity of newcomers to participate more effectively in our communities.

---

[2] http://outreach.mcmaster.ca/#wordathon2019.
[3] http://outreach.mcmaster.ca/#comics2019.

2. To partner with other service providers and organizations to strengthen the response capacity of the settlement sector.
3. To work collectively with other community actors to facilitate better use of newcomers' knowledge and talents in Canadian workplaces.

2.4   Elm Language

We use Elm (https://elm-lang.org/), a language designed for the development of frontend web applications [3], to teach beginners, so it was natural to use it for this project. Its syntax, based on the ML family of languages, is intentionally simple. For example, it has no support for user-defined type classes. In addition to strictly enforcing types, the Elm compiler also forces programmers to follow best practices, such as disallowing incomplete case coverage in case expressions. Elm apps use a model-view-update paradigm that keeps pure code separate from code with side effects without the need for monads as in Haskell. Elm code compiles down to JavaScript which provides many practical advantages for deployment and visualization.

While it may seem like this type of language should be reserved to expert users, many of these features useful to experts (strict types, pure functions) are very useful for beginners. In addition to practical implications of compiling to JavaScript, Elm's combination of simple syntax, strict typing, and purity which matches students' pre-existing intuition about math prove to be an asset to our Outreach program. These features allow the development of tools and curricula which would not otherwise be easy or possible in an imperative language with side effects such as Python.

2.5   Elm Architecture

All Elm programs follow a common architecture, "The Elm Architecture", with different variations enabling or restricting certain features as they are needed. These built-in "app" types interact with Elm's JavaScript-based runtime system, enabling pure code to interact with the outside world in a predictable manner, without runtime errors.

Elm's overall architecture consists of three main components: the *model*, the *view*, and the *update*.

Model. The *model* of the program is a type that encodes all the possible states the program can be in. In this way, it models the problem domain of the application. The type can be as simple as an alias for a basic type, such as `String` or `Int`, or as complex as needed. Since Elm is used to create web apps, it is recommended that the program be subdivided into top-level states or "Pages" using a union type.

For example, one could encode a very simple program having three states: `MainMenu`, `About` and `Contact`, using an algebraic data type. Additionally, we show the addition of a string to the `MainMenu` screen to display the user's name on screen, for example:

```
type Model = MainMenu String
           | About
           | Contact
```

The `view` portion of the Elm Architecture is a pure function which renders the current state of the program in the browser by returning a representation of html capable of sending messages of type `Msg` (see the following *Update* subsection for a discussion on messages): `view : Model -> Html Msg` Elm's runtime then uses a virtual DOM diffing strategy to efficiently display the elements described by the `view` function in the browser window.

The `update` function transforms the model state according to the message received: `update : Msg -> Model -> Model`

In this example, the `Msg` type is a "message" type that describes possible actions or events in this app. In our example from above we could have the following `Msg` type:

```
type Msg = GoToMainMenu
         | GoToAbout
         | GoToContact
         | ChangeName String
```

Together, the `Model` and `Msg` types can be visualized as a state diagram, encoding the states as circles and the transitions as arcs from one state to another state. Figure 2 shows how one might encode this example visually. Note that the type system does not enforce that the user adheres to their design. For example, the user's `update` code must account for the case where the `ChangeName` message is received when the user is in the `About` state, even though that case may be impossible based on the `view` function.

Commands and Subscriptions. In more advanced versions of Elm apps, the update function returns a tuple (`Model`, `Cmd Msg`). Commands (represented as the `Cmd` type in Elm) are a description of an asynchronous action for the Elm runtime to evaluate, passing the result back as a message to the user's `update` function if the command succeeds. This allows the app to perform impure actions, such as sending a message over the Internet or generating a random number.

Additionally, a *subscription* is a passive listener which waits for events and sends a message when the event occurs. For example, an Elm app may subscribe to a timer to receive a message at a set interval, receive a message when the user enters the app from another tab, or when the size of the app's window changes.

2.6 Petri Nets

A Petri net is a particular kind of directed bi-partite graph. There are two kinds of nodes: *transitions* and *places*. Places are *marked* by *tokens* which are consumed from input places and generated into output places upon the *firing* of a transition (which may occur non-deterministically upon fulfilling certain conditions).

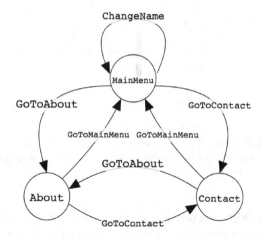

Fig. 2. An Elm app can be encoded as a state diagram, with circles being the top-level states in the app and the transitions being the arcs between them, named by the message sent to initiate the transition. When describing an Elm app this way, the programmer has to take care to follow the state diagram in the logic of the program as it is not enforceable at the type level.

Formal Definition. A Petri net is a 5-tuple,

$$PN = (P, T, F, W, M_0)$$

where [10]

$$
\begin{aligned}
P &= \{p_0, p_1, ..., p_m\} && \text{is a finite set of places} \\
T &= \{t_0, t_1, ..., t_n\} && \text{is a finite set of transitions} \\
F &\subseteq (P \times T) \cup (T \times P) && \text{is a set of arcs (flow relation)} \\
W &: F \to \{1, 2, 3, ...\} && \text{is a weight function} \\
M_0 &: P \to \{0, 1, 2, 3, ...\} && \text{is the initial marking} \\
P &\cap T = \emptyset && \text{and} \\
P &\cup T \neq \emptyset.
\end{aligned}
$$

Petri nets are conventionally represented as graphs with circles for places, rectangles for transitions and dots for tokens. Figure 3 shows a small Petri net example.

The behaviour of a Petri net is determined by the *firing* of transitions according to the following rules

1. A transition t is enabled if each of its input places p is marked with at least $W(p, t)$ tokens (where W is the weighting function of the arc)
2. An enabled transition may or may not fire (nondeterminism)
3. If an enabled transition does fire, $W(p, t)$ tokens are removed from input place p and $W(t, q)$ tokens are added to each output place q.

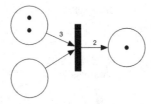

Fig. 3. A Petri net, showing a single transition, represented by the rectangle, two input places, and one output place. The arcs are weighted, meaning the transition requires as one or more tokens as input and produces one or more tokens as output. Tokens are shown as dots within places.

High Level Petri Nets. In order to describe more complex systems in a manageable way, extensions to classical Petri nets such as *Predicate Transition Nets* that utilize predicates in weighting functions and token-colourizing have been developed [9]. "Colouring" of tokens allows the model to distinguish amongst different tokens and the use of predicate expressions in weighting functions allows transitions to fire in several ways based on those colours.

3   Methods

BMC advertised the hackathon through their contacts and nine supporting community organizations, and held interviews and focus groups with interested youth and their parents. Thirty new youth, including new immigrants and refugees, aged 15 to 20 and speaking 10 languages, were selected. Graduate students or graduates in design were tasked with preparing and helping to deliver design-thinking training and the hackathon. Twelve undergraduate mentors were recruited and underwent a one-day Design Thinking together with staff from BMC and community partners.

Through multiple coding sessions, students were introduced to coding and learned to write code in Elm. To further develop their coding and collaboration skills, students worked in groups to code an animated comic book depicting their journeys to Canada. At one of these events, the Peel Regional Diversity Roundtable provided diversity and inclusivity training, for mentors and new youth alike.

NewYouthHack, a two-day "hackathon" was held at McMaster, over a weekend, including an overnight stay. Participants were challenged to use DT to improve the experience of settling into Canada. Twelve teams consisting of two to three youth, one BMC mentor, and one undergraduate mentor were guided through an abbreviated DT training and then asked to consider four themes: access to higher education, access to the labour market, access to information and services, and community connections. They were not directed to look for software solutions to the identified problems, but all of the undergraduates had post-secondary programming experience. A panel of judges was assembled in order to evaluate the effectiveness, business value, and technical feasibility of the designs that each team would develop.

The hackathon activities were modelled after the steps in the DT process. The 12 teams, in an effort to understand the problem from a users point of view, conducted user research by interviewing other participants, with coaching on interviewing provided by mentors. The teams then engaged in the ideation process, by defining their problem space, *how might we?* questions, user persona, and user pain points. At this point, the teams were encouraged to iterate on their ideas, by conducting more user interviews which either corroborated their ideation process results, or informed them that they had to pivot towards a better solution for the user. A practice presentation ended the first day, and a pitch competition the second.

At coding workshops subsequent to the hackathon, the new youth used their coding skills to code illustrations and animations that were incorporated into the app. For instance, students developed new features for an avatar creator, such as glasses and jewelry, and helped prototype the resume format, see Fig. 4. These coding sessions gave the students a means to directly apply their feedback on the app by coding their own contributions.

Fig. 4. Avatar showing a customization developed with the new youth *(left)* and the on-line programming interface, showing the resume template used in teaching, and later included in the app *(right)*.

Focus groups were a way to reach out to newcomer youth and gain their feedback on the current status of the app. Including focus groups in the development process allowed us to take their input into consideration during the development process and adapt the app accordingly. By watching students use the app and holding discussions, we were able to gather information on the usability of features and the user experience. The first focus group consisted of newcomer youth in high school, some of whom had attended NewYouthHack. Students brought up the app on their cellular devices and we displayed the app on a projector. We received feedback on the appearance and usability of the app, and discussed which features they found most helpful. Focus groups afterwards were conducted in a similar manner, with students occasionally using laptops rather than cellular devices. Focus groups were a great way to involve students in the development of the app and ensure the app met their needs and requirements.

4 Platform for User-Driven Innovation

4.1 Introducing Interaction with State Diagrams

In *Software: Tool For Change*, we have found teaching interaction using state diagrams to be an effective way for students to understand and design their programs. The simple graphical representation of the state diagram affords much understanding about the overall design of the application at a glance (see Fig. 2). We first teach them about states and transitions and then how to map both states and transitions to algebraic data types. This recipe produces a one-to-one mapping of states and transitions to constructors, which we have found is easy for students to understand once they have seen an example. One downside to this approach is that all possible transitions have to be handled in all states; "impossible" cases (according to the diagram) must be handled by making no change to the current model.

4.2 Petri App Land

It was our hope to involve the youth in as many phases of product development as possible. Initially, we were hoping that one or more stand-alone web applications would emerge from the Design Thinking phase, because we had a recipe for teaching children how to build such apps in Elm. But the problems surfaced by NewYouthHack clearly called for mentorship, sharing and commenting on resumes, etc., definitely requiring significant client-server interaction. Thus, we expanded upon our state diagrams to create Petri App Land (PAL), a client-server framework. While students did not contribute to the server-side code, we held workshops for students to contribute to the client frontend.

5 Petri App Land Runtime System

PAL contains code on both the client and the server acting as the "runtime system" for all PAL apps. The framework is available as open-source[4].

Client-Side. On the client side, the PAL framework generates code which handles connecting to the server, encoding outgoing messages and decoding incoming messages. It calls the user's `init`, `view`, and `update` functions from generated case expressions, handling the impossible default cases so they do not complicate the user's code. A WebSocket library is used to create a two-way communication channel with the server. Messages in a WebSocket connection always arrive in order, or else the connection is closed and must be restarted.

---

[4] http://github.com/cschank/petri-app-land.

Server-Side. On the server-side, PAL uses a Software Transactional Memory FIFO queue which is read in a state loop, processing messages and updating state atomically, similar to the Elm Architecture. Haskell threads are used to offload the tasks of encoding and decoding values and handling WebSocket connections with clients. In the future, different places on the server could be split into multiple threads to scale to much bigger services. In addition, we support an asynchronous command architecture accessed in a very similar way to Elm's, whose events run in different threads, so complicated calculations can be off-loaded in this way, if necessary.

6   Example Application

Figure 5 shows an example PAL. For NewYouthHack, the PAL network was encoded using Haskell data structures, which also specified the associated message types, and type definitions. Subsequently, we created a graphical specification tool, PALDraw. This example was made using that tool, but PALDraw and data modelling in PAL is beyond the scope of this paper.

6.1   Client-Side Modules

Users must fill in three types of modules on the client side after generating code from their specification, in order to complete their app. These consist of the `Init` module, the `View` modules and the `Update` module.

The `Init` module provides the initial state of the starting place on the client. This is where the user defines the initial data that is associated with the place. Below is an example `ForestPath` place from the example app in Fig. 5 (with imports removed for brevity):

```
init : ForestPath        -- the initial state of the starting place
init = ForestPath 0              -- player's water amount
               (Backpack [] 0) -- player's backpack
               0               -- player's health
```

Each place on the app has an associated view module, with functions corresponding to the Elm Architecture's (see above) `view` function. Note that we provide separate functions for each place, each with a unique model parameter type. This input type is a generated single-constructor version of the constructor describing the client-side state. This enforces at the type level that the user receives the data corresponding to the place in their view. A specialized `Msg` type is generated, limiting (again at the type level) which messages can be sent from which view functions. The programmer can also make use of Elm's subscriptions and change the title bar of the browser inside this module, by modifying the default implementations generated for the functions:

```
subs  : ForestPath -> Sub Msg
view  : ForestPath -> Html Msg
title : ForestPath -> String
```

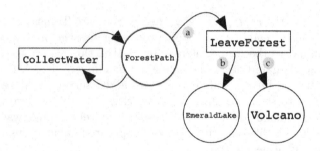

Fig. 5. A small PAL app consisting of three places: ForestPath, EmeraldLake and Volcano, and two transitions: LeaveForest and CollectWater. ForestPath's green outline indicates that it is the place clients are placed in upon connecting to the server. The LeaveForest transition has one incoming place, ForestPath (labeled as a)), and two outgoing places, EmeraldLake and Volcano. Clients in the ForestPath place can trigger the LeaveForest transition, causing the server to respond with either LeaveForest4EmeraldLake or LeaveForest4Volcano (labeled as b and c, respectively), according to rules related to the amount of water a player is carrying. The CollectWater transition keeps the user in the ForestPath and can be used to modify the user's current amount of carried water. (Color figure online)

Update Module. The Update module contains functions for each of the possible transitions the client can make when receiving a message from the server. For example, in our Fig. 5 example, the labels b and c represent the messages LeaveForest4EmeraldLake and LeaveForest4Volcano, respectively. As such, the following function stubs are generated:

```
updateForestPathLeaveForest4EmeraldLakeEmeraldLake : Environment ->
    LeaveForest4EmeraldLake -> ForestPath ->
    (EmeraldLake, Cmd EmeraldLakeT.Msg)

updateForestPathLeaveForest4VolcanoVolcano : Environment ->
    LeaveForest4Volcano -> ForestPath -> (Volcano, Cmd VolcanoT.Msg)
```

Note that, like in the view function, single-constructor types are used to once again enforce adherence to the app's model and to eliminate the need for (visible) case expressions with default cases for impossible cases.

6.2 Server-Side Modules

The Haskell server is structured similarly to the Elm side, but without view modules.

The Init module on the server initializes the place state for each place, as all places must be stored on the server at once. In our simple example, the ForestPath has a certain amount of water, but the other places, which are not shown, have no associated data:

```
initForestPath :: ForestPath
initForestPath = ForestPath 1000 {-initial water in forest-}
```

The **Update** module on the server contains a function for each transition in the PAL diagram. The function is called when a client initiates a transition by sending a message of the same name. The function is similar to the client update functions, but must consider multiple clients and states for all connected places. For example, the **LeaveForest** transition has an associated function on the server whose type signature is:

```
updateLeaveForest :: Environment -> ClientID ->
    LeaveForest -> ForestPath -> EmeraldLake -> Volcano ->
    [ForestPathPlayer] ->
    ( ForestPath, EmeraldLake, Volcano
    , (ClientID, ForestPathPlayer) -> LeaveForestfromForestPath
    )
```

The programmer must return a new state for all involved places, as well as a function that is mapped over all of the players (users) in the **ForestPath** place. This function returns a specialized type (**LeaveForestfromForestPath** in this case — see below) which determines which place to send the user to (or whether to keep them in the same place). In this way, users cannot be placed in multiple places at once or be forgotten.

The **LeaveForestfromForestPath** union type encodes only the possible transitions that are specified in the user's PAL model:

```
data LeaveForestfromForestPath =
    LeaveForest_ForestPathtoVolcano
        -- state of player when they go to volcano
        VolcanoPlayer
        -- message sent back to client
        LeaveForest4Volcano
  | LeaveForest4EmeraldLake
    ... two more cases ...
```

In the **updateLeaveForest** example, the user who issued the message to initiate the transition (determined by their unique **ClientID**) can go to the **Volcano** place if they have enough water in their player state. Otherwise, they stay inside the **ForestPath** place.

6.3   Helper Functions

Places and transitions are generated as constructors with fields for data, with simple data acting as the fields of a record-like structure. Algebraic data types were chosen to have consistency of the data across Elm and Haskell, which share the same basic syntax and semantics. For convenience, we produce **get***, **update***, and **alter*** functions for place states and one-constructor data types.

These helper functions are kept up to date as the specification of the app evolves, which replaces the need to pattern-match to extract information inside of the app's `view` and `update` functions. As such, using these helper functions greatly improves the maintainability of the app as new pieces of data are added. Furthermore, if data is removed or renamed, the helper function will also be removed from, or renamed in, the generated helpers module. The resulting definition error signals to the programmer that changes are required in the app's code in order to meet the new design of the app. Helper functions work the same way on both the client and server, leading to consistent code.

Below, we show the types from the generated templates for selected helper functions to access and update the `backpack` data type contained in the `ForestPath` state (from Fig. 5) generated for use in the client.

```
getBackpack : ForestPath -> Backpack

updateBackpack :
  Backpack -> ForestPath -> ForestPath
```

The argument order makes it easy to compose functions using (|>) : a -> (a -> b) -> b, Elm's left-to-right pipe, as in this fragment:

```
    forestPath -- current client state
        |> updateBackpack newBackpack {- new backpack -}
        |> alterHealth (\h -> h - 1) -- reduce health
```

This produces readable code that self-documents the changes made to models or pieces of data. In particular, the `alter*` functions provide the user with flexibility to compose other semantically-relevant, high-level functions, e.g. one could imagine creating some helper functions for backpacks:

```
addSandwich    : Sandwich -> Backpack -> Backpack
eatNSandwiches : Int -> Sandwich -> Backpack -> Backpack
```

which could then be used in conjunction with the `alterBackpack` function, by partially evaluating all but the final `Backpack` argument.

7   Results

7.1   The Hackathon

The 12 teams each settled on a problem, and made an initial presentation at the end of the first day. Omitting their well-thought-out detail, the ideas were:

1. Technology Learning for Academic Success
2. Information on courses - career pathways
3. Connections, mentorship at institutions
4. An app to make and submit resumes
5. Employer interaction, interviews, networking and hiring

6. Social interaction, services and events
7. Information on transit, maps and attractions
8. Vlog to help with school system and settlement
9. Multi-lingual resource to find friends and resources
10. Find volunteer opportunities activities and interests
11. Community specific multi-lingual interaction
12. Build connections and get information on services

Although NewYouthHack was more of a designathon than a hackathon, we wanted to capture the spirit of a hackathon by producing some prototypes during the weekend. The way we did this was to listen for self-contained app ideas within the presentations of the twelve ideas made at the end of the day on Saturday. A team of three developers then picked what they judged the greatest value/effort ideas, and implemented two of them: a simple chat client, to capture the idea of on-line mentoring, and an interactive high-school math pathway explorer, see Fig. 6.

Of the 12, the top 3 selected by the judges were, the video log, employer interaction app, and post-secondary education navigation.

After the hackathon, a steering group evaluated the twelve ideas with respect to implementation effort, barriers to adoption, privacy and safety issues, and the existence of competing solutions. It was decided that the video log posed safety issues which could be mitigated by restricting access to individual schools, and this idea was communicated to the Peel School Board. Information on courses is already available from myBlueprint.ca, but a focus group determined that new youth knew this, so a presentation to myBlueprint.ca was made, including the MathPathways prototype. Resume builders exist, but new youth needed trusted feedback, so it made sense to duplicate such functionality within a mentoring framework.

7.2   Independent Evaluation

The NewYouthHack project was evaluated using a developmental evaluation approach. It provided timely feedback and data to inform decisions on an ongoing basis, focusing on meeting stated goals, innovating effective solutions and identifying best practices. The newcomer youth and the participating stakeholders were engaged by the independent evaluator through in-person surveys, focus group meetings, key informant interviews, direct observation and informal conversations, to evaluate interaction with stakeholders through the entire process.

We quote the independent evaluator's findings that the NewYouthHack Project achieved its objectives in both developing ideas and empowering youth:

1. Successfully developed an app that aims to assist newcomer youth in multiple areas such as careers, education pathways, volunteer engagement and access to programs and services.
2. The successful launching and implementing of the app now depends on: (1) securing additional funding to further engage in consultation with relevant stakeholders, (2) piloting the app to fine tune, (3) implementing locally in Peel and (4) scale it up by implementing the app in Ontario and Canada.

3. Collaboration and partnership with multiple stakeholders in the community contributed to the successful implementation of the NewYouthHack project that brought sponsorships, stakeholder participation and feedback.
4. The initiative helped engage newcomer youth from diverse background that spoke 10 different languages and included disabled and LGBTQ persons.
5. An environment of trust and safety was created by BMC to address the concerns of parents of the newcomer youth ensuring their full participation.
6. The project provided a platform for newcomer youth to (1) develop a sense of belonging to their new home in Canada, (2) know that they are not alone; (3) open up to share their opinion freely on issues facing newcomer youth at and subsequent to the hackathon; (4) learn, identify, analyse and find solutions to the problems in their day to day life; and (5) expand their social networks.

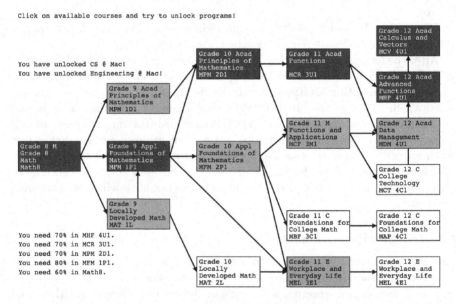

Fig. 6. Interactive Math Pathways explorer. New Youth, who were not used to having as much flexibility as allowed in the Ontario school system, found it difficult to make course selections and understand the implications in terms of post-secondary education. In this prototype tool, we allowed them to pick courses in the math stream one at a time, with new courses opening up once they have taken the prerequisites. At each stage, the selected courses are highlighted in blue, and the courses available to them are highlighted in green. As new courses are chosen, any entrance conditions (i.e. attaining a specific grade in a previous course) are listed, and undergraduate programs whose entrance requirements are met are also shown. This is one pathway for meeting the math requirements for Computer Science at McMaster University. (Color figure online)

Square One

Welcome to Square One (the main menu). Click below to take the GO bus to your desired destination!

Universities and Colleges

Connect with mentors from universities and colleges in Ontario

To Universities and Colleges

Profile Room

Make yourself pretty! Edit your Avatar, name, email address and more here.

To Profile Room

Universities and Colleges

Connect with mentors from universities and colleges in Ontario

To Universities and Colleges

Square One

Welcome to Square One (the main menu). Click below to take the GO bus to your desired destination!

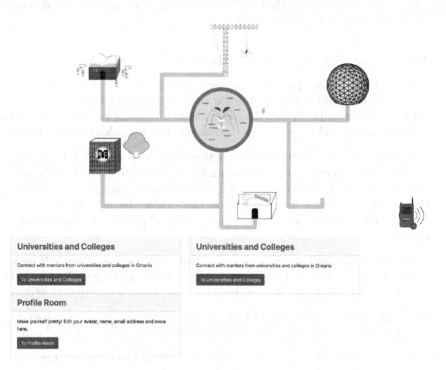

Universities and Colleges

Connect with mentors from universities and colleges in Ontario

To Universities and Colleges

Profile Room

Make yourself pretty! Edit your Avatar, name, email address and more here.

To Profile Room

Universities and Colleges

Connect with mentors from universities and colleges in Ontario

To Universities and Colleges

Fig. 7. Visualization of the landing page as it evolved based on focus group feedback. The initial landing page *(top)* was quite simple, and in response to feedback, we added a map *(bottom)*. Note that Square One is a shopping area and central landmark in Mississauga, the largest municipality from which participants were drawn. *Continued in Fig. 8.*

Square One

Welcome to Square One (the main menu). Click below to take the GO bus to your desired destination!

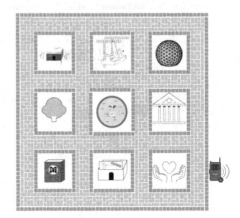

Fig. 8. *Continued from Fig.* 7. The map that was seen as confusing, so we tried to make it look like city blocks. *Continued in Fig.* 9.

We also quote from the evaluator's surveys of the youth:

○ 100% of youth said they have improved their communication skills
○ 96% of youth said they have learned work in group settings
○ 96% of youth said they have learned to design thinking to develop solutions
○ 95% of youth said they have learned about design thinking and its benefits

"Thanks to this experience I have noticed how important my role is in Canada. I have the power to drive change and make a positive impact and other youth can do so wherever they are. Using technology as a tool means that we all can change things and make them better for newcomers across Canada, overseas and for the next generations of people coming into our county."

○ 96% of youth said they have increased their self-confidence and self-esteem
○ 96% of youth said they have expanded their social network with new friends
○ 96% of youth said they have learned to work collaboratively with others

"It means a lot that this time I had the opportunity to design and have a say in creating a solution for barriers I faced as a newcomer youth."

○ 96% of youth said youth and adults have learned from one another
○ 92% said they were able to express their opinion on newcomer youth issues
○ 92% of youth said their opinions were listened and valued by others
○ 88% of youth said the youth and adults worked collaboratively

"STEM has been an interest of mine from an early age but attending Design Thinking, Coding Sessions, and Hackathon made me realize that I might actually look into computer engineering as a career choice."

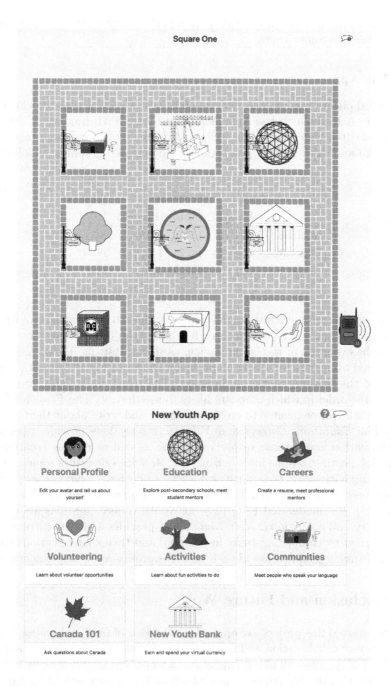

Fig. 9. *Continued from Fig.* 8. The street map introduced a different type of confusion, causing us to add signposts *(top)*, which elicited more concrete feedback and led us to go back to a button interface *(bottom)*, but now with colourful icons.

In one of the final focus groups, 75% reported they would recommend the app to other newcomer youth.

7.3   The App

The final application contained over 55,000 lines of code across the client and server, over half of which was code generated by the PAL framework. Much of the hand-written code was on the client side, defining the user interface which consists of bandwidth-sparing programmatically-created graphics, as follows:

	Spec (Haskell)	Client (Elm)	Server (Haskell)	Total
Written	3621	15498	7418	26537
Generated	N/A	14224	14556	28780
Total	3621	29722	21974	55317

Code generation was critical to development due to the rapid evolution of the design required to respond to user feedback. The changes are most visible through the evolution of the landing page, as shown starting in Fig. 7.

The final app consisted of the main menu shown in Fig. 9 *(bottom)*, leading to each of the features of the application. The icons are roughly ordered to represent the order in which users are likely to use the app. The *Personal Profile* allows the student or mentor to create an avatar and write about their goals or career. The *Education, Careers* and *Volunteering* sections provide mentorship and information about those respective topics, as well as resume creation and sharing, job posting, on-line interviewing, etc. *Activities* describes some common Canadian activities and foods, such as hockey or poutine. *Communities* provides language-based forums for youth to meet others who speak the same language. *Canada 101* is a moderated FAQ page for youth to ask questions about their new country and community. *New Youth Bank* provides a virtual currency that can be earned by completing tasks in the app, and then customizations can be purchased (many gamification ideas from focus groups await implementation).

8   Conclusion and Future Work

When we started this project, we applied for one year of funding because it was a new three-way collaboration and introduced new ideas to all of the participants. At the end of the year, all of our expectations were exceeded, especially in terms of the impact on the participating new youth and the robustness of an app built without requirements. We are seeking funding to continue work on this project.

Building on this experience, we have collectively undertaken follow-on projects: the *#BTCHACK - Re-Imagining Youth Civic Engagement* hackathon, focusing on Reimagining Youth Civic Engagement, was hosted by BMC in partnership with McMaster's Faculty of Engineering and Big Brothers Big Sisters of Peel, funded by the Ontario Trillium Foundation (OTF); and *Software: Tool For Change* hosted an *Internship-Style Summer Camp* over four weeks with 10–12 children ranging from ages 9–14, in which the children were given crash courses in Design Thinking and Cognitive Science and asked to imagine and develop a multi-player math game, with the resulting app[5] exceeding our expectations. In preparation for this camp, we created a prototype visual design tool called PALDraw for modelling the PAL, associated algebraic data types and their documentation, and including embedded state diagrams in each place. PALDraw generates the PAL spec as well as Elm modules which also work stand-alone. As a next step, we will extend PALDraw into an Integrated Development Environment (IDE), merging it with our web-based editor [4].

References

1. Ahmed, F., Fuge, M.: Capturing winning ideas in online design communities. In: Proceedings of the 2017 ACM Conference on Computer Supported Cooperative Work and Social Computing, CSCW 2017, pp. 1675–1687. ACM, New York (2017). https://doi.org/10.1145/2998181.2998249
2. Carroll, M., Goldman, S., Britos, L., Koh, J., Royalty, A., Hornstein, M.: Destination, imagination and the fires within: design thinking in a middle school classroom. Int. J. Art Des. Educ. **29**(1), 37–53 (2010)
3. Czaplicki, E.: Elm: Concurrent FRP for functional GUIs. Senior thesis, Harvard University (2012)
4. d'Alves, C., et al.: Using elm to introduce algebraic thinking to K-8 students. In: Thompson, S. (ed.) Proceedings Sixth Workshop on Trends in Functional Programming in Education, Canterbury, Kent, UK, 22 June 2017. Electronic Proceedings in Theoretical Computer Science, vol. 270, pp. 18–36. Open Publishing Association (2018). https://doi.org/10.4204/EPTCS.270.2
5. Dinant, I., Floch, J., Vilarinho, T., Oliveira, M.: Designing a digital social innovation platform: from case studies to concepts. In: Kompatsiaris, I., et al. (eds.) INSCI 2017. LNCS, vol. 10673, pp. 101–118. Springer, Cham (2017). https://doi.org/10.1007/978-3-319-70284-1_9
6. Gregor, S.: Building theory in the sciences of the artificial. In: Proceedings of the 4th International Conference on Design Science Research in Information Systems and Technology, DESRIST 2009, pp. 4:1–4:10. ACM, New York (2009). https://doi.org/10.1145/1555619.1555625
7. Hajiamiri, M., Korkut, F.: Perceived values of web-based collective design platforms from the perspective of industrial designers in reference to Quirky and openiDEO. ITU AZ **12**(1), 147–159 (2015)
8. IDEO: The field guide to human-centered design (2015). http://www.designkit.org/resources/1
9. Jensen, K.: High-level Petri nets. In: Pagnoni, A., Rozenberg, G. (eds.) Applications and Theory of Petri Nets. INFORMATIK, vol. 66, pp. 166–180. Springer, Heidelberg (1983). https://doi.org/10.1007/978-3-642-69028-0_12

---

[5] Escape From Math Island https://macoutreach.rocks/escapemathisland/.

10. Murata, T.: Petri nets: properties, analysis and applications. Proc. IEEE **77**(4), 541–580 (1989)
11. Natvig, M.K., Wienhofen, L.W.M.: Collaboration support for transport in the retail supply chain. In: Fahrnberger, G., Eichler, G., Erfurth, C. (eds.) I4CS 2016. CCIS, vol. 648, pp. 192–208. Springer, Cham (2016). https://doi.org/10.1007/978-3-319-49466-1_13
12. O'Farrell, B., Anand, C.: Code the future!: teach kids to program in elm. In: Proceedings of the 27th Annual International Conference on Computer Science and Software Engineering, pp. 357–357. IBM Corp. (2017)
13. Optimal Computational Algorithms Inc.: ElmJr (1.0). iOS App Stores (2018). https://apps.apple.com/ca/app/elmjr/id1335011478
14. Pappas, I.O., Mora, S., Jaccheri, L., Mikalef, P.: Empowering social innovators through collaborative and experiential learning. In: 2018 IEEE Global Engineering Education Conference (EDUCON), pp. 1080–1088. IEEE (2018)
15. Plattner, H., Meinel, C., Leifer, L.: Design Thinking: Understand-Improve-Apply. Springer, Heidelberg (2010). https://doi.org/10.1007/978-3-642-13757-0
16. Reis, A., et al.: Tech4SocialChange: technology for all. In: Fahrnberger, G., Eichler, G., Erfurth, C. (eds.) I4CS 2016. CCIS, vol. 648, pp. 153–169. Springer, Cham (2016). https://doi.org/10.1007/978-3-319-49466-1_11
17. Schankula, C.W., Anand, C.K.: GraphicSVG [elm package] (2016–2019). http://package.elm-lang.org/packages/MacCASOutreach/graphicsvg/latest
18. Tschimmel, K.: Design thinking as an effective toolkit for innovation. In: ISPIM Conference Proceedings, p. 1. The International Society for Professional Innovation Management (ISPIM) (2012)
19. Vilarinho, T., et al.: Experimenting a digital collaborative platform for supporting social innovation in multiple settings. In: Hodoň, M., Eichler, G., Erfurth, C., Fahrnberger, G. (eds.) I4CS 2018. CCIS, vol. 863, pp. 142–157. Springer, Cham (2018). https://doi.org/10.1007/978-3-319-93408-2_11

Community Based Emotional Behaviour Using Ekman's Emotional Scale

Debadatta Naik, Naveen Babu Gorojanam, and Dharavath Ramesh$^{(\boxtimes)}$ (iD)

Indian Institute of Technology (ISM), Dhanbad 826004, India
deba.uce03@gmail.com, naveenbabugorojanam@gmail.com,
drramesh@iitism.ac.in

Abstract. In the current era, the analysis of social network data is one of the challenging tasks. Social networks are represented as a graphical structure where the users will be treated as nodes and the edges represent the social tie between the users. Research such as community identification, detection of centrality, detection of fraud, prediction of links and many other social issues are carried out in social network analysis. However, the community plays an important role in solving major issues in a real-world scenario. In a community structure, nodes inside a community are densely connected, whereas nodes between the communities are sparsely connected. Determining the emotional behavior from communities is the major concern because, emotional behavior of community helps us to solve problems like brand reachability, find target audience, build brand awareness and much more. Ekman's emotional scale is a popular categorical model which assumes that there is a finite number of basic and discrete emotions and is used to classify the emotions. In this paper, a novel method is proposed to determine the community-specific emotional behavior of the users related to a particular topic. Communities are formed based on network topology rather than emotions. Girvan Newman algorithm is used to construct the communities of different users, who share their views on twitter media platforms regarding a topic. Then Ekman's emotional scale is used to categorize the emotions of the users of each community. This identifies how the people of different communities react to an incident. The incident can be treated as NEWS/Trending threads on Twitter/Facebook shares. The emotional analysis is done community-specific so that the behavioral analysis of an incident is performed specifically for that community. Further, the comprehensive experimental analysis shows that the proposed methodology constructs influential communities and performs emotional analysis efficiently.

Keywords: Community detection · Emotional analysis · Ekman's emotion scale · Tweet emotions recognition

1 Introduction

The popularity of social media is increasing day by day. This leads to huge research interest and opportunities in the study of communities. The most used

© Springer Nature Switzerland AG 2020
S. S. Rautaray et al. (Eds.): I4CS 2020, CCIS 1139, pp. 63–82, 2020.
https://doi.org/10.1007/978-3-030-37484-6_4

techniques in the study are community detection and sentiment analysis [8]. Community detection finds a group of people who are closely associated with each other, while the sentiment analysis determines the emotional behavior of a person and specifies his perception on a particular topic i.e., states how an individual feels. In social-media-based micro communications, the content individuals produce, and the emotions therein can affect other people's emotional states. Analysis of the social network data for community detection and their behavior has become the fundamental aspect of social network analysis [23]. This gives us an idea about how the users belonging to a particular community interact with each other and how various communities are interacting among themselves too. The analysis of communities is a topic of high research interest due to its wide range of applications. One such important application is to find the communities of interest, then focus only on those communities for marketing [13]. Thus, analyzing, and detecting human emotions based on the behavior exhibited by the communities has a direct effect on social networks [16, 21]. In social networks, people are connected to each other via; social media. One person can easily detect the emotions of the persons who are involved in the group chatting on a particular topic. Safety is one of the main concerns in the present scenario. Based on the emotional status of the community, it can be possible to predict and trap the criminal activities of a particular community. In commercial applications, the organization tries to find out the emotions of people of different communities based on the launched products. For example, when launching a new product into the market, find the communities which are interested in the product. Through the advertisement, companies can focus on the communities which have shown high interest in the product. Apart from this, the organization also tries to find out the problems associated with their product from the reviews of the dissatisfied communities. This gives more exposure to the organization to make future marketing strategies. To solve this, in this work, two real-time issues; one from a commercial application and another from a social application are demonstrated with a different set of data sets.

In the current scenario, WhatsApp, Facebook, Instagram, LinkedIn, Twitter, and other social network sites are the main source for the generation of data. The structure of twitter works as "follow" and "following" relationship between the users. The user following can receive the notifications of the public posts of the other user updates [11]. The present research work focuses primarily on detecting people's positive or negative feelings. However, these approaches fail to detect the other dimensions of emotions like anger, disgust, fear, happiness, sadness, and surprise [15, 24]. Many researchers have proposed methodologies for the extraction of emotions from an individual or considering all the users as a single community. However, the existing methodologies are ineffective, time-consuming and expensive to use in the applications like; study the behavior of people on a product, study the behavior of communities on social issues and many more. It may lead to a huge loss as compared to the profit for the investors. In addition, organizations are also unable to study the emotional behavior of individuals from different communities. It creates a gap for the researchers to conduct analysis on the communities rather than each individual or on a single group. Moreover, the quantifying approach for extracting the emotions of communities is a fast and cost-effective analysis. The aforementioned limitations motivate us to present a novel methodology that is capable enough to capture the emotions of the communities. So, every community's emotional level is monitored. The emotional level of the user is modeled using Ekman's Emotional Scale [10], which classifies human emotions into six in number; anger, disgust, fear, happiness, sadness, and surprise. Later, we calculate how a user's tweet is influencing the emotional behavior of the others following. The main contributions of the proposed work are summarized as follows:

- We propose an algorithm to detect the emotional behavior of communities, giving emphasis to the topological structure of the user's network.
- The more accurate scale of human emotions is determined using Ekman's emotional scale.
- We also demonstrate the impact of influential person's tweets on other people of a community by using two real-life data sets.

The rest of the paper is structured as follows. Section 2 presents the background topics in community detection and sentiment analysis. Section 3 presents the proposed methodology for sentiment analysis as a community wise. Section 4 contains implementation with a sample data set of the tweets, where emotional behavior is obtained for various communities. Section 5 depicts the experimental results and discussion for two different topics. Threats to validity are mentioned in Sect. 6. Conclusion and future work are presented in Sect. 7.

2   Related Work

Social network analysis has been one of the trending topics due to the increasing number of user's day-by-day. Community detection is a method through which it can be achieved that the users who are closely connected to each other are made into communities. In other words, the users inside a community are strongly correlated whereas users between the communities are loosely correlated [20]. One of the primitive algorithms for finding communities was proposed by Girvan and Newman, which forms the communities based on edge betweenness. In this work, edges are removed between the communities until each community gets isolated [17]. There are other community detection algorithms that work based on modularity, where modularity is the density of edges inside the community against the density of edges outside the community [4].

Sentiment analysis is another important topic that is used to recognize the emotion of a person. This analysis has a high significance in social network analysis because most of the people share their opinions on social networks [18]. The opinions of people are classified by Ekman's emotional scale, which classifies the emotions of humans into six categories: Anger, Sadness, Happiness, Disgust, Surprise, and Fear. This is one of the dominant models for classifying emotions based on the sentences [5]. An overview of sentiment analysis approaches has been described in [2]. One of the primitive methods for sentiment analysis on twitter data was carried out by Go et al., where the sentiments are obtained using machine learning algorithms like Naive Bayes, SVM, and maximum entropy [12]. In this work, the method involves prepossessing and post-processing of tweets. In post-processing, the emotions are extracted from the tweets and any tweet with both negative and positive emotion is removed. The retweets are also removed. As a result, the twitter data which has been used for emotional detection are reduced. The main drawback of this method is that it states only two emotional scales. A significant method was proposed by Barbosa and Feng, where the sentiment analysis is carried out through subjectivity classification and polarity detection [3]. Subjectivity classification is done by removing the disagreement approval, the tweets by the same user, and the top opinion words from the twitter data set. The polarity detection classifies the emotion of the tweet into positive or negative by dividing each category of tweets with the total number of tweets. The main drawback of this approach is that filtering of tweets is performed by choosing the specific tweets which satisfy the subjective condition. As a result, the number of original tweet data is significantly reduced and analysis is performed on less number of tweets. Agarwal et al. proposed the methodology, where the twitter data are classified into positive, negative and neutral [1]. The classification in this model is performed with respect to Tree kernel, unigram, and Feature-based models. Parts of speech tagger has been used to classify the emotions in this model. The Tree kernel model and feature-based model outperformed the unigram model, but the emotions are still restricted to three in number i.e., positive, negative and neutral. Xu et al. [24] proposed a method, where sentiment analysis and community detection are combined together to determine sentimental communities. In this work, the emotions are classified based on the opinion of the user towards a product, service, candidate or a topic. This analysis was used for market research to identify the sentiment analysis of the communities. The main drawback of this approach is that the communities are formed either to portray positive emotion or negative emotion. Due to this, the actual behavior of the users could not be determined because this method classifies happiness or surprise both as positive and sadness or disgust both as negative. Further, the classification of emotions was performed by Kanavos et al. [15], where the users are formed into communities based on the post-impact and influence metric. The post-impact of a tweet determines the impact of the tweet posted by the user and the influence metric of the user is calculated based on the influence metric and impact of the post. Emotions are recognized using Ekman's emotional scale and mapped into six different emotional scales. In this work, influential communities are produced based on the emotional analysis. However, in this method, users from different communities may be grouped in a single community because communities are formed based on emotions and influence rather than the topological structure of the users' network. This is because users are formed into groups based on influence metric rather than the connectivity. Dragoni et al. proposed a new approach where emotions are captured based on OntoSenticNet [9]. OntoSenticNet is a commonsense ontology that works based on a SenticNet. The SenticNet is a semantic network consisting of 10,000 primitive concepts. This work states that many lexicon-based knowledge bases are available for sentiment analysis, but there are no sentiment-based ontologies. The same reason is the limitation of this work. In a fast emerging environment, the number of lexicons is increasing rapidly, whereas the primitive concepts used in this model are limited to 10,000 in number. The approach proposed in [7] by Cambria et al. is similar to the approach used in [9]. However, a slight modification was done. While using the same primitive concepts, this method employs context embedding. Context embedding is the process of automatically discovering new conceptual primitives from text and embedding them to the common sense ontologies. This is an improvement in sentiment detection, but this method could not overcome the symbol grounding problem in sentiment analysis. Due to this limitation, this work could not perform sentiment analysis on language independent and symbol independent text data. Also, this approach uses AI for concept prediction. But, if the same concept library is used for any new text data analysis, it might not be fruitful because the new text data might not produce same concept ontology. Kanavos et al. [14] proposed a similar kind of methodology in which author collected and analyzed the tweet's emotions and based on these tweets, influential communities are derived. Each tweet is evaluated using ekman's scale. Then weighted version of communities are formed based on modularity optimization of the network and emotional state of the retrieved tweets. In this work, we propose a method that overcomes the ambiguity of various types of users coming under the same community. The most influential person can alter the emotions of the other users of the same community, i.e., shift emotions of people from the negative side to the positive side or vice versa. This methodology can be of great use in market research because it allows investors to monitor how emotions are being altered due to the tweet by the most influential person of the community.

3   Proposed Method

A social network can be interpreted as a graph structure $G = (V, E)$, where V and E represents the set of users and links between the users respectively. In this work, follow to follow factor analysis is carried out on the user's profile to identify the connections between the users. The user profiles are then mapped into the network of nodes, where they are connected to each other through edges. Then communities are formed in the network by using the Grivan Newman algorithm which uses edge betweenness to remove the edges iteratively. After this, for each of the communities formed, we calculate the emotional levels of each user in each community based on Ekman's emotional scale. Ekman's emotional scale gives the highest dimensions of emotions. This gives us an idea about how the users are reacting to a topic which is trending on Twitter. After this, we find the most influential person from each community using the two parameters; impact factor and influence metric [14]. These two parameters are calculated for each user by using (2) and (3). A user with the highest influence metric value will be treated as the most influential person of the community from which he or she belongs. Tweet of the influential person has a great impact on the emotions of the other users in the community. It mainly helps to alter the emotions of the people of the community. As a result, the emotional behavior of the whole community will be changed. This provides how influential is the community with respect to the tweets by the most influential person of that community. The details of our approach are presented in Algorithm 1. Algorithm 1 is mainly divided into three major subsections: Community formation, Emotional analysis, and Influential impact. These subsections are illustrated as follows.

Algorithm 1. Emotional Analysis based on Community Detection using Ekman's Scale

---

Input: Tweets from the users on a particular topic. This twitter data set is mapped into the graph structure $G = (V, E)$ where V is the set of users and E is the set of connections between the users.

Output: Emotions of each community.

1 Network formation based on follow to follow factor.
2 Community formation based on Girvan Newman algorithm.
3 Analysis of emotions level in communities using Ekman's emotional scale.
4 Identification of the most influential person in each community.
5 Repeat the Step 3 to perform the emotional analysis with new tweet data

---

3.1 Community Formation

In this subsection, the users are grouped into communities based on how strong the connection exists between them. Since, the Girvan Newman algorithm is the simple and standard algorithm used for detecting the non overlapping communities based on the edge betweenness, we have used it for non overlapping community formation [17]. In a graph, edge betweenness centrality represents the number of shortest paths that go through an edge in a graph or network. Each edge in the graph is associated with a betweenness centrality value. An edge with high centrality value represents a bridge between the parts of the graph [6]. Mathematically, betweenness centrality of a node u is defined as:

$$BC(u) = \sum_{u \neq x \neq y} \frac{B_{xuy}}{B_{xy}} \tag{1}$$

where, B_{xuy} is the number of geodesic paths between the nodes x and y that passes through the node u and B_{xy} is the total number of geodesic paths between the node x and y. Normalized betweenness centrality is obtained by dividing the Eq. 1 into $(n-1)(n-2)/2$. Since most of the connections in the twitter are follow to follow type, we use undirected and unweighted edges between the nodes when graphs are constructed. The working principle of the Girvan Newman algorithm for community detection is represented in Algorithm 2. In Algorithm 2, communities are detected by eliminating the edge with high betweenness centrality value iteratively. In a network, edges that are existing between the communities are found to be of high betweenness centrality value. After the removal of an edge having the highest centrality value, betweenness centrality for all the remaining edges is recalculated. The end result of Algorithm 2 shows the dendrogram, representing the different communities.

Algorithm 2. Girvan Newman Algorithm

Input: The network $G = (V, E)$ where $n = |V|$ and $e = |E|$.
Output: Community Structure
1 Edge betweenness is calculated for all the edges present in the network.
2 Edge with the highest betweenness value is removed first.
3 Edge betweenness of affected edges is recalculated after the removal of the edge with the highest value.
4 Step 2 and Step 3 are repeated until no edges remain in the network.

3.2 Emotional Analysis

In this subsection, detailed procedures for the extraction of emotions from the tweets are discussed. Emotions are generated from the tweets of the user using the tool called Emotion recognition tool [19]. The workflow diagram of the Emotion recognition tool is presented in Fig. 1. The tweet is initially divided into

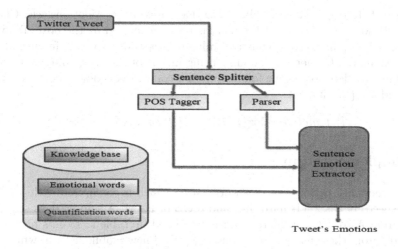

Fig. 1. Emotion recognition tool

words and the words are analyzed using parts of speech tagger and a tree structure is created. After this, stanford parser analyses the words and their relationship between them to create the dependency tree. The tree constructed has triplets namely, the root describing the emotion, the left node representing the governor and the right node representing the dependent. After this step, the triplets are compared with the knowledge base of the tool for further analysis. The knowledge base is a collection of words that portray emotions based on the lexical structure of the words used in the sentences. These emotional words are spotted on WordNet affect source [22]. After this, the sentence emotion extractor outputs the emotional status of the user. The emotions are anger, disgust, fear, happiness, sadness, and surprise according to Ekman's emotional scale.

3.3   Influential Impact

In social media, people's emotional behavior and thoughts are influenced by the people they follow. Often, the users with the highest number of followers term themselves as social media influencers. Anything posted by these people will have an impact on the followers. *Example: if a user with 10,000 followers tweets saying the new X product is totally worth buying. If at least 6000 followers are active and check out the tweet, there are higher chances that at least 30–40% of them might actually buy the product.* So, there is a need to find an influential factor of each user in the community to determine the dominant user. A twitter post has features like a retweet, replies, clicks, favorites, and mentions. Based on these factors, we obtain the influence factor as described in [15] and is shown in (2).

$$post\_impact = ((ret+1) \times (rep+1) \times (fav+1) \times (men+1) \times (cli+1))/directtweets \tag{2}$$

where, ret: Retweets, rep: Replies, fav: Favorites, men: Mentions, cli: Clicks. From (2), we can get how much impact is being generated by the post. To avoid the value becoming zero, a constant value of 1 is added to each feature of the tweet. Similarly, (3) depicts the influencing metric of the users in a community, which mainly depends on the follow to follow count, frequency of posting by the user and the post_impact.

$$Inf\_metric = \log(FtF + 1) \times freq \times post\_impact \tag{3}$$

4   Implementation

Experiments are performed on a workstation which is configured with 3.4 GHz clock speed. It has 2 TB hard disk and 8 GB of RAM. A sample data set of 26 users from A to Z is considered and is presented in Table 1. Tweets have been gathered from these users based on a topic called new mobile launch, which is a different topic from case 1. Users have mentioned their opinions about the product in their tweet. Then communities are formed for these users by implementing the Girvan Newman algorithm. In Fig. 2, it is shown that four communities are formed based on the connectivity between the users and these are; Employees, Freelancers, Students, and Critics. Based on the work profile, names are assigned to the communities for better convenience purpose. The connections between the users are taken in the form of GML file. Geography Markup Language is the XML grammar defined by the Open Geospatial Consortium (OGC) to express geographical features. The community structure is shown in Fig. 2.

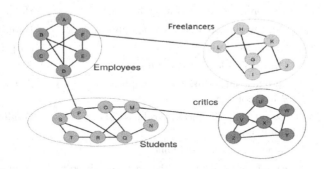

Fig. 2. Community structures

First, users are grouped into their respective communities using Algorithm 2. Each of the above tweets is then analyzed with the emotion recognition tool and the emotion of each tweet is extracted. Emotion levels of these communities are presented in Table 2. It is observed that the opinions of the critics community are mostly positive because they are expressing happiness and surprise mostly. Students are showing the disgust and sadness emotions towards the product. So the students' community should be focused upon in order to improve the sales of the mobile and get a positive impact from the students' community. To achieve this goal, a tweet from the most influential user of a student community must convey happiness emotion. Then the followers will get influenced and they may change their emotion in the retweet. This strategy makes the emotional scale to be shifted towards the positive side. In the students' community, the students R and Q have the highest number of followers, i.e., a good influence in the students' network. If anyone of these users starts tweeting positively about the product, the opinions of the followers will change and the community will head towards the positive side of the emotional scale, i.e., they start expressing surprise or happiness and not disgust, anger or fear.

5   Experimental Results

In this work, we have considered two different cases to validate the proposed methodology. These cases are the *launch of new iphone11* and the *mob lynching* in India. The analysis is done by collecting the tweet data from real users from twitter.

Table 1. Tweets of the users on a mobile launch.

User name	Tweet	Emotions
A	This better have wide lens camera #nophone	Fear
B	Still no bluetooth :-(#nophone #missingbluetooth	Sadness
C	It's gonna be wonderful #nophone	Happiness
D	Can't wait #oneweektogo #nophone	Happiness
E	Wow... the wait is over #nophone	Surprise
F	The camera looks bad #nophone	Sadness
G	No office subscription :-(#nophone #dissapointed	Sadness
H	Except camera, nothing to boast about #nophone	Disgust
I	Same processor #nophone	Angry
J	#nophone ready to be the new flagship killer	Happiness
K	Launching so soon #takenbysurprise #nophone	Surprise
L	One week to go #nophone	Happiness
M	Overpriced :'(#nophone	Sadness
N	#nophone please concentrate on millenials	Fear
O	Uhhh. . . no headphone jack #nophone #nojack	Surprise
P	Please cut down the cost #overpriced #nojack	Fear
Q	Too costly for a phone with no headphone jack #nophone #nojack	Disgust
R	No fast charger included in the box :'(#notfair #nophone	Sadness
S	Is the company accepting kidney as payment #toocostly #nophone	Sadness
T	Same as old #nophone but price +300$	Disgust
U	It should come with amoled display #nophone	Fear
V	Still the old snapdragon chipset #plsupgrade #nophone	Sadness
W	The specs amaze me #surprised #nophone	Surprise
X	Why is it priced twice the previous variant #nophone	Angry
Y	It's surprising that #nophone kept its word regarding camera	Surprise
Z	The best camera about to hit the market #nophone	Happiness

Table 2. Emotional behavior of communities.

Community	Anger	Disgust	Fear	Happiness	Sadness	Surprise
Employees	0%	0%	16.67%	33.34%	33.34%	16.67%
Students	0%	25%	25%	0%	37.50%	12.50%
Freelancers	16.67%	16.67%	0%	33.34%	16.67%	16.67%
Critics	16.67%	0%	16.67%	16.67%	16.67%	33.34%

5.1   Dataset Description

We have taken the data from twitter. These are the real data tweeted by the different users based on two topics. Details of these datasets are given in Table 3. The Girvan Newman algorithm is used for the community formation on the users who have posted the tweet. The users who are involved in posting the tweets related to the topic; Release of the new iPhone 11 are grouped into four different communities and their names are assigned based on the highest number of user's work profile found in these formed communities. These are Youtubers, General Public, News Channels, and Tech Pages. Assignment of names is optional, but for better understanding purpose names are assigned in this work. Similarly, communities of users found in the Mob lynching topic are; Youth, Political parties, News Channels, and Social pages. The emotional analysis is done for these communities using the Emotion recognition tool and Ekman's emotional scale. We then find the influential person in each community of the network to know, how each of these communities is influenced by the tweets of the influential person.

Table 3. Dataset description.

Sl. no.	Tweet topic	No. of tweets analyzed	No. of tweets analyzed after detecting influential node	Source
1	Release of new iPhone 11	193	193	Twitter (Open Source)
2	Mob lynching in India	170	170	Twitter (Open Source)

5.2   Results and Discussions

Release of the new iPhone 11: Initially, emotional levels of 193 users are computed from their tweets, considering all the users as a single community. The analysis categorized the emotions of users into six basic emotions which are shown in Fig. 3. A maximum number of people have shown the surprise emotion

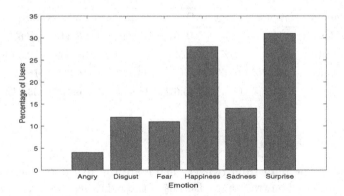

Fig. 3. Emotional levels for *new iPhone 11* launch

Table 4. Communities with emotional levels for *new iPhone 11* launch.

Communities	Angry	Disgust	Fear	Happiness	Sadness	Surprise
Youtubers	4.34%	10.86%	4.34%	32.6%	17.39%	30.43%
General public	7.69%	10.25%	12.82%	33.33%	12.82%	23.07%
News channels	7.89%	13.15%	15.78%	15.78%	15.78%	31.57%
Tech pages	6.06%	15.15%	12.12%	18.18%	18.18%	30.30%

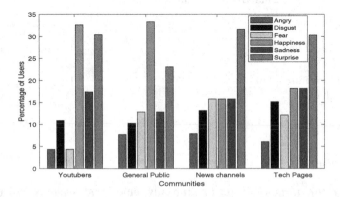

Fig. 4. Emotional levels for *new iPhone 11* launch (Community Specific)

on this topic and it is 31% of the total. The least percentage of people have shown their anger emotion. This analysis shows the emotional levels of all the users without the community-specific and gives us an idea about how the users are reacting to the iPhone 11 launch. However, from this analysis, it is not sure that which category of the people are reacting and how their emotional behavior is being shown. So, no substantial decision can be made based on this analysis. To overcome this problem, the Girvan Newman algorithm is used to categorize the users into different communities. Using this algorithm, four communities named Youtubers, General public, News channels, and Tech pages are formed from the user network. The emotional analysis of these communities gives a clear idea about the emotional behavior of the users. Moreover, the analysis also helps to do good market research and gives an idea of where to focus more. Table 4, shows the general public and News Channels community describes the highest and lowest value of happiness respectively. However, News channel community illustrates the highest anger and Tech pages community shows the highest sadness as compared to other communities. Therefore, investors must pay attention to these communities in marketing strategies. The graphical representation of Table 4 is depicted in Fig. 4. An influential person plays a vital role in changing the emotions of the users of these two communities. A positive tweet (an emotion conveying happiness) of an influential person may change the emotion of users of the same community towards the product. This is illustrated clearly by analyzing a positive tweet from an influential person named Marques Brownlee from You Tuber community. He tweeted about iPhone 11 as: *"NEW VIDEO: The iPhone 11 Models! Youtu.be/rie69pow668 – RT!"*. This tweet has got 731 retweets, 223 replies, 10135 favorites, 46 mentions, 1204 clicks, 193 direct tweets, 3319628 F2F, and 3.4 frequency. Then according to (2), the post_impact factor can be calculated as:

$post\_impact = 4779.94$ (Value is divided by 10^8 to normalize the value)
And the influence metric is calculated as:

$Inf\_metric = 105961.873$

Using (3), the most influential person can be detected for a community and based on his tweet, followers may change their mindset related to a particular topic. The same process is applied to other communities to determine the most influential person. Tweets are again collected from all the users, after the posting of a tweet by the most influential person of each community. Then the emotional levels are re-evaluated for each user. The significant change in the emotional levels of all the communities after the tweet by an influential person of each community are shown in Table 5. As shown in Table 5, in the Youtubers community, disgust feeling decreased by 8%, sadness decreased by 13%, anger decreased to 0%. However, the positive scales of emotions are increased; like happiness increased by 14% and surprise increased by 10%. In the same way, the emotional levels vary in different communities after a tweet by the most influential person from each community. The graphical representation of the modified emotional levels is depicted in Fig. 5.

Table 5. Emotional levels after the tweet by an influential person of each community

Communities	Angry	Disgust	Fear	Happiness	Sadness	Surprise
Youtubers	0%	2.2%	6.6%	46.6%	4.4%	40%
General public	4.87%	19.51%	14.63%	14.63%	9.75%	36.58%
News channels	0%	10.52%	15.78%	10.52%	31.57%	31.57%
Tech pages	5.88%	11.76%	17.64%	29.41%	11.76%	23.52%

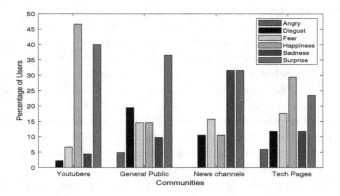

Fig. 5. Emotional levels after the tweet by an influential person of each community

The cumulative analysis of emotional levels is done by considering twitter data of all the users before and after the tweet of the most influential person. The cumulative data presented in Table 6, shows how the emotional levels are actually being portrayed by each community at the present course of time. The graphical representation of these data is depicted in Fig. 6. The analysis shows the significant improvement or deterioration of the emotional levels.

Table 6. Emotional levels for *new iPhone 11* launch (Cumulative)

Communities	Angry	Disgust	Fear	Happiness	Sadness	Surprise
You Tubers	1.48%	8.14%	5.18%	37.77%	13.33%	34.07%
General public	6.72%	13.44%	13.44%	26.89%	11.76%	27.73%
News channels	5.26%	12.28%	15.78%	14.03%	21.05%	31.57%
Tech pages	6%	14%	14%	22%	16%	28%

Mob Lynching: The same procedure is applied to the topic of Mob lynching in India to analyze the emotions of people. The related tweet data are collected to perform the analysis. The normal emotional analysis of the people with respect to the mob lynching is performed using Ekman's emotional scale and is shown in

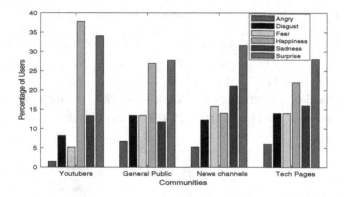

Fig. 6. Emotional levels for *new iPhone 11* launch (Cumulative)

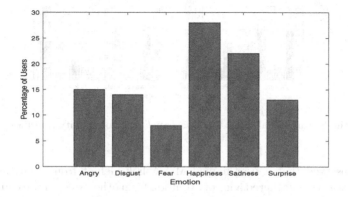

Fig. 7. Emotional levels for *Mob Lynching*

Fig. 7. The main disadvantage of this analysis is that researchers are not able to identify which community of people are reacting and portraying which emotion with respect to the topic. Further, no significant decisions can be made based on this analysis. To overcome these problems, analysis is carried out according to the proposed methodologies. The results shown in Table 7 are illustrating the emotional levels of all the communities.

Using Algorithm 2, four communities have been discovered. These are Youth, Political parties, News channels, and Social pages. Youth and political party's communities show the highest value of happiness emotion, which is never desirable by society. However, the political party's community shows the highest value of sadness emotion. The analysis also states that most of the communities are portraying sadness emotion high as compared to the other emotions. Since this is a controversial topic, most of the user's tweets are displaying such emotions. The graphical representation is depicted in Fig. 8, where emotion levels of all the communities are shown.

Table 7. Communities with emotional levels for *Mob Lynching*

Communities	Angry	Disgust	Fear	Happiness	Sadness	Surprise
Youth	24%	16%	4%	24%	20%	12%
Political parties	12%	4%	4%	24%	48%	8%
News channels	23.52%	17.64%	5.88%	11.76%	17.64%	23.52%
Social pages	10.71%	7.14%	21.42%	14.28%	25%	21.42%

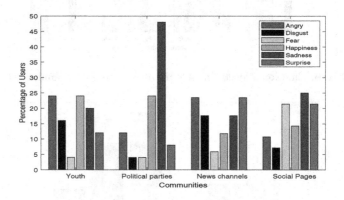

Fig. 8. Emotional levels for *Mob Lynching* (Community Specific)

It is observed that a user named Mr. Ashok Gehlot from political parties posted a tweet that gathered a lot of attention from other users of the community. The tweet is like: *"The #Rajasthan Protection from Lynching Bill, 2019 was passed by the State Assembly today. The Bill has been brought in to provide for strict punishment to curb such incidents".*

The above tweet has got 411 retweets, 61 replies, 2088 favorites, 29 mentions, clicks = 2051, 170 direct tweets, 73007 F2F, and 4.16 frequency. Then post_impact factor is calculated as:

$post\_impact = 183.154$ (Value is divided by 10^8 to normalize the value)
And the influence metric is calculated as:

$Inf\_metric = 4487.717$

The same process is applied to other communities to determine the most influential person. Tweets are again collected from all the users, after the posting of a tweet by the most influential person of each community. Then the emotional levels are re-evaluated for each user. The significant change in the emotional levels of all the communities after the tweet by influential persons are shown in Table 8. As shown in Table 8, the happiness scale has significantly increased from 24% to 54.54% and the anger scale has reduced from 12% to 6.06% in the community of political parties. The emotional scales also varied in other communities. The graphical representation is depicted in Fig. 9, where emotion levels of all the communities are shown.

Table 8. Emotional levels after a tweet by the influential person of a community

Communities	Angry	Disgust	Fear	Happiness	Sadness	Surprise
Youth	17.64%	14.7%	14.7%	29.41%	17.64%	5.88%
Political parties	6.06%	9.09%	0%	54.54%	6.06%	24.24%
News channels	5.88%	29.41%	5.88%	41.17%	11.76%	5.88%
Social pages	13.04%	21.73%	8.69%	13.04%	34.78%	8.69%

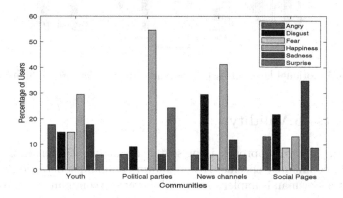

Fig. 9. Emotional levels after a tweet by the influential person of a community

The cumulative analysis of emotions illustrates the overall emotion levels portrayed by each community by considering all the tweets that have been posted by the users, The result of the cumulative analysis is shown in Table 9 and its graphical representation is depicted in Fig. 10. The cumulative analysis is useful for monitoring the emotional levels of each individual community with respect to a topic, whereas the breakdown of tweets before a tweet by the most influential person and after a tweet by the most influential person gives us how the communities are influenced. This can be used as a market research topic by studying the emotional behavior changes in communities in the presence of an influential factor.

Table 9. Emotional levels of each community for *Mob lynching* (Cumulative)

Communities	Angry	Disgust	Fear	Happiness	Sadness	Surprise
Youth	21.42%	15.47%	8.33%	26.19%	19.04%	9.52%
Political parties	8.62%	6.89%	1.72%	41.37%	21.13%	17.24%
News channels	14.7%	23.52%	5.88%	26.47%	14.7%	14.7%
Social pages	11.76%	13.72%	15.68%	13.72%	29.41%	15.68%

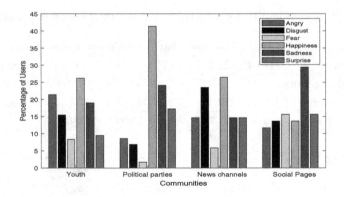

Fig. 10. Emotional levels of each community for *Mob lynching* (Cumulative)

6   Threats to Validity

In this work, a novel approach is presented to analyze the emotion levels of
each user in community-specific. A well-known community detection algorithm
called Girvan Newman is implemented to discover the communities of users. The
method proposed can show how the influence factor can alter the emotions of
the communities in the network. However, there are some limitations associated
with this approach. These are summarized as follows:

- The Twitter extraction tool considers only the tweets which are specifying
  the topic name with #tag.
- Communities with small size are ignored in the analysis because Girvan Newman algorithm unable to detect the small size communities.
- The proposed approach unable to identify the actual emotional scale if sar-
  casm is being portrayed in the tweet.

7   Conclusions and Future Work

In this paper, we have proposed a novel methodology which analyses the community wise emotional behavior of the users in twitter dataset. Initially, the Girvan Newman algorithm is used to detect the communities and then emotions are
determined using Ekman's emotional scale. This shows how various communities
are reacting to a trending topic on Twitter or any other social media platform.
The reactions of the users are analyzed based on their emotional behavior. This
analysis is really helpful for market research as it determines how opinions of
people are divided for a particular event. To improve the opinion on the product or event, the influential users are identified from each community to post
the positive tweet. By doing so, more number of users can be inclined towards
the positive emotional scale. The proposed approach overcomes the limitations
that are associated with the existing methods. In earlier methods, mainly two

emotional scales (positive and negative) were detected and emotions were user-centric rather than community-centric.

As future work, scalability being the major issue needs to be addressed using algorithms which can form communities faster for a larger given data set. Also, a shared-memory approach can be used for the parallel community detection process. Otherwise, techniques like Canopy clustering can be used which gives an estimate of clusters for community detection. In conclusion, we will use faster parallel techniques for community detection in time i.e., Modularity based approaches.

Acknowledgment. This research work is supported by Indian Institute of Technology (ISM), Dhanbad, Govt. of India. The authors wish to express their gratitude and heartiest thanks to the Department of Computer Science & Engineering, Indian Institute of Technology (ISM), Dhanbad, India for providing their research support.

References

1. Agarwal, A., Xie, B., Vovsha, I., Rambow, O., Passonneau, R.: Sentiment analysis of twitter data. In: Proceedings of the Workshop on Language in Social Media (LSM 2011), pp. 30–38 (2011)
2. Aggarwal, C.C., Zhai, C.: Mining Text Data. Springer, Heidelberg (2012). https://doi.org/10.1007/978-1-4614-3223-4
3. Barbosa, L., Feng, J.: Robust sentiment detection on Twitter from biased and noisy data. In: Proceedings of the 23rd International Conference on Computational Linguistics: Posters, pp. 36–44. Association for Computational Linguistics (2010)
4. Blondel, V.D., Guillaume, J.L., Lambiotte, R., Lefebvre, E.: Fast unfolding of communities in large networks. J. Stat. Mech: Theory Exp. **2008**(10), P10008 (2008)
5. Botvinick, M., Jha, A.P., Bylsma, L.M., Fabian, S.A., Solomon, P.E., Prkachin, K.M.: Viewing facial expressions of pain engages cortical areas involved in the direct experience of pain. Neuroimage **25**(1), 312–319 (2005)
6. Brandes, U.: A faster algorithm for betweenness centrality. J. Math. Soc. **25**(2), 163–177 (2001)
7. Cambria, E., Poria, S., Hazarika, D., Kwok, K.: Senticnet 5: discovering conceptual primitives for sentiment analysis by means of context embeddings. In: Thirty-Second AAAI Conference on Artificial Intelligence (2018)
8. Deitrick, W., Hu, W.: Mutually enhancing community detection and sentiment analysis on Twitter networks. J. Data Anal. Inf. Proc. **1**(03), 19 (2013)
9. Dragoni, M., Poria, S., Cambria, E.: Ontosenticnet: a commonsense ontology for sentiment analysis. IEEE Intell. Syst. **33**(3), 77–85 (2018)
10. Ekman, P.: Basic emotions. Handb. Cogn. Emot. **98**(45–60), 16 (1999)
11. Girvan, M., Newman, M.E.: Community structure in social and biological networks. Proc. Natl. Acad. Sci. **99**(12), 7821–7826 (2002)
12. Go, A., Bhayani, R., Huang, L.: Twitter sentiment classification using distant supervision. CS224N Proj. Rep. Stanf. **1**(12), 2009 (2009)
13. Han, M., Yan, M., Cai, Z., Li, Y., Cai, X., Yu, J.: Influence maximization by probing partial communities in dynamic online social networks. Trans. Emerg. Telecommun.Technol. **28**(4), e3054 (2017)

14. Kanavos, A., Perikos, I., Hatzilygeroudis, I., Tsakalidis, A.: Emotional community detection in social networks. Comput. Electr. Eng. **65**, 449–460 (2018)

15. Kanavos, A., Perikos, I., Hatzilygeroudis, I., Tsakalidis, A.K.: Integrating user's emotional behavior for community detection in social networks. In: WEBIST (1), pp. 355–362 (2016)

16. Kreibig, S.D.: Autonomic nervous system activity in emotion: a review. Biol. Psychol. **84**(3), 394–421 (2010)

17. Newman, M.E.: Fast algorithm for detecting community structure in networks. Phys. Rev. E **69**(6), 066133 (2004)

18. Pang, B., Lee, L., et al.: Opinion mining and sentiment analysis. Found. Trends Inf. Retr. **2**(1–2), 1–135 (2008)

19. Perikos, I., Hatzilygeroudis, I.: Recognizing emotion presence in natural language sentences. In: Iliadis, L., Papadopoulos, H., Jayne, C. (eds.) EANN 2013. CCIS, vol. 384, pp. 30–39. Springer, Heidelberg (2013). https://doi.org/10.1007/978-3-642-41016-1_4

20. Pizzuti, C.: GA-Net: a genetic algorithm for community detection in social networks. In: Rudolph, G., Jansen, T., Beume, N., Lucas, S., Poloni, C. (eds.) PPSN 2008. LNCS, vol. 5199, pp. 1081–1090. Springer, Heidelberg (2008). https://doi.org/10.1007/978-3-540-87700-4_107

21. Silberstein, R.B.: Electroencephalographic attention monitor. US Patent 4,955,388, 11 Sep 1990

22. Strapparava, C., Valitutti, A., et al.: Wordnet affect: an affective extension of wordnet. In: Lrec, vol. 4, p. 40. Citeseer (2004)

23. Thelwall, M., Wilkinson, D., Uppal, S.: Data mining emotion in social network communication: gender differences in myspace. J. Am. Soc. Inf. Sci. Technol. **61**(1), 190–199 (2010)

24. Xu, K., Li, J., Liao, S.S.: Sentiment community detection in social networks. In: 6th Annual Conference on 2011 iConference: Inspiration, Integrity, and Intrepidity, iConference 2011, pp. 804–805 (2011)

Non-fear-Based Road Safety Campaign as a Community Service: Contexts from Social Media

Subasish Das[1(✉)], Anandi Dutta[2], Abhisek Mudgal[3],
and Songjukta Datta[1]

[1] Texas A&M Transportation Institute, Bryan, TX 77807, USA
{s-das,s-datta}@tti.tamu.edu
[2] Ohio State University, Columbus, OH 43210, USA
anandixd@gmail.com
[3] Indian Institute of Technology (BHU), Varanasi 221005, UP, India
abhisek.civ@iitbhu.ac.in

Abstract. Traffic crash is a critical health hazard throughout the world. Traffic safety campaigns are important in increasing behavioral safety. Social media makes safety campaigns convenient due to its greater accessibility compared to mass media. Most road safety campaigns are fear-based. There is a need to use these campaigns carefully to reach a wider audience. Non-fear-based safety campaigns are limited in number, and their impact is significant in changing public attitudes towards safety. This study collected YouTube comment data from two non-fear-based safety campaigns and compared their impacts by using natural language processing tools. The findings of this study can help policymakers in understanding public perception and determining appropriate measures to improve road user behavior.

Keywords: Social networks · Social contexts · Natural language processing · Roadway safety campaign · Community service

1 Introduction

Traffic fatalities and injuries continue to be a severe public health hazard, and current trends show that it will remain similar in the upcoming years [1]. According to the World Health Organization (WHO) Global Status Report (2018), "the number of traffic fatalities continues to climb, reaching 1.35 million in 2016. Traffic injuries are the leading killer of children and young adults" [2]. Throughout the world, the road safety campaigns as part of community service aim to reduce traffic crashes and fatalities by influencing road users' behavior.

A majority of the road safety campaigns are fear-based. This approach provokes people by describing the negative consequences of risky driving behaviors by fear mongering. Typically, the fear-based campaigns benefit from the sentiments of the roadway users and apply graphic contents to shock the viewers, or they use strong messages to invoke shame or guilt on certain risky driving behaviors. In many cases, the viewers react differently to fear-based safety campaigns based on their personal

© Springer Nature Switzerland AG 2020
S. S. Rautaray et al. (Eds.): I4CS 2020, CCIS 1139, pp. 83–99, 2020.
https://doi.org/10.1007/978-3-030-37484-6_5

traits. The impact of these campaigns may work to a certain point; however, the long-term impact is still undetermined. It is important to note that the behavioral change of roadway users occurs from the readiness of everyone to adopt safe behavior. Non-fear-based advertisements and campaigns can help in developing long-term behavioral changes by encouraging people to drive safely. The state-of-the-art literature search shows that the examination of the effects on non-fear-based safety campaigns has not received much focus. There is a need to examine the public sentiments and attitudes towards the non-fear-based safety campaigns circulated through social media.

YouTube is a live and constantly fluctuating video-sharing and video-watching platform with more than 2 billion logged-in users (with options to view videos without logged-in also), and every day, these users watch over a billion hours of video [3]. Compared to safety campaigns on television, YouTube offers an alternative, cost-effective, and flexible platform. The mass media campaigns are costly and run only for a limited time. In contrast, road safety campaign videos on YouTube last forever. Additionally, it is impossible to understand public beliefs and sentiments from the televised safety campaigns. YouTube also gives users the choice to provide their opinion about a video with the ability to press a button showing that they like or dislike it. The virtual space created for social interaction and engagement provides public sentiments, opinions, and feedback.

The aim of this study is to examine the public sentiments and opinions towards non-fear-based traffic safety campaigns in YouTube videos. The research team selected two prominent non-fear-based YouTube video safety campaigns (one from India and the other from the UK) to collect relevant comments. By using natural language tools with around 120,000 words from the comments, the sentiments and attitudes are explored to determine the effectiveness of these two campaigns. The insights from this study can help promote non-fear-based safety campaigns more effectively.

2 Research Context

Road safety campaign is an indispensable way to promote roadway safety as well as to educate people about traffic rules and regulations. Many studies over the past several decades have examined the effectiveness of road safety campaigns. Today, traditional media like television, radio, print media, and static roadside advertising are being replaced by various online social media platforms such as Facebook, Twitter, Instagram, Pinterest, YouTube, LinkedIn, and others related platforms [4]. People, specifically the younger generation, are more likely to spend time on social networking sites than watching televisions or reading newspapers. Therefore, in recent days, road safety campaigns have started using social media platforms in addition to traditional media as a medium of raising awareness of road safety issues.

Social media has been widely used in recent years as a quick and real-time medium of broadcasting messages to public. Advertisements on social media are designed to increase sales, attract consumers, and obtain more attention for a brand [5]. Positive advertisements can give individuals positive feelings about the brand, which sometimes leads to a positive attitude towards that brand [6]. Similarly, effective road safety advertising on social media can be very beneficial in promoting a positive attitude towards the issues about road safety. Traditional media are typically one-way interactions that require a mechanism for active engagement with audiences. Information can easily be forwarded to friends and family through social media networks. Social media can spread concise messages as quickly as possible and facilitate the two-way flow of information. It also aims at creating online communities to share information, messages, links, concepts, sentiments, thoughts, and other content.

'Speeding. No One Thinks Big of You' – an important example of an Australian-based traffic safety campaign published on YouTube along with other traditional media sources such as television, print media, and roadside advertising displays [7, 8]. The authority tried online advertising to contact the young generation who has been traditionally difficult to reach. The purpose of online advertising was to show the consequences of speeding on roads that would motivate young driver's behavior change. The campaign received a tremendous response from young people who discussed the issues associated with risky and dangerous driving on social networking platforms but may not be possible through traditional advertising campaigns.

The success of road safety campaigns depends on the well-developed understanding of psychosocial theories of behavior [9]. These theories help the advertising industries as well as the road safety experts to understand their potential audience better and result in the desired change. The theory of planned behavior indicates three significant factors of human characteristics, such as attitudes toward the behavior, social customs, and controls on behavioral aspects [10]. These factors determine whether one should engage him or herself in a specific behavior (e.g., speeding, drinking, and driving, distracted driving, seatbelt use) or not. Health belief theory proposes avoiding an adverse health outcome motivates people to preserve or protect their health [10]. On the other hand, protective motivation theory highlights the human fear of negative consequences, which keeps them away from engaging in a negative behavior [11, 12]. Social norms theory indicates that social perceptions influence human behavior, which may result in inaccurate decision making without thinking about health or safety. According to the elaboration-likelihood theory, individuals will likely to change their behavior if they think it is relevant and sense a high level of social responsibility [13]. All of these theories can be beneficial for the development of road safety advertisings and get a better result out of these safety campaigns.

Fear-based campaigns provide people the negative consequences of risky behaviors (e.g., drinking & driving, speeding), especially with graphic visual displays (for example, crash video footage, crash related severe injuries), and take advantage of the emotions of a target audience [14]. The primary purpose of the fear-based campaigns is to scare and shock individuals and to invoke shame or guilt of their negative behavior. However, past research revealed that fear-based advertising has moderate to low effects on human attitudes, intentions, and behaviors [15–21]. For example, research has shown that young adults recognized fear-based road safety advertising appeals as irrelevant and often believe that the adverse effects are unlikely to happen to them [15, 22]. On the other hand, non-fear-based campaigns that demonstrate individuals how to avoid a negative behavior safely could bring a more significant change than those fear-based campaigns [12, 13, 23]. Additionally, the willingness of humans is the primary key to the positive behavioral change rather than the strength of the fear-based motivation itself [14].

3 Methodology

3.1 Data Collection

Studies on 'transportation related text mining' has been increased in the recent years [24–36]. The current research aimed to use social media platform YouTube to understand the public perception of people on road safety campaigns. The research team used two different non-fear-based advertisements to compare the impacts and insights. These two advertisements are: (1) a series of advertisements by the Ministry of Road Transport and Highways in India, (2) Embrace Life, a British public information film made for the Sussex Safer Roads Partnership (SSRP). As a part of the road safety week campaign in India in 2018, the Ministry of Road Transport and Highways included a popular Indian actor, Akshay Kumar, to spread awareness on traffic rules and road safety in a series of three video advertisements. These non-fear-based safety advertisements gain wide popularity among the viewers. Many media outlets praised the efforts of the Indian Government to raise concerns on roadway safety by these witty and smart advertisements. With the slogan *'Sadak Suraksha Jeevan Raksha'* (*'Safe Roads Save Lives'*) and the title *'Road Kisi Ke Baap Ki Nahi Hai'* (*'Roads Are Not Your Father's Property'*), this series of advertisements won the best advertising campaign (in India) of 2018. The other video *'Embrace Life,'* a traffic safety advertisement on the importance of wearing seat belts released in 2010, became an international sensation after it was distributed through social media such as YouTube. The video has been widely praised for its non-fear-mongering approach, its visual representation, and its impact on public sentiments. It may be argued that the UK advertisement is not completely non-fear-based. However, it illustrates the negative consequences without any graphic display, and it passes positive emotions.

The research team used two tools, tuber and YouTube comment scrapper [37, 38], to download relevant information and developed a list of videos and associated information on these two advertisements. It was found that Indian ads are distributed by many YouTube channels. To acquire adequate comments, the research team selected four video ids for the Indian advertisement and one video id for the UK advertisement. The acquired information includes the number of views, likes, dislikes, original comments as well as replies. The view counts of the Indian and UK advertisements are 3.5 million and 20 million, respectively. The dislike-like ratios for Indian and UK advertisements are 2.02% and 1.60%, respectively. The total number of comments (and replies) Indian and UK advertisements are 4,042 (30,000 words) and 5,598 (90,000 words), respectively (Table 1).

Table 1. Selected videos and view measures.

Country	Focus	Duration	Title	Published on	Video ID	Like	Dislike	Views
India	All	3 min 5 s	Road Kisi Ke Baap Ka Nahi Hai	8/14/2018	BlqOYEXeTyU	106,000	2,100	3,095,595
India	All	4 min 49 s	Road Kisi Ke Baap Ka Nahi Hai	8/14/2018	6YkiMaC4lus	3,400	117	249,184
India	Wrong way	1 min	Sadak Suraksha Jeevan Raksha Road Safety TVC	8/13/2018	8xOVQlqYPjk	970	18	76,191
India	Cell phone	1 min	Sadak Suraksha Jeevan Raksha Road Safety TVC	8/13/2018	xcDnHA5Prko	827	20	82,068
UK	Seat belt	1 min 28 s	Embrace Life - always wear your seat belt	1/29/2010	h-8PBx7isoM	55,000	878	20,171,672

3.2 Exploratory Data Analysis

The research team developed two text corpora from these two campaigns. The final datasets were developed after removing the stop words, numerical values, punctuations, and other relevant words (for example, any word that represents film star, Akshay Kumar).

Odds Ratio Analysis. The odds ratio quantifies the strength of association between two measures and is considered a good statistical tool for finding associations between categorical variables. It represents the ratio of the odds of an event A in the presence of another event B and the odds of event A in the absence of event B.

The strong association is related to higher values. The *odds* of word w in group i's usage can be written as:

$$O_{kw}^{(i)} = e_{kw}^{(i)} / \left(1 - e_{kw}^{(i)} \right) \tag{1}$$

where, $e_{kw}^{(i)} = \frac{y_{kw}^{(i)}}{n_k^{(i)}}$. The term $y_{kw}^{(i)}$ denotes the w-vector of word or term counts from documents of class i for topic k. The odds ratio measure between the two groups is $\theta_{kw}^{(b-a)} = \frac{O_{kw}^{(b)}}{O_{kw}^{(a)}}$ [39]. Figure 1 shows the log odds of the keywords associated with these

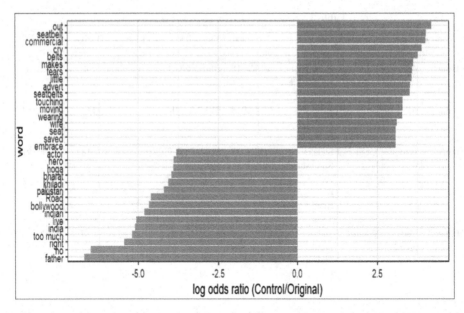

Fig. 1. Log odds ratio (comparison = UK advertisement, reference = Indian advertisement).

video ids. Seatbelt related words have high odds to be presented in the comparison or control dataset (UK data). Emotional terms like 'cry' and 'tears' also have high odds in the UK data. On the other hand, the low odds are associated with the Hindi terms such as hoga (means 'to be') and Bharat (means India). One crucial finding from the log odds analysis is that the positive words are almost common or similar in both text corpora (thus not visible in the log-odds plot).

Word Correlations. The research team developed n-grams (contiguous sequence of n words from a document) to determine the trends of the textual content using R package tidytext [40]. A group of two words in sequence can be defined as a bigram. Tables 2 and 3 provide the top word correlations developed from the significant word pairs. A closer look at both tables showed that many comments included positive sentiments, such as gratitude toward the video participants (for example, many comments associated with Indian advertisement praised the popular actor, Akshay Kumar). Some also admired the campaigner for its effort. Patriotic terms, for example,

Jay Hind (Victory to India) were found at least 63 times in the text corpus of the Indian advertisement. The word pairs in the Indian advertisement do not show any particular interest in any of the key safety issues promoted in the Indian ad (wrong-way driving, helmet, and cell phone usage). As the UK advertisement is based on seatbelt use, many comments are relevant to this topic.

Table 2. Frequency distribution of top word pair patterns (Indian advertisement).

Word	best	good	hai[5]	hind[6]	job	kisi[7]	nice	police	rules	video
road	0	0	0	0	0	164	0	0	0	0
very	0	44	0	0	0	0	76	0	0	0
good	0	0	0	0	49	0	0	0	0	7
nice	0	6	0	0	12	0	0	0	0	62
nahi[1]	0	0	81	0	0	0	0	0	0	0
traffic	0	0	0	0	0	0	0	36	30	0
sir	14	8	0	0	0	0	9	0	0	0
great	0	0	0	0	16	0	0	0	0	0
jai[2]	0	0	0	48	0	0	0	0	0	0
sahi[3]	0	0	24	0	0	0	0	0	0	0
best	0	0	6	0	0	0	0	0	0	8
superb	0	0	0	0	0	0	0	0	0	7
follow	0	0	0	0	0	0	0	0	9	0
always	12	0	0	0	0	0	0	0	0	0
jay[4]	0	0	0	15	0	0	0	0	0	0

Note: 1 nahi (Hindi term) = no, 2 jai (Hindi term)= victory, 3 sahi (Hindi term)= truth, 4 jay (Hindi term)= victory, 5 hai (Hindi term)= have, 6 hind (Hindi term)= Hindustan or India, 7 kisi (Hindi term)= felt certain

Table 3. Frequency distribution of top word pair patterns (UK advertisement).

Word	belt	ad	done	eyes	life	People	safety	Seat belt	seen	time	wear
seat	384	0	0	0	0	0	0	0	0	0	0
ever	0	0	0	0	0	0	0	0	122	0	0
well	0	0	116	0	0	0	0	0	0	0	0
wear	0	0	0	0	0	0	0	247	0	0	0
every	0	0	0	0	0	0	0	0	0	68	0
Embrace	0	0	0	0	46	0	0	0	0	0	0
always	0	0	0	0	0	0	0	0	0	0	41
tears	0	0	0	34	0	0	0	0	0	0	0
best	0	28	0	0	0	0	0	0	0	0	0
ad	0	0	0	0	0	0	0	0	0	0	0
great	0	0	0	0	0	0	0	0	0	0	0
loved	0	0	0	0	0	0	0	0	0	0	0
road	0	0	0	0	0	0	25	0	0	0	0
many	0	0	0	0	0	24	0	0	0	0	0
saved	0	0	0	0	24	0	0	0	0	0	0

4 Sentiment Analysis

It is important to quantify the impact of a safety campaign on a targeted population, and this is one of the key problems surrounding the assessment of safety campaigns. The research team used sentiment analysis as an innovative measure of quantifying the impacts. The research team used AFINN lexicon to identify positive and negative sentiments [41].

4.1 Top Unigrams with Sentiment Measures

Figure 2 shows the top unigrams associated with positive and negative sentiments. It clearly depicts that the negative sentiments are lower in frequency in the Indian ad video comments compared to UK video comments. The top unigrams in both datasets show similarity. Some of the unique positive terms in the Indian corpora are 'salute,' 'super,' and 'superb.' 'Beautiful,' 'powerful,' and 'brilliant' are the unique positive terms in UK corpora. The negative terms are unique for both datasets. For example, terms associated with 'dislike' in the Indian corpora indicates the comments on who disliked the videos. Thus, it implies positive emotion rather than negative emotions. This example particularly calls for individual comment exploration to understand the relevant contexts, which has been shown in the next section.

4.2 Contexts from Representative Comments

In many cases, road safety campaigns are generally not systematically evaluated. The research team randomly selected the top 10 comments (from 300 comments having at least 30 words per comment) to understand the contexts in those comments. Both safety campaigns cover some of the critical behavioral aspects: (1) seatbelt usage, (2) wearing helmets, (3) cell phone usage, and (4) wrong-way driving. Other key behavioral risk factors were not included in these videos, such as speeding and distracted driving. Table 4 lists five randomly selected comments from each dataset. The contexts associated with Indian advertisement are other safety issues (bike riders on sidewalks, overtaking from the left side, driving behavior near bus stops), corruption in police officers, politicians, Bangladesh (regarding a 2018 student movement to promote road safety), and civic sense. The contexts that are associated with the UK advertisement are personal safety precautions and modern in-vehicle safety, death of a relative, teen safety, and negative views on the association between lower speeds in the small towns and relevance of wearing seatbelts. The context associated with lower speed limits and seatbelt use requires further exploration to improve community service through safety campaigns. It is interesting to see that other predominant behavioral risk factors (for example, distracted driving) were not dominant in any of the comments.

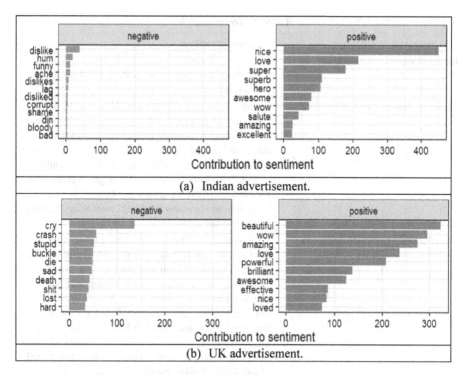

Fig. 2. Top unigrams associated with positive and negative sentiments.

Table 4. Example comments with different contexts

Advertisement (*Context*)	Example comments
Indian (*Context: Other safety issues*)	Good message. Please also pass such message for those bike riders who drives on sidewalks if they see traffic on signal even if they can go only few meters and again waiting for hours in same traffic. One more, people who always over take from left side. People who drives near to bus exit when bus is halting at its designated bus stop risking life of passenger who alight from bus at bus stop
Indian (*Context: Police officers*)	I wish all the officers were honest like these. Even though there will be few no doubt, but the judgment becomes so biased. The majority officers will be wanting to just devour the money and not actually wanting the safety of people
Indian (*Context: politicians*)	Whoever made this video should have included politicians in this video message. They are also citizens of this country and the same traffic laws apples to them too they are not above the law. Thank you

(*continued*)

Table 4. (*continued*)

Advertisement (*Context*)	Example comments
Indian (*Context: Bangladesh*)	This is the ad which reminded me about students raise their voices to safe and follow the traffic laws of roads in Bangladesh
Indian (*Context: Civic sense, and license*)	People get license without any education of driving by Regional Transport Office (RTO), no entry boards are not clear because of posters or not colored on time. So how can we expect people to follow rules just by add. Civics sense is absent which should be taught first, people crossroad when green signal is on for cars. Show civics sense ad in theatre, tv and radio first. This ad is useless till then. Unnecessary honking is another bulls**t
UK (*Context: Personal behavior and in-vehicle safety*)	For some reason, I can't even stand to get in a car without my seat belt on. Just the thought of a body traveling about 50 mph and coming to a complete stop scares me. I will always wear my seat belt because I have seen what it can do. My mother just got a 2011 Mercedes-Benz E550 and it probably is the safest car in the world. It knows when you are about to wreck, and it automatically tightens the seat belts and holds you down in the seat in rollovers, side impacts, and frontal crashes
UK (*Context: Death of a relative*)	Thanks to seat belts my nephew died in a horrible fiery crash because we could not get him out in time. We were powerless to save him as the flames were too intense, We had to watch him and hear him cry suffering a horrific death by flames. His father, my brother-in-law could not take it and took his own life just 6 weeks later. Two lives lost due to the use of seat belts. Sure, seat belts may save some lives, but they also end them. Seat belt laws were created by the insurance companies
UK (*Context: Negative view on wearing seat-belts; small town*)	Respectfully, there is nothing to disagree with. When virtually all small towns the size I live in have never had a fatality in a car there is literally nothing to worry about. It's not impossible to die or get injured here but is so rare that it is pathetic to worry about it so thinking "you never know" really doesn't apply much. People are getting killed just outside of town occasionally where the speed limit is higher than 30 mph. There is very little speeding here unlike the idiots in big cities where enforcement of these stupid seat belt laws would make far more sense. In fact, in Minnesota our last Governor said that 20 to 30% of the fatalities in this state happen in the two largest

(*continued*)

Table 4. (*continued*)

Advertisement (*Context*)	Example comments
	cities and their surrounding seven counties. That means it takes the entire rest of the state to have the other 80% of them which many times as much area as those seven counties. People on this sight should be bitching about speeding in big cities instead of this harping about seat belts all the time! Since I have lived here 65 years wearing seat belts where it matters and am alive to tell about it I'll respectfully ignore all these safety "experts" on YouTube because I like truth better than exaggeration
UK (*Context: Negative view on wearing seat-belts; small town*)	Me stupid? You're so dense that the exact proof, that is all around you, goes right over your head. All you have to do is check anywhere on earth and you will find the exact same thing I find with small towns. It's the speed that makes all the difference. You must be from the big city where there isn't any common sense. Just speeders. Don't be an idiot. Just go to the first small town away from the slum you live in and ask when the last person died in a car in their city limits. They will have to think for a while before they remember the last one or any for that matter. You are the kind that gets these stupid laws enacted because you believe the safety faggot commercials on TV which are extremely exaggerated as to the real danger which just not all over. Get your head out of your ass
UK (*Context: Teen safety*)	First saw this last year. I often forgot to buckle up, but this made me think of my young boy. Now I always remember. Last week I was hit from behind by an SUV going about 50 mph, slamming me into a car in front of me, creating a 6-car pileup That moment where the man's legs, arms & head fly uncontrollably forward is exactly what happens. Fire rescue extricated me. Today, I hurt like hell, but no fractures. Thank you, Sussex Safer Roads. I'm so glad to be hugging and kissing my boy today

4.3   Valence Shift Word Measures

In their study, Dodds and Danforth [42] developed the concept of 'Valence Shift Word Graph.' A brief overview of the theoretical framework of this concept is mostly based on the study of Dodds and Danforth and Doss et al. [42, 43]. Consider two texts T_{ref} (for reference) and T_{comp} (for comparison) with sentiment scores $s_{mean}^{(ref)}$ and $s_{mean}^{(comp)}$ respectively. Comparison of T_{comp} relative to T_{ref} is shown as:

$$s_{mean}^{(comp)} - s_{mean}^{(ref)} = \sum_{i=1}^{N} s_{mean}(w_i) \left[p_i^{(comp)} - p_i^{(ref)} \right]$$

$$= \sum_{i=1}^{N} [s_{mean}(w_i) - s_{mean}^{(ref)}] \left[p_i^{(comp)} - p_i^{(ref)} \right] \quad (2)$$

where,

p_i = the $i-th$ distinct word's normalized frequency of occurrence and which can be inferred as a probability, and

$$\sum_{i=1}^{N} s_{mean}^{(ref)} \left[p_i^{(comp)} - p_i^{(ref)} \right] = s_{mean}^{(ref)} \sum_{i=1}^{N} \left[p_i^{(comp)} - p_i^{(ref)} \right] = s_{mean}^{(ref)} (1-1) = 0, \quad (3)$$

w_i represents the word i in comparison text, p_i represents the percentage of word i in comparison text.

A word's sentiment is associated with text T_{ref} by $+$ sign (positive sentiment) and $-$ sign (negative sentiment), and its relative presence in text T_{comp} versus text T_{ref} with $\uparrow$ sign (more prevalent) and $\downarrow$ sign (less prevalent). By joining these two binary probabilities can lead to four different scenarios [43]:

- $+ \uparrow$: Increasing relatively positive words– If a word/term has more positiveness than text $T_{ref}(+)$ and appears more often in text $T_{comp}(\uparrow)$, then $s_{mean}^{(comp)} - s_{mean}^{(ref)}$ is positive.
- $- \downarrow$: Decreasing relatively negative words– If a word/term has less positiveness than text $T_{ref}(-)$ and appears less often in text $T_{comp}(\downarrow)$, then $s_{mean}^{(comp)} - s_{mean}^{(ref)}$ is also negative.
- $+ \downarrow$: Decreasing relatively positive words– If a word/term has more positiveness than text $T_{ref}(+)$ and appears less often in text $T_{comp}(\downarrow)$, then $s_{mean}^{(comp)} - s_{mean}^{(ref)}$ is positive.
- $- \uparrow$: Increasing relatively negative words– If a word/term has less positiveness than text $T_{ref}(-)$ and appears more often in text $T_{comp}(\uparrow)$, then $s_{mean}^{(comp)} - s_{mean}^{(ref)}$ is also negative.

The normalization of Eq. 3 and conversion to percentages can be described as:

$$\delta s_{mean,i} = \frac{100}{\left| s_{mean}^{(comp)} - s_{mean}^{(ref)} \right|} \underbrace{\left[s_{mean}(w_i) - s_{mean}^{(ref)} \right]}_{+/-} \underbrace{\left[p_i^{(comp)} - p_i^{(ref)} \right]}_{\uparrow/\downarrow} \quad (4)$$

Where $\sum_i \delta s_{mean,i} = \pm 100$, based on the sign value of the difference in sentiment/emotion between two texts, $s_{mean}^{(comp)} - s_{mean}^{(ref)}$, and the terms to which the symbols $+/-$ and $\uparrow/\downarrow$ apply have been indicated. The $\delta s_{mean,i}$ is called the per word sentiment shift of the i th word. Figure 3 can be interpreted by the following interpretations:

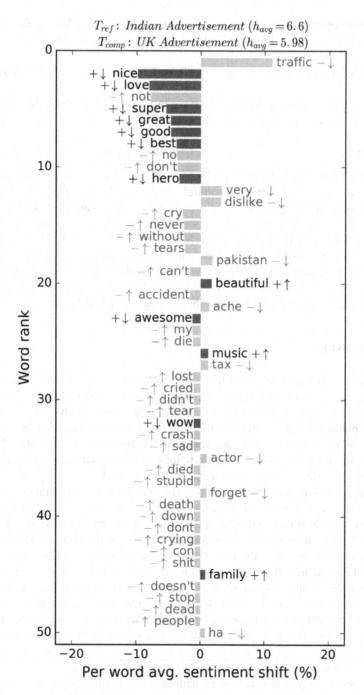

Fig. 3. Valance shift plot. (Color figure online)

- Words on the right contribute to an increase in positive emotions in the corpus
- A yellow bar in the right with a down arrow indicates that a negative emotion was used less
- A purple bar in the right with an up arrow indicates that positive emotion was used more
- Words on the left contribute to a decrease in position emotions in the corpus
- A yellow bar in the left with an up arrow indicates that a negative emotion was used more
- A purple in the left with a down arrow indicates that positive emotion was used less

Figure 3 shows the valence shift plot by using UK data as comparison and Indian data as a reference. Three words (beautiful, music, and family) are in the purple bar with up arrows on the right side. It indicates that these words are more used in the UK dataset. Some of the negative emotions (the yellow bar with down arrows on the right side) that are less used in the UK data are dislike, very, and forget. Some of the positive words that are less used in the UK data (compared to Indian data) include nice, love, super, great, best, hero, awesome, and wow. Some of the negative emotions that are more used in the UK data include cry, tears, accident, crash, and death. The average happiness index (h_{avg}) of Indian data is higher than the UK data.

5   Conclusions

Promotional videos are considered as a significant tool to promote traffic safety campaigns. Researchers consider safety campaigns using videos more effective because of their influential appeals and storytelling power. The current study was designed for acquiring public interactions from a case study on two non-fear-based safety campaign videos using YouTube comment data. The main contribution of the current study is that it has developed an intuitive text mining framework to measure the public sentiments associated with the selected video data. The framework can be applied to other effectiveness measure determination works. The analysis points to sentiments, different contexts, and valence shift paradigms by individual data from these datasets. The general findings show that comments in the Indian context are less insightful due to the presence of noise in the dataset that incorporates praise of the film star. However, key issues such as corruption of the police officers, the influence of politicians, sidewalk issues, and nationalism (for example, the utterance of Jai Hind or Victory to India) are vigilant in different analysis outcomes. The UK video is mostly associated with seatbelt and the sublime version of the advertisement itself. One issue requiring more attention for the UK context is to increase public awareness regarding lower speeds in small towns and the importance of seatbelt wearing. The valence shift plot provides a word-based emotion shifts in both datasets. The results show that there is a different pattern of word usage when expressing emotions related to these videos.

The current study is not without limitations. First, the investigation in the current study was limited to two non-fear-based safety campaign videos. Future studies should expand the scope of the current study by extending the list of the videos (by quantity and quality) on a wide range of social media platforms. Second, non-user (those who do not use social media or do not comment in case they use) feedback is undetermined in the current study. Lastufka and Dean [44] showed that the mean video views to comment ratios on YouTube is about 5%. Other types of analysis, such as survey design and analysis, can help comprehend the impacts of the campaign on roadway users. However, comments on YouTube are mostly unobtrusive (compared to other social media platforms) and easily retrievable data that can be used to understand public perception towards road safety campaigns. Future studies can investigate on the penetration rate of the collected comments to measure effectiveness of a campaign with the use of advanced algorithms and tools.

References

1. World Health Organization: International Classification of Diseases – 10th Revision. Geneva, World Health Organization (1990)
2. World Health Organization: Global Status Report on Road Safety 2018. Geneva, World Health Organization (2018)
3. YouTube: YouTube for press. https://www.youtube.com/yt/press/statistics.html. Accessed 29 Aug 2019
4. Wundersitz, L., Hutchinson, T.: Road safety advertising and social marketing. J. Australas. Coll. Road Saf. **22**(4), 34–40 (2011)
5. Stafford, P.: Top social media campaigns and what you can learn from them. http://www. smartcompany.com.au/advertising-and-marketing/20110113-top-social-mediacampaigns-what-you-can-learn-from-them.html. Accessed 29 Aug 2019
6. Homer, P., Yoon, S.: Message framing and the interrelationships among ad-based feelings, affect and cognition. J. Advertising **21**(1), 19–33 (1992)
7. Watsford, R., Roads, N.S.W.: The success of the Pinkie campaign 'Speeding. No one thinks big of you': a new approach to road safety marketing. In: Annual Conference of the Australasian College of Road Safety, High Risk Road Users-Motivating Behavior Change: What Works and What Doesn't Work, pp. 18–19 (2008)
8. Smart, W., et al.: The Newell Highway road safety review. In: Australasian Road Safety Research, Policing and Education conference, New South Wales (2009)
9. Elliott, B.: Road Safety Mass Media Campaigns: A Meta-Analysis. Federal Office of Road Safety, Canberra (1993)
10. Delhomme, P., De Dobbeleer, W., Forward, S., Simões, A.: Manual for designing, implementing, and evaluating road safety communication campaigns: Part I. In: Campaigns and Awareness Raising Strategies in Traffic Safety, Institut Belge pour la Sécurité Routière (IBSR) (2009)
11. Rogers, R.W.: Cognitive and physiological processes in fear appeals and attitude change: a revised theory of protection motivation. In: Cacioppo, J.T., Petty, R.E. (eds.) Social Psychophysiology, Guilford, New York, NY, pp. 153–176 (1983)
12. Cismaru, M., Lavack, A.M., Markewich, E.: Social marketing campaigns aimed at preventing drunk driving: a review and recommendations. Int. Market. Rev. **26**(3), 292–311 (2009)
13. Wundersitz, L.N., Hutchinson, T.P., Woolley, J.E.: Best practice in road safety mass media campaigns: A literature review. Centre for Automotive Safety Research. Adelaide, Australia (2010)

14. SWOV: SWOV Fact sheet: Fear-based information campaigns. Leidschendam, the Netherlands, Institute for Road Safety Research (2009)
15. Brennan, L., Binney, W.: Fear, guilt, and shame appeals I social marketing. J. Bus. Res. **63**, 140–146 (2010)
16. Hastings, G., Stead, M., Webb, J.: Fear appeals in social marketing: strategic and ethical reasons for concerns. Psychol. Market. **21**, 961–986 (2004)
17. Laroche, M., Toffoli, R., Zhang, Q., Pons, F.: A cross-cultural study of the persuasive effect of fear appeal messages in cigarette advertising: China and Canada. Int. J. Advertising **20**, 297–317 (2001)
18. Meneses, G.D.: Refuting fear in heuristics and in recycling promotion. J. Bus. Res. **63**, 104–109 (2010)
19. Mowen, J.C., Harris, E.G., Bone, S.A.: Personality traits and fear response to print advertisements: theory and an empirical study. Psychol. Market. **21**, 927–943 (2004)
20. Rossiter, J.R., Thornton, J.: Fear-pattern analysis supports the fear-drive model for anti-speeding and road safety TV ads. Psychol. Market. **21**, 45–60 (2004)
21. Arnett, J.J.: Optimistic bias in adolescent and adult smokers and nonsmokers. Addict. Behav. **25**, 625–632 (2000)
22. Kempf, D.S., Harmon, S.K.: Examining the effectiveness of proposed cigarette package warning labels with graphic images among U.S. college students. Acad. Market. Stud. J. **10**, 77–93 (2006)
23. Tay, R., Watson, B.: Changing drivers' intentions and behaviors using fear-based driver fatigue advertisements. Health Market. Q. **19**(4), 55–68 (2002)
24. Das, S., Sun, X., Dutta, A.: Text mining and topic modeling of compendiums of papers from transportation research board annual meetings. Transp. Res. Rec.: J. Transp. Res. Board **2552**, 48–56 (2016)
25. Das, S., Dixon, K., Sun, X., Dutta, A., Zupancich, M.: Trends in transportation research. Transp. Res. Rec.: J. Transp. Res. Board **2614**, 27–38 (2017)
26. Casas, I., Delmelle, E.C.: Tweeting about public transit — gleaning public perceptions from a social media microblog. Case Stud. Transp. Policy **5**(4), 634–642 (2017)
27. Das, S., Mudgal, A., Dutta, A., Geedipally, S.R.: Vehicle consumer complaint reports involving severe incidents: mining large contingency tables. Transp. Res. Rec.: J. Transp. Res. Board **2672**, 72–82 (2018)
28. Trueblood, A., et al.: A semi-automated tool for identifying agricultural roadway crashes in crash narratives. Traffic Injury Prev. **20**(4), 413–418 (2019)
29. Das, S.: #TRBAM: Exploring Knowledge Management, Research Trends, and Networks by Social Media Mining. TR News, November-December Issue (2019)
30. Cottrill, C., Gault, P., Yeboah, G., Nelson, J.D., Anable, J., Budd, T.: Tweeting transit: an examination of social media strategies for transport information management during a large event. Transp. Res. Part C: Emerg. Technol. **77**, 421–432 (2017)
31. Das, S., Dutta, A., Medina, G., Minjares-Kyle, L., Elgart, Z.: Extracting patterns from Twitter to promote biking. IATSS Res. **43**(1), 51–59 (2019)
32. Das, S., Griffin, G.: Big data and transportation safety: connecting the dots. In: The Proceedings of Transportation Research Board Annual Meeting, Washington DC, 12–16 January 2020
33. Haghighi, N.N., Liu, C., Wei, R., Li, W., Shao, H.: Using Twitter data for transit performance assessment: a framework for evaluating transit riders' opinions about quality of service. Public Transp. **10**(2), 363–377 (2018)
34. Das, S., Jha, K., Dutta, A.: Vision zero hashtags in social media: understanding end-user needs from natural language processing. In: the Proceedings of Transportation Research Board Annual Meeting, Washington DC, 12–16 January 2020

35. Pender, B., Currie, G., Delbosc, A., Shiwakoti, N.: Social media use during unplanned transit network disruptions: a review of literature. Transp. Rev. **34**(4), 501–521 (2014)
36. Das, S., Dutta, A., Brewer, M.: Transportation research record articles: a case study of trend mining. In: The Proceedings of Transportation Research Board Annual Meeting, Washington DC, 12–16 January 2020
37. Sood, G.: tuber: Access YouTube from R. http://soodoku.github.io/tuber/authors.html Accessed 29 Aug 2019
38. Klostermann, P.: YouTube Comment Scrapper. https://github.com/philbot9/youtube-comment-scraper. Accessed 29 Aug 2019
39. Monroe, B., Colaresi, M., Quinn, K.: Fightin' words: lexical feature selection and evaluation for identifying the content of political conflict. Polit. Anal. **16**, 372–403 (2008)
40. Silge, J., Robinson, D.: Text Mining with R: A Tidy Approach. O'Reilly Media, Newton (2018)
41. Nielsen, F.: A new ANEW: evaluation of a word list for sentiment analysis in microblogs. In: Proceedings of the ESWC2011 Workshop on 'Making Sense of Microposts': Big Things Come in Small Packages 718 in CEUR Workshop Proceedings, pp. 93–98 (2011)
42. Dodds, P., Danforth, C.: Measuring the happiness of large-scale written expression: songs, blogs, and presidents. J. Happiness Stud. **11**(4), 441–456 (2010)
43. Doss, P., Harris, K., Kloumann, I., Bliss, C., Danforth, C.: Temporal patterns of happiness and information in a global social network: hedonometrics and Twitter. Plos One **6**(12), e26752 (2011)
44. Lastufka, A., Dean, M.: YouTube: An Insider's Guide to Climbing the Charts, 1st edn. O'Reilly Media, Newton (2008)

Survey on Social Networks Data Analysis

Soufien Jaffali[1]([⊠]) [iD], Salma Jamoussi[2] [iD], Nesrine Khelifi[3] [iD],
and Abdelmajid Ben Hamadou[2] [iD]

[1] Computing Department, Community College,
Imam Abdulrahman Bin Faisal University, Dammam 34212, Saudi Arabia
smjaffali@iau.edu.sa.com
[2] Sfax University, 3029 Sfax, Tunisia
jamoussi@gmail.com, abdelmajid.benhamadou@gmail.com
[3] Computing Department, Deanship of Preparatory Year and Supporting Studies,
Imam Abdulrahman Bin Faisal University, Dammam 34212, Saudi Arabia
nmkhelifi@iau.edu.sa.com

Abstract. Social networks are the most successful Web 2.0 applications, where users share and create over 2.5 quintillion bytes of data daily. This data can be exploited to retrieve many kinds of information which will be used in several applications. In fact, social networks have attracted considerable attention from researchers in different domains. This paper serves as an introduction to social network data analysis. In this work we present the recent and representative works in social network data analysis in an analytical fashion. We also highlight most important applications and used methods in the context of structural data analysis. Then, we list the major tasks and approaches proposed to analyse added-content in social media.

Keywords: Social network · Data analysis · Structural analysis · Added-content analysis

1 Introduction

Recently, there has been a growing interest in social networks, given their impact on society, economy and many sides of user lives. One of the most important characteristics of social networks is the huge amount of data. This data represents a precious mine of information which attracted researchers from different domains. In this context, most of literature works focused on the social network topology or the communications between individuals [24], which represents the linkage information. Several purposes motivated researchers to analyze link information in social networks such as studying the network evolution [84], predicting future links [47] and discovering communities within the social network [19]. Other works analyze the added-content to social networks such as text and multimedia. This content has an important added-value to the analysis.

Previous surveys studying social network data analysis focused on a single analysis axis such as community detection [19] or sentiment analysis [41]. Few

© Springer Nature Switzerland AG 2020
S. S. Rautaray et al. (Eds.): I4CS 2020, CCIS 1139, pp. 100–119, 2020.
https://doi.org/10.1007/978-3-030-37484-6_6

surveys tried to present the state of the art of social network data analysis in general without focusing on a special field [2]. The literature review in these surveys organizes works according to the application like community discovery and node classification. [69] presents a survey on social networking data analysis frameworks classified according the kind of analysis.

In this paper, a new social network data analysis survey is proposed, in which we organize works according to the nature of the analysed data. Thus, we cluster the most representative works into structured-based analysis and added-content based analysis. The remainder of the paper is organized into three sections. Section 2 outlines the most representative works focused on social network structural data analysis. Section 3 describes methods and approaches used to analyze the added-content. Section 4 concludes the paper.

2   Structural Analysis

The basic idea of the structural analysis approaches is that the users are rather characterized by their relations than by their attributes (name, age, social class, etc.) or their added-content (what they share) [57].

The density of relationships and the distances or the number of hops between users within the social network are variable. Furthermore, some actors occupy more central positions than others.

The purpose of structural analysis is therefore to study these phenomena, to identify strong links and weak links, structural holes and central nodes. In this context, some researchers studied links within the social network to extract nodes with higher impact and to determine communities and regions in evolution. Among the major research scopes relying on structural analysis, we can cite link prediction, community detection, user classification, social network evolution analysis, the link inference and visualization.

2.1   Community Detection

There is no universal or exact definition of a "community". Communities are also called groups, clusters, coherent subgroups, or modules in different contexts. In sociology, a community is formed by individuals interacting with each other more often than those outside the community. Community detection and tracking [19] can facilitate other social analytic tasks and its results are exploited in many real-world applications. For example, bringing together customers with similar interests in social media can lead to more effective recommendations that expose customers to a wide range of relevant articles. Communities can also be used to compress a huge network, by treating the set of users forming a community as a single node. In other words, problem-solving is done at the group level, instead of the user level. In the same vein, an extensive network can be viewed at different resolutions, providing an intuitive solution for network analysis and visualization.

Some methods create communities in social networks based on similarities or distances between nodes (users) within the network [53]. Other works retrieve communities by dividing the social network into a set of high densely interconnected nodes [28]. The majority of community detection methods deals with static networks [24], ignoring the time dimension in social networks. To overcome this drawback, some new methods are proposed to take into consideration the dynamic aspect [68].

2.2   User Classification

User classification is a task closely related to community detection. The huge amount of information collected about users, their connections, opinions, activities and thoughts can be modeled as labels associated with individuals. Several forms of labels are possible such as demographic labels (age, gender and place), political labels, labels that encode religious beliefs, labels that represent interests, preferences, and affiliations.

Unfortunately, this information is not available about all users. Some of users are either partially labeled or unlabeled. The classification task aims to infer the unknown user labels based on correlated labeled users. In literature, several models and methods are proposed for user classification such as Relational Neighbor classifier [52], latent group model [59] and Copuler Latent Markov model [83].

2.3   Social Network Evolution Analysis

The dynamism is one of the most important aspects of social networks, which is a manifestation of interactions between individuals. Indeed, the structure of the network can evolve over time thanks to the change of roles, social status and even user preferences. There are a variety of approaches and algorithms available to analyze the evolution of social networks. Guandong et al. [84] classify these algorithms into two families.

The first family uses an additional temporal dimension with the traditional graphic representation (two-dimensional graph, where the two dimensions of the graph can be *"author × keyword"* or *"user × user"*) [7,74]. In this approach, the network in the different stamps is modeled as a two-dimensional graph, represented by a matrix. The new representation is thus in the form of a three-dimensional cube of each data slice corresponding to the matrix representing the network in a specific stamp.

The second category consists in simultaneously discovering the structure of communities and the dynamic network evolution. Unlike classic methods of network evolution analysis and community detection, this category takes into account both network evolution and community detection to analyze the social network. These approaches are based on the assumption that the evolution of community structures in a social network from one stage to its next will not be a dramatic change. In [48], Lin et al. provide a general framework for the analysis of communities and their evolution in dynamic networks. In their approach, the authors measure the quality of a community structure at a certain time t using a cost function *Cost*. The formation of a stable community structure depends on the minimization of the cost function. The latter is composed of an instantaneous cost CI and a time cost CT.

$$Cost = \alpha \cdot CI + (1 - \alpha) \cdot CT \tag{1}$$

The instantaneous cost CI is then determined by the difference in distribution between the similarity matrix of the nodes in the network and the calculated similarity matrix of the community structures formed. In other words, the instantaneous cost is the Kullback-Leibler divergence between the aforementioned similarity matrices. On the other hand, the time cost CT indicates the difference in distribution between the similarity matrices at two consecutive time stamps using the same formula. Thus, the analysis of community structures and their evolution is converted into an optimization problem to find appropriate communities that minimize the total cost.

2.4   Link Prediction

As we have already explained, social networks are dynamic and in continuous evolution. Indeed, it is always possible to add nodes and links in the network. Understanding evolution and, above all, being able to predict the next links that will be established in social networks is a very active topic of research, known as link prediction. According to [47], the prediction techniques of links in social networks can be categorized into two main approaches. The first approach includes proximity-based methods, which use node information, topology, or social theory to compute the similarity between a pair of nodes. In the second approach, we find learning-based methods of predicting links based on machine learning.

Proximity-Based Methods

Nodal Proximity-Based Method: Intuitively it's the simplest idea: the probability of having link in the future between two nodes is proportional to the similarity between them [6]. This idea is consistent with the fact that a person tends to establish relationships with people who resemble him in religion, location or education.

A node in a social network is usually represented by its name, publications, interests, or demographic information. It is therefore sufficient to use these attributes to measure the similarity between a pair of nodes. The greater the similarity between an unconnected pair of nodes, the greater the likelihood that they will be linked. On the other hand, a low similarity indicates that it is very likely that the pair of nodes will not be bound in the future.

In the work of Anderson et al. [5], the similarity between the nodes is measured using the overlap between the users' interests. User interests are extracted from their actions such as editing an article on *Wikipedia* or asking a question about *Stack Overflow*. The interests of each user are represented as a vector, and the similarity between two users is calculated using the cosine as a measure of difference between their vectors of interest.

Topology Based Method: In addition to the characteristics of nodes in social networks, the network topology can also be used to determine the similarity between two nodes, and predict the possibility of linking them. Depending on their characteristics, topology-based link prediction method can be categorized into neighbor-based method, path-based method, and random walk method.

- *Neighbor-based methods:* Among these methods we can cite *Common Neighbors (CN)*. This method, known for its simplicity, is widely used to predict links [60]. His principle is simple; to measure the similarity between two nodes x and y, it is enough to calculate the number of nodes in direct interaction with the nodes x and y at a time. The *CN* measure is defined as follows:

$$CN(x,y) = |\Gamma(x) \bigcap \Gamma(y)| \tag{2}$$

With $\Gamma(x)$ (respectively $\Gamma(y)$) is the set of neighboring nodes of the x node (respectively) y), and $|\Gamma(x)|$ is the number of nodes in the $\Gamma(x)$ set. The higher the value of *CN*, the more the x and y nodes have a chance to be linked. Since the *CN* measure is not normalized, it reflects a relative similarity between the pairs of nodes. Several methods are proposed to normalize it. We cite as an example the measure of *Leicht-Holme-Nerman(LHN)* [45], defined as follows:

$$LHN(x,y) = \frac{|\Gamma(x) \bigcap \Gamma(y)|}{|\Gamma(x)| \cdot |\Gamma(y)|} \tag{3}$$

Thus, we assign a higher similarity to nodes having a large number of neighbors in common compared to the total number of their neighbors.

- *Path-Based Methods:* These methods consist of calculating the number of paths between the x and y nodes to measure the similarity between them. Lü et al. [51] use the *Local Path (LP)*, to measure the similarity between a pair of nodes. This measure consists of calculating the number of paths of length 2 and length 3 between the two nodes Given that paths of length 2 are more relevant, a factor of α (small value close to 0) is applied to adjust the importance given to paths of length equal 3.

$$LP(x,y) = A^2 + \alpha A^3 \tag{4}$$

Where A^i is the adjacency matrix of the nodes separated by paths of length i. The *FrienLink (FL)* method proposed in [62] provides a faster and more efficient prediction. It follows the principle that two people in a social network can use all the paths between them to establish a direct link proportionally to the lengths of these paths. *FL* is defined by the following function:

$$FL(x,y) = \sum_{i=1}^{l} \frac{1}{i-1} \cdot \frac{|path_{x,y}^i|}{\prod_{j=2}^{i}(n-j)} \tag{5}$$

With l is the path length between x and y (excluding paths containing cycles), n is the number of vertices in the network, $path_{x,y}^i$ is the set of all paths of length i between x and y.

– *Random walk-based methods:* The random walk technique consists of calculating a probability for each neighbor of the node x, to determine to which node a random walker located at x will move. Some methods are based on the random walk to measure the similarity between a pair of nodes. Among these methods *Time of Strike (TS)* [25] calculates the expected number of steps a random walker do to reach the node y starting from x. This measure is given by the following function:

$$TS(x,y) = 1 + \sum_{w \in \Gamma(x)} P_{x,w} TS(w,y) \tag{6}$$

With $P = D_A^{-1} A$, where D_A is the diagonal matrix of A.

Social Theories Based Metrics: Some recent works like [50,77] introduce social theories such as *triadic closure* and *homophily* to refine the quality of link prediction. In [77], Valverde et al. combine topology-based methods (*Common Neighbors*) with user behavior and interest information to predict future links in *Twitter*.

Liu et al. [50] propose another model of link prediction using the notion of node centrality[1]. In this model, neighboring nodes participate in the establishment of new links in proportion to their centrality. The introduced module is given by:

$$S(x,y) = \sum_z (w(z) \cdot f(z))^\beta, \quad with \; f(z) = \begin{cases} 1 & if \quad z \in \Gamma(x) \bigcap \Gamma(y) \\ 0 & otherwise \end{cases} \tag{7}$$

Where $w(z)$ presents the centrality weight of the node z, and β is a constant between -1 and 1 used to adjust the contribution of each common neighbor to the probability of linking the nodes x and y.

Learning-Based Link Prediction. Some recent works propose models based on machine learning for the prediction of links [14,46,54]. These models can be classified into three categories, namely: classification according to characteristics, probabilistic graph models and matrix factorization.

Characteristic-Based Classification: Let $G(N, E)$ be a graph corresponding to a social network, with N being the set of nodes and E being the set of edges between N. $l^{(x,y)}$ is the label corresponding to the instance of nodes (x, y). Each pair of nodes corresponds to an instance that includes a tag l and a set features describing the pair of nodes. If there is a link between the nodes x and y, the label $l^{(x,y)}$ is a positive value, otherwise it is negative.

$$l^{(x,y)} = \begin{cases} +1 \; if \; (x,y) \in E \\ -1 \; if \; (x,y) \notin E \end{cases} \tag{8}$$

---

[1] A measure to capture the vague notion of importance in a graph, used to identify the most significant vertices.

To classify the instance labels, several classification methods can be used, such as *SVM* and *decision trees*. To adopt the classification results to predict links, it is necessary to define and extract an appropriate set of characteristics from the social network. These characteristics are given by methods based on the topology and social theories.

In this context, [46] present a machine-learning model based on a graph kernel and properties of nodes such as age, grade level, and so on. This model is used to predict the links between users and items in a bipartite network.

In the work of Wu et al. [82], the authors propose a three-step model for predicting links: *(i)* choose candidate nodes using methods based on social theory (*homophilia*). *(ii)* refine the list of candidates using a factor graph template to adjust the ranking of candidate nodes. *(iii)* Use the interactive learning method *RankFG +*, which uses users' feedback to effectively update the existing prediction model.

Probabilistic Graph Models: In this type of method, a social network can be represented with a graph, in which one assigns probability values (such as the probability of transition of a random walker, the topological similarity, etc.). The probabilistic graph obtained is widely used for predicting links.

Clauset et al. [14] propose a model of probabilistic graph to infer the hierarchical structure of a network, and apply it for link prediction. Let H be a dendrogram corresponding to the hierarchical structure of the G probability graph. Each leaf of the dendrogram corresponds to a node of the graph and each internal node of the dendrogram corresponds to a probability p_r (the probability of connecting a pair of nodes having r as ancestor).

Let E_r be the number of edges in H, where the closest common ancestor is r and let R_r (respectively L_r) the number of leaves in the right sub-tree (respectively left) rooted at r. Then, the probability of the hierarchical graph is given by:

$$L(H, \{p_r\}) = \prod_r p_r^{E_r} (1 - p_r)^{R_r L_r - E_r} \tag{9}$$

For a given graph G, there are several possible dendrograms. Assuming that all hierarchical random graphs are priory equiprobable, the likelihood that a given model $(H, \{p_r\})$ is the right explanation of the data in G is proportional to the likelihood $L(H, \{p_r\})$ with which this model generates the observed network. To predict whether two unconnected nodes x and y will be connected in the future, we consider a set of dendrogram samples, with probability proportional to their likelihood. Then, we calculate the average of the p_{xy} probabilities on the dendrogram samples.

Matrix Factorization Based Models: Menon et al. [54] treat the prediction of links as a matrix completion problem and extend a method of factorizing the matrix to solve the problem of predicting links. They factorize the graph $G \approx L(U \Lambda U^T)$: With $U \in \mathbb{R}^{n \times k}$, $\Lambda \in \mathbb{R}^{k \times k}$ and $L(\cdot)$ a link function (n is the number of nodes and k is the number of latent characteristics).

Each node x has a latent vector corresponding to $u_x \in \mathbb{R}^k$. Thus, the predicted score for the pair of nodes (x, y) is $L(u_x^T \Lambda u_y)$. This model combines the latent characteristics with explicit characteristics of the nodes and the links in the graph via a bilinear regression model.

2.5   Social Network Visualization

Social network visualization may be an alternative solution to better understand social networks if a list of statistics does not offer a clear vision. In this context, several representations has been proposed where graphic elements represent the individuals and lines to symbolise the links between individuals. We can distinguish four classes of social media visualization methods depending on the purpose of the visualization and the knowledge to be identified.

Structural Visualization. The structural visualization of the social network focuses on the network structure, which can be considered as the graph topology that represents individuals and links in the social network. The two main structural visualization approaches are the *node-link diagram* and the *oriented matrix* method.

The first approach is to represent the actors by nodes taking geometric shapes (circles, triangles, etc.) and the relationships between the actors by links between these geometric shapes. In the *diagram node-link*, different properties of the social network such as the importance of a node and the strength of the friendship bond can be expressed via several geometric properties such as color, size, shape, or thickness [26].

The *oriented matrix* method consists of an explicit display of the adjacency or incidence matrix of a social network. In this representation, each link is in the form of a location on a grid having the Cartesian coordinates corresponding to the nodes of the network concerned by the link. Colors and opacity are often used in this kind of visualization to represent important structural or semantic quantities [23].

Semantic Visualization. It is a visualization that uses ontologies to represent the types of actors and relationships in the network. The purpose of this representation is the visualization of the attributes of nodes and links.

Ontovis [72] is an example of ontology-based visualization, where a *diagram node-link* is enriched by an ontology graphic representation.

Temporal Visualization. Time is an important semantic information that has attracted the researchers attention. Indeed, individual's behavior and relations are time-dependent. Thus, the time dimension should be visualized to enhance the comprehension. In this context, several types of visualizations are proposed.

Moody et al. [56] propose two types of dynamic visualization, namely; *flip-books* and *movies*. In the first representation, the nodes remain static and relationships change over time. In the second representation, the nodes may vary as the relationships change.

In *Movibis* [71] an ontology-based visualization is enriched by a time graph, which includes spatiotemporal information about the actors in the network.

Statistic Visualization: Another aspect that seems interesting for the visualization of social networks is the statistical aspect. Social network statistics represent the degree, centrality, and coefficient of clustering in networks or communities of users.

One way to understand these statistical distributions is via visual summaries, such as histograms that show the variation of a variable. An additional insight can be obtained by analyzing the joint distribution between two variables at once. This overview is usually obtained through scatter plots, where the points are mapped into a Cartesian coordinate system based on the values of the two variables in question.

In the context of social networks, scatterplots are useful, especially in the representation of edge correlations. This technique has been explored by Kahng et al. [29] to study the correlation of intermediate centrality in a social network.

3 Added Content-Based Analysis

The amount of user-added information in certain networks, such as *"Youtube"*, *"Flickr"*[2] and email networks, is gigantic. Therefore, the exploitation of this information is very important to improve the quality of the analysis. In addition, in some networks, more knowledge can be derived from the added-content than through links between nodes. In addition, by analyzing the content of social networks we can better understand the opinions of users on a given subject, identify groups among the masses of users and detect influential people.

Research axis on content-based analysis can classified according to the nature of the analyzed data. Thus we find text mining in social networks, multimedia mining and sensors and flows mining.

3.1 Text Mining in Social Networks

Social networks are rich in text as they offer users a variety of ways to contribute with text. *Facebook*[3], for example, allows users to create different textual content, such as publications on the wall, comments on publications and links to other web pages. This fact encouraged researchers to invest in modeling text mining tools to analyze social networks content. In the literature, a variety of algorithms are developed in the context of text mining. However, social networks present

---

[2] https://www.flickr.com/.
[3] https://www.facebook.com/.

new challenges because the network structure intervenes to add information to search. In the remainder of this paper, we designate by textual publications all types of textual contributions possible on social networks (tweets, comments, statutes).

Keyword Research. In a keyword research, we specify a set of terms to identify the nodes in a social network that are relevant to a given query. The main challenge for keyword research in social networks is how to effectively explore the social network and find the sub-network that contains all the keywords in the query. To cope with this challenge, we use the content and the links together to improve the search result, following the assumption that "documents containing similar terms are often linked" [2].

We can classify keyword research algorithms in social networks into two categories. The algorithms of the first category search the sub-network corresponding to the keywords by exploring all the links of the network, without exploiting any index [39]. The algorithms in the second category are based on a network index, which is used to guide the exploration of the network [32].

Classification. In the classification problem, the nodes in the social network are associated with classes. These tagged nodes are subsequently used for learning. There is a whole range of textual content classification algorithms, but the presence of links often provides useful help for classification.

In the case of social networks, there are some of additional challenges to text classification algorithms. These challenges are:

- Social networks contain a much broader and non-standard vocabulary, compared to conventional text collections.
- Tags in social networks are often very rare. Thus, data from social networks are often much more sparse than in other standard text collections.
- The presence of links between nodes can be useful to guide the classification process.

Irfan et al. [34] distinguish three families of text classification methods in social networks:

Ontology-Based Methods: Ontologies can be used for text classification [85], in order to introduce an explicit specification of concepts and their semantic relations [22]. However, semantic analysis is very expensive and difficult in the context of classification of large body of text, as is the case of social networks online [85].

Machine Learning-Based Methods: In this family, we can cite the most used supervised learning algorithms in the text classification context, such as *Rocchio's algorithm* [67], *learning-based 'instances'* [11], *artificial neural networks* [35,37] and *genetic algorithms* [43].

Hybrid Methods: In the literature, some studies show that the combination of different classification algorithms gives better results and improves the performance of text classification compared to the application of a unique classification method [1,55]. However, the result of applying a hybrid approach depends largely on test data sets. Therefore, there is no guarantee that we will achieve the same performance by changing the test set [34].

Clustering. The clustering problem arises quite often in the context of node grouping. It is closely related to the traditional problem of graph partitioning. Some recent works use text content in social network nodes to improve the quality of grouping [30,63]. The problem of categorization has been widely studied by the research community in text mining. In this context, a variety of algorithms have been proposed [3]. These algorithms use several variants of traditional categorization algorithms for multidimensional data. Most of these algorithms are variants of the *K-means* method [2].

According to the study by Irfan et al. [34], text categorization methods can be grouped into three large families:

Hierarchical Clustering: Hierarchical categorization organizes a group of documents in a tree structure (dendrogram) where parent/child relationships can be considered topic/subtopic relationships [42].

Partitional Clustering: Partitional clustering groups probabilistic *partitioning* methods such as the *maximization of hope* [8], the *single-pass* [66], *K-means* variations such as *C-means* [12], *k-medoid* [36] and *C-medoid* [86].

Semantic Clustering: Consists of using an external semantic source (*WordNet, Wikipedia*), if it exists, or creating a source and using it to find the correlation between the terms. In the context of categorizing short text (such as mini-blogs like *Twitter*), limited knowledge is available, hence it is important to create semantic relationships based on internal semantics [70].

Topic Detection. Topic detection and tracking is one of the emerging subject in social network data analysis. It consists on discovering the latent patterns or structures of textual content within social networks. Several methods are proposed to discover topics in the literature. *Latent Dirichlet Allocation* and *Author-Topic Model* are widely used to identify topics in social network [33]. Authors in [15] proves that SVMs are efficient to predict users political alignment based on *Twitter* hashtags.

Learning Transfer. Many social networks contain heterogeneous content, such as text, video, and images. Some types of content may have more or less difficulty in the process of learning classification or categorization. Indeed, several forms of data can not be available to the user in certain fields. For example, it is relatively easy to obtain learning data for textual content. However, this is not always true in the case of images, where there are fewer collections for learning. In this case, the learning transfer is useful for solving classification or grouping problems caused by the lack of data availability. Also, learning transfer is often useful for transferring knowledge from one form of data to another by using the concept of *mapping*. A similar observation applies to the case of text classification problems in cross languages. Indeed, the amounts of learning data available for some languages are not always sufficient. For example, a large amount of labeled textual content may be available in the English language; which is not true in some other languages such as Arabic [44]. Pan and Yang [61] distinguish three categories of techniques used for learning transfer, namely: *Inductive Learning Transfer* [65], *Transductive Learning Transfer* [20,88] and *Unsupervised Learning Transfer* [18,79].

3.2 Multimedia Data Mining

A multimedia information network is a structured collection, where multimedia documents, such as images and videos, are conceptually represented by nicknames tied by links. These links correspond either to real hyperlinks in social networks and web pages, or to logical relationships between the nodes that are implicitly defined through meta-information such as user identifiers, location information or other labels.

Multimedia news networks are seen as a marriage between multimedia content and social networks. They are richer in information thanks to the information stored in the interaction between these two types of entities. To understand multimedia information networks, we must not consider the visual characteristics of each node, but also explore the network structure with which they are associated. Recently, several studies have been carried out in this field, but which have not yet reached the desired maturity. It is important to note that the link structure in multimedia information networks is essentially logical. These links are created from logical common points in the characteristics and relationships between the different entities of the network. Aggarwal [2] distinguishes four sources of logical links that can be used to create a multimedia information network besides the hypertext links often present in social networks.

Ontologies. In multimedia information networks created from ontologies, some studies have focused on the hierarchical classification of concepts. Kamvar et al. [40] associates each node of the network with a binary classifier that calculates the conditional probability given the previous node. the network is constructed by exploiting the semantic relationship "is-a" and "part of" in a general graph, since the graph may not be a tree, there may be several paths from the node (concept) root to any target concept. Each path is associated with the minimum conditional probabilities associated with all edges of the trajectory. The marginal probability of any target concept is defined as the maximum of all likely paths connecting the root concept to the target concept. The same classifier is used for the classification of concepts in the network *ImageNet* [21]. Another method of more sophisticated hierarchical classification is proposed by Cai and Hoffman [10]. This method consists in encoding the root-to-target concept path through a fixed-size binary vector, and treat it as a multi-label classification problem using SVM.

Media Communities. In media communities, users play a central role in multimedia content indexing and retrieval. The basic idea is quite different from a multimedia system centered on traditional content. Web sites that provide media communities are not only run by site owners, but by millions of amateur users who provide, share, edit, and index content.

In this context, some works have focused on the development of multimedia search systems by exploiting the tags provided by users [64,78]. As a result, two basic problems must be solved. First, user tags are often very noisy or semantically meaningless [13]. More specifically, user tags are known to be ambiguous, limited in terms of completeness, and too personalized [2]. Secondly, the tags associated with an image, for example, are generally in random order without any information of importance or relevance, which limits the effectiveness of these tags in the search and other applications.

To remedy the first problem, Tang et al. [76] suggest building an intermediate space of concepts from user tags. This space can be used as a means of deducing and detecting new concepts more generic in the future. The work in [80] provides a probabilistic framework for resolving ambiguous tags that are likely to occur, and which appear in different contexts. There are also many tag suggestion methods that allow users to annotate media with more informative labels, and avoid low-quality or meaningless labels [4,73].

To overcome the second problem, Liu et al. [49] propose a tag classification system that aims to automatically classify the tags associated with a given image according to their relevance to the image content. This system estimates the initial tags relevance scores based on an estimations of likelihood density, followed by a random walk on a tag similarity graph to refine the relevance scores.

Personal Photo Albums. Among the major lines of research that are interested in personal photo albums in social networks, we can mention the discovery of relationships between people in the same photos. Wu et al. [81] took advantage of face categorization technology to discover the social relationships of subjects in personal photo collections. The co-occurrence of identified faces as well as the distances between the faces in the personal photos are used to calculate the strength of the connection between two identified persons. Also, social classes and the social importance of individuals can be calculated.

The labeling and categorization of personal photo albums in social networks is another attractive area of research. In this context, some works are interested in the labeling and categorization of personal photos by exploiting the information on the date and place of taking photos [16,75]. The motivation behind this work is that events and location are among the best clues that people remember and use when searching for photos [58].

Geographical Information. Thanks to the progress of low-cost GPS (Global Positioning System[4]), cell phones and cameras have become equipped with GPS receivers, and so are able to save locations by taking pictures. As a result, the use of geographic information has become increasingly popular. Furthermore, social networks allow users to specify the location of their shared pictures. As a result, millions of new geo-tagged images are added each month to *Flickr*.

Geographical annotation is a rich source of information that can be used in many applications. Among these applications, we find the use of geographic information for a better semantic understanding of the image. Joshi and Luo [38] propose to explore databases of geographic information systems (SIG^5) using a given geographical location. They use descriptions of small local neighborhoods to form *geo-tags* bags. The association of *geo-tags* with visual features is used as a basis for learning to derive the label of an event or activity such as "natural disaster" or "marriage". The authors demonstrate that the context of geographic location is a good indicator for recognition of an event. Yu and Luo [87] improves the accuracy of region recognition by using a probabilistic graphical model. At the entrance of the model, they provide the information of the merged visual and non-visual context. Information on location and time is obtained through image metadata automatically.

Another line of research is devoted to the estimation and deduction of geographic information. The work in this area is motivated by the fact that many web users may be interested in where a beautiful photo is taken and want to know where exactly it is. Also, if a user plans to visit a place, he may want to discover places of interest nearby. In this context, Hays and Efros [31] collected millions of geolocated *Flickr* images. Using a comprehensive set of visual features, they used nearest neighbor search in the reference set to locate the image. Motivated by the work of Hays and Efros [31], Gallagher et al. [27] incorporate text tags to estimate the geographic locations of images. Their results show that text tags perform better than visual content, but they do better by combining visual content with text tags. Crandall et al. [17] estimate the approximate location of a new photo using an SVM classifier. The new image is geolocated by assigning it to the best cluster based on its visual content and annotations.

3.3 Sensors and Data Flows Mining

Driven by the explosive development of online social networks such as *"Facebook"*, *"Twitter"*, and the growing popularity of smartphones, and even the rapid evolution of sensor networks, mobile social networks are likely to become the future key direction for mobile computing. Beach et al. [9] defines mobile social networks as a distributed system that combines the three components: telephone,

---

[4] https://en.wikipedia.org/wiki/Global_Positioning_System.

[5] https://en.wikipedia.org/wiki/Geographic_information_system.

social and sensor. Telephone devices are ubiquitous and can provide information on the identity or location of the user. In addition, smartphones are equipped with a variety of sensors such as accelerometers, microphones, cameras and even digital compasses, which can be leveraged to infer user orientations and preferences. However, telephone devices alone can not produce a complete picture of the context, especially user preferences. On the other hand, social networks are rich in detailed contextual information describing an individual's personal interests and relationships, but they can not locate users. Sensor networks provide the desired third dimension of the data and thus provide a better understanding of the context. Taking the example of information provided by sensors such as temperature, humidity, sound and video and everything characterizing the individual's context. In addition, data from the three classes: telephones, social, and sensors when archived together can improve the context understanding. Therefore, it is the combination of these three data streams that allows the consideration of the current location and the current preferences of the user to be able to perform conscious actions of the user's context, such as movie recommendation or friend suggestion.

4   Conclusion

In this paper, we presented a state of the art of social network analysis methods. We organized these methods, according to the type of analyzed data, in two main classes, namely: structural analysis methods and added-content methods. The first class of methods mainly studies the structure of the social network, where the users present the nodes of the network. The links between the nodes vary according to the purpose of the analysis; they can be friendships, professional relationships or kinship ties. The second class groups the methods that are more interested in the content added by users than in the structure of the network.

Clearly, further research will be needed to cover in detail all social network analysis axis and methods. Several tasks in this context can be cited such as opinion and sentiment analysis or grouping like-minded users. On the basis of the findings presented in this paper, many issues in social network analysis need to be addressed and several methods and techniques could be improved.

References

1. Aci, M., İnan, C., Avci, M.: A hybrid classification method of k nearest neighbor, Bayesian methods and genetic algorithm. Expert Syst. Appl. **37**(7), 5061–5067 (2010)
2. Aggarwal, C.C.: Social Network Data Analytics, 1st edn. Springer, Heidelberg (2011). https://doi.org/10.1007/978-1-4419-8462-3
3. Aggarwal, C.C., Han, J., Wang, J., Yu, P.S.: A framework for clustering evolving data streams. In: Proceedings of the 29th International Conference on Very Large Data Bases. VLDB 2003, vol. 29, pp. 81–92. VLDB Endowment, Germany (2003)

4. Ames, M., Naaman, M.: Why we tag: motivations for annotation in mobile and online media. In: Proceedings of the SIGCHI Conference on Human Factors in Computing Systems, pp. 971–980. ACM, New York (2007)

5. Anderson, A., Huttenlocher, D., Kleinberg, J., Leskovec, J.: Effects of user similarity in social media. In: Proceedings of the Fifth ACM International Conference on Web Search and Data Mining, WSDM 2012, pp. 703–712. ACM, New York (2012)

6. Aouay, S., Jamoussi, S., Gargouri, F.: Feature based link prediction. In: 11th IEEE/ACS International Conference on Computer Systems and Applications, Qatar, AICCSA, pp. 523–527 (2014)

7. Bader, B., Harshman, R., Kolda, T.: Temporal analysis of semantic graphs using ASALSAN. In: Seventh IEEE International Conference on Data Mining (ICDM), USA, pp. 33–42 (2007)

8. Banerjee, A., Dhillon, I., Ghosh, J., Sra, S.: Expectation maximization for clustering on hyperspheres. Technical report, University of Texas at Austin, USA (2003)

9. Beach, A., et al.: Fusing mobile, sensor, and social data to fully enable context-aware computing. In: Proceedings of the Eleventh Workshop on Mobile Computing Systems and Applications, HotMobile 2010, pp. 60–65. ACM, New York (2010)

10. Cai, L., Hofmann, T.: Hierarchical document categorization with support vector machines. In: Proceedings of the Thirteenth ACM International Conference on Information and Knowledge Management, CIKM 2004, pp. 78–87. ACM, New York (2004)

11. Chang, M., Poon, C.K.: Using phrases as features in email classification. J. Syst. Softw. **82**(6), 1036–1045 (2009)

12. Chen, W., Wang, M.: A fuzzy c-means clustering-based fragile watermarking scheme for image authentication. Expert Syst. Appl. **36**(2), 1300–1307 (2009)

13. Chua, T., Tang, J., Hong, R., Li, H., Luo, Z., Zheng, Y.: NUS-WIDE: a real-world web image database from National University of Singapore. In: Proceedings of the ACM International Conference on Image and Video Retrieval, CIVR 2009, pp. 48:1–48:9. ACM, New York (2009)

14. Clauset, A., Moore, C., Newman, M.E.J.: Hierarchical structure and the prediction of missing links in networks. Nature **453**, 98–101 (2008)

15. Conover, M., Gonçalves, B., Ratkiewicz, J., Flammini, A., Menczer, F.: Predicting the political alignment of Twitter users, pp. 192–199, October 2011

16. Cooper, M., Foote, J., Girgensohn, A., Wilcox, L.: Temporal event clustering for digital photo collections. ACM Trans. Multimedia Comput. Commun. Appl. **1**(3), 269–288 (2005)

17. Crandall, D.J., Backstrom, L., Huttenlocher, D., Kleinberg, J.: Mapping the world's photos. In: Proceedings of the 18th International Conference on World Wide Web, WWW 2009, pp. 761–770. ACM, New York (2009)

18. Dai, W., Yang, Q., Xue, G., Yu, Y.: Self-taught clustering. In: Proceedings of the 25th International Conference on Machine Learning, ICML 2008, pp. 200–207. ACM, New York (2008)

19. Dakiche, N., Tayeb, F.B.S., Slimani, Y., Benatchba, K.: Tracking community evolution in social networks: a survey. Inf. Process. Manag. **56**(3), 1084–1102 (2019)

20. Daumé, I.I.I., Marcu, D.: Domain adaptation for statistical classifiers. J. Artif. Int. Res. **26**(1), 101–126 (2006)

21. Deng, J., Dong, W., Socher, R., Li, L., Li, K., Fei-fei, L.: ImageNet: a large-scale hierarchical image database. In: Computer Society Conference on Computer Vision and Pattern Recognition CVPR, USA, pp. 248–255 (2009)

22. Dong, J., Zhao, Y., Peng, T.: Ontology classification for semantic-web-based software engineering. IEEE Trans. Serv. Comput. **2**, 303–317 (2009)

23. Du, J., Xian, Y., Yang, J.: A survey on social network visualization. In: International Symposium on Social Science (ISSS 2015), China, pp. 275–279 (2015). Atlantis Press
24. Fortunato, S.: Community detection in graphs. Phys. Rep. **486**(3–5), 75–174 (2010)
25. Fouss, F., Pirotte, A., Renders, J., Saerens, M.: Random-walk computation of similarities between nodes of a graph with application to collaborative recommendation. IEEE Trans. Knowl. Data Eng. **19**(3), 355–369 (2007)
26. Freeman, L.C.: Visualizing social networks. J. Soc. Struct. **1**, 4 (2000)
27. Gallagher, A., Joshi, D., Yu, J., Luo, J.: Geo-location inference from image content and user tags. In: 2009 IEEE Computer Society Conference on Computer Vision and Pattern Recognition Workshops, USA, pp. 55–62 (2009)
28. Girvan, M., Newman, M.E.: Community structure in social and biological networks. Proc. Natl. Acad. Sci. **99**(12), 7821–7826 (2002)
29. Goh, K.I., Oh, E., Kahng, B., Kim, D.: Betweenness centrality correlation in social networks. Phys. Rev. E **67**, 017101 (2003)
30. Hannachi, L., Asfari, O., Benblidia, N., Bentayeb, F., Kabachi, N., Boussaid, O.: Community extraction based on topic-driven-model for clustering users tweets. In: Zhou, S., Zhang, S., Karypis, G. (eds.) ADMA 2012. LNCS (LNAI), vol. 7713, pp. 39–51. Springer, Heidelberg (2012). https://doi.org/10.1007/978-3-642-35527-1_4
31. Hays, J., Efros, A.A.: IM2GPS: estimating geographic information from a single image. In: Proceedings of the IEEE Conference on Computer Vision and Pattern Recognition (CVPR), pp. 1–8. IEEE Computer Society, Washington, D.C. (2008)
32. He, H., Wang, H., Yang, J., Yu, P.S.: Blinks: ranked keyword searches on graphs. In: Proceedings of the 2007 ACM SIGMOD International Conference on Management of Data, SIGMOD 2007, pp. 305–316. ACM, New York (2007)
33. Ho, K.T., Bui, Q.V., Bui, M.: Dynamic social network analysis using author-topic model. In: Hodoň, M., Eichler, G., Erfurth, C., Fahrnberger, G. (eds.) I4CS 2018. CCIS, vol. 863, pp. 47–62. Springer, Cham (2018). https://doi.org/10.1007/978-3-319-93408-2_4
34. Irfan, R., et al.: A survey on text mining in social networks. Knowl. Eng. Rev. **30**, 157–170 (2015)
35. Jaffali, S., Jamoussi, S.: Principal component analysis neural network for textual document categorization and dimension reduction. In: 6th International Conference on Sciences of Electronics. Technologies of Information and Telecommunications (SETIT), pp. 835–839. IEEE, Tunisia (2012)
36. Jain, A.K.: Data clustering: 50 years beyond k-means. Pattern Recogn. Lett. **31**(8), 651–666 (2010)
37. Jo, T.: Neural text categorizer for exclusive text categorization. Int. J. Inf. Sci. **34**(1) (2010)
38. Joshi, D., Luo, J.: Inferring generic activities and events from image content and bags of geo-tags. In: Proceedings of the 2008 International Conference on Content-Based Image and Video Retrieval, CIVR 2008, pp. 37–46. ACM, New York (2008)
39. Kacholia, V., Pandit, S., Chakrabarti, S., Sudarshan, S., Desai, R., Karambelkar, H.: Bidirectional expansion for keyword search on graph databases. In: Proceedings of the 31st International Conference on Very Large Data Bases, VLDB 2005, pp. 505–516. VLDB Endowment, Norway (2005)
40. Kamvar, S., Haveliwala, T., Manning, C., Golub, G.: Exploiting the block structure of the web for computing pagerank. Technical report 2003–17, Stanford InfoLab, UK (2003)
41. Kashfia, S., Alhajj, R.: Emotion and sentiment analysis from Twitter text. J. Comput. Sci. **36**, 101003 (2019)

42. Kavitha, V., Punithavalli, M.: Clustering time series data stream - a literature survey. Int. J. Comput. Sci. Inf. Secur. IJCSIS **8**(1), 289–294 (2010)
43. Khalessizadeh, S.M., Zaefarian, R., Nasseri, S., Ardil, E.: Genetic mining: using genetic algorithm for topic based on concept distribution. Int. J. Math. Comput. Phys. Electr. Comput. Eng. **2**(1), 35–38 (2008)
44. Khemakhem, I.T., Jamoussi, S., Hamadou, A.B.: POS tagging without a tagger: using aligned corpora for transferring knowledge to under-resourced languages. Computación y Sistemas **20**(4), 667–679 (2016)
45. Leicht, E.A., Holme, P., Newman, M.E.J.: Vertex similarity in networks. Phys. Rev. E **73**(2), 026–120 (2006)
46. Li, X., Chen, H.: Recommendation as link prediction in bipartite graphs. Decis. Support Syst. **54**(2), 880–890 (2013)
47. Li, Z.L., Fang, X., Sheng, O.R.L.: A survey of link recommendation for social networks: methods, theoretical foundations, and future research directions. ACM Trans. Manag. Inf. Syst. **9**(1), 1:1–1:26 (2017)
48. Lin, Y., Chi, Y., Zhu, S., Sundaram, H., Tseng, B.L.: FacetNet: a framework for analyzing communities and their evolutions in dynamic networks. In: Proceedings of the 17th International Conference on World Wide Web, WWW 2008, pp. 685–694. ACM, New York (2008)
49. Liu, D., Hua, X.S., Yang, L., Wang, M., Zhang, H.: Tag ranking. In: Proceedings of the 18th International Conference on World Wide Web, WWW 2009, pp. 351–360. ACM, New York (2009)
50. Liu, H., Hu, Z., Haddadi, H., Tian, H.: Hidden link prediction based on node centrality and weak ties. EPL (Europhys. Lett.) **101**(1), 18004 (2013)
51. Lü, L., Jin, C., Zhou, T.: Similarity index based on local paths for link prediction of complex networks. Phys. Rev. E **80**, 046–122 (2009)
52. Macskassy, S.A., Provost, F.: A simple relational classifier. In: Proceedings of the Second Workshop on Multi-Relational Data Mining (MRDM-2003) at KDD-2003, pp. 64–76 (2003)
53. McPherson, M., Smith-Lovin, L., Cook, J.M.: Birds of a feather: homophily in social networks. Annual Rev. Sociol. **27**(1), 415–444 (2001)
54. Menon, A.K., Elkan, C.: Link prediction via matrix factorization. In: Gunopulos, D., Hofmann, T., Malerba, D., Vazirgiannis, M. (eds.) ECML PKDD 2011. LNCS (LNAI), vol. 6912, pp. 437–452. Springer, Heidelberg (2011). https://doi.org/10.1007/978-3-642-23783-6_28
55. Miao, D., Duan, Q., Zhang, H., Jiao, N.: Rough set based hybrid algorithm for text classification. Expert Syst. Appl. **36**(5), 9168–9174 (2009)
56. Moody, J., McFarland, D., Bender-deMoll, S.: Dynamic network visualization. Am. J. Sociol. **110**(4), 1206–1241 (2005)
57. Moradabadi, B., Meybodi, M.R.: Link prediction in weighted social networks using learning automata. Eng. Appl. Artif. Intell. **70**, 16–24 (2018)
58. Naaman, M., Harada, S., Wang, Q., Garcia-Molina, H., Paepcke, A.: Context data in geo-referenced digital photo collections. In: Proceedings of the 12th Annual ACM International Conference on Multimedia, MULTIMEDIA 2004, pp. 196–203. ACM, New York (2004)
59. Neville, J., Jensen, D.: Leveraging relational autocorrelation with latent group models. In: Fifth IEEE International Conference on Data Mining (ICDM 2005), p. 8. IEEE (2005)
60. Newman, M.E.J.: Clustering and preferential attachment in growing networks. Phys. Rev. E **64**, 025–102 (2001)

61. Pan, S.J., Yang, Q.: A survey on transfer learning. IEEE Trans. Knowl. Data Eng. **22**(10), 770–783 (2010)
62. Papadimitriou, A., Symeonidis, P., Manolopoulos, Y.: Fast and accurate link prediction in social networking systems. J. Syst. Softw. **85**(9), 2119–2132 (2012)
63. Qi, G., Aggarwal, C.C., Huang, T.S.: Community detection with edge content in social media networks. In: Kementsietsidis, A., Salles, M.A.V. (eds.) Proceedings of the 2012 IEEE 28th International Conference on Data Engineering, pp. 534–545. IEEE Computer Society, Washington, D.C. (2012)
64. Qi, G., Hua, X., Zhang, H.: Learning semantic distance from community-tagged media collection. In: Proceedings of the 17th ACM International Conference on Multimedia, MM 2009, pp. 243–252. ACM, New York (2009)
65. Raina, R., Battle, A., Lee, H., Packer, B., Ng, A.Y.: Self-taught learning: transfer learning from unlabeled data. In: Proceedings of the 24th International Conference on Machine Learning, ICML 2007, pp. 759–766. ACM, New York (2007)
66. Rao, Y., Li, X.: A topic-based dynamic clustering algorithm for text stream. In: International Conference on Artificial Intelligence and Industrial Engineering (AIIE 2015), Thailand, pp. 480–483 (2015)
67. Rocchio, J.J.: Relevance feedback in information retrieval, pp. 313–323 (1971)
68. Rossetti, G., Cazabet, R.: Community discovery in dynamic networks: a survey. ACM Comput. Surv. **51**(2), 35:1–35:37 (2018)
69. Sapountzi, A., Psannis, K.E.: Social networking data analysis tools and challenges. Future Gen. Comput. Syst. **86**, 893–913 (2018)
70. Seifzadeh, S., Farahat, A.K., Kamel, M.S., Karray, F.: Short-text clustering using statistical semantics. In: Gangemi, A., Leonardi, S., Panconesi, A. (eds.) Proceedings of the 24th International Conference on World Wide Web, pp. 805–810. ACM, New York (2015)
71. Shen, Z., Ma, K.: MobiVis: a visualization system for exploring mobile data. In: Proceedings of MobiVis: A Visualization System for Exploring Mobile Data, pp. 175–182. IEEE, Japan (2008)
72. Shen, Z., Ma, K., Eliassi-Rad, T.: Visual analysis of large heterogeneous social networks by semantic and structural abstraction. IEEE Trans. Vis. Comput. Graph. **12**(6), 1427–1439 (2006)
73. Sigurbjörnsson, B., van Zwol, R.: Flickr tag recommendation based on collective knowledge. In: Proceedings of the 17th International Conference on World Wide Web, WWW 2008, pp. 327–336. ACM, New York (2008)
74. Sun, J., Tao, D., Faloutsos, C.: Beyond streams and graphs: dynamic tensor analysis. In: Proceedings of the 12th ACM SIGKDD International Conference on Knowledge Discovery and Data Mining, KDD 2006, pp. 374–383. ACM, New York (2006)
75. Tang, F., Gao, Y.: Fast near duplicate detection for personal image collections. In: Proceedings of the 17th ACM International Conference on Multimedia, MM 2009, pp. 701–704. ACM, New York (2009)
76. Tang, J., Yan, S., Hong, R., Qi, G., Chua, T.: Inferring semantic concepts from community-contributed images and noisy tags. In: Proceedings of the 17th ACM International Conference on Multimedia, MM 2009, pp. 223–232. ACM, New York (2009)
77. Valverde-Rebaza, J.C., de Andrade Lopes, A.: Exploiting behaviors of communities of Twitter users for link prediction. Social Netw. Analys. Mining **3**(4), 1063–1074 (2013)
78. Wang, X.J., Zhang, L., Li, X., Ma, W.Y.: Annotating images by mining image search results. IEEE Trans. Pattern Anal. Mach. Intell. **30**(11), 1919–1932 (2008)

79. Wang, Z., Song, Y., Zhang, C.: Transferred dimensionality reduction. In: Daelemans, W., Goethals, B., Morik, K. (eds.) ECML PKDD 2008. LNCS (LNAI), vol. 5212, pp. 550–565. Springer, Heidelberg (2008). https://doi.org/10.1007/978-3-540-87481-2_36

80. Weinberger, K.Q., Slaney, M., Van Zwol, R.: Resolving tag ambiguity. In: Proceedings of the 16th ACM International Conference on Multimedia, MM 2008, pp. 111–120. ACM, New York (2008)

81. Wu, P., Tretter, D.: Close & closer: social cluster and closeness from photo collections. In: Gao, W., et al. (eds.) ACM Multimedia, pp. 709–712. ACM, New York (2009)

82. Wu, S., Sun, J., Tang, J.: Patent partner recommendation in enterprise social networks. In: Proceedings of the Sixth ACM International Conference on Web Search and Data Mining, WSDM 2013, pp. 43–52. ACM, New York (2013)

83. Xiang, R., Neville, J.: Collective inference for network data with copula latent Markov networks. In: Proceedings of the Sixth ACM International Conference on Web Search and Data Mining, WSDM 2013, pp. 647–656. ACM, New York (2013)

84. Xu, G., Zhang, Y., Li, L.: Web Mining and Social Networking: Techniques and Applications, 1st edn. Springer, New York (2011). https://doi.org/10.1007/978-1-4419-7735-9

85. Xu, X., Zhang, F., Niu, Z.: An ontology-based query system for digital libraries. In: Pacific-Asia Workshop on Computational Intelligence and Industrial Application, China, pp. 222–226 (2008)

86. Yamamoto, T., Honda, K., Notsu, A., Ichihashi, H.: A comparative study on TIBA imputation methods in FCMdd-based linear clustering with relational data. Adv. Fuzzy Syst. **2011**, 265170:1–265170:10 (2011)

87. Yu, J., Luo, J.: Leveraging probabilistic season and location context models for scene understanding. In: Proceedings of the 2008 International Conference on Content-Based Image and Video Retrieval, CIVR 2008, pp. 169–178. ACM, New York (2008)

88. Zadrozny, B.: Learning and evaluating classifiers under sample selection bias. In: Proceedings of the Twenty-First International Conference on Machine Learning, ICML 2004, pp. 114–121. ACM, New York (2004)

Information and System Security

ReFIT: <u>R</u>eliability Challenges and <u>F</u>ailure Rate Mitigation Techniques for <u>IoT</u> Systems

Sukanta Dey$^{(\boxtimes)}$ (ID), Pradeepkumar Bhale, and Sukumar Nandi

Department of Computer Science and Engineering,
Indian Institute of Technology Guwahati, Guwahati 781039, Assam, India
{sukanta.dey,pradeepkumar,sukumar}@iitg.ac.in

Abstract. As the number of Internet-of-Things (IoT) devices increases, ensuring the reliability of the IoT system has become a challenging job. Apart from the emerging security issues, reliable IoT system design depends on many other factors. In this work, for the first time, we have shown all the reliability challenges of an IoT system in details, which may arise due to the random faults. We have also proposed a mathematical formulation of the lifetime of the IoT system. Subsequently, we devise an algorithm which uses Lévy distribution-based duty cycling approach to improve the IoT network lifetime. We have validated our proposed method using Cooja simulation software. The simulation results show $1.5 \times$ increment in network lifetime for the IoT system using our proposed method than the state-of-the-artwork. We have also demonstrated that our proposed method does not degrade the network performance.

Keywords: Duty cycle · Internet-of-Things · Lévy flight · Lifetime · Low power · Reliability · VLSI

1 Introduction

With the inception of Industry 4.0, the human race is experiencing a new age revolution, where all the devices, things, and equipment are connected and controlled with the help of the internet. The establishment of the Internet of Things (IoT) in the industrial sector, has enabled the industry in the automatic, intelligent, and digitalized decision-making process over the internet with wireless components. It has also allowed the industry to perform time-critical cyber-physical operations [1] over the internet. Works related to IoT-based frameworks, its requirements, and its architectures are started to gain attention, which is described in work [2].

Different IoT nodes, for example, smartphones, smart cameras, wearable, house electronics, electric vehicles, smart door lock, garden irrigation systems, can be connected wirelessly to form an IoT network. An illustrative example of IoT nodes forming an IoT network is shown in Fig. 1. These IoT nodes are,

© Springer Nature Switzerland AG 2020
S. S. Rautaray et al. (Eds.): I4CS 2020, CCIS 1139, pp. 123–142, 2020.
https://doi.org/10.1007/978-3-030-37484-6_7

in turn, connected to the sink/border router, through which the IoT nodes are connected to the internet. From this illustrative example, it is clear that for the successful functioning of the IoT system, it is essential for the proper functioning of every IoT nodes. However, the nodes near to border router remain active most of the time and discharge a large amount of energy. Due to which the battery lifetime of the nodes near to border router is decreased. This problem is termed as *energy hole* problem. In this work, we have proposed a solution to address this energy hole problem and to increase the battery-operated lifetime. Apart from that, for the successful deployment of the IoT system, it is also necessary to study different reliability challenges for an IoT system. Therefore, we have also considered various reliability issues for an IoT system and formulated an analytical expression for lifetime calculation.

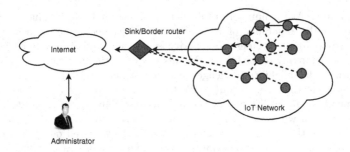

Fig. 1. An illustrative example of IoT system

Motivation: As the critical autonomous decision making depends on the IoT system, ensuring the reliability of the IoT system has become essential. The objectives of the reliable IoT system should be (1) provide seamless connectivity (2) long-lasting IoT system (3) non-stop working of the IoT system. Without these objectives, the aspiration of Industry 4.0 can not be fulfilled. Considering that, the study of reliability challenges of these IoT systems is very much necessary. Further, the reliability study of the IoT system also helps in designing reliable systems. It also helps in providing seamless and non-disruptive communication among the IoT devices of the system. Further, it is also necessary to alleviate any runtime reliability issues which may arise in an IoT system to increase the lifetime of the IoT system. Therefore, our work focuses on the reliability study of the IoT system, considering various factors. The major contribution of the paper,

- Different reliability challenges for Low Power IoT nodes and systems are discussed in detail in this paper. An analytical expression for mean-time-to-failure (MTTF) calculation of the IoT system is formulated for considering different parameters.
- A Methodology using Lévy Distribution-based duty cycling approach is proposed to decrease the failure rate and to improve the lifetime of the IoT nodes and systems.

– The proposed methodology is validated using simulation with the help of Cooja tool in Contiki OS. The obtained results show that the lifetime increases using our proposed approach.

The rest of the paper is arranged in the following way. The background of the paper is explained in Sect. 2, which contains a brief description of low power IoT nodes, and the previous related work. The reliability challenges of IoT node and systems are mentioned in Sect. 3. Mathematical modeling for the reliability prediction of the IoT system is also discussed in the section. The proposed methodology using a Lévy flight-based duty cycling technique for lifetime improvement of the IoT system is discussed in Sect. 4. The experimental results are listed in Sect. 5. The work is concluded in Sect. 6.

2   Background

A pictorial representation of a low power IoT node is shown in Fig. 2. A significant characteristic of the low power IoT node is that all the components of the IoT node should consume low power, and the power supply range must be less than 1 V.

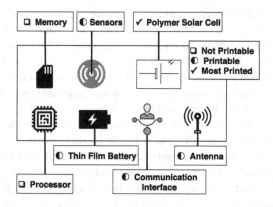

Fig. 2. An ideal IoT node with different components [3]

2.1   Low Power IoT Nodes

A low power IoT node contains, the following components,

– processor: used to process the data of the IoT node.
– memory: used to store the data.
– thin-film battery: used as the power supply to the IoT node.
– communication interface: used for communication with the hardware.

- antenna: used for communication with the other IoT nodes.
- sensor: used for collecting data.
- polymer solar cell: alternative non-conventional power source.

These are essential components of low power IoT nodes. Some of these components are printable, and some are not printable. For the seamless connectivity of the IoT system, all these components of IoT nodes must work correctly. Any transient or permanent damage to any of the parts due to random faults may create risk for the proper functioning of the IoT system.

2.2 Related Works

There are very few works that discussed the reliability challenges of IoT nodes and systems. Most of the papers in the literature concentrate more on the cyber-security perspective of the IoT. There are few works which tried to enhance the IoT network lifetime by giving solution from the security perspective.

A few works which deal with the reliability issues of IoT systems are trying to demonstrate the reliability measures of the IoT systems using different metrics. For e.g., Ahmad [4], in his work, proposed a methodology to deal with the hardware and software-based system-level reliability of the IoT. He validated his work on different case studies using hardware and software. Rosing [5], in his presentation, demonstrated different approaches for the reliability and maintainability of IoT systems. Xing et al. [6] have demonstrated the failure analysis of the IoT system, considering the cascade effect of functional dependency. Thomas and Rad [7] have shown different reliability metrics for the IoT car tracking system. No work in the literature has an objective to model the reliability of the IoT system analytically. In this work, we propose an analytical model for measuring the reliability of the IoT system for lifetime estimation.

There are also a few works that try to maximize the lifetime of the IoT system using different heuristics. Raptis et al. [8] in their work proposed an offline centralized solution of integrated service in order to increase the network lifetime considering latency constraints. They evaluated the performance of their approach using testbed. Valls et al. [9] in their work proposed solutions for the allocation of bandwidth and resources for the data processing using the IoT network, which is used for lifetime maximization. Morin et al. [10] has done a comparative study of the lifetime of different devices in the IoT wireless network. Airehrour et al. [11] in work has done a detailed survey on different energy optimization techniques of IoT nodes using the energy harvesting method. Fafoutis et al. [12] have demonstrated a real-world experiment on the lifetime prediction of the battery for the IoT devices. Cao et al. [13] have proposed an offline solution of mobility-aware network lifetime maximization under quality-of-service (QoS) constraints. Li et al. [14] have intended to improve the IoT network lifetime by introducing the hierarchical cluster-based duty cycle approach. Our proposed method works on top of the framework proposed in [14].

3   Reliability Challenges in IoT

IoT systems can fail due to the one or more of the following reasons:

– Due to system-level random failure
  • Errors caused by user.
  • Errors while installation.
  • Problems in communication interface or with the transceiver.
  • Problems with the sensor.
  • Issues with the power (Battery lifetime).
  • Software or firmware failure.
  • Hardware failure (Memory and processor)
    * Soft errors (transient in nature)
    * Hard errors (permanent in nature)
– Due to intended cyber attack on the IoT systems
  • Cyber attack can cause all the system-level failures mentioned above.

These problems may arise due to different attacks by the attacker on an IoT system, which reduces the reliability of the IoT system. Without any pertinent attack by an attacker, the problems mentioned above still can occur, due to some random faults, which also reduces the reliability of the IoT system. Therefore, our objective is to mathematically model the reliability of the IoT system, depending on different parameters. Once the mathematical model is formed, then we can analyze the IoT system in order to reduce the above issues and to increase the lifetime of the IoT system. In this work, we assume that we are not proposing any solution to prevent different attacks on the IoT. However, we are concentrating on those reliability issues which may occur due to random faults.

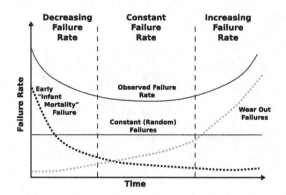

Fig. 3. Reliability Bathtub curve.

3.1   Mathematical Modeling of Reliability of IoT System

These errors can occur in any of the IoT nodes, which in turn can affect the total IoT network/system. The occurrence of these errors can happen during any instance of its lifetime. Therefore, depending on these issues, the reliability of the IoT nodes and system can be defined as the time-varying function $R(t)$. It defines the probability function that an IoT node operates correctly in time $[0, t\}$. Mean-time-to-failure(MTTF) of the IoT node can be defined as the following:

$$MTTF_{IoT\ Node} = \int_0^\infty R(t)dt \tag{1}$$

Generally, the reliability of any device is modeled with the reliability bathtub curve, as shown in Fig. 3. The bathtub curve is divided into three parts with respect to the lifetime of a certain design of a device. In the first part, the infant mortality rate keeps on decreasing from an initial higher value. When the infant mortality of rate decreases, the lifetime of the device remains almost constant in the second part of the curve. In the end, due to the wear-out failures, the failure rate increases. From the reliability bathtub curve and a deformed version of Weibull distribution [15], we can obtain a mathematical expression for the reliability of an IoT node by the following:

$$R(t) = e^{(-\lambda_f t)}, \tag{2}$$

where λ_f is the constant failure rate of the IoT device, which is determined by observing the failure rate pattern of the IoT devices. From (1) and (2), we get that

$$MTTF_{IoT\ Node} = \frac{1}{\lambda_f} \tag{3}$$

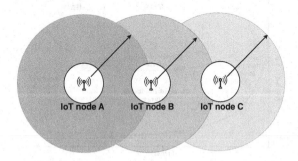

Fig. 4. IoT nodes A, B, and C are in series

To obtain the lifetime of the IoT system, we have to observe the connections of the IoT nodes. Considering the IoT nodes are connected in an ad-hoc network mode. If the n IoT nodes are connected in series (as shown in Fig. 4) then all the nodes must work correctly in order to keep the system in working condition. In this case, MTTF of the IoT system is defined as follows,

$$MTTF_{IoT\ Series\ System} = \int_0^\infty \prod_1^n R_i(t)dt \tag{4}$$

$$= \frac{1}{\sum_{i=1}^n \lambda_{f_i}} \tag{5}$$

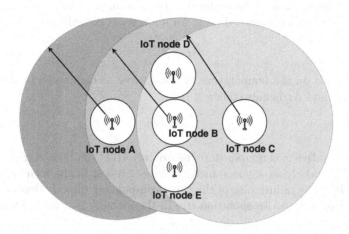

Fig. 5. IoT nodes B, D, and E, are in parallel. If all the three nodes, B, D, and E fail, then no communication between node A and C is possible. As a result, the IoT system fails.

If the n IoT nodes are connected in parallel (as shown in Fig. 5) then the IoT system fails if the all the IoT node fails, then rate of failure $F_s(t)$ is defined by the following,

$$F_s(t) = \prod_1^i F_i(t), \tag{6}$$

where $F_i(t) = 1 - R_i(t)$. Therefore, the MTTF of a parallel IoT system is given by,

$$MTTF_{IoT\ Parallel\ System} = \int_0^\infty \left(1 - F_s(t)\right) dt \tag{7}$$

However, in reality the IoT systems are neither series system or parallel system. Real IoT system forms a hybrid combination of the series and parallel systems. Therefore, the MTTF of real IoT system can be defined as follows:

$$MTTF_{IoT\ System} = \int_0^\infty \prod_1^i R_i(t)dt + \int_0^\infty \left(1 - F_s(t)\right) dt, \tag{8}$$

where it is assumed that i devices are connected in series and another i devices are connected in parallel.

3.2 Modeling Constant Failure Rate, λ_f

MTTF of the IoT system can be obtained if we know the constant failure rate, λ_f. The value of λ_f depends on many factors. If the number times a IoT node is used by the user is K in an hour, then the number of errors caused by the user can assumed to be in the order of $log(K)$ in an hour. λ_f is directly proportional to $log(K)$.

$$\lambda_f \propto log(K) \tag{9}$$

If the IoT node is running on uniform duty cycle mode, the let d times be the number of time device is turned on in an hour. λ_f is directly proportional to d.

$$\lambda_f \propto d \tag{10}$$

λ_f also depends on the temperature of the devices as mentioned in the Black's equation [16] and Arrhenius equation [17].

$$\lambda_f \propto e^{(-\frac{E_a}{kT})} \tag{11}$$

Due to the negative bias temperature instability(NBTI) and hot carrier injection (HCI) of the underlying semiconductor devices present in the memory and the processor [18]. The failure rate of the these components directly depends on the number of times the write operation (w) in the memory is done in an hour.

$$\lambda_f \propto w \tag{12}$$

Due to power supply noise and electromigration also failure can happend in the processor [19,20], which directly depends on the current density(J) of the IoT node

$$\lambda_f \propto J \tag{13}$$

From the above equations, we have got that the

$$\lambda_f = Clog(K)de^{(-\frac{E_a}{kT})}wJ \tag{14}$$

where C is a proportionality constant. Equation (14) is an analytical expression of the failure-rate calculation.

3.3 Mitigation Techniques of Failure Rate

The failure rate can be mitigated by decreasing those terms of (14), which is directly proportional to the failure rate. The failure rate can also be decreased by increasing those parameters, which are inversely proportional to the failure rate. Different solutions can be proposed to mitigate the failure rate by considering various parameters, and the lifetime of the IoT system can be evaluated accordingly. Some of the parameters are inter-dependent, i.e., if one parameter increases, then the other parameter decreases. For such settings, a trade-off between the parameters has to be maintained in order to reduce the failure rate.

In this work, we are only considering the failure of the IoT system due to IoT network failure, which can occur due to the battery failure or discharging of the power sources. The *network lifetime of IoT system* can be defined as given in Definition 1. It is to be noted that the network lifetime of the IoT system is different from the MTTF expression formulated earlier. The MTTF is the mean-time-to-failure of the IoT system, which can be caused by random faults. However, MTTF also depends on the network lifetime, as mentioned in Remark 1. In this work, we are only considering the network lifetime improvement for an IoT system.

Definition 1. *When one of the nodes of an IoT system fails to work properly due to the discharge of its battery power, then the time elapsed from the beginning of communication to the first node failure is termed as* **network lifetime of an IoT system** *($T_{Nlifetime}$).*

Remark 1. The network lifetime of an IoT system is directly related to the MTTF caused by random faults. In other words, network lifetime is related inversely to the failure rate of an IoT system.

Proof. If p is the probability of failure of the power system of IoT network, then we can establish a relationship between $T_{Nlifetime}$ and MTTF.

$$T_{Nlifetime} = p * MTTF \tag{15}$$

If random faults occur in the power supply system of IoT network (meaning $p = 1$), then the IoT network fails. For such a case, MTTF can be equivalent to the network lifetime. Therefore, from this, we can see that MTTF and network lifetimes are related. It also implies that network lifetime and failure rate (λ_f) of an IoT system are related. As MTTF and λ_f are inversely related. Hence, $T_{Nlifetime}$ and λ_f are inversely related to each other.

In the next section, the proposed methodology for failure rate mitigation is described.

4   Proposed Methodology for Failure Rate Mitigation

4.1   System Model

We are considering n nodes for our IoT network. These n nodes are connected to the internet via border router. The nodes are clustered hierarchically, as shown in Fig. 6. The nodes are clustered in different layers with a cluster head node for each cluster. Cluster heads are responsible for the communication to the successive layers. The nodes which are near to the border router drain out its energy quickly. Our system model of hierarchical clustering is similar to one the used in [14]. We also adapted the energy model used in [14].

In this work, we propose to improve the lifetime of the IoT system by incorporating an adaptive duty-cycling approach on the similar system model and energy model as used in [14]. We have used Lévy distribution for our proposed adaptive duty-cycling approach.

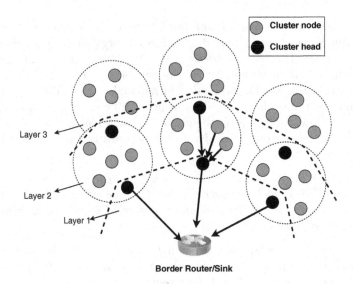

Fig. 6. Hierarchical clustering of nodes.

4.2   Problem Formualation

Our objective here is to improve the network lifetime of the IoT nodes and systems, which can be mathematically interpreted as

$$\text{maximize} \quad T_{Nlifetime}$$

However, energy constraints of the IoT nodes need to be satisfied. In order to improve the network lifetime we can formulate the same problem in terms of failure rate, λ_f. As $T_{Nlifetime}$ and λ_f are inversely related to each other as showed in Proposition 1. Therefore, we have to minimize the constant failure rate, λ_f for increasing the IoT network lifetime. Mathematically it can be represented as,

$$\underset{d_i}{\text{minimize}} \quad \lambda_f$$

$$\text{subject to} \quad E_i(d_i) \leq e_i, \ i = 1, \ldots, m.$$

where d_i represents the layer ID, $E_i(d_i)$ represents the energy consumed by the nodes of the d_i layer, and e_i is the maximum energy allowed in i^{th} layer. We use an adaptive duty cycle-based approach using Lévy Distribution which is described in next.

4.3   Lévy Distribution and Lévy Flight

The Lévy distribution is heavy-tailed stable distribution used extensively in the probability theory. The distribution can be approximated as follows [21],

$$L(d) \sim d^{-1-\beta} \tag{16}$$

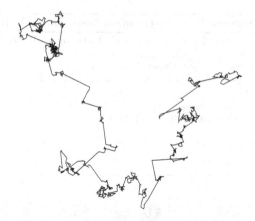

Fig. 7. An illustrative example of Lévy flight with $\beta = 1.5$ for 1000 steps

where $0 < \beta < 2$ and d is the distance vector. A random walk which follows the Lévy distribution is known as Lévy flight. An illustrative example of Lévy flight is shown in Fig. 7. From the figure we can see that Lévy flight is a combination of walks with many small step-sizes and few large step-size which follows heavy-tailed distribution. We can use the concept of Lévy flight to obtain the duty cycling of the IoT nodes.

4.4 Proposed Lévy Distribution-Based Duty Cycling

Our proposed algorithm for failure-rate mitigation is mentioned in the Algorithm 1. We have used Lévy distribution to obtain the duty cycling of the IoT nodes. We have used similar energy models and system models for our work, as used in [14]. Our objective is to use the duty cycle ratio of the nodes optimally in order to decrease the system failure rate and to increase the system's lifetime. Therefore, initially, the nodes are hierarchically clustered, and to obtain the duty cycles of each node; we use the Lévy flight strategy. The nodes which are nearer to the sink (border router) uses the Variable duty cycle ratio, which corresponds to the Lévy flight strategy. The duty cycle varies similar to the Lévy distribution such that after a series of many small duty cycles, it exhibits fewer larger duty cycle. This methodology helps in reducing the energy hole problem and increases the lifetime of the IoT system without decreasing the system performance. The algorithm is summarized in the Algorithm 1. From the algorithm, we can see that initially hierarchical clustering is done IoT node containing clusters are placed in different layers ($i = 1, 2, \cdots, n$). Subsequently, a random number is generated using Lévy distribution to obtain the duty cycle ratio (T_r) of the nodes near to the border router. If the energy required for this duty cycle ratio ($E(T_r)$) is less than the stored energy of the nodes ($E(T_{left})$), then the communication keeps on happening, else if $E(T_r) \geq E(T_{left})$ the communication stops and the IoT system fails. The lifetime is calculated depending on its time elapsed from the beginning.

Algorithm 1. Proposed Lévy Distribution-based Duty Cycling

---

1 IoT Nodes are partitioned with hierarchical clustering with clusters placed in
  different layers ($i = 1, 2, \cdots, n$), as shown in Fig. 6 ;
2 **while** *IoT nodes near to border router active* **do**
3   Generate a random number (r) using the Lévy distribution;
4   Duty cycle ratio (T_r) $\leftarrow r$;
5   **if** $E(T_r) < E(T_{left})$ **then**
6   Communication happens in IoT nodes;
7   **else**
8   IoT System fails;
9   Calculate the lifetime;

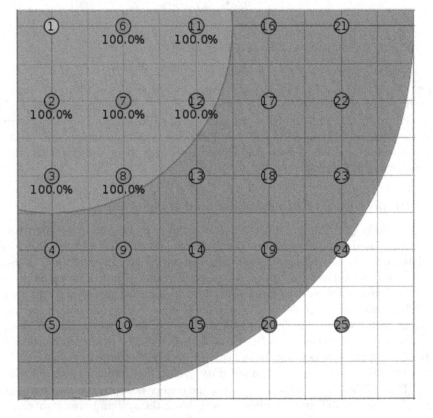

Fig. 8. Radio environment of 25 nodes used in simulation with Cooja simulator

5   Experiments and Results

5.1   Experiments Setup

The evaluation of the proposed methodology for failure rate mitigation and lifetime improvement is done using real hardware parameters of the IoT systems.

Table 1. Experimental setup for the Cooja simulator

Item name	Value
Operating system	Contiki 3.0
Simulator	Cooja
Target area	$100\,m \times 100\,m$
Radio environment	UDGM
Node type	Tmote Sky
Routing protocol	RPL
Adaptation layer	6LoWPAN
Transmitter output power	0 to 25 dBm
Receiver sensitivity	94 dBm
Radio frequency	2.4 GHz
Mobility scenario	Random distribute, No mobility
Simulation duration	Variable

The simulation is performed in Contiki Operating System-based Cooja simulator in a machine with Intel i5 processor. We have done our simulation for 15 nodes, 20 nodes, and 25 nodes for the evaluation of lifetime of the IoT system. The experimental parameters are fixed, as mentioned in [14]. The simulation parameters for the Cooja software is done as given in Table 1. The radio environment of the simulated nodes of the Cooja simulator are shown in Fig. 8.

The average power consumption of all the 25 simulated nodes for uniform duty cycling is shown in Fig. 9. The initial duty cycle ratio for all the 25 nodes are shown in Fig. 10. From Figs. 9 and 10, we can get an idea about the average power consumption of the IoT nodes and its duty cycle ratio used initially.

5.2   Results and Discussion

We have implemented the Algorithm 1 in the Cooja simulation tool to obtain the effects of the proposed Lévy flight-based duty cycling approach. Accordingly, duty cycles are varied adaptively using the Lévy distribution, and for that, the codes are modified in the Cooja simulation software, and simulations are performed. We also compare our results with the hierarchical clustering approach of EnergyIoT [14] and the uniform duty cycling approach. Comparative representation of the duty cycles used in all the three methods mentioned is shown in Fig. 11. In [14], the authors have utilized the energy consumption in the idle listening in the network construction phase and data processing phase, which saves energy and increases the IoT network lifetime. In our method, the energy consumption in idle listening is utilized with the help of Lévy distribution, which saves the energy much more than the EnergyIoT. The minimum required active time for proper operations of the IoT node is ensured while assigning the duty cycle using the Lévy distribution.

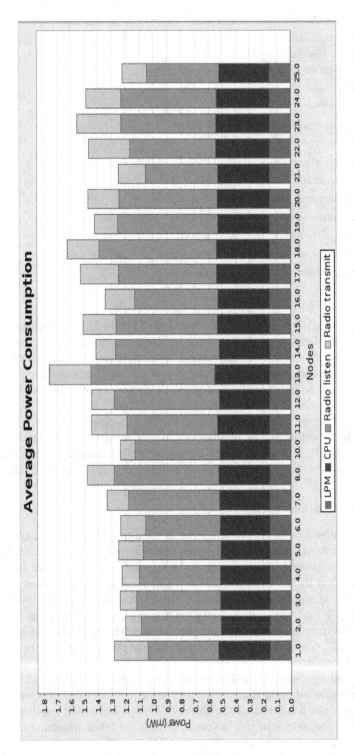

Fig. 9. Average power consumption of 25 nodes used in simulation with Cooja simulator.

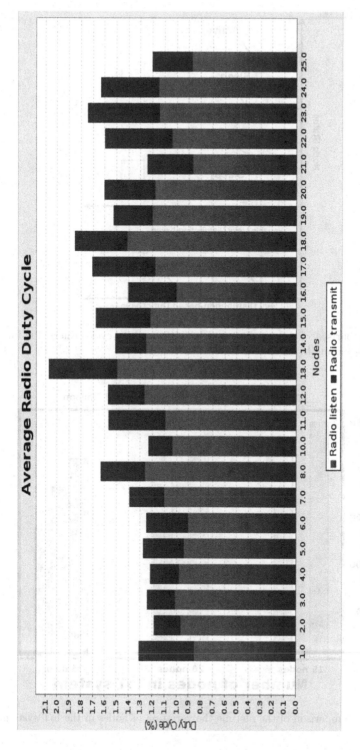

Fig. 10. Duty cycle ratio of 25 nodes used in simulation with Cooja simulator.

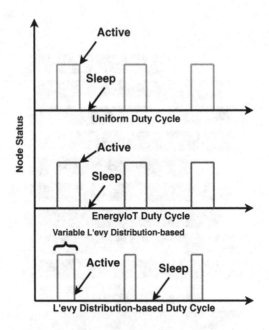

Fig. 11. Comparison of duty cycles used in uniform duty cycle, EnergyIoT method and our proposed method.

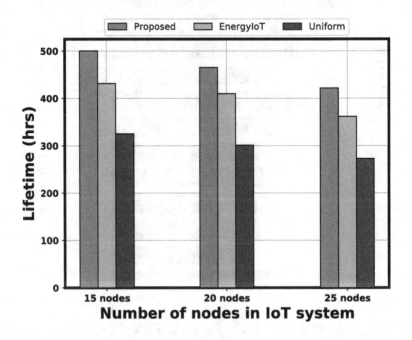

Fig. 12. Comparison of the lifetime the variation of nodes in the IoT system.

Comparison of Lieftime: The result of the comparison of the lifetime of the IoT system is shown in Fig. 12. From the experiment, we have obtained that the lifetime obtained by our proposed method is longer than that of [14] and a uniform duty cycling approach. One of the main reasons behind this, we have used Lévy flight-based duty cycling, which helps in the reduction of the failure rate of the node near to border router, which helps in the increase in lifetime. It can also be observed from Fig. 12 that when the number of nodes increases, then the lifetime of the IoT system decreases. The increase of lifetime implies the decrease in failure rate.

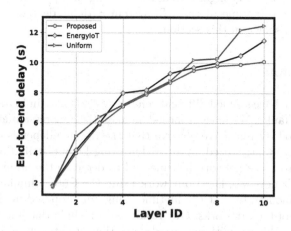

Fig. 13. Variation of end to end delay for different layers

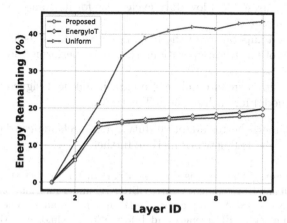

Fig. 14. Percentage of energy remaining for different layers

Network Performance Evaluation: We have also evaluated the performance of the network for our proposed approach. For that, we have evaluated the end-to-end delay for each of the layers for the 25 node configuration. We have also evaluated the remaining energy for each of the layers. We compare these parameters with the work of [14] and the uniform duty cycling approach. From the result, it can be seen that our approach does not degrade the end-to-end delay as compared to [14], as shown in Fig. 13.

The percentage of energy remaining for different layers of the IoT system is also similar using our approach compared to the [14], as shown in Fig. 14. Therefore, using our Lévy flight-based duty cycling the approach we have gained an increase in the lifetime of the IoT system without degrading the network performance, as shown in this section.

6 Conclusion

In this paper, we have studied different reliability challenges in IoT system design due to random faults. We have proposed an analytical expression for the lifetime evaluation of IoT systems. We observe that the lifetime depends on the failure rate. We have also introduced an algorithm using Lévy distribution-based duty cycling to improve the network lifetime and to decrease the failure rates of the IoT system. We have validated our work using the Cooja simulation software. The results demonstrate that the lifetime using our proposed method increases than the state-of-the-art works. Our results also include that lifetime improvement has been achieved without any degradation in network performance. We have also observed that as the number of nodes increases in the IoT systems, the network lifetime decreases. From our work, for designing a reliable IoT system following recommendation should be followed,

- The IoT nodes must use a low duty cycle ratio for its transceivers in order to save battery power.
- The operating temperature of the IoT system should be as low as possible.
- Few numbers of hardware operations should be performed for a better lifetime.
- IoT network with a small number of nodes should be designed with a border router (sink node) for each of the IoT networks.

In the future, a much better adaptive duty cycling scheme can be proposed in order to improve the IoT network lifetime further.

Acknowledgements. The work is done as a part of the project title "Information Security Research and Development Centre (ISRDC)" under Information Security Education and Awareness (ISEA) Project (Phase-II) at IIT Guwahati. The authors would like to thank Ministry of Electronics and Information Technology (MeitY) and IIT Guwahati for the support.

References

1. Wollschlaeger, M., Sauter, T., Jasperneite, J.: The future of industrial communication: automation networks in the era of the internet of things and industry 4.0. IEEE Ind. Electron. Mag. **11**(1), 17–27 (2017)
2. Lucas-Estañ, M.C., Raptis, T.P., Sepulcre, M., Passarella, A., Regueiro, C., Lazaro, O.: A software defined hierarchical communication and data management architecture for industry 4.0. In: 2018 14th Annual Conference on Wireless On-Demand Network Systems and Services (WONS), pp. 37–44. IEEE (2018)
3. Shao, L., et al.: Compact modeling of thin film transistors for flexible hybrid IoT design. IEEE Des. Test **36**, 6–14 (2019)
4. Ahmad, M.: Reliability models for the Internet of Things: a paradigm shift. In: 2014 IEEE International Symposium on Software Reliability Engineering Workshops, pp. 52–59. IEEE (2014)
5. Rosing, T.S.: Reliability and maintainability of IoT systems (2018)
6. Xing, L., Zhao, G., Wang, Y., Mandava, L.: Competing failure analysis in IoT systems with cascading functional dependence. In: 2018 Annual Reliability and Maintainability Symposium (RAMS), pp. 1–6. IEEE (2018)
7. Thomas, M.O., Rad, B.B.: Reliability evaluation metrics for Internet of Things, car tracking system: a review. Int. J. Inf. Technol. Comput. Sci. (IJITCS) **9**(2), 1–10 (2017)
8. Raptis, T.P., Passarella, A., Conti, M.: Maximizing industrial IoT network lifetime under latency constraints through edge data distribution. In: 2018 IEEE Industrial Cyber-Physical Systems (ICPS), pp. 708–713. IEEE (2018)
9. Valls, V., Iosifidis, G., Salonidis, T.: Maximum lifetime analytics in IoT networks. In: IEEE INFOCOM 2019-IEEE Conference on Computer Communications, pp. 1369–1377. IEEE (2019)
10. Morin, E., Maman, M., Guizzetti, R., Duda, A.: Comparison of the device lifetime in wireless networks for the Internet of Things. IEEE Access **5**, 7097–7114 (2017)
11. Airehrour, D., Gutiérrez, J., Ray, S.K.: Greening and optimizing energy consumption of sensor nodes in the Internet of Things through energy harvesting: challenges and approaches (2016)
12. Fafoutis, X., Elsts, A., Vafeas, A., Oikonomou, G., Piechocki, R.J.: On predicting the battery lifetime of IoT devices: experiences from the sphere deployments. In: RealWSN@ SenSys, pp. 7–12 (2018)
13. Cao, K., Xu, G., Zhou, J., Wei, T., Chen, M., Hu, S.: Qos-adaptive approximate real-time computation for mobility-aware IoT lifetime optimization. IEEE Trans. Comput.-Aided Des. Integr. Circuits Syst. **38**, 1799–1810 (2018)
14. Li, Q., Gochhayat, S.P., Conti, M., Liu, F.: EnergIoT: a solution to improve network lifetime of IoT devices. Pervasive Mob. Comput. **42**, 124–133 (2017)
15. Weibull, W., et al.: A statistical distribution function of wide applicability. J. Appl. Mech. **18**(3), 293–297 (1951)
16. Black, J.R.: Electromigration–a brief survey and some recent results. IEEE Trans. Electron Devices **16**(4), 338–347 (1969)
17. Laidler, K.J.: Chemical Kinetics, vol. 42. Harper & Row, New York (1987)
18. Guo, X., Verma, V., Gonzalez-Guerrero, P., Stan, M.R.: When "things" get older: exploring circuit aging in IoT applications. In: 2018 19th International Symposium on Quality Electronic Design (ISQED), pp. 296–301. IEEE (2018)
19. Dey, S., Dash, S., Nandi, S., Trivedi, G.: PGIREM: reliability-constrained IR drop minimization and electromigration assessment of VLSI power grid networks using

cooperative coevolution. In: 2018 IEEE Computer Society Annual Symposium on VLSI (ISVLSI), pp. 40–45. IEEE (2018)

20. Dey, S., Nandi, S., Trivedi, G.: PGRDP: reliability, delay, and power-aware area minimization of large-scale VLSI power grid network using cooperative coevolution. In: Mandal, J.K., Sinha, D. (eds.) Intelligent Computing Paradigm: Recent Trends. SCI, vol. 784, pp. 69–84. Springer, Singapore (2020). https://doi.org/10.1007/978-981-13-7334-3_6

21. Dey, S., Dash, S., Nandi, S., Trivedi, G.: Markov chain model using lévy flight for VLSI power grid analysis. In: 2017 30th International Conference on VLSI Design and 2017 16th International Conference on Embedded Systems (VLSID), pp. 107–112. IEEE (2017)

The Ultimate Victory of White- over Blacklisting for the Editing of Encrypted Instant Messages Without Decrypting Nor Understanding Them

Günter Fahrnberger[✉][iD]

University of Hagen, Hagen, North Rhine-Westphalia, Germany
guenter.fahrnberger@studium.fernuni-hagen.de

Abstract. The European Union Agency for Law Enforcement Cooperation (hereinafter denominated as Europol) has constantly warned society about the unbowed growth of child sexual exploitation in its six issued IOCTAs (Internet Organised Crime Threat Assessments). If already all attempts succeed to thwart grooming as the initiation of contacts between pedophiles and adolescents, then CSEM (Child Sexual Exploitation Material) cannot accrue and SGEM (Self Generated Explicit Material) does not find its way to perpetrators. IM (Instant Messaging) spearheads the list of preferred communication tools that render grooming possible. The consensual editing of encrypted instant messages without decrypting nor understanding them based on black- or whitelisting commits itself to the thwarting of grooming. Existing literature attests whitelisting better functionality and worse performance than blacklisting. In contrast, recent related work objects to the inferior performance of whitelisting, since former experiments for both paradigms happened under incomparable conditions, and demands their remake under fair circumstances. This scholarly piece refutes the inferiority of whitelisting by exhibiting the results of a new test series in which blacklisting screens the complementary set of words that whitelisting does not incorporate. At the end, it corroborates that whitelisting outplays blacklisting and emerges victorious.

Keywords: Blacklisting · Blind computing · Cyberbullying · Cyberharassment · Cyberstalking · Flaming · Grooming · Instant Messaging · Pedophilia · Whitelisting

1 Introduction

Europol has recently published the sixth annual IOCTA [12]. Just as its predecessors [7–11], the recent edition again reports on a continuously growing amount of detected CSEM [12]. Furthermore, the survey explicates the reasons for this ostensibly ineradicable kind of crime.

© Springer Nature Switzerland AG 2020
S. S. Rautaray et al. (Eds.): I4CS 2020, CCIS 1139, pp. 143–157, 2020.
https://doi.org/10.1007/978-3-030-37484-6_8

The most evident reason for the rising number of cases of online sexual coercion and extortion of minors is their increasing accessibility to the Internet and, concurrently, to social media platforms [11]. Topical statistics evidences that this ubiquity of the Internet additionally leads to the circumstance that victims and culprits in such cases steadily get younger in the course of time. While young children are rather sexually abused by family members or someone else in their close vicinity, a considerable threat for older children and teenagers stems from sexual exploitation by someone they have never met in real life. Irrespective of the victims' age, the lack of parental control and awareness amplifies the risk of being approached by pedophiles.

Grooming terms the initiation of sexual contacts to kids and juveniles. Once successful, offenders might meet their victims and record explicit videos and images. Even easier and more common is SGEM produced by youths and initially shared voluntarily with peers or posted on social networks. If such SGEM ends up in the possession of online child sexual offenders, they have a field day to commence subsequent sexual extortion in order to generate new SGEM.

First and foremost, delinquents primarily place CSEM on the Darknet before the impious content tends to eventually find its way to the surface Internet. The sole remedy for already published CSEM is to seek and destroy it. The Canadian Centre for Child Protection has deployed the automated website crawler *Arachnid* for such quests.

While villains mainly took advantage of P2P (Peer-to-Peer) platforms in the past to share their CSEM, this means of communication has become risky for them due to improved law enforcement detection. Therefore, they were coerced to find secure communication media. Since anonymization and privacy-preserving technologies have become easier to access and use, and evildoers gradually come from a younger generation, they more and more shift from P2P to everyday communication applications with E2E (End-to-End) encryption. The usage of IM (such as WhatsApp) ranks first, but also VPN (Virtual Private Networks) and TOR (The Onion Router) nowadays require very little technical skill. The IOCTA 2018 refers to creative wrongdoers who do not even flinch from hiding CSEM in the distributed ledger of Bitcoin's block chain.

In interplay with E2E encipherment, felons also benefit from the online storability of instant messengers. They tend to erase CSEM on their local devices once they have seen it. Nonetheless, they still have access to their historical (E2E-enciphered) messages by logging in to their IM accounts. It challenges law enforcement to detect and investigate criminals without locally stored CSEM as evidence. Hence, the tackling of saved E2E-encrypted CSEM in the repositories of instant messengers makes the cooperation of CSPs (Communication Service Providers) indispensable.

A series of associated scientific publications focuses on the consensual editing of encrypted instant messages without decrypting nor understanding them, i.e. on how CSPs can *blindly* filter out explicit content of ciphertext instant messages without standing any chance of obtaining plaintext for unscrupulous data mining [16, 19–22, 24]. Consensual editing means the modification of instant messages by CSPs with the agreement of addressers and addressees. The approaches in all these scholarly pieces rest upon blacklisting [13–15,17,18,23] and/or whitelisting [19]. While blacklisting cuts dedicated words out of instant messages, whitelisting lets merely pass instant messages that solely comprise whitelisted terms.

Of all the cited references, only the dissertation about *editing encrypted messages without decrypting nor understanding them* juxtaposes the particulars of black- and whitelisting [22]. On the one hand, it red-flags the vulnerability of blacklisting to filter circumvention. On the other hand, it unexpectedly diagnoses whitelisting with an overall longer computing time than blacklisting. This disparity can be attributed to totally diverging cardinalities of the employed plaintext dictionaries. While the blacklisting prototype only considers a single blacklist word at a time, the experiment for whitelisting operates with a realistic cardinality of 128,656 whitelist words. Thus, this treatise adjusts the blacklisting prototype with a more faithful PBD (Plaintext Blacklist Dictionary) cardinality of 148 blacklist words and compares it again with its whitelisting counterpart in order to gain more coherent results. In addition to the already descried risk of filter circumvention, it can be expected that blacklisting also succumbs to whitelisting in terms of its performance.

Prior to the verification of this conjecture, Sect. 2 starts with an explication of the previously mentioned citations about black- and whitelisting ideas usable for the editing of encrypted instant messages without decrypting nor understanding them. Section 3 delves into the methodology of the very last versions for black- and whitelisting. Section 4 continues with the proof of an inferior blacklisting performance compared to whitelisting. Section 5 summarizes the ultimate victory of white- over blacklisting for the editing of instant messages without decrypting nor understanding them and proposes worthwhile future work.

2   Related Work

As announced in the very previous paragraph, this section recapitulates the history of black- and whitelisting for the editing of encrypted instant messages without decrypting nor understanding them [20]. The scientifically experienced reader might claim a representative extent of contrastable literature for this section rather than content themselves with the perusal of one research thread. The author of this series soothes the peruser at this point by referring to the sections about related work in the cited predecessors with an abundance of comparable literature.

2.1   SecureString 1.0 – The First Approach for Blacklisting

SecureString 1.0 was the first blacklisting approach to overcome extra hardware resources with a pure software solution [13]. It belongs to the kind of cryptosystems for the blind computing on nonnumerical data. It bases upon a topical underlying symmetric cryptosystem and polyalphabetical encryption. The ciphering scheme encrypts each n-gram (character string of length n) of a word together with the beginning position of the n-gram within the word. Thereby, the start index of each n-gram stipulates the applied alphabet (alphabet = encryption transformation) on it. SecureString 1.0 brings the ciphertext n-grams out of sequence after their encryption without losing the possibility to operate on them because their order can be restored after their decryption through their enveloped position information.

Due to the finiteness of character string lengths that can be fully supported through querying and replacing operations, every SecureString 1.0-object deliberately contains exactly one word. Disadvantageously, this discloses the string boundaries and abets repetition pattern attacks on them.

2.2   SecureString 2.0 – The More Flexible Successor

The detection of these considerable limitations by SecureString 1.0 caused the construction of the improved SecureString 2.0 [14,15,17]. SecureString 2.0 permits an arbitrary number of cohered words per SecureString 2.0-object. In detail, SecureString 2.0 heads for monoalphabetical (substitutional) encryption within each character string, but every utilized alphabet must not become effective for more than one word. Normally, each encryption transformation depends on a dedicated key, but SecureString 2.0 enciphers each character of the same plaintext character string together with an identical salt (salt = arbitrary nonce). If the salt always transmutes from word to word, then the encryption transformation also changes from word to word, even in case the same key would be employed for all character strings. Automatic salt updating [1,16] is applicable, which means that each salt serves as the input for a hash function that outputs the salt for the encryption of the successive plaintext word. This non-size-preserving behavior of SecureString 2.0 entails the advantage that the decryption scheme can simply ignore salts rather than must care about them. Optionally, for flow control, the salts can be shortened to make room for an appended sequential number that becomes verified during the decryption scheme.

SecureString 2.0 acts as the cryptosystem for four applications: SecureSIP for computing on confidential character strings in an enhanced SIP (Session Initiation Protocol) framework [6], SecureSMPP for computing on confidential character strings in an enhanced SMPP (Short Message Peer to Peer) framework [25], SafeChat as a tool to shield children's communication from explicit messages [24], and SIMS (Secure Instant Messaging Sifter) [16].

The most recent treatise about SecureString 2.0 suggests to develop an advancement of the cryptosystem that converts every arbitrary plaintext into pangram ciphertext and, thereby, impedes any recurrences of ciphergrams [17].

2.3   SecureString 3.0 – The Abolition of Ciphertext Repetitions

On these grounds, SecureString 3.0 as the next generation of the cryptosystem hardened SecureString 2.0 with better authenticity, integrity, and privacy [18,23]. As its predecessors SecureString 1.0 and SecureString 2.0, SecureString 3.0 poses a non-size-preserving cryptosystem. The encryption scheme does nothing else but to salt each individual plaintext character of a string, i.e. to append an arbitrary character sequence, and to encipher the amalgamation of plaintext character and salt with a contemporary high-performing cryptosystem in ECB (Electronic CodeBook) mode [28]. The encryption algorithm may prolong as many characters with the same salt as no ciphertext repetition appears. Therefore, before it would scramble a dedicated character with an equal salt twice, it had to switch to another salt and, thereby, defused the hazardousness of repetitions despite the usage of ECB mode. Automatic salt updating by inputting the recent salt in a (trapdoor) hash function denotes an easy and secure alternative to obtain a fresh salt from an RNG (Random Number Generator) [1]. This kind of salt production does not only perpetuate backward security i.e. no salt can be concluded from its successors, but also lets a TTP (Trusted Third Party) prepare homomorphic computations for an untrustworthy CSP just with a starting salt per cohesive text body.

To make a long story short, SecureString 3.0 achieves non-repetitive ciphertexts with controlled randomness attained through hashed salts in lieu of haphazardly compiled ciphertexts through the contents of foregoing blocks.

2.4   Secure Whitelisting of Instant Messages

Blacklisting connotes the search and eradication of unsolicited terms. Unfortunately, already explicit phrases in spaced form can circumvent any blacklist filters, not to mention resourceful fake character insertions and uppercase-lowercase-combinations [35]. For this purpose, a secure whitelisting technique has emerged that securely scans instant messages and forwards only those with solely harmless words to their destinations [19]. It amalgamates the following six principles.

- **White- instead of blacklisting to impede circumvention:** Only instant messages with merely approved words including their declined or conjugated variants become delivered to their intended targets.
- **Secret sharing between CSP and TTP to maintain privacy:** A CSP only becomes aware of the source and the destination accounts of instant messages, but not of their plaintext content. A TTP just processes a multitude of addressless ciphertext character strings.
- **PKI (Public Key Infrastructure) to sustain authenticity:** Asymmetric cryptography assures consignees of the consigners' authenticity. On the one hand, this applies if asymmetrical cryptography protects the secret keys for symmetrical cryptography. On the other hand, a sender of an instant message convinces the receiver of their authenticity by signing a hash value of the ciphertext instant message with their private key.
- **Training mode to enforce resilience:** Every IM client can covertly recommend vocables to the TTP that should be included in the whitelist in future or excluded from there.

- **One-time secret keys to assure privacy:** The symmetric encipherment of each instant message respectively of each batch of individual words draws on a unique arbitrary secret key to reach nondeterministic encryption and to avert collision attacks, which would be a consequence of ciphertext repetitions.
- **Onionskin paradigm to warrant authenticity, integrity, and privacy:** A topical hybrid cryptosystem for transport cryptography between all involved components ensures an extra umbrella against menaces during data transmission.

2.5   Editing Encrypted Messages Without Decrypting nor Understanding Them

The design science in information systems research of Hevner and Chatterjee abstractly recommends developing and evaluating a design artifact for a relevant problem with rigorous methods [21,22,26]. This abstraction requires adopting well-proven IT security concepts, or adapting them to ultimately finalize an adequate framework design [21,22]. For that purpose, the thesis about *editing encrypted messages without decrypting nor understanding them* and its preceding disquisition about the blind censoring for IM amalgamate two such IT security concepts as a methodological basis for black- and whitelisting. The NIST (National Institute of Standards and Technology) penned one of them with a framework to ameliorate the cybersecurity of critical infrastructure by outputting an action plan [21,22,30]. Boyd's OODA loop as the second contributive concept leaves its mark by offering a crafty template for the activities of this action plan [2,21,22].

The below-mentioned Sect. 3 explicates the action plans for black- and whitelisting, whose algorithms finally ran for a contrasting juxtaposition of their performance in Sect. 4.

3   Methodology

This section continues the methodological basis in the paper about the blind censoring for IM [21]. It concretizes the abstract framework to serviceable expedients for the editing of encrypted instant messages without decrypting nor understanding them. Figure 1 zones a rudimentary IM architecture inclusive their threats into the four OODA loop activities *observation, orientation, decision,* and *action* [22].

The dissertation about *editing encrypted messages without decrypting nor understanding them* specifies two algorithms for the observation phase and one for each of the other three phases as hereinafter given.

- Observation
  - IM Session Initialization
  - Instant Message Initialization

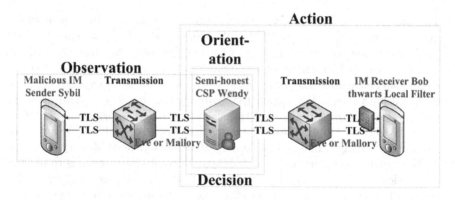

Fig. 1. Action plan

- Orientation
    - Instant Message Analysis
- Decision
    - Instant Message Determination
- Action
    - Instant Message Delivery

For lack of space, this disquisition takes the liberty to redirect the interested reader to [22] for the perusing of the algorithmic details. Nevertheless, the remainder of this section explains the players of black- and whitelisting in a rudimental IM architecture. The itemization below introduces seven of them that assume a role in both scenarios.

- **Bob** is the endpoint that receives instant messages [21,22].
- **Sybil** replaces the ordinary IM consigner **Alice** by adopting several identities and insistently harassing Bob [5,21,22].
- **Wendy** represents an ordinary CSP that has become semi-honest(-but-curious) [3,31] and capable of divulging plaintext instant messages [21,22]. In spite of this unwanted behavior, Wendy assumes the responsibility for storing and forwarding an incoming instant message to the designated Bob. In the presented scenario, Wendy forms a heterogeneous secret-sharing cluster together with a scenario-specific TTP. Each of the both cluster entities must strictly run in its own isolated environment in order to ensure privacy.
- The **CA (Certification Authority)** provides assurance of Alice's identity to the TTP and Bob through the establishment of a common PKI (Public Key Infrastructure) [22]. Thus, Bob is also made aware of spurious instant messages. The CA generally is a passive entity providing validation when required. Its function is comprised of issuing certificates vouching for the identity of Alice and Bob by signing their CSRs (Certificate Signing Requests) as well as revoking any compromised certificates.

- The passive eavesdropper **Eve** tries to grab valuable data in transmissions between Alice and Bob [16,21,22]. The unimpeded propagation of freely available packet sniffers combined with careless or antagonistic transmission providers (which ignore or negate any prophylactic measures or responsive countermeasures, and/or conspire with intelligences, or exploit customer data) permits even a low-skilled Eve (equipped with access to transmission elements) with direct glimpses of transferred plaintext information [21,22].
- The active eavesdropper **Mallory** trumps Eve's passive grabbing behavior by varying or denying valuable data [16,21,22]. An experienced Mallory performs brute intrusions with man-in-the-middle attacks into data streams to exploit authentication flaws in link protocols [21,22]. In other words, Mallory cracks the poorly secured IM sessions, studies Alice's writing style, and replaces the originally intended messages toward Bob with feigned ones in order to elicit confidential knowledge (such as Bob's passwords or credit card details) or personal data (like nude pictures of Bob). Naturally, the latter (falling into the wrong hands) could lead to exploitation through blackmail for financial gain.
- **Transmission** allegorizes the backbone of an IM topology as noticeably opaque pathways interconnecting all the labeled items in Fig. 2 respectively Fig. 3 [22]. This opaqueness in conjunction with lack of control impairs the trustworthiness of transmission. Due to the conjoint exertion of insecure communication paths (vulnerable to eavesdropping and manipulation by Eve respectively Mallory) and secure ones, hybrid cryptography must outweigh any insecurity for all sessions within OODA loop activities.

Subsections 3.1 and 3.2 add the specific actors of black- respectively whitelisting.

3.1 Blacklisting

Compared with the generic action plan in Fig. 1, the PBD and the TTP appear as the two additional units in Fig. 2.

- The **PBD** (such as WordNet [29]) provides a reliable online repository of illicit terms, i.e. it keeps up-to-date with rapid changes in online terminology [22]. Beyond that, it maintains the morphed variants of offensive nouns and verbs.
- The **TTP** downloads a customized set of plaintext matching pattern strings from the PBD for each IM session [22]. The composition of such a set depends on Bob's profile. The TTP assumes the responsibility of processing the laborious encipherment of the downloaded plaintext matching pattern strings and, thereby, relieves the CSP as well as the interface between Alice and the CSP of voluminous uploads. This distribution of labor yields secret-sharing, i.e. the TTP discovers the plaintext-ciphertext-relations, however, nothing with regards to the contents of instant messages is revealed.

3.2 Whitelisting

Just as blacklisting, whitelisting also works with two tailored constituents (see Fig. 3).

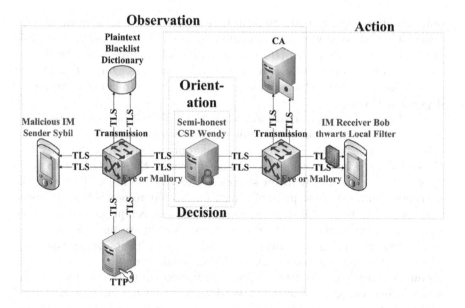

Fig. 2. Activities of blacklisting

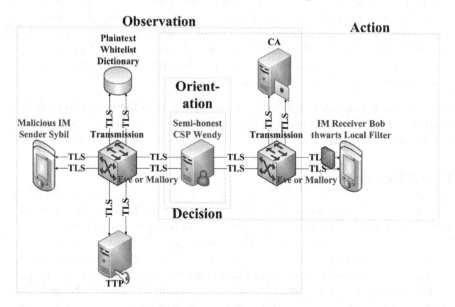

Fig. 3. Activities of whitelisting

– The **PWD** appears as an available online database with the unencrypted, unobjectionable character collections of all supported languages [22]. For example, it also must embrace the digits from zero to nine to facilitate the TTP allowing instant messages with numeric parts, like times, dates, and other numbers. Additionally, the database supplier must actively update the whitelist vocabulary with newly emerging, innocuous expressions to avoid upsetting contemporary writers whose texts could inadvertently be flagged as malevolent. Undoubtedly, it requires resilient defense against DoS attacks as well as unauthorized manipulations to serve as a reliable platform for dependent CSPs.

– The **TTP** as the counterpart alongside the CSP within their established secret-sharing cluster can be denominated as a simple ciphertext comparator and may be placed into a tamper-proof microprocessor [34] of the CSP [22]. Generally, its primary task is focused on informing the CSP about the containedness of ciphered character strings (retrieved from the CSP) within the encrypted whitelist. More precisely, the TTP is solely responsible for the positive acknowledgment of instant messages exclusively comprised of whitelisted words. Each time before the TTP executes such comparisons, it must release the hybrid encryption of a processed word packet with its own private key, which an Alice has imposed with the fitting public key.

As an auxiliary job, the TTP receives suggestions from Bob in the training mode for expressions that ought to be added to or deleted from its enciphered whitelist. If the number of trustworthy advocates exceeds a predefined threshold, then the suggestion gets added to the (ciphertext) TTP repository as a new buzzword. In the same way, an entry is removed from the whitelist in the event that the predefined threshold for negative associations is reached. The reliability of the categorization of these proponents and objectors can be vouched for as long as the rate of barred outbound instant messages does not rise above a predetermined percentage.

The experimental setup for the performance analysis in the successional Sect. 4 incorporates all described but the antagonistic roles, i.e. Alice in lieu of Sybil, an innocuous CSP in place of Wendy, and no influence of Eve or Mallory.

4 Performance Analysis

Each of the above-mentioned protagonists (as well as a Java remote object registry) was simulated by means of a separate Java 8 process running on a HP DL380 G5 server utilizing eight 2.5 GHz cores and 32 GB main memory whilst supporting a Fedora 64 bit Linux operating system [22]. The simulation was deliberately deployed on a single isolated computer for the purpose of keeping volatile network latencies out of the equation. During the trial each Linux process was running at the lowest nice level and, therefore, with the highest priority to eliminate any potentially negative effects caused by concurrently launched processes.

The communication sequences between the elements took advantage of AES-128/CBC/PKCS7Padding (Advanced Encryption Standard [4] with Cipher Block Chaining [28] and padding based upon the Public Key Cryptography Standard number 7 [27]) as the symmetrical cryptosystem and RSA (Rivest, Shamir, and Adleman) [32] as well as ECC (Elliptic Curve Cryptography) [33] (each utilizing three differing key sizes) for asymmetrical encryption.

128,804 genuine English vocables from WordNet [29] were imported into a MariaDB table and subsequently partitioned disjunctively into two further MariaDB tables, 148 blacklist words for the PBD and 128,656 whitelist words for the PWD. After the accomplishment of the preparatory observation phase, Alice combinatorially assembled 1,000,000 haphazard instant messages out of the 128,804 vocables per word count from 1 to 16 for each of the three selected key lengths of RSA, and also for each of the three chosen key sizes of ECC. Altogether, Alice sent 1,000,000 * 16 * 6 = 96,000,000 instant messages for blacklisting and, once more, 96,000,000 instant messages for whitelisting to the CSP. Figure 4 substantiates real-world average instant message lengths up to 168 characters during the remade tests.

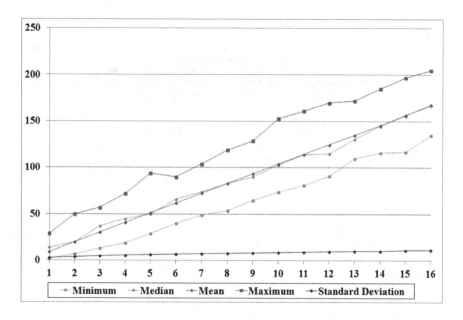

Fig. 4. Characters per Instant Message

Since a chart comprising twelve different data arrays would negatively affect its legibility, it makes more sense to separately observe the mean running time of instant messages from Alice to Bob in ns (nanoseconds) with RSA-support in Fig. 5 and with ECC-support in Fig. 6.

The application of RSA for instant messages comprised of merely a sole word cannot declare an unambiguous winner because of their interlaced data points. In the case of filtering instant messages containing multiple words, white- dominates blacklisting with lower cycle time. The more words an instant message comprises, the higher the time saving factor turns out and, therewith, the dominance of white- over blacklisting. This circumstance occurs because of a stronger linear growth rate of blacklisting in comparison to whitelisting. Accordingly, the most lead time in Fig. 5 is reduced for 16 words long instant messages. While blacklisting needs approximately 50.50 s (seconds) per instant message on average,

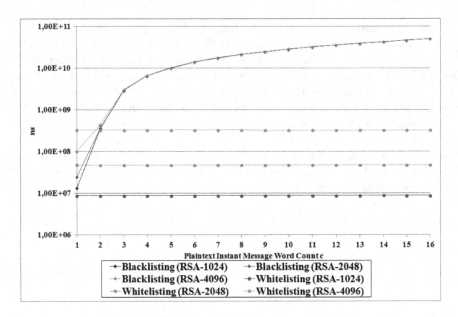

Fig. 5. Performance with RSA-support

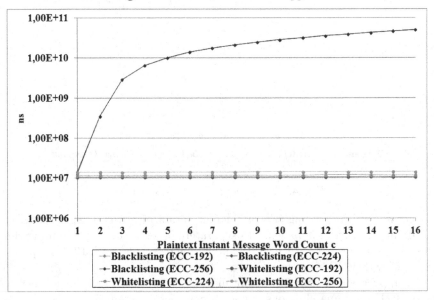

Fig. 6. Performance with ECC-support

whitelisting merely consumes between 8.66 ms (milliseconds) for RSA-1024 and 317.07 ms for RSA-4096.

Figure 6 reveals an even unequivocal domination of white- over black-listing for ECC-support. While blacklisting merely underperforms slightly in comparison with whitelisting for one-word instant messages, the processing time gapes between both paradigms the more the amount of words per instant message increases. Moreover, ECC-support even quickens whitelisting when juxtaposed to RSA-support. Considering all three key sizes and all amounts of words, the mean throughput time remains in the narrow bandwidth between 7.39 ms and 12.68 ms. On the contrary, the worse performance of blacklisting with ECC-support behaves similarly to that with RSA-support. It again culminates in an Alice-to-Bob time of 50.50 s at an average.

Both figures convey the clear recommendatory message to a reader to save computation resources by favoring white- over blacklisting. The succeeding Sect. 5 recaps the process that redounds to this recommendation.

5 Conclusion

The thesis about *editing encrypted messages without decrypting nor understanding them* contrasts the performance of the both paradigms black- and whitelisting with the help of historic experimental results. At first glance, white- defeats blacklisting concerning functionality, and vice versa pertaining to performance. At the same time, the dissertation doubts the latter finding since it descries too unequal test conditions. Consequently, it calls for equitably reevaluating the door-to-door time of instant messages from Alice to Bob in future work.

This scientific publication satisfies the desire for an equitable reevaluation. For the sake of verification, the fresh evaluation occurred for two completely independent asymmetric cryptosystems, which need computationally intensive operations. What is more, the experiment incorporated three commonly used key lengths for each asymmetrical cryptosystem. Irrespective of the exerted asymmetric cryptosystem, key size, and word count, the outcome always confirms the thesis' surmise of suboptimal performance by blacklisting juxtaposed with whitelisting.

In the face of this whitelisting's superiority, there is nothing else for it but to suggest the further development of whitelisting, for instance, by amalgamating it with prudent topic detection.

Acknowledgments. Many thanks to Bettina Baumgartner from the University of Vienna for proofreading this paper!

References

1. Anderson, R.J.: Security Engineering - A Guide to Building Dependable Distributed Systems, 2nd Edn. Wiley (2008). https://www.cl.cam.ac.uk/~rja14/book.html
2. Angerman, W.: Coming full circle with Boyd's OODA loop ideas: an analysis of innovation diffusion and evolution. Master's thesis, Defense Technical Information Center, March 2004. http://www.dtic.mil/get-tr-doc/pdf?AD=ADA425228

3. Chai, Q., Gong, G.: Verifiable symmetric searchable encryption for semi-honest-but-curious cloud servers. In: 2012 IEEE International Conference on Communications (ICC), pp. 917–922, June 2012. https://doi.org/10.1109/ICC.2012.6364125
4. Daemen, J., Rijmen, V.: The Design of Rijndael: AES - The Advanced Encryption Standard. Springer, Heidelberg (2001). https://doi.org/10.1007/978-3-662-04722-4
5. Douceur, J.R.: The Sybil attack. In: Druschel, P., Kaashoek, F., Rowstron, A. (eds.) IPTPS 2002. LNCS, vol. 2429, pp. 251–260. Springer, Heidelberg (2002). https://doi.org/10.1007/3-540-45748-8_24. http://www.cs.rice.edu/Conferences/IPTPS02/101
6. Elgaby, M.: Computing on confidential character strings in an enhanced SIP-framework. Master's thesis, University of Hagen, February 2013. https://doi.org/10.13140/2.1.2059.4241
7. Europol: Internet Organised Crime Threat Assessment (IOCTA) 2014, January 2016. https://doi.org/10.2813/16
8. Europol: Internet Organised Crime Threat Assessment (IOCTA) 2015, June 2016. https://doi.org/10.2813/03524
9. Europol: Internet Organised Crime Threat Assessment (IOCTA) 2016, December 2016. https://doi.org/10.2813/275589
10. Europol: Internet Organised Crime Threat Assessment (IOCTA) 2017, September 2017. https://doi.org/10.2813/55735
11. Europol: Internet Organised Crime Threat Assessment (IOCTA) 2018, January 2019. https://doi.org/10.2813/858843
12. Europol: Internet Organised Crime Threat Assessment (IOCTA) 2019, October 2019. https://www.europol.europa.eu/sites/default/files/documents/iocta_2019.pdf
13. Fahrnberger, G.: Computing on encrypted character strings in clouds. In: Hota, C., Srimani, P.K. (eds.) ICDCIT 2013. LNCS, vol. 7753, pp. 244–254. Springer, Heidelberg (2013). https://doi.org/10.1007/978-3-642-36071-8_19
14. Fahrnberger, G.: SecureString 2.0 - a cryptosystem for computing on encrypted character strings in clouds. In: Eichler, G., Gumzej, R. (eds.) Networked Information Systems, Fortschritt-Berichte Reihe 10, vol. 826, pp. 226–240. VDI, Düsseldorf, June 2013. https://doi.org/10.13140/RG.2.1.4846.7521/5
15. Fahrnberger, G.: A second view on securestring 2.0. In: Natarajan, R. (ed.) ICDCIT 2014. LNCS, vol. 8337, pp. 239–250. Springer, Cham (2014). https://doi.org/10.1007/978-3-319-04483-5_25
16. Fahrnberger, G.: SIMS: a comprehensive approach for a secure instant messaging sifter. In: 2014 IEEE 13th International Conference on Trust, Security and Privacy in Computing and Communications (TrustCom), pp. 164–173, September 2014. https://doi.org/10.1109/TrustCom.2014.25
17. Fahrnberger, G.: Repetition pattern attack on multi-word-containing SecureString 2.0 objects. In: Natarajan, R., Barua, G., Patra, M.R. (eds.) ICDCIT 2015. LNCS, vol. 8956, pp. 265–277. Springer, Cham (2015). https://doi.org/10.1007/978-3-319-14977-6_26
18. Fahrnberger, G.: A detailed view on securestring 3.0. In: Chakrabarti, A., Sharma, N., Balas, V.E. (eds.) Advances in Computing Applications, pp. 97–121. Springer, Singapore (2016). https://doi.org/10.1007/978-981-10-2630-0_7
19. Fahrnberger, G.: Secure whitelisting of instant messages. In: Fahrnberger, G., Eichler, G., Erfurth, C. (eds.) I4CS 2016. CCIS, vol. 648, pp. 90–111. Springer, Cham (2016). https://doi.org/10.1007/978-3-319-49466-1_7

20. Fahrnberger, G.: Secure filtering techniques for instant messaging. In: Unger, H., Halang, W.A. (eds.) Autonomous Systems 2017, Fortschritt-Berichte Reihe 10, vol. 857, pp. 226–240. VDI, Düsseldorf, October 2017. https://doi.org/10.13140/RG.2.2.29962.77761/1
21. Fahrnberger, G.: Blind censoring for instant messaging. In: Kubek, M.M., Li, Z. (eds.) Autonomous Systems 2018, Fortschritt-Berichte Reihe 10, vol. 862, pp. 62–80. VDI, Düsseldorf, October 2018. https://doi.org/10.13140/RG.2.2.21331.63520/1
22. Fahrnberger, G.: Editing encrypted messages without decrypting nor understanding them. Ph.D. thesis, University of Hagen, June 2019. https://doi.org/10.18445/20190616-221209-3
23. Fahrnberger, G., Heneis, K.: SecureString 3.0. In: Natarajan, R., Barua, G., Patra, M.R. (eds.) ICDCIT 2015. LNCS, vol. 8956, pp. 331–334. Springer, Cham (2015). https://doi.org/10.1007/978-3-319-14977-6_33
24. Fahrnberger, G., Nayak, D., Martha, V.S., Ramaswamy, S.: SafeChat: a tool to shield children's communication from explicit messages. In: 2014 14th International Conference on Innovations for Community Services (I4CS), pp. 80–86, June 2014. https://doi.org/10.1109/I4CS.2014.6860557
25. Freitag, D.: Erweiterung eines SMPP-Frameworks zur sicheren Verarbeitung vertraulicher Zeichenketten. Master's thesis, University of Hagen, September 2013. https://doi.org/10.13140/2.1.4680.8641
26. Hevner, A., Chatterjee, S.: Design science research in information systems. In: Hevner, A., Chatterjee, S. (eds.) Design Research in Information Systems. Integrated Series in Information Systems, vol. 22, pp. 9–22. Springer, Boston (2010). https://doi.org/10.1007/978-1-4419-5653-8_2
27. Housley, R.: Cryptographic Message Syntax (CMS). RFC 5652 (Proposed Standard), September 2009. https://www.ietf.org/rfc/rfc5652.txt
28. ISO/IEC 10116:2006: Information Technology - Security Techniques - Modes of Operation for an n-Bit Block Cipher. International Organization for Standardization, February 2006. https://www.iso.org/iso/catalogue_detail?csnumber=38761
29. Miller, G.A.: WordNet: a lexical database for English. Commun. ACM **38**(11), 39–41 (1995). https://doi.org/10.1145/219717.219748
30. National Institute of Standards and Technology (NIST): Framework for Improving Critical Infrastructure Cybersecurity. National Institute of Standards and Technology (NIST), February 2014. https://www.nist.gov/document-3766
31. Örencik, C., Savas, E.: An efficient privacy-preserving multi-keyword search over encrypted cloud data with ranking. Distrib. Parallel Databases **32**(1), 119–160 (2014). https://doi.org/10.1007/s10619-013-7123-9
32. Rivest, R.L., Shamir, A., Adleman, L.: A method for obtaining digital signatures and public-key cryptosystems. Commun. ACM **21**(2), 120–126 (1978). https://doi.org/10.1145/359340.359342
33. Stebila, D., Green, J.: Elliptic Curve Algorithm Integration in the Secure Shell Transport Layer. RFC 5656 (Proposed Standard), December 2009. https://www.ietf.org/rfc/rfc5656.txt
34. Waksman, A., Sethumadhavan, S.: Tamper evident microprocessors. In: 2010 IEEE Symposium on Security and Privacy (SP), pp. 173–188, May 2010. https://doi.org/10.1109/SP.2010.19
35. van der Zwaan, J.M., Dignum, V., Jonker, C.M., van der Hof, S.: On technology against cyberbullying. In: van der Hof, S., van den Berg, B., Schermer, B. (eds.) Minding Minors Wandering the Web: Regulating Online Child Safety. ITLS, vol. 24, pp. 211–228. T.M.C. Asser Press, The Hague (2014). https://doi.org/10.1007/978-94-6265-005-3_12

Code-Tampering Defense for Internet of Things Using System Call Traces

Rajesh Kumar Shrivastava[✉] and Chittaranjan Hota

Department of Computer Science, Birla Institute of Technology and Science, Pilani, Hyderabad Campus, Hyderabad, India
{p20150005,hota}@hyderabad.bits-pilani.ac.in

Abstract. This paper proposes a novel method to prevent an attack mounted by an adversary on an IoT device by executing suspicious system calls. An adversary in such cases would want to modify the behavior of an IoT device for hijacking the control by mounting malicious code. This paper uses system call traces to find out illegal accesses made on an IoT node. We develop a kernel-level processor tracing method for jeopardizing adversary's activities. The method is rigorously tested on various IoT nodes like Raspberry Pi 3, Intel Galileo Gen 2, Arduino Uno etc.

Keywords: IoT security · Kernel tracing · Embedded device security

1 Introduction

Internet of Things (IoT) is an emerging domain used widely in deploying embedded systems in the real world. This deployment provides fascinating opportunities for future applications. IoT devices include home alarm systems, medical devices, cameras, cell phones, vehicles, smart cities, buildings, running shoes, refrigerators and ovens etc. Such deployments also have their own short comings [19]. IoT nodes capture valuable data and provide smart services that may be of value to adversaries. Adversaries may tamper with the device, insert malicious payload or intervene overall operation of the IoT device. Unfortunately, embedded system vendors are careless about the software security because of which adversaries often cause damage to the IoT device. The common vulnerabilities present inside a code sample of an IoT device are buffer overflow, array out of bound, illegal pointer access etc. These vulnerabilities allow an adversary to execute code reuse attack and tamper with the devices, intervene their communication channels, or clone the devices, to instrument the data gathering and overall operation for their own interest [4]. Estimation of secure state in a device is the dynamic problem of estimating the state of a system and detect an adversary's attack. Secure state estimation problem is basically focused on brute force attack, but this type of algorithm can terminate in polynomial time. In this paper, we proposed a novel algorithm that uses an attack detection module based approach to identify these attacks while a program is executing continuously.

© Springer Nature Switzerland AG 2020
S. S. Rautaray et al. (Eds.): I4CS 2020, CCIS 1139, pp. 158–170, 2020.
https://doi.org/10.1007/978-3-030-37484-6_9

Existing works [1,9,14] on securing embedded devices are focused on system settings and injecting run-time checks into the binary. In their work, they assumed that, an adversary can tamper the control flow [14], hijack the control from vulnerable function [1] and perform code reuse attack [17], DoS attack [2], memory corruption attack [8], etc. These settings and assumptions primarily focus on the following points:

- How to verify control flow with low overhead in presence of control flow hijack attack [14,17]?
- Mount perfect buffer overflow attack, identify their conditions of existence, analyse the effect of code reuse attack and there mitigation policies [3,10].

Present solutions prevent control flow integrity and apply these attack-defense matrices in a special type architecture i.e. x86, but most of the IoT devices use a heterogeneous architecture like ARM and Intel. In this paper, we present an architecture independent solution, which is suitable for all the available architectures of IoT nodes.

```
ppoll([{fd=3, events=POLLIN}], 1, NULL, [], 8) = 1
([{fd=3, revents=POLLIN}])
recvmsg(3, {msg_name(0)=NULL, msg_iov(1)=[{"L\2\0\0
\0\0\0\0\10\0\0\0renderer\r\0\0\0\16\0\0\0/pro"...,
8192}], msg_controllen=40, [{cmsg_len=40, cmsg_level=
SOL_SOCKET, cmsg_type=SCM_RIGHTS, [17, 18, 19, 20, 21,
22]}], msg_flags=0}, 0) = 592
pipe([23, 24]) = 0
clone(child_stack=0x7ffd0405ebb0, flags=CLONE_NEWPID|
SIGCHLD) = 2484
close(23)                                      = 0
close(17)                                      = 0
recvmsg(3, {msg_name(0)=NULL, msg_iov(1)=[{"\10\0\0\0\4\0
\3426\0\0", 8192}], msg_controllen=0, msg_flags=0}, 0)=12
write(24, "\3426\0\0", 4)                      = 4
close(24)                                      = 0
```

The above listing, shows system call traces of an IoT device showing a series of system calls executed on the IoT device. We evaluated the implications of intermittent attacks on IoT devices similar to Fig. 1 and estimated the system call execution probability. With the help of quantitative knowledge about the system call tracing and detection of an attack from kernel level, we propose a non-intrusive tracking of an attack in IoT environment such that resultant IoT devices are robust against such kind of attacks. The proposed method tracks all illegal executions and ensures the stability of the IoT device with minimal overhead, based on the software deployment irrespective of extra hardware support.

Rest of the paper is organized as follows: Sect. 2 shows the threat model used for this research. Section 3 contains the problem statement that is solved in this

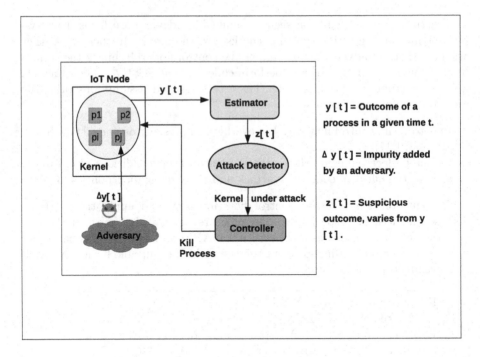

Fig. 1. Attack detection model

research. Section 4 focuses on our proposed model. This section also discusses our mathematical model to identify an attack in IoT environments. Section 5 gives detailed information of the test-bed setup and functionality of each module deployed in this proposed approach. Section 6 discusses, how proposed model is suitable to detect an attack from the kernel level traces and also presents the result analysis. Section 7 discusses the related research and the contribution of other researchers to securing embedded devices. Section 8 concludes the work and provides direction for the future aspects of this work.

2   Threat Model

We used a hostile host threat model [5, 13] to evaluate the proposed work. In this model, attacker can execute any program and control memory and execution environments. An attacker can also modify existing binary by using debugging tools.

Additionally, as part of the threat, an attacker is assumed to be capable of the following actions:

1. Collecting information about the system through some reverse engineering techniques.
2. Identifying the presence of already available system level defences such as ASLR, DEP, etc.

3. Injecting faulty data and mounting an attack from remote location to hijack an IoT node.

The primary objective of an adversary is to perform code tampering with the executable code and modify the functionality of the software. A hostile host model allows an user to perform reverse engineering methods to alter the existing code or add new functionalities into the code. The objective of our code tamper-proofing method is to protect the code tampering by non-intrusive monitoring. It traces attempts made by the adversary to tamper the protected binary.

The threat model assumes that the running program must have memory corruption vulnerabilities that allows an attacker to write random values to random memory locations including stack and heap and also leaks some information by arbitrary read primitive.

3   Problem Formulation

The objective of this paper is to build a kernel-based monitoring solution that supports a non-intrusive monitoring of running processes and threads at the operating system level. This monitoring method must trace all the activities carried out in an IoT device without affecting the running program. It would use a method that allows the kernel to register all events related to processes and threads. For example, Process creation, Process termination, Execution of a system call, etc. The most important thing that we consider, is that, the deployment exhibits high performance with low overhead.

We formulate our objective as a linear time invariant system problem. A time-invariant system does not directly relate to time, but the state of a system varies between two different time intervals on the basis of input and output of a function. In this work, we consider a system which has an output function $y(t)$, and an input function $x(t)$. Both functions are dependant on time and hold a relation like $y(t) = x(t + \delta)$, where δ is the difference between start and end time. Then, we can detect any illegal activity or an attack performed on an IoT device by analysing the input and the output functions.

4   Proposed Model

The objective of this paper is to detect adversary's activities by tracking the kernel activities in real time. We consider a discrete linear time-invariant model [2,9] to demonstrate our proposed problem. Let us assume,

$$x[t + 1] = \alpha x[t] + u[t] \tag{1}$$

and the output is presented by,

$$y[t] = \beta x[t] \tag{2}$$

where, $x[t]$ is the matrix which contains system calls executed by each process in a given time t. $y[t]$ is the expected output or state of all the processes with respect to system calls within a given time t. α and β are constant values set by the administrator to calculate the next state. The $u[t]$ is the estimated update of individual process state. $u[t] = \gamma \hat{x}[t]$, where γ is the estimated count of a system call at time t in a specific process. The $\hat{x}[t]$ is the expected process state generated by the estimator using kernel output $y[t]$. The estimator function has a predefined threshold value θ. If the value of $u[t]$ is higher than θ, then, estimator function transfers $u[t]$ matrix to attack detector module which analyzes $y'[t]$ (received output instead of $y[t]$). If the attack detector module detects malicious activity in the kernel, then, it initiates a signal to the controller and the controller can kill the malicious process. Figure 1 shows the proposed approach. This model uses the hostile host attack model. This model assumes that an adversary has control over execution environments and he/she can execute malicious program to eavesdrop on the kernel activity and system calls, which are responsible to produce $y[t]$. The adversary can inject an impurity Δy into any running process by identifying vulnerability [9]. Due to this malicious attack, the estimated output value $\hat{x}[t]'$ is different from the predicted value $\hat{x}[t]$. $z[t] = (\hat{x}[t]' - \hat{x}[t]) > \theta$, is a sufficient condition to raise an alarm. The controller function determines the process id, which is malicious, and sends a kill signal to the kernel to terminate the process.

5   Experimental Set-Up

Figure 2 shows the test-bed setup. Raspberry Pi 3, and Intel Galileo Gen 2, devices have been used in this experiment. The "strace -p" command is used to collect real time logs of process executions. All the logs are transferred to server by using socket programming. A daemon process running in the back-end continuously collects logs and transfers them to the server. A centralized server is maintained for collecting all the logs and processing the data for extracting useful information. The experiment can be classified into the following phases.

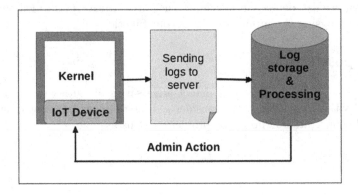

Fig. 2. Test-bed

5.1   Kernel Trace

This phase captures process events like process creation ($PROC\_EVENT$ $\_FORK$), execution of system call ($PROC\_EVENT\_EXEC$), change in user id ($PROC\_EVENT\_UID$), process termination ($PROC\_EVENT\_EXIT$), thread creation and thread exit. The kernel level traces allow event registration related to processes and threads. It also generates the log of each process id (pid). In this module, the kernel traces each newly created process. Once the kernel tracer receives pid, it collects system calls executed by pid and sends to the server. The server has multiple monitoring processes to monitor each syscall trace generated by the process.

5.2   Estimator

The IoT device can execute predefined tasks like read, pre-process and write sensor values. This phase processes prior knowledge about system calls executed by specific process in a given time interval, i.e., $x[t + 1] = \alpha\, x[t] + u[t]$ and expected output $y[t]$. The threshold value θ is used to differentiate between attacks and system noise. Now we define, τ, such that, $\theta = \{x[t] + \tau\}$, i.e., in a given time t, if $count(x)$, i.e., total number of system call count in a given time interval, crosses θ, then this can be labelled as an attack. If $x[t+1] - x'[t+1] > 0$, where $x[t + 1]$ is expected value and $[x + 1]'$ is real value provided by kernel, then there is a chance of an attack. Then the value of $x'[t + 1]$ is sent to attack detector module to verifying the attack.

5.3   Attack Detector

Once the quantifier threshold θ is decided, the attack detector revisits log file of suspicious pid and evaluates all system calls executed by the process within the given time. Attack detection can be computed as follows:

$x_1 = s[t + 1] - s[t];$
$x_2 = s[t + 2] - s[t + 1];$
...
$x_n = s[t + n] - s[t + n - 1];$
i.e., $\forall x_i - (x_i - 1) \approx \theta \pm \tau$

If there is any sudden increase in the existing system call count or any suspicious system call, such as, `memcpy`, `syscall_handler`, `ptrace`, etc. getting detected by the attack detector, then $\forall a \in x_i\, and\, x_i \cap a \neq x_{i-1}$, "a" can be labelled as unregistered. An alert is raised in accordance to the list given below:

```
si_signo=SIGCHLD,  si_code=CLD_TRAPPED,
si_pid=1709,  si_uid=1000,   si_stime=1
si_status=SIGTRAP,  si_utime=4
```

In the above listing, "pid 1709" tries to debug ptrace signal of another process. The controller module issues a kill signal to the processor for the suspicious pid.

6   Result Analysis

Figure 3 shows an analysis of system call traces for a process. It indicates run time execution and call counts, which are monitored by the proposed model.

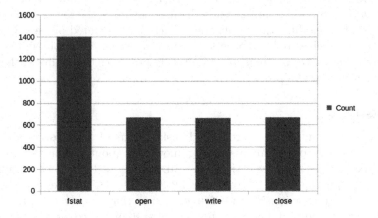

Fig. 3. Syscall traces of a process

6.1   Attack Matrix

– **ROP (Return Oriented Programming) Attack:** The binary running on an IoT device may contain a vulnerable function that can be attacked by an adversary. We exploit this binary using buffer overflow by uploading malicious payload. This malicious payload is stored in the stack. It tries to execute another program with the help of "exec" system call. This attack also uses system() function to invoke another program. The common system calls used by this attack are system(), execve() etc. The return address of a function subvert the control flow and launch a new shell to replace the current running program.

– **JOP (Jump Oriented Programming) Attack:** This attack uses functions which are vulnerable to buffer overflow such as memcpy(), strcpy(), sprintf(), strcat(), sscanf() and fscanf() etc. The JOP attack uses setjmp() and longjmp() functions to mount the attack. In JOP, the adversary used "jmp_buf" structure available in "setjmp.h" and calls setjmp(), which keep the current IP value and longjmp() returns control flow back to setjmp(). Our adversarial program overwrites this "jmp_buf" buffer and then calls longjmp() to transfer the control flow to another location. This attack executes new system call into the kernel and bypasses some existing system calls.

– **Process Tracing:** Reverse engineering tools like "ptrace" is used to trace the running processes. Adversary can control or analyse and manipulate the internal state of user program.

Our attack module attaches malicious binary to the running process. The attack module performs manipulation of file descriptors, memory, and register values. This module observes and intercepts system calls and their results. It can also manipulate the signal handlers and can also receive and send signals.

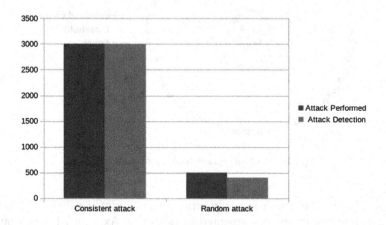

Fig. 4. Attack Evaluation

Figure 4 depicted the attack detection by our proposed approach, we execute attacks in following two different approaches:

- Consistent attack [15]: Consistent attack is a type of bias attack, it continuously attacks the target program and tries to modify binary. We ran a program which continuously execute "ptrace" and collect debugging information. This type of attack is identified by the work done in this paper with 100% success rate.
- Random attack [15]: In this attack, attacker randomly tries to modify or mount an attack. We applied the same program for executing attack, but the program repeat itself in random time interval. This attack is detected only when an attacker's program crosses the binary count threshold value. Our work, in this detects random attacks with 80% success rate.

6.2 Attack Countermeasures

The experiment environment executes only one user program "P" in the kernel for monitoring, which reads sensor value and after pre-processing sends it to the server. With the kernel output for a sampling period "T", such that the kernel state $x[t+1]$ during the $(t+1)^{th}$ sampling period as given in Eq. 1. Let us assume S = {y=x}, i.e., initial state as shown in Eq. 2 and there is no attack on

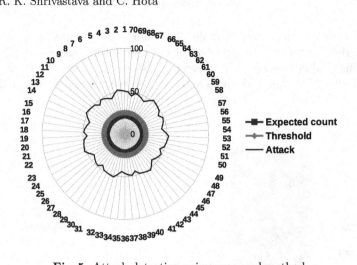

Fig. 5. Attack detection using proposed method

the kernel. In this case, we can easily estimate the updated value u[t]. Updated value of a single program is represented as $\{x[t+1] = Ax + u; P\}$ such that $\{$ [x = Ax + u; P]$^n\}$ represents n^{th} state of user program P and "A" is an execution count of "x".

Figure 5 shows a scenario of an attack detection using system call count within the time interval. Let the signal (system call count) for a given time interval is r, so $x[t] = r$ is the acceptable threshold. But in some cases we have $x[t] = r + \tau$ for some $\tau \in \theta$, and $x[t] \in S$, where S is kernel space with variation τ having expected value r. Hence, an adversary is allowed to inject maximum τ values in each time interval. But there exists no mathematical model to estimate τ for an adversary to inject malicious payload.

Table 1. Process id and system call count

Process Id	System call	Count
1898	recvmsg	33980
2220	gettid	32546
13275	ptrace	2386
13296	ptrace	34862
13317	rt_sigprocmask	360

Table 1 shows the system call count made by an individual process. When an adversary executes malicious code, the kernel tracer identifies new "pid" which uses "exec()" or "system()" calls. This unregistered "pid" and system calls alert the attack detector module and controller module and sends a kill signal to the kernel.

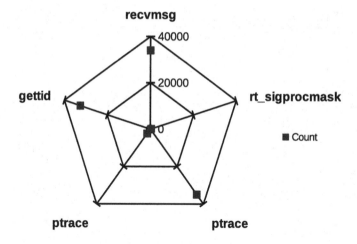

Fig. 6. Top 5 system call trace

Figure 6 exhibits traces of top 5 system calls, here system calls "recvmsg", "gettid", "rt_sigprocmask", "ptrace" are used by kernel trace program. But there is one more "ptrace" command executed by unregistered pid. This system call increases the count of expected "ptrace" system call count and attack-detector module raises an alarm for the controller.

6.3 Performance Overhead

Figure 7 shows the memory graph of the proposed method. All experiments were performed on Raspberry Pi 3 and Intel Galileo Gen2 IoT boards. Here the target program executes constantly and is not interrupted by the kernel trace program. The kernel monitor program collects information of each process and transfers it to the server. This kernel program runs like a daemon process and does not generate overhead for a running process.

7   Related Work

Nagarkatte et al. [12] proposed a hardware-based solution. They generated a meta-data of each pointer used in the program binary. This meta-data contained the base addresses for a pointer. At the time of execution the pointer memory range was verified by base address and the maximum allowable bound. The pointer based method had some loopholes, such as, more than one pointer variable reference a single memory location. Each pointer had its own memory location and meta-data which increase performance overheads and make programming more complex. Tsoutsos et al. [18] discussed various memory safety issues with respect to embedded devices, and described different attacks especially ROP that can hijack the control flow. They also suggested some attack

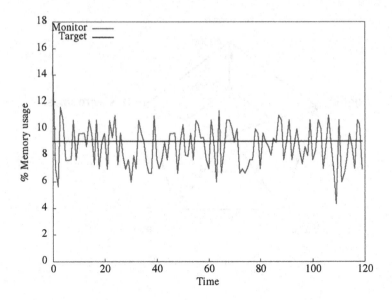

Fig. 7. Performance overhead

avoidance method like buffer bounds checking, instruction set randomization, and inline reference monitors etc. Krishnakumar et al. [8] developed a tool "Gandalf" which is the software based hardware extension to prevent memory corruption attack for the openRISC processor. Their solution depends on system's hardware and attacks are determined by the hardware at runtime. Bresch et al. [1] presented a hardware based solution to prevent ROP attacks. The author has focused on micro-controller based devices to prevent code reuse attacks by modifying return addresses. Isenberg et al. [6] proposed a method for software verification against AC hardware. They performed array bound checking within the loop to avoid buffer overflow attacks. Shoukry et al. [16] proposed a solution for secure state estimation problem. In that solution they developed a simulation based attack on sensors in a linear dynamical systems with the presence of noise. Mo et al. [11] proposed a method to analyzed the effect of replay attacks on a tiny systems. They executed replay attacks to hijack the control flow of an embedded device. In that work, they injected an external input to hijack the sensors and record their readings. After a certain interval the attacks are repeated. They discovered that, for some systems, the classical estimation, control, failure detection strategies are not resilient to prevent replay attacks. They proposed a discrete time invariant model to discover the replay attacks. Jovanov et al. [7] used secure state estimator to prevent network-based attacks. They also proposed a sporadic data integrity enforcement method to prevent message authentication from stealthy attacks.

Most of the related work, focused on detecting the malicious attacks instead of taking action against these attacks. We proposes the complete solution, i.e attack detection and kill the malicious process. Our solution is independent from hardware and the architecture of IoT board.

8 Conclusion

The experiments carried out in this paper are mainly used for diagnostic and debugging kernel space utilities for IoT nodes. The proposed solution monitors any adversarial attack by monitoring the kernel's traces, which include system calls, signal deliveries, and change of process states. In future, we intend to improve kernel tracing for multi-process non-linear systems.

Acknowledgement. This work was supported by Ministry of Electronics and Information Technology (MeitY), Govt. of India and Netherlands Organization for Scientific research (NWO), Netherlands under grant number: 13(1)/2015-CC&BT.

References

1. Bresch, C., Hély, D., Papadimitriou, A., Michelet-Gignoux, A., Amato, L., Meyer, T.: Stack redundancy to thwart return oriented programming in embedded systems. IEEE Embed. Syst. Lett. **10**(3), 87–90 (2018)
2. Ghosh, S.K., Dey, S., Mukhopadhyay, D.: Performance, security trade-offs in secure control. IEEE Embed. Syst. Lett. **11**, 102–105 (2018)
3. Habibi, J., Panicker, A., Gupta, A., Bertino, E.: DisARM: mitigating buffer overflow attacks on embedded devices. Network and System Security. LNCS, vol. 9408, pp. 112–129. Springer, Cham (2015). https://doi.org/10.1007/978-3-319-25645-0_8
4. Ho, J.-W.: Efficient and robust detection of code-reuse attacks through probabilistic packet inspection in industrial iot devices. IEEE Access **6**, 54343–54354 (2018)
5. Hota, C., Shrivastava, R.K., Shipra, S.: Tamper-resistant code using optimal ROP gadgets for IoT devices. In: 2017 13th International Wireless Communications and Mobile Computing Conference (IWCMC), pp. 570–575. IEEE (2017)
6. Isenberg, T., Jakobs, M.-C., Pauck, F., Wehrheim, H.: Validity of software verification results on approximate hardware. IEEE Embed. Syst. Lett. **10**(1), 22–25 (2017)
7. Jovanov, I., Pajic, M.: Sporadic data integrity for secure state estimation. In: 2017 IEEE 56th Annual Conference on Decision and Control (CDC), pp. 163–169. IEEE (2017)
8. Krishnakumar, G., Slpsk, P., Vairam, P.K., Rebeiro, C., Veezhinathan, K.L.: Gandalf: a fine-grained hardware-software co-design for preventing memory attacks. IEEE Embed. Syst. Lett. **10**(3), 83–86 (2018)
9. Li, Y., Shi, D., Chen, T.: A stackelberg-game analysis, false data injection attacks on networked control systems. IEEE Trans. Autom. Control **63**, 3503–3509 (2018)
10. Liu, J., Sun, W.: Smart attacks against intelligent wearables in people-centric Internet of Things. IEEE Commun. Mag. **54**(12), 44–49 (2016)
11. Mo, Y., Sinopoli, B.: Secure control against replay attacks. In: 2009 47th annual Allerton Conference on Communication, Control, and Computing (Allerton), pp. 911–918. IEEE (2009)

12. Nagarakatte, S., Martin, M.M.K., Zdancewic, S.: WatchdogLite: hardware-accelerated compiler-based pointer checking. In: Proceedings of Annual IEEE/ACM International Symposium on Code Generation and Optimization, p. 175. ACM (2014)

13. Nickerson, J.R., Chow, S.T., Johnson, H.J.: Tamper resistant software: extending trust into a hostile environment. In: Proceedings of the 2001 Workshop on Multimedia and Security: New Challenges, pp. 64–67. ACM (2001)

14. Nyman, T., Ekberg, J.-E., Davi, L., Asokan, N.: CFI CaRE: hardware-supported call and return enforcement for commercial microcontrollers. In: Dacier, M., Bailey, M., Polychronakis, M., Antonakakis, M. (eds.) RAID 2017. LNCS, vol. 10453, pp. 259–284. Springer, Cham (2017). https://doi.org/10.1007/978-3-319-66332-6_12

15. Park, J., Ivanov, R., Weimer, J., Pajic, M., Lee, I.: Sensor attack detection in the presence of transient faults. In: Proceedings of the ACM/IEEE Sixth International Conference on Cyber-Physical Systems, pp. 1–10. ACM (2015)

16. Shoukry, Y., Nuzzo, P., Puggelli, A., Sangiovanni-Vincentelli, A.L., Seshia, S.A., Tabuada, P.: Secure state estimation for cyber-physical systems under sensor attacks: a satisfiability modulo theory approach. IEEE Trans. Autom. Control **62**(10), 4917–4932 (2017)

17. Shrivastava, R., Hota, C., Shrivastava, P.: Protection against code exploitation using ROP and check-summing in IoT environment. In: 2017 5th International Conference on Information and Communication Technology (ICoIC7), pp. 1–6. IEEE (2017)

18. Tsoutsos, N.G., Maniatakos, M.: Anatomy of memory corruption attacks and mitigations in embedded systems. IEEE Embed. Syst. Lett. **10**(3), 95–98 (2018)

19. Zhao, K., Ge, L.: A survey on the internet of things security. In: 2013 Ninth International Conference on Computational Intelligence and Security, pp. 663–667. IEEE (2013)

Cloud and Network Security

Binary Binomial Tree Based Secure and Efficient Electronic Healthcare Record Storage in Cloud Environment

Rahul Mishra[1], Dharavath Ramesh[1(✉)], Damodar Reddy Edla[2], and Manoj Kumar Sah[3]

[1] Indian Institute of Technology (ISM), Dhanbad 826004, India
rahul.18DR0107@cse.iitism.ac.in, drramesh@iitism.ac.in
[2] National Institute of Technology, Goa, Farmagudi 403401, India
dr.reddy@nitgoa.ac.in
[3] BP Mandal College of Engineering, Madhepura 852113, Bihar, India
emanojcse@gmail.com

Abstract. Electronic Health Records (EHRs) is a key form of health-care records that attracts a great deal of attention. It is regarded that the sharing of healthcare records is a vital strategy for improving the quality of healthcare services and reducing medical expenses. Presently, the cloud computing paradigm supports many significant characteristics in Electronics Health Records (EHRs). However, in the cloud model, the patients have no longer control over their crucial healthcare records after outsourcing the records to cloud servers, which can lead to severe data integrity related concerns. Therefore, in this manuscript, we introduce a novel secure and efficient cloud based EHR data storage system by constructing Binary Binomial Tree like data structure. Furthermore, we extend the proposed model to attain significant cloud model based public auditing characteristics such as data dynamics, batch auditing, privacy preserving, blockless verification, data traceability, and recoverability. Extensive experiments and results demonstrate that the proposed cloud based EHR system is secure and efficient over other existing strategies.

Keywords: Electronic health records (EHRs) · Public auditing protocol · Data dynamics · Batch auditing · Data traceability and recoverability

1 Introduction

Electronic healthcare records (EHRs) are often extremely sensitive personal data for clinical analysis and treatment in healthcare. The sharing of EHRs seems like a successful strategy for improving the quality of healthcare related facilities and reducing medical expenses [1,2]. However, most private hospitals and organizations generally use their individual inner networks to maintain records of their patients but, don't enforce record sharing with other hospitals and organisations

© Springer Nature Switzerland AG 2020
S. S. Rautaray et al. (Eds.): I4CS 2020, CCIS 1139, pp. 173–186, 2020.
https://doi.org/10.1007/978-3-030-37484-6_10

which causes difficulties and burden of expenses to healthcare services. The latest development of cloud based EHR schemes [3,4] provides several facilities along with cost-effectiveness, remote access, and limited IT necessities. In cloud based EHR storage systems, every patient outsources their medical records to cloud servers (CSP). So, the doctors have access these records to provide enough prescription needed. However, the group of patients and cloud servers (CSP) are mistrust on each other. Therefore, the patient's EHRs should be encrypted form before outsourcing to CSP; to maintain the proper security to EHRs. Apart from this, sometimes the CSP may conceal sudden data loss and may also delete the rarely accessed healthcare records to manage the space. So, these types of mishappenings might also lead to numerous form of dangers which causes the patient's life at risk. Therefore, it is important to verify the ownership of healthcare records at CSP. In the case of cloud based EHR storage system, the conventional cryptographic methods may not be implemented as these methods needed to download the whole outsourced EHRs to verify the ownership. Thus, a large number of public auditing protocols have been discussed where a trusted third party auditor (TPA) may manage the complete auditing task [5–7]. In these methodologies, whenever any doctor wants to verify their EHRs, then they would deliver such auditing task to TPA. However, these methodologies are not support batch auditing for muiltiple doctor at the same time as well as also fail to aid proper data dynamics for dynamic updation or deletion. On the other hand, the latest concern of data traceability and recoverability should also be taken into consideration. Thus, to solve these issues, we introduce a novel secure and efficient auditing protocol to aid data dynamics, proper batch auditing, data traceability, data recoverability, and blockless verification for crucial EHRs. The proposed methodology diverges the concepts of a Binary Binomial tree like (BBT) data structure with Boneh-Lynn-Shacham signature based Homomorphic Verifiable Authenticators (BLS-HVA). The total communication overhead and computation cost of proposed model records less than the existing schemes. In addition to this, we also present the security analysis to validate the unforgeability of the proposed model.

The rest of the paper is systemized as follows; Sect. 2 illustrates the related work on secure EHRs storage models. Section 3 describes the system model, whereas Sect. 4 describes the complete auditing model with proper functionality. Further, in Sect. 5 we illustrate the security analysis with appropriate methodologies. Section 6 describes the performance analysis with appropriate metrics. Section 7 concludes the whole model. At last, Sect. 8 illustrates the acknowledgement about research work.

2   Related Work

To attain secure EHR sharing and data integrity in the cloud environment, previously, several conventional methodologies have been presented to address the issue of secure EHRs storage and sharing [8–10]. These methodologies make easier for the patient to encrypt their crucial medical records and then outsource these records to CSP. However, these works are suffer to attain proper integrity and data dynamics to EHRs. Initially, the concept of public auditing was introduced by Ateniese et al. [11] to attain proper integrity to EHRs. However, this model suffers in framing the data dynamics. In 2013, Wang et al. [12], proposed a methodology based on HVA with random masking for identity preserving. But, this model also suffers from the proper data dynamics and efficient privacy-preserving during auditing procedure. In 2016, Wang et al. [13], compiled a work for an independent identity and incentive based PDP method. This methodology aided the efficient privacy preserving to patients and permit the users to reveal any type of malicious activities. But, this methodology lacks from the point of data dynamics, blockless verification, proper data recoverability, and traceability. Shacham et al. [14] proposed a model for secure auditing of outsourced data by using the concept of q-SDH based secure BLS signature scheme. However, this model requires much time for an auditing procedure which reduces the effectiveness of this model. To reduce the communication overhead, a secure and efficient model was proposed to support batch auditing and data dynamics [15,16]. As a consequence, the TPA can be handled multiple auditing requests simultaneously. But these models fail to aid data traceability and recoverability. Further, Erway et al. [17] discussed a model to attain full data dynamics by constructing a novel rank based authentication dictionaries refrerred as skip list. However, this newly designed data structure needs large intermediate information of outsourcing the data blocks during the auditing tasks. So, this model also suffers from large computation and communication overhead. In 2017, Tian et al. [18] constructed a DHT (dynamic hash table) based auditing model, where DHT stores data with timestamp_value to preserve from reply attack. However, this methodology endures from collusion attacks from TPA side and users. In 2018, Zhang et al. [19] proposed a model as ID based proxy oriented outsourcing with public auditing protocol to attain secure auditing without pairing and proper data dynamics. This methodology has low computation and communication overhead at TPA side than other existing models as it has no pairing operations. However, this model fails to trace any type of data corruption during the verification procedure. To handle all these conditions mentioned above, this manuscript proposes a secure and efficient cloud based EHR storage system. This proposed model attain proper data dynamics, data traceability, data recoverability, and efficient remote public auditing.

3   System Model

As described in Fig. 1, any traditional cloud based EHR storage model include four elementary entities; the cloud service provider (CSP), the patient's group, the trusted third party auditor (TPA) and the doctor's group. The CSP entity is an entity that offers limitless storage and computing resources on pay-per-use model. The patient's group entity refers to the group who outsources their crucial medical or health related records to CSP. The doctor's entity usually accesses the outsourced EHRs that are stored at CSP by patients. However, prior to usage, the doctors must check the integrity of EHRs to assure about the correctness of stored EHRs as any type of defective healthcare records may pose life threats to the patients. Thus, a trusted third party auditor (TPA) is maintained to manage all auditing works to check the integrity of the patient's EHRs.

Initially, the patient's entity fragment the whole EHRs into n- blocks as $EHR\_seg = \{ms_1, ms_2, ..., ms_i\}$ and then outsources these EHRs blocks with their timestamp_value (Tm), version no (Vr). Moreover, in order to maintain proper data integrity, all EHRs are associated with tag_value and signature_value. At CSP, EHRs records are stores in Binary Binomial Tree (BBT) like data structure with unforgeable signature scheme to attain proper data traceability and recoverability [20,21]. The TPA also manage an index table with timestamp_value (Tm), version no (Vr) to store abstract information about the EHRs. As illustrated in Fig. 1, during auditing procedure the doctor's group delegates such auditing task to trusted TPA. Then, the TPA sends challenges to CSP. After receiving these challenges, the CSP first validate the TPA then form proof_value as a response to TPA. At last, the TPA validate these proof_value to check the correctness of outsourced EHRs. Apart from that, we assume that the trusted third party is trustworthy in nature, but the CSP may be dishonest or may conceal any type of modifications in EHRs of any patient. We also recognize this instance that none of the doctor is collude with CSP in order to disprove the integrity.

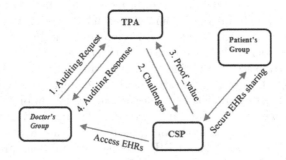

Fig. 1. System model

3.1 Security Model

In the security model, we consider three types of attacks- forge attack, reply attack and replace attack. The proposed model needs to resist the CSP from producing invalid tag_values for the stored data files. Thus, in the proposed scheme, the proper authentication from CSP side is being used to fulfill this security necessity. Further, in the proposed model, we assume that TPA is reliable but inquisitive. By the way of explanation, the TPA honestly performs the auditing work on behalf of the users, but may be interested about the user's data. Apart from this, the CSP can also be dishonest or may hide any type of the user's data modification. So, the server may launch the following attacks.

(a) Forge attack: The cloud service provider may forge the data values or their tag value to mislead the trusted auditor.
(b) Replace attack: The cloud service provider may generate another valid and uncorrupted pair of data blocks with its corresponding tag_value and try to pass the verification process by replacing the challenged pair of data blocks with its tag_value.
(c) Reply attack: The CSP may attempt to pass the auditing process by using the previously generated proofs or other former information, without fetching the user's data.

4   The Proposed Model

As a proposed model, the strategy of Binary Binomial Tree (BBT) is shown in Fig. 2, initially all EHRs records $EHR_{seg} = \{ms_1, ms_2, ..., ms_i\}_{encrypted}$ are arranged in Binary Binomial Tree (BBT) like data structure with their corresponding signature_value $(\sigma_1, \sigma_2, ..., \sigma_w)$ and a pair of $\{Vr_i, Tm\}$ at root (w) of BBTs. Moreover, as described in Fig. 3, whenever any i^{th} block of BBTs has been modified 3 times, then the current modified EHRs records $\{(ms_i^3, \sigma_i^3), (Vr_3, Tm_3)\}$ is always at root of the BBTs and the old EHRs records are in the internal node. On the other hand, whenever any EHR data blocks are deleted, then the CSP only maintains track of this specific EHR or medical records with no extra records. In addition, the CSP will no longer acknowledge which medical record or EHR has been deleted. Furthermore, as illustrate in Fig. 4 whenever an EHR is added by a new patient between ms_{i-1} and ms_i in constructed BBTs, then the CSP may only create a new root value for the new EHR. Moreover, if any latest updated signature_value is damaged then the patients may trace any sort of modifications just by implementing post-order traversal method on designed BBTs at CSP side.

Due to the unforgeability of the signature scheme, any corrupted signature_value can't pass the verification step. Thus, during the verification step whenever the patients found any corrupted signature_value, then the patient's group apply the post-order traversal on BBTs and continue to verify the next signature_value until the correct one is not found. For example, if σ_i^3 signature_value is damaged, then the patient's group execute the post-order traversal method to trace any type of modifications amongst all the previous versions $\{(ms_i^2, \sigma_i^2), (ms_i^1, \sigma_i^1), (ms_i^0, \sigma_i^0)\}$. Afterwards, the patient's group checks the signature_values in post-order traversal method to trace the latest accurate data block through the TPA.

Fig. 2. Construction of BBTs

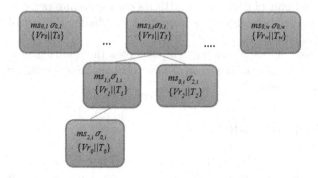

Fig. 3. Updated BBTs when i^{th} block has been modified 3 times

Fig. 4. Insertion of kth - EHR record block

The proposed method consists mainly three phases- key_generation phase, signing_phase, and auditing_phase. The complete description of the proposed public auditing model is described in the following manner.

1. Key_generation phase: Initially, with the security parameter $\lambda > 1$, a group G of order p with generators u, g; the patients randomly selects *signing_key_pair* as *(spriv_key, spub_key)* for the generation of signature_value and tag_value. Further, select $r \in \mathbb{Z}_p^*$ and compute $v = g^r$. At last, calculates *pub_key* = {g, u, v, *spub_key*} and *priv_key* = {r, spriv_key}.
2. Signing_phase: At this phase, the patients produce fragmented EHRs records with their corresponding signature_values (σ_i) where $\sigma_i = h((Vr_i || Tm), u^{ms_i})^r$ and aggregate signature_value (σ) = {σ_i}$_{i \in [1,...,n]}$ then calculate the corresponding tag_value,
$\delta = (Patient\_ID || EHR\_ID || Sig(Patient\_ID || EHR\_ID_{spriv\_key}))$
Where Patient_ID is patient's ID. Finally, the patient's group uploads (σ, δ, w) to CSP.
3. Auditing_phase: To check the correctness of EHRs records the TPA randomly selects sub-set of EHRs records as $d \in [1, ..., n]$ then again selects from sub-set d, so the challenge_value is $chal = (i, t_i)_{i \in [1,...,d]}$ and sends it to CSP. After receiving these challenges from TPA, the CSP generates a set of proofs as proof_value as a response through unforgeable bilinear pairing [22]. The CSP calculates,

$$Tag\_proof(TP) = \prod_{i \in [1,...,d]} \sigma_{t_i}^i$$

$$Data\_proof(DP) = \sum_{i \in [1,...,d]} ms_i \cdot t_i$$

then the , $main\_data\_proof = e(h(Vr_i||Tm), v)$, and $aggregate\_main\_data\_proof = \prod_{i \in [1,...,d]} AP_i$. Finally set proof values as proof_value = {TP,DP,AP} then it send to TPA for verification process. After that, the TPA checks the validation of this proof_value by taking chal, proof_value and the abstract value of EHRs as inputs. At last, the TPA verifies either the following condition hold or not. Displayed equations are centered

$$e(TP, g) \doteq AP \cdot e(u^{DP}, v) \tag{1}$$

If this final verification holds true, then the proofs are accepted otherwise rejected.

4.1   Batch Auditing

Public auditing for outsourced EHRs records is a sustainable task in the cloud paradigm that helps the doctors to check the integrity of their crucial EHRs at CSP. In this present time, due to the existence of a large number of doctors, the TPA can receive multiple auditing requests from many doctors simultaneously. Thus, the TPA may combine all these auditing requests together and execute the batch auditing for the number of doctors at the same time. The whole batch auditing task is divided into two subsections, (1) multiple auditing request from a single doctor (2) many auditing requests from many doctors simultaneously. Now, we suppose that $doctor_i \in [1, Doctor]$ where $Doctor$ describes the total number of doctors in doctors's group and send multiple auditing requests $EHR_i \in [1, ..., EHR_d]$ to TPA simultaneously. We now consider Case 1, whenever only a single doctor sends auditing request, then the doctor would be described as $doctor_i = 1$. Then, the proper validation for this case is described as,

$$\prod_{EHR_i \in [1,...,EHR_d]} e(TP, g) \doteq \prod_{EHR_i \in [1,...,EHR_d]} AP \cdot e(u^{DP}, v)$$

Now, for case 2, whenever multiple patients become $patient_i \subseteq Patient$, then the validation is described as,

$$\prod_{doctor_i \in [1,Doctor]} \prod_{EHR_i \in [1,...,EHR_d]} e(TP, g)$$
$$\doteq \prod_{doctor_i \in [1,Doctor]} \prod_{EHR_i \in [1,...,EHR_d]} AP \cdot e(u^{DP}, v)$$

If these final verification holds true, then the proofs are accepted otherwise rejected.

4.2 Blockless Verification

To demonstrate that the proposed model fulfills the blockless verification, we shows that the TPA may validate the correctness of all n blocks of outsourced EHRs records just by verifying the integrity of only a single block of EHR. Such a single block of EHR is a linear combination of all n blocks of outsourced EHRs records. Given, total n blocks of EHRs i.e. $\{ms_1, ms_2, ..., ms_n\}$ then the linearly combined block (α) may be generated with a randomly choose number i.e.$\{t_i = t_1, t_2, ..., t_n\}$ as;

$$(\alpha) = \sum_{i \in [1,...,n]} ms_i \cdot t_i$$

Afterwards, the TPA can verify the integrity of this combined block (α) just by validating the following Eq. (2),

$$e(\prod_{i \in [1,...,n]} \sigma_i \cdot t_i) \doteq AP \cdot e(u^\alpha, g^r) \tag{2}$$

5 Security Analysis

The following theorems describe the security and correctness analysis of the proposed secure cloud based EHR storage model.

Theorem 1. *(Public Auditing) Given healthcare record $\{ms_i\}$ and its signature_value (σ_i), the TPA is capable to publicly and efficiently verify the integrity of crucial EHR under the proposed model.*

Proof: Besides the doctor's group, the TPA may carry out the auditing task by randomly selecting a subset of outsourced EHRs without having to retrieve all EHRs from the CSP that achieve the objective of public auditing.

$$
\begin{aligned}
e(TP, g) &= e(\prod_{i \in [1,...,d]} (h(Vr_i || Tm_i), (u^{ms_i})^{r \cdot t_i}, g) \\
&= e(\prod_{i \in [1,...,d]} (h(Vr_i || Tm_i), (u^{ms_i})^{\cdot t_i}, g^r) \\
&= e(\prod_{i \in [1,...,d]} (h(Vr_i || Tm_i) \cdot e(u^{\sum_{i \in [1,...,d]}^{ms_i \cdot t_i}}, v) \\
&= \prod_{i \in [1,...,d]} AP_i \cdot e(u^{DP}, v) \\
&= AP \cdot e(u^{DP}, v)
\end{aligned}
$$

Theorem 2. *(Privacy Preserving) Given that, the outsourced EHRs $\{ms_i\}$ and its signature_value (σ_i); the proposed model is computationally infeasible for trusted TPA to reveal the real identity of the patients.*

Proof: Because the trusted TPA may not conclude the private key as $priv\_key$ = $\{r, spriv\_key\}$ from the established values $v = g^r$ and (σ, δ). Thus, it is computationally unforgeable for TPA to reveal the real identity of patients from signature_value. Furthermore, the private key value as v which is used to verify the signature_value (σ_i) and the patients share the same secret value r. Therefore, this signature_value (σ_i) of all the patients are the same. For this reason, the TPA may not be capable to conclude the actual identity of any patients from signature_value.

Theorem 3. *(Unforegability) The BLS-HVA based aggregate signature_value used in the proposed model may not be forged by any adversary if the unforgeable bilinear pairing holds the Co-CDH assumption.*

Proof: This theorem shows that the counterfeiting on BLS-HVA is totally computationally unforgeable. As illustrated in the security analysis part of Wang et al. [12] and Boneh et al. [20], it has been shown that HVA based authenticator tag is unforgeable in nature. The main reason for this is that BLS signature method is infeasible until the Co-CDH assumption is hard in bilinear pairing. The detailed proof to show the unforegability of BLS signature may be found in [12].

Theorem 4. *(Reply and replace attacks) In the proposed model, any type of reply and replace attacks may never be effective during the auditing phase i.e. (1) If any malicious CSP may attempt to pass the auditing phase with the previously stored EHRs record while sending the proof_value as a response to TPA. (2) If any malicious CSP will produce some other valid and uncorrupted EHRs records and signature_value (σ_i) with its associated $\{Vr_i, Tm\}$ replace it with the original EHRs records. Then, it is totally impossible for the CSP to pass the auditing phase with the replaced values to maintain its credibility.*

Proof: As per the situation illustrates for reply attack's game during the auditing procedure, the doctor's group delegate all type of auditing task to TPA. After that, the TPA sends challenges (chal) to CSP and CSP produces proof_value as a response for TPA. But, in the current situation, we believe that the CSP is experiencing a reply attack. Thus, some part of the CSP's proof_value could be modified by the previously stored EHRs. Now, we conclude that the jth-block of EHRs records where $j \in [1, ..., d]$ is replace with any previous EHR's records $\{ms_j^{\dagger}\}$. So, the computed values are,

$$TP^{\dagger} = \prod_{i \in [i, j-1] \cup [j+1, d]} \sigma_i^{t_i} \cdot \sigma_i^{t_{j\dagger}}$$

$$DP^{\dagger} = \sum_{i \in [i, j-1] \cup [j+1, d]} ms_i \cdot t_i + ms_{j\dagger} \cdot t_{j\dagger}$$

Afterwards, the TPA check the validation of these proof_value; if this validation holds true then it proofs the CSP experiencing a reply attack and wins the game otherwise fails. To become more definitive, we further evaluate the Eq. (1) to demonstrate that the reply attack on the proposed model is impossible. Then, the L.H.S. of Eq. (1) includes the Tag_proof as.

$$e(TP^\dagger, g) = e(\prod_{i\in[i,j-1]\cup[j+1,d]} \sigma_i^{t_i} \cdot \sigma_i^{t_{j^\dagger}}, g)$$

$$= e(\prod_{i\in[i,j-1]\cup[j+1,d]} (h(Vr_i||Tm_i), (u^{ms_i})^{r \cdot t_i} \cdot (h(vr_{j^\dagger}||Tm_{j^\dagger}) \cdot u^{ms_{j^\dagger}})^{r \cdot t_{j^\dagger}}, g)$$

$$= e(\prod_{i\in[i,j-1]\cup[j+1,d]} (h(Vr_i||Tm_i)) \cdot (h(vr_{j^\dagger||Tm_{j^\dagger}}))$$

$$\cdot u^{\sum_{i\in[i,j-1]\cup[j+1,d]} ms_i \cdot t_i + ms_{j^\dagger} \cdot t_{j^\dagger}}, v)$$

Further, the R.H.S. includes the main_data_proof as,

$$AP \cdot e(u^{DP^\dagger}, v) = \prod_{i\in[i,j-1]\cup[j+1,d]} \cdot AP_i \cdot e(u^{DP^\dagger}, v)$$

$$= e(\prod_{i\in[i,j-1]\cup[j+1,d]} (h(Vr_i||Tm_i)) \cdot (h(vr_{j^\dagger||Tm_{j^\dagger}}))$$

$$\cdot u^{\sum_{i\in[i,j-1]\cup[j+1,d]} ms_i \cdot t_i + ms_{j^\dagger} \cdot t_{j^\dagger}}, v)$$

So, on comparing these equations of both parts (L.H.S and R.H.S) may be equal iff; $h(Vr_{j^\dagger}||Tm_{j^\dagger}) = h(Vr_j||Tm_j)$ i.e. $Vr_{j^\dagger} = Vr_j$ and $Tm_{j^\dagger} = Tm_j$ However, the timestamp_value and version number may never be equal to any previous version of timestamp_value and version number values. Thus, the L.H.S. and R.H.S. parts can never be equal.

Now, for replace attack we consider the situation; when any doctor sends auditing request to TPA then the TPA perform auditing task as described above manner. However, replace the EHRs and signature_value; generates the Tag_proof and Data_proof with modified values. Here, we exclude the detailed validation step which is same as numerical evaluation of earlier mentioned equations for the impossibility of reply attack. Finally, through these outcomes, we demonstrate that the replace attack and reply attack could never be succeed in the proposed model.

6   Performance Analysis

The Overall performance of the proposed model is mentioned in terms of computation and communication overhead. Further, describes the comparison of computation and communication overhead at distinct phases of the proposed model with other existing methodologies. As demonstrated above, the constructed auditing protocol performs the secure auditing through key_generation, signing_phase, and auditing_phase, where the TPA randomly chooses the EHRs records block to sends the set of challenges to CSP. After receiving, these challenges the CSP produces the proof_value then the TPA validates these proof_value to check the correctness of EHRs. Thus, only the verification phase presents a major part of the communication overhead during the whole auditing task. So, the total communication overhead from TPA to CSP is only $O(d)$. After that, the CSP produces proof_value as response and sends to TPA with communication cost only $O(1)$. Therefore, the overall communication cost is $O(d)$.

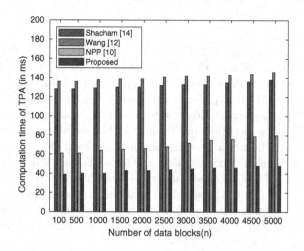

Fig. 5. Computation cost of TPA for EHRs records.

Table 1. Comparison of different existing schemes

Design objectives	Shacham [14]	Wang [12]	NPP [10]	Li [5]	Proposed
Public Auditing	Yes	Yes	Yes	Yes	Yes
Data Dynamics	No	No	Yes	Yes	Yes
Traceability and Recoverabilty	No	No	Yes	No	Yes
Privacy Preserving	No	Yes	Yes	Yes	Yes
Unforgeability	Yes	Yes	Yes	Yes	Yes
Impossibilty of Reply and Replace Attack	No	No	No	No	Yes
Communication Cost	$O(d)$	$O(d\log(n))$	$O(d)$	$O(d)$	$O(d)$

To compute the overhead of the proposed model, all the experimental cases are implemented on Linux OS with secure PBC pairing (0.5.14) based cryptography library. The signature_value and tag_value are implemented on OpenSSL crypto libraries. Figure 5 illustrate the total computation overhead required by CSP and the TPA for auditing work by constantly increasing the number of outsourced EHRs records. The total computation cost for key_generation phase is

Table 2. Computation cost of different existing schemes

Different schemes	Total computation Cost
Shacham [14]	$2 \cdot PO + (2 \cdot n + 2 \cdot d + 2)E_p + (n + 3 \cdot d + 1)SC\_M + (n + d) \cdot H$
Wang [12]	$3 \cdot PO + (2d + 1) \cdot E_p + (2 \cdot d + n + 1)SC\_M + 2n \cdot H$
NPP [10]	$2 \cdot PO + 22 \cdot E_p + (2 \cdot n + d)SC\_M + (n + d) \cdot H + 2 \cdot MP$
Li [5]	$2 \cdot PO + (n + d) \cdot E_p + (n + d + 1)SC\_M + n \cdot H$
Proposed	$2 \cdot PO + 9 \cdot E_p + (n + d) \cdot H + 6 \cdot Pt\_A + (n + d + 1) \cdot SC\_M$

$1 \cdot E_p$ only, and signing_phase is $2 \cdot E_p + n \cdot SC\_M$. Finally, the overall computation overhead for auditing task is $2 \cdot PO + 9 \cdot E_p + (n+d) \cdot H + 6 \cdot Pt\_A + (n+d+1) \cdot SC\_M$ where SC_M = scalar multiplication, PO= pairing operation, H=hash function, Pt_A = point addition in G_1, E_p = Exponentiation operation, d = randomly selected data blocks for verification n = total number of outsourced EHRs record blocks, Pt_A = point addition in G_1 and MP = point multiplication. Thus, Table 1 shows that the overall communication overhead of the proposed model is less in comparison of other existing methods. Table 2 illustrates that total computation cost of the proposed model is less than the previously designed model. This may be due to the situation that the proposed model contains only 2- pairing with very less number of exponential and multiplication operations, whereas a large number of pairing operation and multiplication operations have been regarded by the existing models.

7   Conclusion

In this manuscript, a novel secure and efficient cloud based EHR storage system which is relying on BBTs construction with BLS-HVA is introduced. The most attractive aspects of this model are the timestamp_value (TM) and version no. (Vr) fields are concatenating with EHRs records in BBTs to ensure the inevitability of reply and replace attacks. Exceptionally, our construction guarantees that patient's group can trace any type of data modifications through the constructed BBT and also easily recover the current accurate data block whenever the latest data block is corrupted. The proposed model effectively supports proper auditing, data dynamics, proper privacy preserving, authorized auditing, blockless verification, adequate data traceability, and recoverability. Further, adequate and standardized theoretical proofs indicate the security of the proposed methodologies. Moreover, this model offers less computation and communication overhead to the TPA as compared to the existing model.

Acknowledgement. This research work is supported by Indian Institute of Technology (ISM), Dhanbad, Govt. of India. The authors wish to express their gratitude and heartiest thanks to the Department of Computer Science & Engineering, Indian Institute of Technology (ISM), Dhanbad, India for providing their research support.

References

1. Xia, Q.I., Sifah, E.B., Asamoah, K.O., Gao, J., Du, X., Guizani, M.: MeDShare: trust-less medical data sharing among cloud service providers via blockchain. IEEE Access **5**, 14757–14767 (2017)
2. Joshi, M., Joshi, K.P., Finin, T.: Delegated authorization framework for EHR services using attribute based encryption. IEEE Trans. Serv. Comput. (2019). https://doi.org/10.1109/TSC.2019.2917438
3. Wang, H., Song, Y.: Secure cloud-based EHR system using attribute-based cryptosystem and blockchain. J. Med. Syst. **42**(8), 152 (2018)
4. Ying, Z., Wei, L., Li, Q., Liu, X., Cui, J.: A lightweight policy preserving EHR sharing scheme in the cloud. IEEE Access **6**, 53698–53708 (2018)
5. Li, A., Tan, S., Jia, Y.: A method for achieving provable data integrity in cloud computing. J. Supercomput. **75**(1), 92–108 (2019)
6. Qureshi, B., Koubaa, A., Al Mhaini, M.: A lightweight and secure framework for hybrid cloud based EHR systems. In: Mehmood, R., Bhaduri, B., Katib, I., Chlamtac, I. (eds.) SCITA 2017. LNICST, vol. 224, pp. 197–206. Springer, Cham (2018). https://doi.org/10.1007/978-3-319-94180-6_20
7. Nayak, S.K., Tripathy, S.: Privacy preserving provable data possession for cloud based electronic health record system. In: 2016 IEEE Trustcom/BigDataSE/ISPA, pp. 860–867. IEEE, August 2016
8. Cai, Z., Yan, H., Li, P., Huang, Z.A., Gao, C.: Towards secure and flexible EHR sharing in mobile health cloud under static assumptions. Cluster Comput. **20**(3), 2415–2422 (2017)
9. Deshmukh, P.: Design of cloud security in the EHR for Indian healthcare services. J. King Saud Univ.-Comput. Inf. Sci. **29**(3), 281–287 (2017)
10. Fu, A., Yu, S., Zhang, Y., Wang, H., Huang, C.: NPP: a new privacy-aware public auditing scheme for cloud data sharing with group users. IEEE Trans. Big Data (2017). https://doi.org/10.1109/TBDATA.2017.2701347
11. Ateniese, G., et al.: Provable data possession at untrusted stores. In: Proceedings of the 14th ACM Conference on Computer and Communications Security, pp. 598–609. ACM, October 2007
12. Wang, C., Chow, S.S., Wang, Q., Ren, K., Lou, W.: Privacy-preserving public auditing for secure cloud storage. IEEE Trans. Comput. **62**(2), 362–375 (2013)
13. Wang, H., He, D., Yu, J., Wang, Z.: Incentive and unconditionally anonymous identity-based public provable data possession. IEEE Trans. Serv. Comput. **12**, 824–835 (2016)
14. Shacham, H., Waters, B.: Compact proofs of retrievability. In: Pieprzyk, J. (ed.) ASIACRYPT 2008. LNCS, vol. 5350, pp. 90–107. Springer, Heidelberg (2008). https://doi.org/10.1007/978-3-540-89255-7_7
15. Ramesh, D., Mishra, R., Edla, D.R.: Secure data storage in cloud: an e-stream cipher-based secure and dynamic updation policy. Arab. J. Sci. Eng. **42**(2), 873–883 (2017)
16. Ramesh, D., Mishra, R., Pandit, A.K.: An efficient stream cipher based secure and dynamic updation method for cloud data centre. In: Zelinka, I., Senkerik, R., Panda, G., Lekshmi Kanthan, P.S. (eds.) ICSCS 2018. CCIS, vol. 837, pp. 505–516. Springer, Singapore (2018). https://doi.org/10.1007/978-981-13-1936-5_53
17. Erway, C.C., Kupcu, A., Papamanthou, C., Tamassia, R.: Dynamic provable data possession. ACM Trans. Inf. Syst. Secur. (TISSEC) **17**(4), 15 (2015)

18. Tian, H., et al.: Dynamic-hash-table based public auditing for secure cloud storage. IEEE Trans. Serv. Comput. **10**(5), 701–714 (2017)
19. Zhang, X., Zhao, J., Mu, L., Tang, Y., Xu, C.: Identity-based proxy-oriented outsourcing with public auditing in cloud-based medical cyber-physical systems. Pervasive Mob. Comput. **56**, 18–28 (2019)
20. Boneh, D., Gentry, C., Lynn, B., Shacham, H.: Aggregate and verifiably encrypted signatures from bilinear maps. In: Biham, E. (ed.) EUROCRYPT 2003. LNCS, vol. 2656, pp. 416–432. Springer, Heidelberg (2003). https://doi.org/10.1007/3-540-39200-9_26
21. Boneh, D., Lynn, B., Shacham, H.: Short signatures from the Weil pairing. J. Cryptol. **17**(4), 297–319 (2004)
22. Nguyen, L.: Accumulators from bilinear pairings and applications. In: Menezes, A. (ed.) CT-RSA 2005. LNCS, vol. 3376, pp. 275–292. Springer, Heidelberg (2005). https://doi.org/10.1007/978-3-540-30574-3_19

Energy Efficient Approach to Detect Sinkhole Attack Using Roving IDS in 6LoWPAN Network

Pradeepkumar Bhale[1]([⊠]), Sukanta Dey[1], Santosh Biswas[1,2], and Sukumar Nandi[1]

[1] Department of Computer Science and Engineering,
Indian Institute of Technology, Guwahati, Guwahati 781039, India
{pradeepkumar,sukanta.dey,santosh_biswas,sukumar}@iitg.ac.in
[2] Department of Electrical Engineering and Computer Science,
Indian Institute of Technology, Bhilai, Bhilai 492015, India

Abstract. The *Internet of Things (IoT)* has become a widespread technology where everyday objects are being transferred toward intelligent devices. These smart devices incorporate sensing, computing, and networking abilities into them. A smartphone, a smartwatch can be utilized for various tasks other than calling and timekeeping. Even home appliances also incorporate a midrange computer. Therefore, the most advanced applications and services have considerably risen. Despite numerous gains, security threats increased in terms of recorded catastrophic events as well as attack severity. There are multiple threads in 6LoWPAN and related routing protocol. In our research paper, we perform and assess an energy-efficient, lightweight intrusion detection system (IDS) for the 6LoWPAN network. The primary goal of this paper to target routing attacks (i.e., selective-forwarding, sinkhole, etc.). Our intended energy-efficient lightweight defense solution which identifies sinkhole attack in the IoT ecosystem. The defense method is executed with the help of *Cooja network simulator* on the *Contiki OS*. The experimental outcomes show that the solution is lightweight and can identify the sinkhole attack with a noteworthy performance, and provides 95.86% TPR and 94.31% TNR rate. It also shows minimum memory (RAM/ROM) utilization and energy consumption, which is comparable.

Keywords: Internet of Things (IoT) · Sinkhole attack · IPv6 over Low-Power Wireless Personal Area Networks (6LoWPAN) · Intrusion detection system (IDS)

1 Introduction

Kevin Ashton is a British technology pioneer who invented the *Internet of Things (IoT)*. The IoT is a giant network of connected machines or objects. The connecting objects might be resource-constrained devices which can share and communicate by wired or radio technology.

© Springer Nature Switzerland AG 2020
S. S. Rautaray et al. (Eds.): I4CS 2020, CCIS 1139, pp. 187–207, 2020.
https://doi.org/10.1007/978-3-030-37484-6_11

According to a different study [1–3], IoT growth opportunities and market shares increase by 31% from 2016, and the IoT devices are estimated to be 8.4 billion in 2017. The resource persons determine that the IoT ecosystem will comprise 30 billion devices by 2020 [4]. This points the alarming rate out at which we are incorporating them into our daily lives and at the same time illustrates us why it is essential to take their security seriously.

There are some startling cases of spiteful IoT attacks that happened in the past. In Finland on November 2016 [5], the heating of two buildings in the city of Lappeenranta has been shut down by the cybercriminals. This was a result of a *DDoS (Distributed Denial of Service)* attack where the assailants achieved to make the heating controllers reboot the system so the heating never truly propelled continually. This scenario points out the scary situation where hackers can remotely create this kind of damage.

In another story in 2016, the world witnessed a notable hack involving IoT devices called the *Mirai botnet* [5,6]. The botnet contaminated several IoT devices, mainly IP Cameras, and old routers then utilized them to flood DNS contributor Dyn with a DDoS assault. It leveraged the significant number of devices in the network to perform a more massive DDoS attack ever recorded. The botnet took down many major company websites like Etsy, GitHub, Net-Flix, Twitter, etc. The wicked code took benefit of devices operating outdated versions of the Linux kernel and relied on the fact that the maximum number of the users do not change the default credential (i.e., username and password) [7,8]. Many companies cut costs by not providing enough storage on the device because of which they cannot be updated to the latest *Linux Kernels*.

Considering the recent trends in technology and hacking it will not be a surprise if hackers are going to use IoT devices to hack and use them to provoke catastrophic crashes in the IoT ecosystem. To get access into a secure network and carry out even more sophisticated attacks like *DODAG Inconsistency, Sybil, Selective Forwarding, Wormhole,* and *CloneID* to target the 6LoWPAN network in particular.

Existing network attack detection and mitigation technique for 6LoWPAN networks takes vast amounts of battery and computational power due to this IoT network lifetime is reduced. Our research work aims to propose a lightweight energy efficient security solution, which is straightforward to implement and identify the sinkhole attack in IoT ecosystems. The novelty of the intended defense approach included as follow:

1. The given proposal curtail the number of IDSs without compromising its effectiveness using power utilization profile analysis.
2. Through simulation, we prove that significant savings in memory utilization (ROM/RAM) and average energy consumption.
3. The proposed approach uses the 6LoWPAN devices local knowledge, consequently making it scalable and distributed.
4. Our intended solution maximizes the lifetime of 6LoWPAN network with High *True Positive Rate (TPR)* and *True Negative Rate(TNR)*.

The remaining part of the paper is organized as follows. In Sect. 2, we explain background knowledge regarding IoT network architecture, routing protocol, sinkhole attack, and intrusion detection system. Section 3 describes recent literature in defense mechanisms for the IoT ecosystem. In Sect. 4, the description of the proposed method is presented. Section 5 illustrates the experimental circumstances and results analysis of the aimed approach. Finally, Sect. 6 gives the conclusion and future work.

2 Background

2.1 Network IoT Architecture

The IoT network architecture is quite different from that of a standard network since it comprises of five layers the lowest Perception Layer, then IoT Access Network Layer, then IoT-Internet Connection Layer, then Processing Layer, Application Layer, and last the Business Layer [9,10]. As shown in Fig. 1, the basic idea behind the network stack is the same except some changes such as addition of the 6LoWPAN adaptation layer, changing the routing algorithm at the network layer, usage of IEEE 802.15.4 as MAC layer, etc.

In Fig. 1 for the layers and their designated functionalities. The network layer is basically the same as in standard networks with the exception of the added

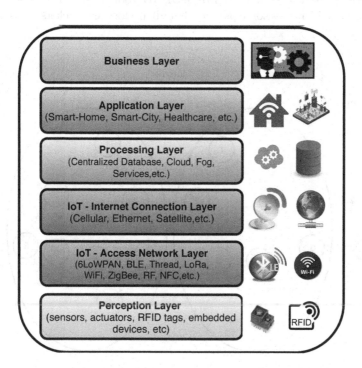

Fig. 1. Network stack of IoT ecosystem

6LoWPAN adaptation layer. The Application layer in IoT generally uses *CoAP (Constrained Application Protocol)* specially designed for constrained devices such as LLN devices. The routing protocol used is as stated before the RPL algorithm.

2.2   Routing Protocol Low Power and Lossy Network (RPL)

This is routing protocol for *Low Power and Lossy Networks (LLN)*-based IoT ecosystem. RPL is a convenient protocol that permits one-to-one, one-to-many, and many-to-one communication. There are two kinds of RPL in IoT like Reactive and Proactive RPL: Reactive RPL yields routes when required. Its downside is that whenever the routes are required to the IoT Node, searching time of routes is raising [11]. Proactive RPL gives the routes ere it is needed by another IoT node. It also exchanges different control messages to partake local information of the neighborhood and discover new routes [12].

The RPL protocol forms DODAG *(Destination Oriented Directed Acyclic Graph)*. It is a tree-like topology and carries various modes of services: unidirectional DODAG service carries all traffic directed to the root node (6BR), and bi-directional *DODAG* service contains all traffic among IoT nodes and 6BR node. A standard *DODAG RPL* is illustrated in Fig. 2 where every node is connected with each other by RPL protocol. All interconnections among nodes have particularized direction towards *DODAG* root as shown in Fig. 2. Every LLN RPL node identifies some parents that all are forward packets to its parents.

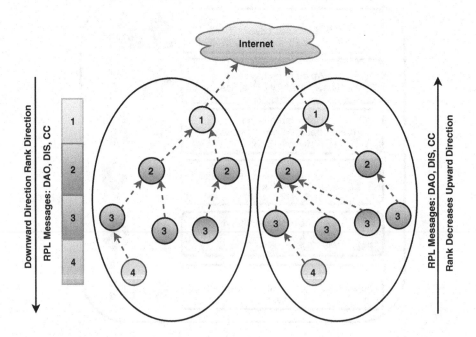

Fig. 2. RPL protocol.

A node's rank relates the position of a particular node in its neighborhood. Rank stringently rises downwards and stringently reduces upwards. This is the operation in the RPL implementation in the *Contiki cooja* [13,14], that we adopt in this research paper to evaluate our security approach.

2.3 Routing Attack in 6LoWPAN

The principal goal of this section is to describe the two most relevant routing based attacks. Attacks are classified into three main classes depending on the traffic, topology, and resources as shown in Fig. 3. In this paper, the sinkhole attack have been performed and examined in a smart home scenario.

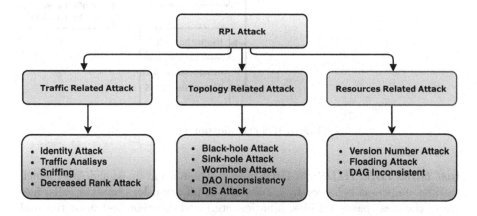

Fig. 3. Routing attack

- **Sinkhole Attack:**

The *sinkhole attack* utilizes the rank based *DODAG* formation method which RPL uses. In RPL there is no way of knowing if the rank that a node is communicating is actually the correct one and so a malicious node can surreptitiously show lower rank than they actually have thus warping the routes towards them and then either dropping all packets thus essentially forming a black hole attack node, or selectively forwarding some packets and dropping others according to the sender or randomly. Since all packets travel from nodes of higher rank to nodes of lower rank so, all packets from the nodes "below" the malicious node in the *DODAG* lose either all or some percentage of their transmitted packets.

2.4 Intrusion Detection System (IDS)

The IDS is a collection of interacting components that are used to detect an attack and malicious activity. IDSs can be categorized as follows [15–18] (Fig. 4):

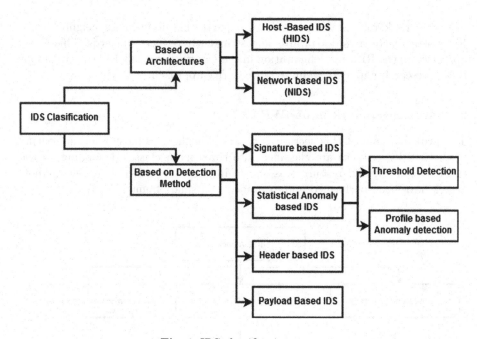

Fig. 4. IDS classification tree.

Host-based IDS (HIDS): A HIDS consists of an agent on a single host which identifies malicious behavior by monitoring application logs, system calls, filesystem changes (password files, binaries, etc.) and different host activities and state.

Network-based IDS (NIDS): A NIDS is an autonomous platform which identifies malicious behavior by analyzing network traffic and monitors multiple hosts.

Signature-based IDS: Signature-based IDS utilizes database of observed intrusion detection signatures. Every intrusion drops a fingerprint behind e.g. file and folder access, nature of data packets and failed logins etc. These IDS examines network or system behavior against known attack patterns (signatures) or malicious signature set. If a signature match is detected, a warning takes place for suitable actions.

Statistical anomaly-based IDS: Statistical anomaly-based IDS collects network or system information (under normal condition) and learn legitimate user behavior. The statistical tests are applied to perceived behavior to decide whether that behavior is legitimate or not. Statistical anomaly-based IDS falls into two broad categories (i.e., Threshold detection and Profile-based anomaly detection) [19].

Header-based IDS: In this IDS, we analyze only the packet header part of the network packets during training (under normal condition). The statistical tests are applied to perceived network packet payload is compared.

Payload-based IDS: In this IDS, we analyze payload information for particular direction (inbound/outbound). The statistical tests are applied to the network packets.

3 Related Works

Loo et al. [20] have shown a different class of routing attack naming *Topology Attack*, which modifies the node execution by splitting the optimal topology of the nodes. For this type of attack, they have proposed two sub-classes of the attacks like *Local Repair Attack* and *Rank Attack*. They have further introduced an IDS architecture utilizing RPL finite state machine to monitor the nodes. However, the shortcoming of this approach is the extra memory and power consumption.

Wallgren et al. [21] authors have implemented various attacks such as selective forwarding attack, sinkhole attack against RPL in Cooja simulation software. They have also demonstrated different features of IPv6 protocol, and its use in the intrusion detection mechanism of the IoT environment. The foremost disadvantage of this solution is an added power-utilization than local processing.

Pongle et al. [22] have surveyed *6LoWPAN* and *RPL* attacks. They have demonstrated that different attacks are possible in the resource-constrained devices, on account of the lightweight characteristics of the IoT protocols.

Cervantes et al. [23] have proposed a lightweight solution, known as *INTI (Intrusion detection of SiNkhole attacks on 6LoWPAN for InterneT of ThIngs)*. This approach is a sandwich of different strategies (i.e., trust, reputation, and watchdog). They also considered the mobility of the IoT nodes while implementing the solution for the IoT environment. The INTI considers FPR, FNR, and resource cost as a performance attribute. However, the prominent limitation of this solution is that it demands extra computational power and resources. Therefore, this solution reduced the lifetime of the IoT Ecosystem.

Glissa et al. [24] have offered a secure routing protocol based on RPL known as SRPL. This method stops misbehaving nodes from creating a fraudulent topology by manipulating the ranks of the nodes. They have added a hash chain authentication and rank threshold strategy which alleviates the internal attacks (i.e., Selective forwarding, black hole, and sinkhole attack). The outcome of this research paper is to resist internal attacks based on malicious RPL metrics. However, SRPL approach introduces some drawbacks. The very first drawback is controlled messages created by SRPL added extra overhead compared with RPL. It also takes more computing power and storage capacity.

Hatzivasilis et al. [25] in their research paper offered a trust-based system (TBS). This TBS is adopting five metrics (i.e., energy metric, topology metric, channel-health, reputation metric, and trust metric) to achieve trustworthy routing for intelligent *ad-hoc networks*. The comprehensive assessment of the proposed approach introduces the extra overhead with adequate security.

Raoof et al. [26] have considered three types of routing attacks naming blackhole attacks, selective forward attacks, and Sybil attacks. The assessment of different attack based on diverse metrics (e.g., power consumption, data packet delay, and data packet delivery rate, etc.). This research article decreases the consequences of routing attack without having added defense mechanism for routing protocol. However, the shortcoming of this paper is low TPR and TNR.

Kamble et al. [27] have proposed a recent survey on different Security attacks and secure routing protocols in RPL-based IoT. They have classified the assaults in two broad class (i.e., direct and indirect assault). During a direct assault, the intruder is directly implicated in the assault, like routing table overload assault and flooding attacks in IoT Ecosystem. In indirect assaults, the intruder is not directly involved in the attack. Instead, the wicked node requires the other nodes to create overload to the IoT networks, like version number attack, DAG inconsistency attack, and increased rank attacks.

4   Proposed Works

In this section, we present the intended approach to recognize *sinkhole attacks* in the *6LoWPAN network*. This network comprises different devices with various storage and computing capacity. Our proposed method execute intelligent IDS roving approach. It also performs an energy-efficient strategy to identifies *sinkhole attacks*.

4.1   Assumption

Before explaining the security model and the algorithms, we would like to consider the following assumptions:

1. All the resource constraint devices in the IoT ecosystem are heterogeneous (i.e. memory, battery power, computation, communication capacity).
2. Although, there might be billions and trillions of small IoT devices connected over a wireless network. However, we will propose our approach for a system holding a constant number of the devices (i.e., 8, 16, 32, 64).
3. We also assume that every resource constraint device has the finite amount of power on which it can run.

4.2   Security Model

The 6LoWPAN network comprises of *Legitimate Node (LN)* and *Malicious Node (MN)*. The entry point of the *6LoWPAN* is border-router (6BR). Moreover, 6BR is a bridge between the internal network with the Internet. The 6BR is a resource-rich node, and it can be a *laptop* or *personal computer (PC)*. Nowadays, there is no laptop and personal computer equivalent IEEE 802.15.4 devices. Therefore, we execute *6Mapper module* on the Linux system and interact with *Cooja simulator* by serial socket plugin. Figure 5 shows the IoT setup topology for our experiment.

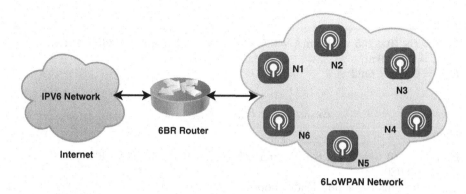

Fig. 5. Experimental setup topology

4.3 Energy Model

The network energy consumption E_{net} model derived from [1,2]. the energy consumption for handling 6Mapper response event and packet lost correction event 0.1468 mJ and 0.0483 mJ respectively at resource constraint node.

$$E_{net} = [\{(TT \times 19.5\,\text{mA}) + LT \times 21.8\,\text{mA} + CT \times 1.8\,\text{mA} + LP \times 0.545\} \times 3\,\text{V} \div 4096] \times 8 \quad (1)$$

where,

TT = Time spent on transmitting the message
LT = time spent on receiving only
CT = CPU time
LP = low power mode

The total energy consumption measured using Eq. 2. This formula incorporates three energy parameters (i.e. network energy (E_{net}), overhead energy (E_{over}), and IDS execution energy (E_{ids})).

$$E = E_{net} + E_{over} + E_{ids} \quad (2)$$

The E_{net} already presented in Eq. 1, E_{over} is the average of all the IoT devices as shown in Eq. 4, and E_{ids} is a energy measured during IDS executed on the resource constraint node.

$$E_{over} = AVG(overhead of all machines) = 0.0809\,\text{mJ} \quad (3)$$

The leader and non-leader further estimate energy pattern using Eqs. 4 and 5 separately. The TT, RT are taken as 0.5 of total CPU Time in low power mode. E_{over} defined using Eq. 2. Here we assume that the IDS executed on the leader nodes, and transmission energy for leader becomes zero. The leader takes 0.5% energy when non-leader takes 0.2 energy.

$$E_{leader} = E_{net} + E_{over} + E_{ids} \quad (4)$$

where,

$E_{net} = t \times (0 + 0.5 \times 21.8\,\text{mA} + 0.5 \times 1.8\,\text{mA} + 0.545\,\text{mA})3\,\text{V}/4096\} \times 8$
$E_{over} = 0.0809\,\text{mj}$
$E_{ids} = 0.215 \times t\,\text{mJ}$

$$E_{nonleader} = E_{net} + E_{over} + E_{ids} \qquad (5)$$

where,

$E_{net} = t \times (0 + 0.5 \times 21.8\,\text{mA} + 0.5 \times 1.8\,\text{mA} + 0.545\,\text{mA})3\,\text{V}/4096\} \times 8$
$E_{over} = 0.0809\,\text{mj}$
$E_{ids} = 0$ (This is for non-leader node)

4.4   Proposed Solution

The intended security approach executes lightweight IDS with roving nature. The placing of lightweight IDS is a crucial part of our approach. By observing

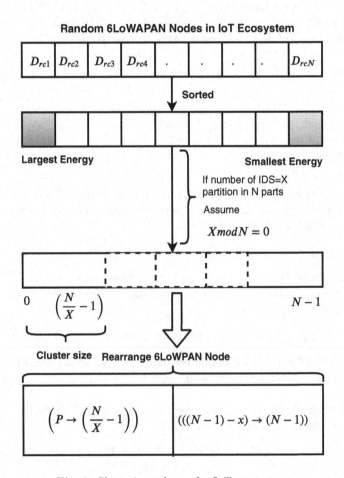

Fig. 6. Clustering scheme for IoT ecosystem.

6LoWPAN characteristics (i.e., lossy, resource-constrained, and battery power), we adopt both roving and static lightweight IDS modules which placed in constrained nodes and 6BR router, respectively. The roving IDS using clustering mechanism as shown in Fig. 6. We sort all resource constraint device (D_{rc}) based on residual energy in descending order. The sorted D_{rc} devices divided into a various cluster and equivalent count of IDS initiate at a time. To make energy-efficient lightweight roving IDS, we order D_{rc} devices one by one as explained in Fig. 6. We separate the first cluster (F_{CL}) elements and last cluster (L_{CL}) elements in a different collection. The ith and ($2 * CL - 1 - i$) element chose in each iteration. Suppose, 'i' value is odd then place the D_{rc} in the first cluster (F_{CL}), and 'i' value even then places the D_{rc} in the second cluster (S_{CL}).

The cluster formation repeats recursively for $F_{CL} = F_{CL} + CL\_size$ and $L_{CL} = L_{CL} - CL\_size$. This procedure ensures merging of the heterogeneous IoT devices (i.e., computing and battery power) into each CL and hence ensures balancing.

The Algorithm 2 shows IoT devices sorting mechanism and perform proper cluster utilizing rearrange function. Keep repeating this process until node dead. The first element of the cluster is the leader. The leader node are those who have the highest energy in it's CL. All leaders and non-leader nodes calculate and update their energy consumption value. Suppose same CL contain comparable energy level node, then we choose the first element to be the leader. Shortly, others will get a turn to become leaders as a result of the Algorithm 1.

After updating the energy value of the IoT nodes, we initiate the sorting function and perform clustering. It ensures the dynamic nature of the real network as nodes will not necessarily be in the same cluster all the time. This approach gives a chance to become a leader to all nodes and exhibits fairness in the system. A newly formed cluster leader is incompatible with executing IDS when the first node is dead, repeat this process until the first dead node discovered.

5   Experiments and Results Analysis

For the impact of Sinkhole attack analysis, two scenarios are generated with the help of *Contiki cooja simulator* [14, 15]. These scenarios consider the smart home as the use case. The complete explanation of the entire scenarios is given below.

5.1   Experiment 1: Non-attack Scenario

In this experiment, we consider a different number of nodes (i.e., 4 to 64 node). The parameters used for simulating the scenario have been recorded in Table 1, and the network topology for the simulation has been depicted in Fig. 7a.

The DODAG building process of regular (non-attack) network is normal, as shown in Fig. 7b. Figure 7c shows the power consumption profile. We observed that the power consumption for the nodes when there is no malicious node which is increasing the rank, and so the network is usually performed. The power consumption values lie within the range 0.75 mW–1.25 mW for the non-attack scenario.

Algorithm 1. Working of the clustering mechanism

1: **procedure** REARRANGE($D_{rc}, D_{rc\_size}, CL\_size, f, l$)
2:　　▷ f is first index of first cluster (F_{CL})　　▷ l is first index of last cluster (L_{CL})
3:　　**if** $f < l$ **then**
4:　　　　Copy all elements of both cluster in an array a.
5:　　　　**while** $i \neq CL\_size$ **do**　　　　　　　　▷ Runs for cluster size times
6:　　　　　　**if** CL_size *is even* **then**
7:　　　　　　　　**if** i *is even* **then**
8:　　　　　　　　　　Add i and $2 * (CL\_size - 1 - i)$ indexed element in (S_{CL}).
9:　　　　　　　　**else**
10:　　　　　　　　　　Add i and $2 * (CL\_size - 1 - i)$ indexed element in (F_{CL}).
11:　　　　　　**else if** $i \neq CL\_size - 1$ **then**
12:　　　　　　　　**if** i *is even* **then**
13:　　　　　　　　　　Add i and $2 * (CL\_size - 1 - i)$ indexed element in (S_{CL}).
14:　　　　　　　　**else**
15:　　　　　　　　　　Add i and $2 * (CL\_size - 1 - i)$ indexed element in (F_{CL}).
16:　　　　　　**else**
17:　　　　　　　　Add i^{th} element in (S_{CL}) and $(i + 1)^{th}$ element in (F_{CL}).
18:　　**else**
19:　　　　Return
20:　　Rearrange ($D_{rc}, D_{rc\_size}, CL\_size, f + 1, l - 1$)

Algorithm 2. Residual energy estimation

1: time = 0.
2: flag = false
3: **while** *true* **do**
4:　　time++
5:　　$j = 0$
6:　　**while** $j \neq n$ **do**
7:　　　　**if** $j \% CL\_size = 0$ **then**
8:　　　　　　$arr[j].R\_energy- = 0.0723 + 0.0809 + 0.215$　　　　▷ Derivation shown
9:　　　　　　j++
10:　　　　**else**
11:　　　　　　$arr[j].R\_energy- = 0.0665 + 0.0809$　　　　　　▷ Derivation shown
12:　　　　　　j++
13:　　Sort array arr by R_energy
14:　　Call rearrange function (Algorithm 1)　　　　　　▷ To make new clusters
15:　　**while** $j < n$ **do**
16:　　　　**if** $arr[j].R\_energy < 0.215$ **then**　　　　▷ At least 1 cluster is low
17:　　　　　　$flag = true$
18:　　　　$j+ = CL\_size$
19:　　**if** $flag = true$ **then**
20:　　　　break

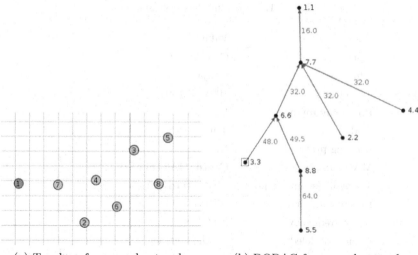

(a) Topology for normal network   (b) DODAG for normal network

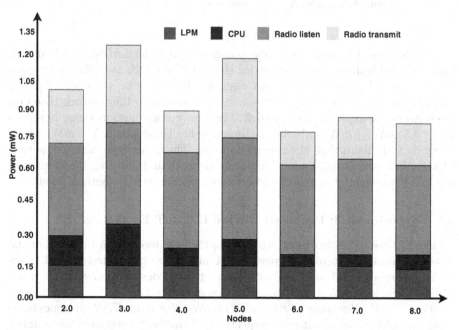

(c) Power consumption profile when 7 normal nodes and no malicious node

Fig. 7. Non attack analysis with topology, DODAG, power consumption profile.

5.2 Experiment 2: Attack Scenario

In this experiment, we consider the same topology and simulation parameter as Experiment 1 with a different number of *Legitimate node (LN)* and *Malicious node (MN)*.

Table 1. Cooja simulator parameters.

Parameter name	Value
Operating system	Contiki 3.0
Simulator	Cooja
Target area	100 m × 100 m
Radio environment	UDGM
Node type	Tmot Sky
Routing protocol	RPL
MAC/adaptation layer	ContikiMAC/6LoWPAN
Transmitter output power	(dBm) 0 to −25
Receiver sensitivity	(dBm) −94
Radio frequency	2.4 GHz
Attack modeled	Sinkhole attack
Mobility scenario	Randomly distribute, No mobility
Simulation duration	Variable

We examine IoT network traffic generated from the *LM* and *MN* nodes. Figure 8a and b shows the topology for the sinkhole attack and DODAG formation for the sinkhole attack scenario, respectively. In Fig. 8c, we observed power consumption of nodes when there is a malicious node in the network based on the outcome of experiments 1, and 2. The power consumption range has gone up to 3.5 mW–5.5 mW with the maximum value being about 5.52 mW, which is significantly more than the normal scenario. Thus, this type of attack is very effective in both causing packet loss in the network and reducing the lifetime of the IoT ecosystem by increasing power consumption to unacceptable levels.

5.3   Experiment 3: Proposed Roving IDS IoT Ecosystem

To identify the sinkhole attack, we execute the IDS module on the basis of the power consumption profile. Experiment 1 and 2 are conducted several times with a different number of IoT nodes and power consumption analysis using *Collect-View application* of the *Contiki Cooja Simulator*.

The *True Positive Rate (TPR)* and *True Negative Rate (TNR)* are calculated using specificity and sensitivity, respectively. Sensitivity estimates the number of *Compromise Nodes (CN)* recognized accurately, and specificity measures the number of *legitimate nodes (LN)* identified rightly. Both sensitivity and specificity are defined as follows:

$$Sensitivity = \frac{p}{p + q} \tag{6}$$

and

$$Specificity = \frac{r}{r + s} \tag{7}$$

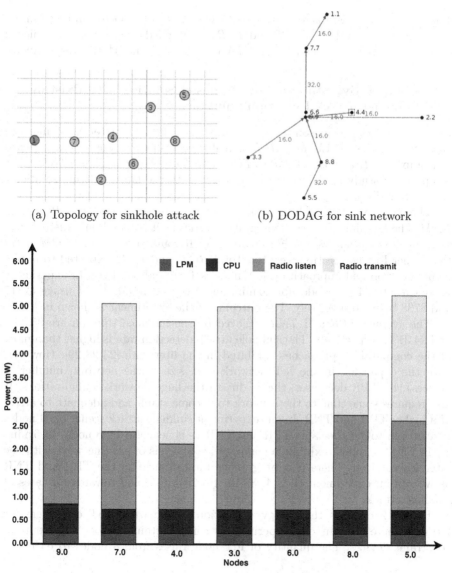

(a) Topology for sinkhole attack   (b) DODAG for sink network

(c) Power consumption profile when 7 normal nodes and one malicious node

Fig. 8. Sinkhole attack analysis with topology, DODAG, power consumption profile.

Where

$p = $ CN detected accurately, $q = $ CN classify wrongly as legitimate, $r = $ LN detected accurately, $s = $ LN classify wrongly as malicious.

For an accurate sinkhole attack detection system, both TPR and TNR can be calculated based on experiments 1, and 2 with LN and CN. To verify every

202 P. Bhale et al.

situation in experiment is recursively redone 70 times with the expanding number of IoT nodes. The values of *TPR* and *TNR* are intended every time. The achieved experimental result of the *TPR* and *TNR* are 95.86% and 94.31% respectively.

5.4 Comparative Study of the Proposed Solution with Existing Sinkhole Attack Detection Solutions

In this subsection, the comparative study is performed in terms of memory consumption (i.e., *RAM* and *ROM*), real-time traffic analysis, average power consumption, *True Positive Rate (TPR)* and *True Negative Rate (TNR)*. The comparative study of the intended approach with the latest existing solutions, as shown in Table 2.

The memory usage analysis of the proposed approach takes extra *ROM* and *RAM*. The baseline of every configuration varies as it is based on a distinct element of the Contiki system. For example, 6BR router needs more *ROM/RAM* than other IoT nodes. However, the Total *ROM* and *RAM* expected to implement the proposed approach on IoT node is 1760 and 365 byte. In experiment 3, we execute 64 IoT nodes for 20 min. and recorded *ROM*, *RAM* usage 42317 and 8738 bytes, respectively. The outcome of the experiment is shown in Fig. 9.

The average *TPR* and *TNR* achieved by the intended solution are 95.86% and 94.31%, respectively. The sinkhole attack detection rate is higher than most of the comparable approaches exhibited in the literature [23,28,29]. However, with the expansion in the IoT network (i.e., size of the network, number of devices) the TPR decreases; this is due to the huge network configurations. It also requires some time to the network to become stable and adequate to arrive at a higher TPR and TNR. In our experiment sinkhole attack scenario, 64 nodes take 20 min to get the same TPR and TNR as is achieved by 8 nodes in 6 min.

In Figs. 10 and 11 exhibits a comparative analysis of existing work with the intended solution. There is a progressive improvement in the TPR and TNR as we run an experiment (i.e., 4, 8, 12, 16, 20 min) going towards all cases of sinkhole attack.

Figure 12 exhibits the energy utilization of the whole IoT ecosystem for 20 min, where we run our experiment with a certain number of resources-constraint devices. The quantity of IoT node raises from 8 nodes to 64 nodes

Table 2. The comparative study of intended approach with the existing solutions

Method applied	Experimet environment	Memory utilization (in byte)		Avg. energy consumption (mJ)	Detection rate (%)	
		ROM	RAM		TPR	TNR
SVELTE [28]	Contiki cooja	45672	9832	52250	87.38%	90.57%
INTI [23]	Contiki cooja	48759	11638	67750	91.54%	92.39%
DL [29]	Testbed	54914	12587	73000	94.8%	93.00%
Proposed method	Contiki cooja	42317	8738	43250	95.86%	94.31%

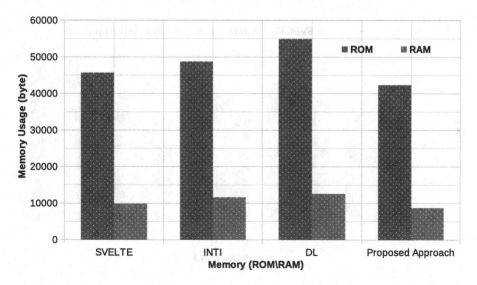

Fig. 9. ROM and RAM usage for handling sinkhole attack detection approach

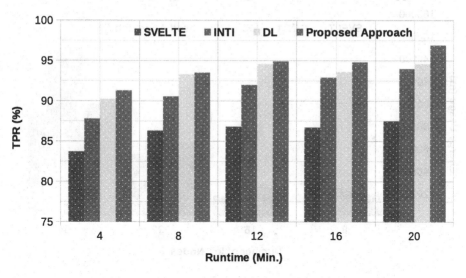

Fig. 10. True Positive Rate (TPR)

corresponding energy consumption also increase. Our proposed solution minimizes energy usage up to 90000 mJ.

Figure 13 shows the average power consumption of an individual node. The small size IoT network individual power consumption is minimized. However, each IoT node average power consumption increases with resources-constraint node network of diverse sizes and more resources-constraint nodes serve as routers.

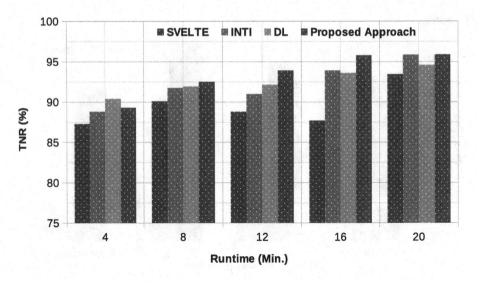

Fig. 11. True Negative Rate (TNR)

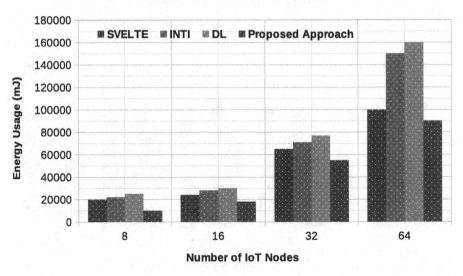

Fig. 12. Energy usage for whole IoT ecosystem in 20 min.

The proposed approach does not require any assistance from all routers and devices that require high computational power. Using the clustering mechanism, we select appropriate router and devices for IDS implementation. Therefore, the solution is lightweight. The IoT nodes do not undergo any additional workload due to the execution of the proposed attack detection solution.

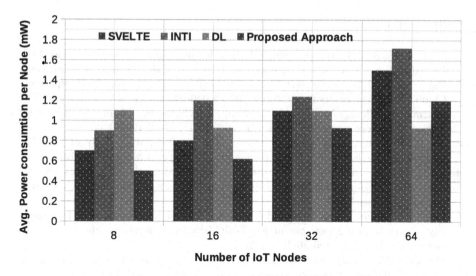

Fig. 13. Avg. power consumption of individual node in IoT ecosystem

6 Conclusion and Future Work

The aim of this research paper is to develop an energy-efficient roving IDS which detect sinkhole attacks using power consumption profile-based clustering strategies. The performance analysis of the intended approach is measured on *Contiki cooja simulator*. The comparative study of the aimed solution with the existing research contributions is also exhibited. Experimental outcomes confirm that the proposed solution observes the IoT traffic and can recognize the sinkhole attacks. Since the methods identify the sinkhole attack using power consumption profile, the associated memory consumption, and average energy consumption minimizes as compared to literature study. The *TPR* and *TNR* rate is high. The experimental outcomes prove that the average values of *TPR* and *TNR* are 95.86% and 94.31% respectively, which are comparable with the existing approaches.

Future work incorporates the various network layer attacks (i.e., Black Hole attack, Version attack, DIS attack, etc.). Future work also contains the implementation of lightweight energy-efficient defense methods and estimates the gain of improved security.

Acknowledgments. We thank the anonymous reviewers for their helpful feedback that served to improve this paper. The research work has been conducted under Information Security Education and Awareness (ISEA) Project Phase - II. The authors would like to thank MeitY and IIT Guwahati India, for the support.

References

1. Sharma, N., Shamkuwar, M., Singh, I.: The history, present and future with IoT. In: Balas, V.E., Solanki, V.K., Kumar, R., Khari, M. (eds.) Internet of Things and Big Data Analytics for Smart Generation. ISRL, vol. 154, pp. 27–51. Springer, Cham (2019). https://doi.org/10.1007/978-3-030-04203-5_3
2. Sharma, S., Chang, V., Tim, U.S., Wong, J., Gadia, S.: Cloud and IoT-based emerging services systems. Cluster Comput. **22**(1), 71–91 (2019)
3. Mekki, K., Bajic, E., Chaxel, F., Meyer, F.: A comparative study of LPWAN technologies for large-scale IoT deployment. ICT Express **5**(1), 1–7 (2019)
4. Cisco: IoT to drive growth in connected devices through 2022. https://www.zdnet.com/article/iot-to-drive-growth-in-connected-devices-through-2022-cisco/. Accessed 26 July 2019
5. Cold in Finland: Five nightmarish attacks that show the risks of IoT security. https://www.zdnet.com/article/5-nightmarish-attacks-that-show-the-risks-of-iot-security/. Accessed 26 July 2019
6. Mirai-Botnet: Mirai Botnet DDoS. https://www.zdnet.com/article/5-nightmarish-attacks-that-show-the-risks-of-iot-security/. Accessed 26 July 2019
7. Passos, L., et al.: A study of feature scattering in the Linux kernel. IEEE Trans. Softw. Eng. (2018)
8. Gershuni, E., et al.: Simple and precise static analysis of untrusted Linux kernel extensions. In: Proceedings of the 40th ACM SIGPLAN Conference on Programming Language Design and Implementation, pp. 1069–1084. ACM (2019)
9. Krčo, S., Pokrić, B., Carrez, F.: Designing IoT architecture(s): a European perspective. In: 2014 IEEE World Forum on Internet of Things (WF-IoT), pp. 79–84. IEEE (2014)
10. Radanliev, P., De Roure, D., Nicolescu, R., Huth, M.: A reference architecture for integrating the industrial Internet of Things in the industry 4.0. arXiv preprint arXiv:1903.04369 (2019)
11. Airehrour, D., Gutierrez, J.A., Ray, S.K.: SecTrust-RPL: a secure trust-aware RPL routing protocol for Internet of Things. Future Gener. Comput. Syst. **93**, 860–876 (2019)
12. Raoof, A., Matrawy, A., Lung, C.H.: Routing attacks and mitigation methods for RPL-based Internet of Things. IEEE Commun. Surv. Tutor. **21**(2), 1582–1606 (2018)
13. Zikria, Y.B., Afzal, M.K., Ishmanov, F., Kim, S.W., Yu, H.: A survey on routing protocols supported by the Contiki Internet of Things operating system. Future Gener. Comput. Syst. **82**, 200–219 (2018)
14. IoT-Simulator: Cooja. https://anrg.usc.edu/contiki/index.php/CoojaSimulator. Accessed 29 July 2019
15. Modi, C., Patel, D., Borisaniya, B., Patel, H., Patel, A., Rajarajan, M.: A survey of intrusion detection techniques in cloud. J. Netw. Comput. Appl. **36**(1), 42–57 (2013)
16. Butun, I., Morgera, S.D., Sankar, R.: A survey of intrusion detection systems in wireless sensor networks. IEEE Commun. Surv. Tutor. **16**(1), 266–282 (2013)
17. Khandelwal, M., Gupta, D.K., Bhale, P.: DoS attack detection technique using back propagation neural network. In: 2016 International Conference on Advances in Computing, Communications and Informatics (ICACCI), pp. 1064–1068. IEEE (2016)

18. Agrawal, N., Pradeepkumar, B., Tapaswi, S.: Preventing ARP spoofing in WLAN using SHA-512. In: 2013 IEEE International Conference on Computational Intelligence and Computing Research, pp. 1–5. IEEE (2013)
19. Anantvalee, T., Wu, J.: A survey on intrusion detection in mobile ad hoc networks. In: Xiao, Y., Shen, X.S., Du, D.Z. (eds.) Wireless Network Security. SCT, pp. 159–180. Springer, Boston (2007). https://doi.org/10.1007/978-0-387-33112-6_7
20. Le, A., Loo, J., Luo, Y., Lasebae, A.: Specification-based IDS for securing RPL from topology attacks. In: 2011 IFIP Wireless Days (WD), pp. 1–3. IEEE (2011)
21. Wallgren, L., Raza, S., Voigt, T.: Routing attacks and countermeasures in the RPL-based internet of things. Int. J. Distrib. Sens. Netw. 9(8), 794326 (2013)
22. Pongle, P., Chavan, G.: A survey: attacks on RPL and 6LoWPAN in IoT. In: 2015 International Conference on Pervasive Computing (ICPC), pp. 1–6. IEEE (2015)
23. Cervantes, C., Poplade, D., Nogueira, M., Santos, A.: Detection of sinkhole attacks for supporting secure routing on 6LoWPAN for Internet of Things. In: 2015 IFIP/IEEE International Symposium on Integrated Network Management (IM), pp. 606–611. IEEE (2015)
24. Glissa, G., Rachedi, A., Meddeb, A.: A secure routing protocol based on RPL for Internet of Things. In: 2016 IEEE Global Communications Conference (GLOBECOM), pp. 1–7. IEEE (2016)
25. Hatzivasilis, G., Papaefstathiou, I., Manifavas, C.: SCOTRES: secure routing for IoT and CPS. IEEE Internet Things J. 4(6), 2129–2141 (2017)
26. Raoof, A., Matrawy, A., Lung, C.H.: Secure routing in IoT: evaluation of RPL secure mode under attacks. arXiv preprint arXiv:1905.10314 (2019)
27. Kamble, A., Malemath, V.S., Patil, D.: Security attacks and secure routing protocols in RPL-based Internet of Things: survey. In: 2017 International Conference on Emerging Trends and Innovation in ICT (ICEI), pp. 33–39. IEEE (2017)
28. Raza, S., Wallgren, L., Voigt, T.: SVELTE: real-time intrusion detection in the Internet of Things. Ad Hoc Netw. 11(8), 2661–2674 (2013)
29. Thamilarasu, G., Chawla, S.: Towards deep-learning-driven intrusion detection for the Internet of Things. Sensors 19(9), 1977 (2019)

BRAIN: Buffer Reservation Attack PreventIoN Using Legitimacy Score in 6LoWPAN Network

Pradeepkumar Bhale[1(✉)], Satya Prakash[1], Santosh Biswas[1,2], and Sukumar Nandi[1]

[1] Department of Computer Science and Engineering,
Indian Institute of Technology, Guwahati, Guwahati 781039, India
{pradeepkumar,satya.prakash,santosh_biswas,sukumar}@iitg.ac.in
[2] Department of Electrical Engineering and Computer Science,
Indian Institute of Technology, Bhilai, Bhilai 492015, India

Abstract. Internet of Things (IoT) is a network of tangible objects forming a Low-Power Network with each connected device having limited resources and computing power, and each entrusted with a task of data acquisition and transmission to controller devices or users. IoTs are taking over the networking world fast and are bringing the physical and the virtual world ever closer. The most prominent security threat with IPv6 over Low-Power Wireless Personal Area Networks (6LoWPAN) is the *Buffer Reservation Attack*. In this paper, this attack has been extensively described, simulated using Contiki cooja simulator and proposed an energy efficient solution named *BRAIN* that defend against buffer reservation attack. We observe that the legitimacy score based *BRAIN* approach is improved by 4–35% packet dropping rate and 36.16% average throughput. Along with it reduces 0.09 mJ CPU Energy Computation (CPUENC), 0.14 mJ Transmission Energy (ETX), and 0.08 mJ Reception Energy (ERX).

Keywords: Internet of Things (IoT) · 6LoWPAN · Buffer reservation attack

1 Introduction

The *Internet of Things (IoT)* has started growing exponentially. It is a giant network of connected machines or objects. The connecting object might be resource-constrained devices such as sensors and actuators, with the Internet using IPv6 protocol [1,2]. The networks of the resource-constrained devices also named as *6LoWPAN* networks. Using this network we build smart automation and control, intelligent sensor etc. Despite various gains, it suffers scalability, availability, affordability, security, and privacy.

The TCP/IP based network protocols that we use were developed over a long period of time in which a lot of problems and vulnerabilities were found

© Springer Nature Switzerland AG 2020
S. S. Rautaray et al. (Eds.): I4CS 2020, CCIS 1139, pp. 208–223, 2020.
https://doi.org/10.1007/978-3-030-37484-6_12

and mitigated and then improved upon again and again till acceptable and usable methods were found to implement various aspects of the network. Thus, there are still many aspects in IoTs that remain to be worked upon and to be made actually implementable in real life and usable by all. Many sources predict that IoTs will become the networks of the future where everything will be connected to everything else passing on data and taking actions based upon information gleaned from the data, without any human intervention making almost everything automatic and configurable, thus making everyone's life infinitely easier and comfortable [3–5]. Since IoTs are a rather new concept, developed in late 20th century and that too not to a far extent, there are a lot of problems that still persist in these networks, most of which are related to security.

As the IoT networks grow larger, while handling much more data that may be sensitive and critical in nature the need for security and privacy methods that have been implemented till now are called into question. The generic IoT architecture comprises of five layers the lowest Perception Layer, then IoT Access Network Layer, then IoT-Internet Connection Layer, then Processing Layer, Application Layer, and last the Business Layer. As shown in Fig. 1.

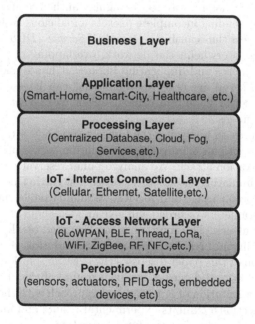

Fig. 1. Generic IoT architecture

There are many security threats at all layers of IoT but many of the Application Layer and the Service Layer security concerns can be handled by the already developed security methods such as SSL, TLS, DTLS, etc., but the Network Layer and Perception Layer require particular analysis and work since they implement their own unique algorithms and architecture, meaning that there are no already in place security measures for these layers [6–11].

The Network Layer of IoT architecture consists of IPv6 protocols with 6LoW-PAN as an abstraction layer between the network and the MAC layer, since the IEEE 802.15.4 doesn't support packets as large as IPv6 (since IPv6 packets require an MTU size of 1280 bytes and the maximum size of a MAC layer frame in IEEE 802.15.4 is 127 bytes which gives just 102 bytes for an IPv6 packet which means that using IPv6 with 802.15.4 directly is just not possible). However, IPv6 is necessary since even now when there is no wide range IP allocation to IoT devices the IPv4 addresses are being exhausted and such IPv4 will not be in any case be able to sustain the huge address space that is required for future IoT growth. So, 6LoWPAN is used as an abstraction layer that has the job of fragmenting and reassembling the fragments for the packet received from the IP layer [12]. Now, though this is a very efficient and flawless method of data transmission, it carries with it some unwanted consequences relating to security, privacy and availability.

The fragmentation algorithm that 6LoWPAN uses has some security flaws in it, since there is no authentication mechanism built in the system at this layer 6LoWPAN layer has no way to distinguish authentic and malicious packets meaning that by sending incomplete packets a malicious node can overwhelm the reassembly process thus causing a *Denial Of Service (DOS)*. Similarly, flooding of fragments to overwhelm the network, overlapping of fragments to corrupt authentic fragments and duplicating important handshaking fragments to disrupt connection setup are other methods that can be used to take up the resources of the receiver node and cause DOS or to prevent connection setup between authentic nodes.

This paper focuses on analyzing the buffer reservation attack on the 6LoW-PAN layer and propose an energy efficient solution which prevents a different type of buffer reservation attack. We analyze buffer reservation attack in *6LoW-PAN Network* by simulating these attacks to see how the IoT devices will behave, by assessing their power usage and service availability while the attack is going on. The various parameters recorded will give an idea about the severity and the feasibility of these attack. The solution is implemented on the Contiki OS and provided the experimental results of our proposed solution.

The next section of this paper discusses the existing solutions for the adaptation layer attack. Section 3 describes the background of the 6LowPAN network. In Sect. 4 the implementation of our proposed approach with the Contiki OS and cooja simulator. Section 5 exhibits experimental results and analysis. In Sect. 6 we conclude the paper indicating the future direction.

2   Related Work

Various research works have been done in IoT Ecosystem and related attacks in all layers from Application Layer to Perception Layer. In this section, we exhaustively study adaptation layer attack mitigation techniques. Every mitigation scheme has its benefits and weaknesses outlined as follows.

The paper [13], implement Nonce and Timestamp with fragmented packets in IoT adaptation layer. Using this approach authenticate the fragments. However, the drawback of this method is the assailant can simply spoof fragmented data.

A split buffer solution is suggested in [14] to allocating fragment-sized buffer space for every anew arrived fragment. In this approach, fragments are not reserving the buffer size for the entire packet using initial FRAG1. This solution prevents an assailant from holding the buffer just by sending one single $FRAG1$. Whenever a buffer overload happens they drop one of the packets from the reassembly buffer based on some unusual behavior. It also discards slow burst packets of the sender. However, the weakness of this technique is that it uses a cryptographic approach to verify received fragments. And it takes more computational cost and memory.

In [15], identified an IP design vulnerability using spoofed fragments with perfectly selected IP-ID field. The security appliances and commodity operating systems are insecure due to Incomplete packets. During transmission of big packets extended reassembly timeout enables to malevolent hold limited buffer resources.

The SPIN protocol proposed by Perrig et al. in [16], has a couple of building blocks i.e TESLA and SNEP. TESLA gives authenticated facility to broadcast message in wireless network environments. SNEP provides data freshness indication, data authentication, and data confidentiality. However, the shortcoming of the SPIN protocol is strenuous to improve MAC data authentication.

In SecuPAN security solution proposed by Hossain et al. in [17]. This approach mainly focuses on the adaptation layer attacks. The solution incorporates fragment authentication and integrity check based on Message Authentication Code. It also gives a solution to compute IPv6 and datagram tag using the crypto strategy to alleviate impersonation attacks. SecuPAN also defends resource-constrained devices from buffer reservation vulnerabilities. This approach gives comparable performance against adaptation layer attacks with a reliable throughput and packet delivery ratio. However, the drawback of this security solution takes more energy consumption, extra computational cost, and memory.

In comparison with the earlier research work, Our solution gives security to the adaptation layer attacks. Many of the existing work only treated one types of buffer reservation attack. However, our intended solution defends against two types of buffer reservation attack. We describe FRAG 1 and FRAG N-1 attack in Sect. 4.

3   Background

3.1   Fragmentation Process Overview

Since the IPv6 protocol requires a minimum MTU of 1280 Bytes and the 802.15.4 MAC layer supports only 127 bytes out of which 25 is gone in frame overhead, and another 21 Bytes for minimum required security measures, leaving only 81

Bytes for the IPv6 packet thus the packet needs to be fragmented into multiple fragments of size that can be sent over the 802.15.4 system.

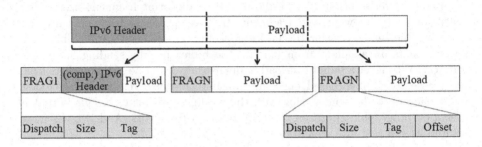

Fig. 2. Fragmentation process overview

The fragment contains the fragment header, IPv6 compressed header, and in the payload the original IPv6 header and the first payload fragment of packet. Subsequent fragments contain the fragment header and the data payload. The fragment header in the first fragment contains Fragment Type, the Datagram Tag and the Datagram Size, while the header in the other fragments contain an additional Fragment Offset field. as shown in Fig. 2.

The first fragment contains the end-to-end routing information, and the rest don't, to relate the remaining fragments with the first fragment there is the Datagram Tag unique to the sender and the packet. The Datagram Size parameter is used for reserving the buffer for final reassembly of the fragments, and the offset is for specifying in which order the fragments must be reassembled.

3.2 6LoWPAN Based Buffer Reservation Attack

This attack uses a different aspect of fragmentation and reassembly process, which deals with buffering of fragments at the receiver for reassembly. All fragments pertaining to the current packet are buffered in the receiver's buffer till that packet is completely received after which it is passed to the layer above (Network Layer), and the buffer is cleared to receive new packets. But, if the malicious node just sends one fragment and then doesn't send anything else, the receiver will keep waiting for the rest of the fragments till timeout after which the malicious node can again send one fragment and reserve the buffer till next timeout thus completely denying access to other nodes.

4 Proposed Solution

Algorithm 1 elucidates in detail the proposed Buffer Reservation Prevention mechanism. This mechanism uses a legitimacy score calculation rule for determining how much buffer to allocate to a certain node's packets. It basically

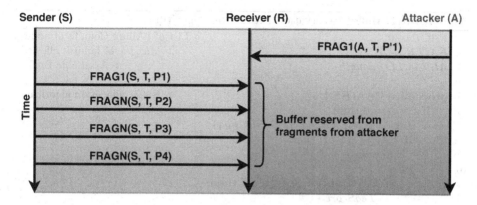

Fig. 3. Attack scenario for buffer reservation attack

Table 1. Notation description

Notation	Description
BAA	Buffer Allocation Algorithm
$LAPD$	LAst Packet received from nodes
LOB	6LoWPAN Buffer for reassembly
$T.out_{reass}$	6LoWPAN Reassembly timeout
$FACT$	List of FAilure CounTs of nodes
$FAITH$	Max no. of failures allowed
ALB	AvaiLable Buffer
LIS	LIgitimate Score
L_{FRAR}	Fragment Length
O_{FRA}	Fragment Offset

calculates a score based upon the behavior of a node after every new packet reception. The mechanism allocates buffer to the node in chunks of a quarter of the total buffer so that no node can monopolize the buffer as a precaution. The size of a chunk i.e. $\frac{1}{4}$ was chosen in accordance to the performance of the mechanism during a simulated attack. Table 1 presented the notations with description seen in this research paper.

$$A = Max(\beta_1 \times LIS + (1 - \beta_1) \times LAPL, \frac{ALB}{4}) \qquad (1)$$

$$B = Min(\beta_2 \times LIS - (1 - \beta_2) \times \frac{LAPL}{\Delta t - T.out_{reass} + \epsilon}, \alpha) \qquad (2)$$

$$C = Min(LIS, L_{FRAR}, \alpha) \qquad (3)$$

$$D = Min(LIS, L_{FRAR} - O_{FRA} \times S_{FRA}) \qquad (4)$$

Algorithm 1. Buffer Reservation Prevention Algorithm

```
1: FACT ← 0                                        ▷ List of FAilure CounTs of nodes
2: FAITH ← 5                                         ▷ Max no. of failures allowed
3: ALB ← LOB.length                                          ▷ AvaiLable Buffer
4:
5: procedure BAA(FRA)                                 ▷ Buffer allocation algorithm
6:     if O_FRA = 0 then
7:         LAP ← GetLAPD(LAPD, SRC_FRA)
8:         if LAP = NULL then
9:             LegScore ← ALB/4
10:        else
11:            if LAP.status = SUCCESS then
12:                LegScore ← A
13:            else if LAP.status = T.out_reass then
14:                LegScore ← B
15:            end if
16:        end if
17:        if LegScore = α then
18:            Counter ← GetFACT(FACT, SRC_FRA)
19:            Counter ← Counter + 1
20:            if Counter > FAITH then
21:                BlackListNode(SRC_FRA)
22:            end if
23:            return False
24:        end if
25:        Allocation ← C
26:    else
27:        if ALB < S_FRA then
28:            Allocation ← D
29:        end if
30:    end if
31:    Allocated ← AllocateBuffer(Allocation)
32:    if Allocated = True then
33:        ALB ← ALB − Allocation
34:        return True
35:    else
36:        return False
37:    end if
38: end procedure
```

When the first fragment of a first time node is received it is trusted and a quarter of the Buffer is allocated. If the packet is received successfully then the next time the node's legitimacy score is increased proportional to the length of the packet successfully received. This increase is done in a smoothed out moving window average way so as to control the reward awarded to the node. Higher the β_1 value, more the speed with which the score increases. On the contrary, if the packet is not sent completely and the Reassembly Timer times out then the next time the legitimacy score of the node is decreased. Again the decrease is proportional to the total length of the packet which was partially received. Also, another factor is added, based on the behavior of Malicious nodes. A node carrying Buffer reservation attack generally keeps reserving the buffer by sending another partial packet immediately after Reassembly Timer Timeout. Thus, the closer the next packet is to the Timeout the more effective the attack is going to be and so the more penalty should be incurred by the node. Thus, the closer Δt, which is the time difference between two consecutive First Fragments, is to the Timeout the more the penalty. So, score decrease must be proportional to $\frac{1}{\Delta t - T.out_{reass}}$. We add a ϵ parameter to control this penalty and also to prevent it from becoming too large. Higher ϵ means lower penalty and lower ϵ means a more severe penalty. β_2 similar to β_1 can be used to control the speed of the score decrease (Fig. 3).

The two types of Buffer Reservation attacks which are listed below are both prevented using this algorithm:

1. When the attacker sends a single fragment FRAG1 and then stops sending. It again sends FRAG1 after some time (preferably $T.out_{reass}$) to reserve the buffer again. This attack
2. When the attacker sends $N - 1$ fragments and then abstains from sending the last fragment. Thus the node behaves normally till the second to last fragment and then disrupts transmission.

Our proposed algorithm prevents both these attacks, since the score keeps decreasing in both these cases till the it becomes α. If the node keeps attacking then the score stays at α and after five instances the node is blocked. Between reaching α and being blocked the node is allowed some buffer, but α being very low (1 or 2 frag_size) means that such attack doesn't affect the attacked node much. If the attacker node then becomes genuine or the fragment loss was due to some legitimate reason then the node has a chance to gain back it's score and a larger allocation of buffer.

5   Experiments, Results, and Discussion

For the analysis of adaptation layer attack in smart agriculture, two experiments have been carried on the Contiki OS and Cooja simulator [18,19]. Two set of circumstances are produced in the experimental setup: non-attack circumstance and adaptation layer attacks circumstance. The complete explanation of individual experiments described below. The simulation parameters of Contiki cooja are presented in Table 2.

5.1   Experiment 1: Non-attack Circumstance

In the non-attack circumstance, all IoT nodes are legitimate and send MQTT request for getting their services (e.g., light intensity and temperature values).

The experiment is conducted on 8, 16, 32, 64, 128 nodes. The 6LoWPAN traffic is taken into consideration using *Wireshark* at the sensor node for further study. It is seen that packet loss is evenly distributed for the non-attack circumstance.

Table 2. Cooja simulator parameters

Parameter name	Value
Operating system	Contiki 3.0
Simulator	Cooja
Radio environment	UDGM
Node type	Tmot Sky
Routing protocol	RPL
MAC/adaptation layer	ContikiMAC/6LoWPAN
Transmitter output power	(dBm) 0 to −25
Receiver sensitivity	(dBm) −94
Radio frequency	2.4 GHz
Attack modeled	6LoWPAN buffer reservation attack
Simulation duration	Variable

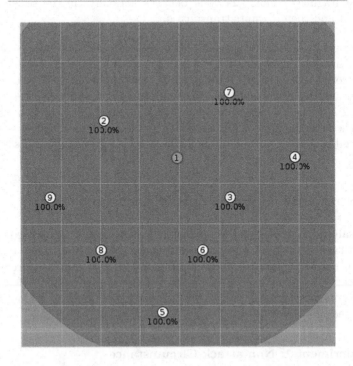

Fig. 4. Topology for non-attack circumstance

When the non-attack simulation process, a couple of parameters examined were throughput and packet interval (packet generating rate) with the different number of IoT Nodes. Topology for non-attack circumstance as shown in Fig. 4. The Contiki uses the RPL as a routing protocol in the 6LoWPAN. The exhaustive execution of the experiment throughput values achieved by a different count of IoT nodes exhibited in Fig. 5a and b respectively.

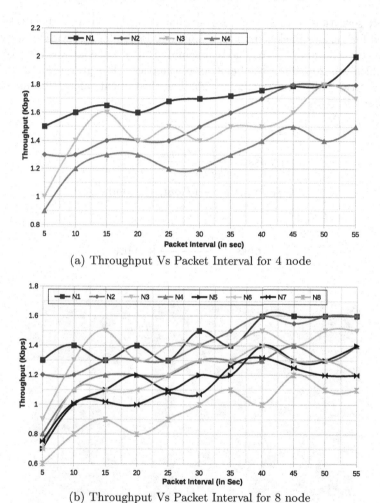

(a) Throughput Vs Packet Interval for 4 node

(b) Throughput Vs Packet Interval for 8 node

Fig. 5. Comparison of packet loss and throughput (during non-attack circumstance)

The experimental result shows that throughput increased at a packet interval of 15 s and continuously reduce when we introduce new nodes in the 6LoWPAN network. This can be delineated to experiences of larger packet loss caused by immense incoming 6LoWPAN traffic.

Figure 5a, and b which depicts throughput against packet interval with the number of IoT nodes. The simulated result indicates a throughput drop with increase in IoT nodes, caused by to the distance among all nodes and atmospheric noise where the 6LoWPAN network is installed.

5.2   Experiment 2: 6LoWPAN Buffer Reservation Attack

Buffer Reservation Attack was also simulated on Cooja and the packet loss recorded for various packet intervals. Topology for buffer reservation attack circumstance as shown in Fig. 6. The Reassembly Buffer Timeout was left to default value which was 20 s. Thus the behavior of the packet loss graph would be different on the two sides of $T.out_{reass} = 20$. The theoretical calculation for various time intervals:

for $T_m < T.out_{reass}$,

$$\%Loss = \frac{T.out_{reass}}{T.out_{reass} + \alpha} \times 100\% \tag{5}$$

$$where \quad \alpha = T_m - (T.out_{reass} \bmod T_m)$$

for $T_m >= T.out_{reass}$,

$$\%Loss = \frac{T.out_{reass}}{T_m} \times 100\% \tag{6}$$

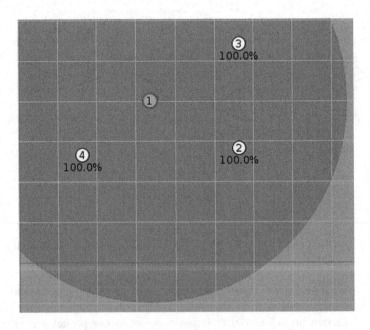

Fig. 6. Topology for buffer reservation attack

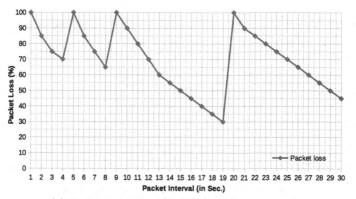

(a) Packet loss Vs packet interval (Theoretical)

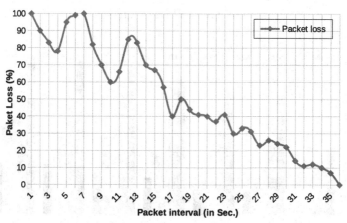

(b) Packet Loss Vs Packet Interval

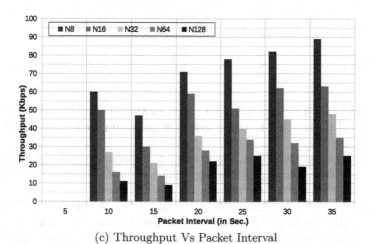

(c) Throughput Vs Packet Interval

Fig. 7. Comparison of packet loss and throughput (during buffer reservation attack)

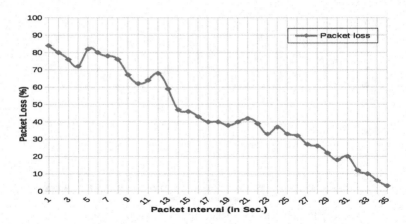

(a) Packet Loss Vs Packet Interval

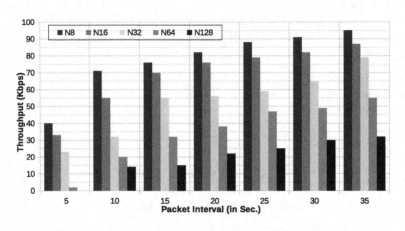

(b) Throughput Vs Packet Interval

Fig. 8. Comparison of packet loss and throughput (after implementation of BRAIN)

The graph for this derivation has been plotted in Fig. 7a. As can be seen the empirical packet loss response graph is quite similar to the one obtained theoretically.

This packet loss trend is as expected since if the interval for malicious fragments is less than $T.out_{reass}$ then the malicious node sends multiple packets within a single timeout, these packets are rejected since it has already captured the reception buffer with the first packet say at time t_0. So, till time $t_0+T.out_{reass}$ the buffer will be reserved by the malicious node. Then as soon as the next malicious fragment is sent the buffer will be reserved again but there will be a lag in between which will allow other nodes to take the buffer. The size of this lag directly corresponds to the fraction of packets that are not being lost. The lag

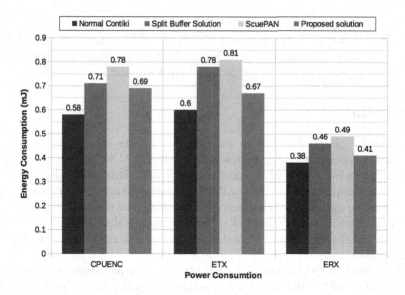

Fig. 9. Analysis and comparison of energy computation

can be easily calculated to be $\alpha = T_m - (T.out_{reass} \bmod T_m)$ which is the time remaining for the next malicious fragment after $T.out_{reass}$. So, the approximate fraction of packets lost will be $\frac{T.out_{reass}}{T.out_{reass}+\alpha}$ as depicted by (Eq. 5).

For intervals more than $T.out_{reass}$ once a malicious fragment reaches it will reserve the buffer for $T.out_{reass}$ time, and then will only attempt recapture after T_m time which means after the buffer is free again. So, the more the malicious node waits after $T.out_{reass}$ the less will be the fraction of packet loss. Here, fraction of packet loss is approximately the portion of T_m for which the buffer was reserved, which is depicted by (Eq. 6) [20].

During the buffer reservation attack simulation method, similar parameters consider as we consider in the non-attack process. In this experiment, we additionally examine theoretical packet loss with respective packet generation rate as shown in Fig. 7a. The experimental packet loss and throughput with the different number of IoT nodes are described in Fig. 7b and c.

From the derived experimental result, it is noted that packet loss and throughput with the packet generating time is decreased as compared to non-attack scenarios. This packet loss occurred due to different buffer reservation attack. Existing split buffer and SucePAN approach, it is obvious that several legitimate or spiteful alike packets were dropped. In *split buffer* approach improved packet dropping rate (9–28%). The average improvement in dropping is 17.25%. And it takes 0.71 mJ CPUENC, 0.78 mJ ETX, and 0.45 mJ ERX. In *SecuPAN* improved packet dropping rate compare to split buffer but it takes more CPUENC, ETX, and ERX.

Our proposed legitimacy score based approach gives an effective difference between legitimate and spiteful packets, and It enhanced packet dropping rate

(4–35%) and Throughput (19.6–52.71%) compares to normal Contiki, Split buffer, and SecuPAN with minimum CPUENC, ETX, and ERX. The performance study of the proposed approach (i.e., Packet dropping rate, Throughput, CPUENC, ETX, and ERX) are shown in Figs. 8a, b and 9, respectively.

6   Conclusion

The objective of the paper is to exhibit the impacts of a buffer reservation attack and proposed an energy efficient solution (BRAIN), that can protect the 6LoWPAN device from a buffer reservation attack. This paper also reveals to recognize the implications of the 6LoWPAN attacks so that the researcher can be offered feasible mitigation techniques. The experimental and theoretical analysis shows that normal and attacked IoT network behaviors (like Throughput, Packet Loss with a different number of nodes) which are not available in the existing state-of-the-art.

Future work is divided into two part, the very first part remains to detection and mitigation of 6LoWPAN attacks so that autonomy can be preserved. The second part encompasses the implementation of lightweight resource constraint security solutions and evaluates the gain of the improved security scheme by launching a network layer attack (i.e DIS attack, Version attack, Black Hole attack, etc.)

Acknowledgments. We thank the anonymous reviewers for their helpful feedback that served to improve this paper. The research work has been conducted under Information Security Education and Awareness (ISEA) Project Phase - II. The authors would like to thank MeitY and IIT Guwahati India, for the support.

References

1. Ziegler, S., et al.: IoT6 – moving to an IPv6-based future IoT. In: Galis, A., Gavras, A. (eds.) FIA 2013. LNCS, vol. 7858, pp. 161–172. Springer, Heidelberg (2013). https://doi.org/10.1007/978-3-642-38082-2_14
2. El Ksimi, A., Leghris, C.: A new IPv6 security approach for a local network. In: Khoukhi, F., Bahaj, M., Ezziyyani, M. (eds.) AIT2S 2018. LNNS, vol. 66, pp. 17–26. Springer, Cham (2019). https://doi.org/10.1007/978-3-030-11914-0_2
3. Zanella, A., Bui, N., Castellani, A., Vangelista, L., Zorzi, M.: Internet of things for smart cities. IEEE Internet Things J. 1(1), 22–32 (2014)
4. Diaz-Rozo, J., Bielza, C., Larrañaga, P.: Clustering of data streams with dynamic gaussian mixture models: an IoT application in industrial processes. IEEE Internet Things J. 5(5), 3533–3547 (2018)
5. Pace, P., Aloi, G., Gravina, R., Caliciuri, G., Fortino, G., Liotta, A.: An edge-based architecture to support efficient applications for healthcare industry 4.0. IEEE Trans. Ind. Inform. 15(1), 481–489 (2018)
6. Pradeepkumar, B., Talukdar, K., Choudhury, B., Singh, P.K.: Predicting external rogue access point in IEEE 802.11 b/g WLAN using RF signal strength. In: 2017 International Conference on Advances in Computing, Communications and Informatics (ICACCI), pp. 1981–1986. IEEE (2017)

7. Arış, A., Oktuğ, S.F., Voigt, T.: Security of internet of things for a reliable internet of services. In: Ganchev, I., van der Mei, R.D., van den Berg, H. (eds.) Autonomous Control for a Reliable Internet of Services. LNCS, vol. 10768, pp. 337–370. Springer, Cham (2018). https://doi.org/10.1007/978-3-319-90415-3_13

8. Abdul-Ghani, H.A., Konstantas, D., Mahyoub, M.: A comprehensive IoT attacks survey based on a building-blocked reference model. Int. J. Adv. Comput. Sci. Appl. (IJACSA) 9(3), 355–373 (2018)

9. Ammar, M., Russello, G., Crispo, B.: Internet of Things: a survey on the security of IoT frameworks. J. Inf. Secur. Appl. 38, 8–27 (2018)

10. Agrawal, N., Pradeepkumar, B., Tapaswi, S.: Preventing ARP spoofing in WLAN using SHA-512. In: 2013 IEEE International Conference on Computational Intelligence and Computing Research, pp. 1–5. IEEE (2013)

11. Khandelwal, M., Gupta, D.K., Bhale, P.: DoS attack detection technique using back propagation neural network. In: 2016 International Conference on Advances in Computing, Communications and Informatics (ICACCI), pp. 1064–1068. IEEE (2016)

12. Kushalnagar, N., Montenegro, G., Schumacher, C.: IPv6 over low-power wireless personal area networks (6LoWPANs): overview, assumptions, problem statement, and goals. Technical report (2007)

13. Kim, H.: Protection against packet fragmentation attacks at 6LoWPAN adaptation layer. In: 2008 International Conference on Convergence and Hybrid Information Technology, pp. 796–801. IEEE (2008)

14. Hummen, R., Hiller, J., Wirtz, H., Henze, M., Shafagh, H., Wehrle, K.: 6LoWPAN fragmentation attacks and mitigation mechanisms. In: Proceedings of the Sixth ACM Conference on Security and Privacy in Wireless and Mobile Networks, pp. 55–66. ACM (2013)

15. Gilad, Y., Herzberg, A.: Fragmentation considered vulnerable: blindly intercepting and discarding fragments. In: Proceedings of the 5th USENIX Conference on Offensive Technologies, p. 2. USENIX Association (2011)

16. Perrig, A., Szewczyk, R., Tygar, J.D., Wen, V., Culler, D.E.: SPINS: security protocols for sensor networks. Wirel. Netw. 8(5), 521–534 (2002)

17. Hossain, M., Karim, Y., Hasan, R.: SecuPAN: a security scheme to mitigate fragmentation-based network attacks in 6LoWPAN. In: Proceedings of the Eighth ACM Conference on Data and Application Security and Privacy, pp. 307–318. ACM (2018)

18. Contiki: IoT Simulator. http://www.contiki-os.org/start.html. Accessed 15 Aug 2019

19. Cooja: IoT Simulator. http://anrg.usc.edu/contiki/index.php/Cooja_Simulator. Accessed 15 Aug 2019

20. Yang, Y., Wu, L., Yin, G., Li, L., Zhao, H.: A survey on security and privacy issues in internet-of-things. IEEE Internet Things J. 4(5), 1250–1258 (2017)

Communication and Networks

TA-ACS: A Trust Aware Adaptive Carrier Selection Scheme for Reliable Routing in Delay Tolerant Networks

Amrita Bose Paul[1]($\boxtimes$), Susmita Mondal[2], Santosh Biswas[2],
and Sukumar Nandi[2]

[1] Department of Computer Applications, Assam Engineering College,
Guwahati 781013, Assam, India
amritabosepaul@gmail.com
[2] Department of Computer Science and Engineering,
Indian Institute of Technology Guwahati, Guwahati 781039, Assam, India
{susmita,santosh_biswas,sukumar}@iitg.ernet.in

Abstract. Delay Tolerant Network (DTN) is an infrastructure-less wireless network characterized with sporadic link connectivity and probable co-existence of high end-to-end delay. It relies on opportunistic contacts for message forwarding and builds an overlay atop disconnected networks to combat network disruptions through persistence storage. The lack of infrastructure and opportunistic contacts make DTN highly vulnerable for misbehaving (both malicious and selfish) nodes. Existence of such nodes have disadvantageous contributions (in terms of network throughput and message overhead) to the network. This paper proposes a novel *Trust Aware Adaptive Carrier Selection* (TA-ACS) scheme for assuring reliable routing in DTN. The efficiency of TA-ACS is evaluated through extensive simulations study in the presence of misbehaving nodes. Further, a comparative analysis of TA-ACS with other existing schemes has been carried out in terms of *message delivery ratio, removed messages count*, and *message overhead*. Results generated from the simulations verified the usability and efficacy of TA-ACS in DTN.

Keywords: Delay tolerant network · Carrier selection · Reliable routing · Misbehaving nodes · Trust · Adaptive

1 Introduction

In recent years, delay tolerant networks (DTNs) [1] have gained popularity in research as a new communicating perspective for addressing the routing issues of challenged networks. These networks are characterized by intermittent connectivity, non contemporaneous end-to-end paths, and probable existence of long and variable delivery latency between the communicating nodes. DTNs are originally conceived for interplanetary use, but recently the technology have become

© Springer Nature Switzerland AG 2020
S. S. Rautaray et al. (Eds.): I4CS 2020, CCIS 1139, pp. 227–244, 2020.
https://doi.org/10.1007/978-3-030-37484-6_13

a potential solution for diverse terrestrial applications, where disruption toler-
ance is the greatest need [2]. The terrestrial applications span over a broad range
of military and intelligence applications, vehicular networks, rural connectivity,
environmental and wildlife monitoring, mobile social networks (MSNs), pocket
switched networks (PSNs), and many more applications to include [3]. The DTN
approach is based on building an overlay atop disconnected networks to combat
network disruptions or disconnections through persistence storage. Thus, to tolerate network disruptions in DTNs, researchers have recommended a message
propagation scheme popularly known as "store-carry-forward" [4]. According to
this scheme, the in-transit messages are physically carried by intermediate nodes
(known as carriers or forwarders). The carriers are expected to become custodian of the messages until they get delivered or find a suitable next-hop carrier.
The conventional routing protocols developed for DTNs assume that nodes are
always willing to accept custody or forward messages whenever they got a chance
to do so. Although, these assumptions of "store-carry-forward" scheme appear
promising and perform well in a congenial (i.e., friendly) DTN environment,
but may not perform well in a people centric hostile networking scenario, (e.g.,
in the presence of "malicious" and "selfish" users in PSNs.), where behavior
of nodes (i.e., human carried mobile devices like smartphones, PDAs, laptops
etc.) are unpredictable and change with time [5,6]. The intermediate nodes in
the transmission path may act selfishly to conserve their power, buffer or other
resources and may become reluctant to forward a bundle unless the forwarding
activity directly benefits them [7]. Again, DTN being a structure less distributed
system, lacks existence of any central control authority. These make the routing
protocols vulnerable for different types of attacks by malicious nodes. A node
having malicious intention can pull messages from a legitimate node and then
drop those messages which in turn detrimentally worsen DTN's routing performance [6]. Thus, the misbehaving nodes can cause considerable message loss and
adversely affect quality and reliability of data. Accordingly, an interacting node
has to be careful when selecting a next-hop message carrier for delivering them
to the intended recipient nodes. Further, the interacting node has to rely on some
sort of uncertainty about the goodness of the selected carrier after forwarding
a message to it. As such, selection of a suitable next-hop carrier for ensuring
routing security and reliability in DTNs still remain an open research issue.

The use of conventional cryptographic techniques for assuring routing security are ineffective in DTNs because of their assumptions of uninterrupted network availability. Although, the application of substantial cryptographic technique can render integrity, confidentiality, and authentication to the routing protocols, but it goes wrong in the presence of selfish and insider attackers. Further,
the characteristics of delayed or disrupted network conditions of DTN makes it
harder for implementing the key management and key distribution services for
assuring routing reliability and security. Moreover, integration of credit based
mechanisms are inefficient in DTNs as easy dissemination of credit values as
well as end-to-end acknowledgements can not be promised due to node sparsity,
infrequent and intermittent node connectivity etc. These situations motivate the

application of trust based strategy for secure and reliable routing in DTNs. In general, "Trust" is the level of confidence or assurance that an entity will act in an anticipated manner, despite the lack of ability to observe or control the environment on which it operates [8]. In DTNs, "Trust" enables network entities to cope with the uncertainty and uncontrollability caused by the node sparsity and frequent link disruptions. Therefore, a trust aware adaptive carrier selection framework is the main objective for deciding a next-hop message carrier to ensure security and reliability for routing protocols in DTNs.

In the literature of DTNs, few trust based schemes have been introduced for detecting or avoiding malicious nodes in the next-hop carrier selection process and thus, to ensure security for routing protocols [9–13]. However, none of these approaches have focused on the possible violations or vulnerabilities that could occur in "store-carry-forward" paradigm of DTN routing due to the existence of selfish nodes. Furthermore, some of these schemes are based on the assumptions of (i) use of watchdog mechanism for monitoring packet forwarding behavior of nodes [9,12], (ii) reputation building using feedback mechanisms [11] and (iii) existence of centralized trusted authority [13] to judge nodes behavior etc. These assumptions, however, restrict the behavior of DTNs where connectivity is intermittent and communication is opportunistic in nature. Again, some routing protocols made available in the literature [14,15] have considered the issues of selfish nodes for message forwarding in people centric opportunistic DTNs. These protocols have analyzed the forwarding behavior of users from a social networking perspectives and try to optimize the social characteristics (such as friendship, social selfishness etc.) of mobile users for avoiding misbehaving nodes in the forwarding path. However, they did not focus on the reliability issues (viz., mobility, buffer, energy etc.) that are of significant importance in DTN routing protocols. To summarize, all these trust based and social-aware routing schemes available in DTN literature are found beneficial in their respective domain, but none of them have addressed together the inherent uncertainty involved in the "store-carry-forward" paradigm and the reliability issues of DTN routing protocols in presence of misbehaving nodes.

To address such issues, a novel *Trust Aware Adaptive Carrier Selection* (TA-ACS) scheme for assuring security and reliability to DTN routing in an hostile environment has been proposed. In this scheme, each node in the network periodically evaluates its own *Belief Trust* about other nodes in the network and maintains a dynamically updated trust zone. Formulation of such zone is based on the evidences acquired by each node on contact with other nodes from various perspectives, such as, (i) node's willingness to act as a message custodian (ii) disparity, if any, in information exchange procedure, and (iii) consistency in self estimated trust with the received recommended trust for an observed node. These collective evidences are aggregated together to form a composite metric called *Multidimensional Trust Value* (MTV) and represent a quantified measure of *Belief Trust* associated with each node in the network. A node is considered to be the part of the trust zone if its MTV is greater than a predefined threshold. In our proposed TA-ACS, whenever a source node has a message to forward, it announces IP Neighbor Discovery (IPND) beacon [16] to discover its neighbor nodes. Once the neighbors are discovered, the source node computes the *Reliability Trust* of its neighbor nodes with respect to the intended destinations of the messages. During this computation process, every trusted node can render their full capabilities for being selected as a potential carrier if they have adequate usable resources in terms of (i) buffer occupancy and (ii) connectivity with destination node. Thus, the capability of each potential neighbor is evaluated adaptively for being selected as a next hop message carrier. The proposed enhancements not only assure security for DTN routing, but also take intelligent decisions to make the carrier selection process adaptive and thus, to improve reliability. The novelty of this approach lies in the fact that all information for trust computation are entirely obtained from local information base, which significantly reduces the overhead of proposed TA-ACS. The performance of the proposed scheme is evaluated through large scale simulation results.

The rest of the paper is organized as follows. Section 2 details the available literature for secure routing in DTNs. The system model is represented in Sect. 3 that includes the network as well as the attack model. The proposed TA-ACS scheme is presented in Sect. 4. Section 5 details the performance analysis of TA-ACS against attacks with different routing metrics viz., message delivery ratio, removed messages count, and message delivery overhead. Finally, Sect. 6 concludes the work.

2 Existing Works

In the existing literature, few approaches based on trust or reputation have been proposed for assuring reliable delivery of messages in presence of misbehaving nodes in DTNs. In addition, some social-aware routing protocols have been proposed to ensure reliability in message delivery while optimizing social characteristics of mobile users. These available approaches are detailed next.

The work in [10] has utilized reputation building mechanism to address the problem of misbehaving carriers in DTNs. The proposed mechanism is based on the condition that the system is capable of keeping track of intermediate carriers as a whole for message delivery. But this assumption is not practical since the network is characterized by frequent link disruptions leading to non-availability of contemporaneous links on an end-to-end path. The authors in [11] have introduced an Iterative Trust and Reputation Mechanism (ITRM) system to detect and isolate malicious nodes from the network. Their work is solely intended for defending Byzantine types of attacks in DTNs. Further, the authors in [12] have proposed a reputation assisted framework to evaluate an encounter's competency for being selected as message carrier. The proposed framework is based on gathered evidences of nodes' packet-forwarding behavior. In another approach [13], the authors have presented a probabilistic misbehavior detection scheme (iTrust) that adopts the concept of "Inspection Game" to stimulate the behavior of misbehaving nodes. The scheme considers a periodically available central Trusted Authority (TA) to judge the nodes' packet forwarding behavior. However, the existence of central trusted authority is impractical in DTNs because of its distributed nature.

The authors in [14] have proposed a trust based routing for people centric DTNs, where they have considered the social and quality of service (QoS) trust properties to analyze the trust level of a node in the network. But the questions arise, how to decide on a situation, when a node having good QoS trust carries low social trust and vice versa. Moreover, the work failed to address the prevailing uncertainty in "store-carry-forward" message propagation paradigm of DTNs. Further, the work has not explored the behavioral aspects of the mobile devices in a people centric opportunistic communication scenario. In a very recent work [15], a Trust Based Intelligent Routing (TBIR) using artificial neural network (ANN) is proposed for DTNs which exploits the "Call Data Record" from "Call Detail Record" in socially active communities. However, no attention has been given for reliable delivery of the messages to the destinations.

Therefore, compared to the works cited above, the research work presented in this paper intends to design an integrated scheme for secure and reliable routing amidst prevailing uncertainty in hostile DTNs. To achieve these, two different trust measuring components viz., *Belief Trust* and *Reliability Trust* have been proposed for analyzing a node's trust level from different perspectives. The *Belief Trust* component is responsible for ensuring security for DTN routing in presence of misbehaving nodes, and the *Reliability Trust* has been introduced to reduce the chances of message dropping and thus, to improve the reliability of message delivery.

3   System Model

3.1   Network Model

The proposed work focuses on trust-aware adaptive next-hop carrier selection scheme for message forwarding and its subsequent reliable delivery to the intended destination in an hostile DTN environment. Each node in the network uses DTN IPND [16] to learn about the existence, availability, and addresses of other nodes within their wireless transmission range. All nodes in the network have similar capability and identical processing requirements. There is no existence of central trusted authority. All nodes are mobile, resource constrained, calculate their trust table independently and update it periodically. Each time two nodes encounter each other, they exchange encounter history information along with previously computed trust values about other nodes. To avoid malicious nodes from supplying incorrect information to attract messages, the exchanged information is certified by encounter tickets as mentioned in [17]. After the initial phase of handshaking, each node calculates the *Belief Trust* and *Reliability Trust* of the encountered nodes to evaluate their potentiality for being selected as a next-hop message carrier in the forwarding path.

3.2   Attack Model

The network consists of good nodes and misbehaving nodes. Good nodes are those that follow the normal protocol functionalities and misbehaving nodes deviate from it. The misbehaving nodes include both malicious and selfish nodes. Depending on malicious behavior, the system may face a wide range of attacks viz., *black hole attacks* (i.e., intentional dropping of messages), *ballot-stuffing attacks* (i.e., providing good recommendations for other malicious nodes to increase their trust value), *bad-mouthing attack* (i.e., providing bad recommendations to the good nodes in order to decrease their trust value) etc. Again, the good nodes may become reluctant to act as a carrier and might act selfishly to conserve their power, buffer or other computational resources and thus exhibit forwarding misbehavior.

4   Proposed TA-ACS Scheme

This section elaborates the proposed *Trust Aware Adaptive Carrier Selection* (TA-ACS) scheme for reliable delivery of messages in a hostile DTN environment. The proposed scheme has its two trust components viz., *Belief Trust* and *Reliability Trust*, which are obtained through collective evidences and estimated information. The *Belief Trust* component is responsible for assuring security for DTN routing in the presence of misbehaving nodes. However, only ensuring belief trust in a uncongenial environment is not sufficient. Let us consider a situation, where a node has enough belief trust to depend on, but has no reachability towards the destination or does not have enough buffer space to hold a message. Eventually, this situation may result in dropping of messages and leads to performance degradation of the underlaying DTN routing protocols. Furthermore, the simulation study carried on the existing conventional routing protocols for DTNs viz., "Epidemic" [18] and "First Contact" [19], exhibit that there is a significant amount of message dropping either because of overloaded buffer or due to the message's time-to-live (TTL) expiration. Therefore, to reduce the chances of message dropping and thus, to improve the reliability in message delivery, we introduce another component called *Reliability Trust*. This trust component of TA-ACS is obtained in a reactive manner during the protocol's runtime. In our proposed scheme, whenever a source node has a message to forward, it announces IPND beacon [16] packets to discover its neighbor nodes. After receiving the beacon packets, the neighbors reply back with a feedback packet informing their available buffer capacity to carry messages in the network. Depending on the received feedback packets, the source node does extra computations to approximate link quality of potential neighbors with the designated destinations. Thus, the *reliability trust* component is obtained dynamically in runtime and from these acquired evidences and estimated information the source nodes in TA-ACS select a suitable next-hop carrier adaptively that ensures a secure and reliable communication in a hostile DTN. The evaluation methods of *Belief Trust* and *Reliability Trust* components are detailed next.

4.1   Determining Belief Trust

Each node in TA-ACS obtains the *Belief trust* about other nodes in the network through collective evidences of nodes behaviors on contact. To evaluate the *Belief trust* of each node in the network, three different trust measuring criteria viz., "Custodian Willingness", "Maliciousness", and "Consistency" are proposed. The trust criteria "Custodian Willingness" reflects a node's willingness to act as a message custodian, "Maliciousness" represents a node's behavioral disparity, if any, in information exchange procedure, and "Consistency" measures the coherency in self estimated trust with received recommended trust for an observed node. The derivation of each criteria is a *subjective judgment* carried by each node based on the observations made on nodes' behavior for assessing their potentiality as a trustworthy message carrier. We represent this *Belief trust* component as a composite trust metric called *Multicriteria Trust Value* (MTV) and represented as

$$\mathfrak{T}_{\mathcal{A}}^{MTV}(\mathcal{B}) = w(CW) * T_{\mathcal{A}}^{CW}(\mathcal{B}) + w(MAL) * T_{\mathcal{A}}^{MAL}(\mathcal{B}) + w(CON) * T_{\mathcal{A}}^{CON}(\mathcal{B}) \quad (1)$$

where $\mathfrak{T}_{\mathcal{A}}^{MTV}(\mathcal{B})$ is the *Belief trust* of trustor node $\mathcal{A}$ about trustee node $\mathcal{B}$. The term w in Eq. (1) is the correction factor that balances the significance of evidences associated with each trust criteria viz., "Custodian Willingness", "Maliciousness", and "Consistency", respectively. Each node in TA-ACS stores the MTV value about other encountered nodes in their own TRUST_TABLE, along with the storage timestamp for further processing of TA-ACS. The TRUST_TABLE is updated periodically during each refresh interval of the protocol. This process helps each node of TA-ACS to maintain a dynamically updated trust zone. The MTV of each node is defined as a continuous real number in the range of $[-1, 1]$, with 1 indicating complete trust, 0.5 ignorance, and -1 complete distrust. The belief trust computation process of TA-ACS assumes a minimum trust threshold as $\mathfrak{T}_{min}^{MTV}$ and the threshold-limit is set to $(\delta = 0.5)$. A positive trust evaluation for a node depends on whether the MTV computed for that node is above the threshold-limit (δ). A node is considered to be the part of the trust zone if its MTV is greater than a threshold (δ). For example, if $\mathfrak{T}_{\mathcal{A}}^{MTV}(\mathcal{B}) > \mathfrak{T}_{min}^{MTV}$, node $\mathcal{A}$ will consider node $\mathcal{B}$ as a member of its trust zone. Now, the derivation mechanisms of different trust measuring criteria for obtaining the MTV value of each node in TA-ACS are detailed next.

Custodian Willingness. We introduce this metric to measure the willingness factor of a node to become custodian for a message. This has been derived from monitoring the bundle protocol execution behavior. According to bundle protocol specification [20], whenever a DTN node requests for a custody transfer to another DTN node, the requested node sends the requesting node a custody acceptance status report to inform that the node has accepted custody. But in a hostile environment this assumption may deviate from normal protocol functionality. This observation is based on the fact that a malicious node can delete a bundle after providing false custody acceptance status report. Again, a selfish node that always tries to save its power will stop from sending custody acceptance status report. In addition, an honest node with very low remaining battery power can resist itself from sending this status report and can get a low trust value. Therefore, to measure the custodian willingness metric of a trustee node $\mathcal{B}$ by a trustor node $\mathcal{A}$, we observe the bundle protocol execution behavior and evaluate it as

$$T_{\mathcal{A}}^{CW}(\mathcal{B}) = \begin{cases} \dfrac{B_{\mathcal{A}}^{CS}(\mathcal{B}) - B_{\mathcal{A}}^{CF}(\mathcal{B})}{B_{\mathcal{A}}^{CS}(\mathcal{B}) + B_{\mathcal{A}}^{CF}(\mathcal{B})} & \text{if } B_{\mathcal{A}}^{CS}(\mathcal{B}) + B_{\mathcal{A}}^{CF}(\mathcal{B}) \neq 0 \\ 0 & \text{otherwise} \end{cases} \qquad (2)$$

Where $B_{\mathcal{A}}^{CS}(\mathcal{B})$ and $B_{\mathcal{A}}^{CF}(\mathcal{B})$ denote the number of successful custody acceptance status report received from $\mathcal{A}$ and number of custody acceptance status not received from $\mathcal{B}$, respectively as observed by $\mathcal{A}$. Theoretically $-1 \geq T_{\mathcal{A}}^{CW}(\mathcal{B}) \leq 1$.

Maliciousness. On encounter, each node exchanges information regarding its own encounter history and trust values about other nodes in the network. To protect this information from being forged, each node uses encounter tickets as mentioned in [17]. However, a misbehaving node may violate this assumption. Therefore, to measure the uncertainty in information exchange procedure, we introduce the metric called "Maliciousness", represented by T^{MAL}, to derive the trust related to this criteria and evaluated as

$$T_{\mathcal{A}}^{MAL}(\mathcal{B}) = \frac{B_{\mathcal{A}}^{EC}(\mathcal{B}) - B_{\mathcal{A}}^{EF}(\mathcal{B})}{B_{\mathcal{A}}^{EC}(\mathcal{B}) + B_{\mathcal{A}}^{EF}(\mathcal{B})} \qquad (3)$$

where $B_{\mathcal{A}}^{EC}(\mathcal{B})$ signifies number of times the encounter history ever exchanged certified by encounter tickets. $B_{\mathcal{A}}^{EF}(\mathcal{B})$ denotes number of times encounter history was not exchanged or exchanged but with entries not certified by encounter tickets. This measured criteria can show the existence of selfish and malicious behavior in a node. Our proposed trust evaluation method is based in the assumption that encounter history without certification by encounter tickets shows malicious behavior while not exchanging trust value and encounter history information on contact exhibits selfish behavior of nodes in hostile DTNs.

Consistency. As every node is continuously monitoring its neighbor nodes, the direct estimated trust value for the neighbors and the recommended trust value (for the same set of neighbors) from another node possibly does not differ too much in general. But, if the recommended trust values differ too much with the direct estimated trust values, the recommender appears to be a malicious node trying to impose a *bad-mouthing* or *ballot-stuffing* attacks. Therefore, to detect such activity, we introduce a similarity measure based on pearson correlation coefficient [21] to determine the inconsistency between the direct calculated trust with the recommended trust value of a node under consideration. The consistency measure between calculated trust values of node $\mathcal{A}$ and recommended trust values from node $\mathcal{B}$ is evaluated as

$$T_{\mathcal{A}}^{CON}(\mathcal{B}) = \frac{\sum_{i \in I}(T_{\mathcal{A}}(i))(T_{\mathcal{B}}(i))}{\sqrt{\sum_{i \in I}(T_{\mathcal{A}}(i))^2}\sqrt{\sum_{i \in I}(T_{\mathcal{B}}(i))^2}} \tag{4}$$

where $T_{\mathcal{A}}^{CON}(\mathcal{B})$ represents the similarity between node $\mathcal{A}$'s direct estimated trust value with $\mathcal{B}$'s recommended trust value and I is the set of nodes for whom trust values are determined by both $\mathcal{A}$ and $\mathcal{B}$. $T_{\mathcal{A}}(i)$ is the trust value of node i determined by node $\mathcal{A}$ and $T_{\mathcal{B}}(i)$ is the recommended trust value of node i provided by node $\mathcal{B}$. The results obtained from this correlation formula range from -1 for negative correlation to +1 for positive correlation.

4.2   Determining Reliability Trust

Here we detail the different qualifying criteria and their derivation methods to obtain *Reliability trust* of a potential node for selecting it as a next-hop message carrier in DTN routing. The different criteria proposed for obtaining *Reliability trust* of a potential node are (i) node's available buffer capacity to avoid unnecessary message drops (ii) its contact probability with the destination and (iii) the received message delivery acknowledgement from potential nodes. The potential nodes are the member nodes in each DTN nodes' trust zone and confirm the *Belief trust* component of TA-ACS scheme.

Buffer Capacity. In TA-ACS, IP Neighbor Discovery (IPND) [16] protocol is used to learn the existence, availability, and addresses of other DTN participants in the network. Each DTN node in TA-ACS sends and receives small IP UDP announcement beacon to detect its neighborhood. In TA-ACS buffer availability information is incorporated as a parameter in the feedback IPND beacon to inform about the nodes' available buffer space for accommodating incoming messages. A trustor node selects a trustee neighbor from its own trust zone only if the trustee has sufficient buffer space to hold incoming messages. In this process, dropping of messages due to buffer overloading can be avoided. Each node in TA-ACS calculates its available buffer information as

$$\mathrm{BUF}_{\mathcal{A}} = \frac{\text{No. of Buffered Messages}}{\text{Buffer Size}} \tag{5}$$

where $\mathrm{BUF}_{\mathcal{A}}$ is the available buffer capacity of node $\mathcal{A}$.

Contact Probability. This criteria of *reliability trust* component in TA-ACS is responsible for providing information about contact probability of a trusted potential forwarder with the destination node. In TA-ACS scheme, each DTN node maintains an encounter history matrix which contains the information about number of contacts with other DTN nodes and the information regarding message delivery acknowledgement. The encounter matrix is updated regularly to ensure the freshness of information. Whenever a DTN node has a contact with other DTN node, they exchange their history matrix. If node $\mathcal{A}$ behaves as source node and wants to send messages to destination $\mathcal{D}$, and $\mathcal{B}$ happens to be the potential trusted forwarder confirming "buffer capacity" criteria, then $\mathcal{A}$ calculates the "contact probability" of node $\mathcal{B}$ with destination $\mathcal{D}$ from the encounter history matrix as,

$$P_{\mathcal{A}}^{contact}(\mathcal{B}, \mathcal{D}) = \frac{E_{\mathcal{B},\mathcal{D}}}{\sum_{v \in V} E_{\mathcal{B},*}} \qquad (6)$$

where $E_{\mathcal{B},\mathcal{D}}$ denotes number of previous encounter of node $\mathcal{B}$ with destination $\mathcal{D}$ and $E_{\mathcal{B},*}$ signifies total number of encounters of node $\mathcal{B}$ with any other arbitrary destination. The value of $P^{contact}$ always lies within $[0, 1]$.

Message Delivery Acknowledgement. This trust criteria enhances the possibility of message delivery and hence improves reliability of DTN routing. This comes into operation in absence of "contact probability" criteria of *Reliability Trust*. In general, DTN is a sparse network and exhibits infrequent and intermittent connectivity patterns between the nodes. Therefore, in a situation where the trusted potential forwarder fails to provide "contact probability" with the intended destination and no alternate competent forwarder is available, i.e., $P^{contact} = 0$ for all neighbors belonging to trustor's trust zone, then the "message delivery acknowledgement" criteria is looked into for choosing a probable forwarder. This is accomplished by processing the message delivery acknowledgement information stored in the encounter matrix against each node. The delivery acknowledgements from the destination node stored in the candidate potential forwarder's list indirectly implies that previously some messages were delivered to that destination through this node. Therefore, in near future there is a possibility of contact between the potential forwarder and the destination for which the message is designated. Therefore, while choosing a candidate node as a message forwarder from the trust zone, if no node is available with positive $P^{contact}$, it can be forwarded to a neighbor that confirms the "message delivery acknowledgement" criteria of TA-ACS. This can minimize the chances of message droppings due to TTL expiration. The flowchart as provided in Fig. 1 exhibits the working functionality of proposed TA-ACS.

5   Simulation of TA-ACS and Performance Analysis

This section encloses the distinct sets of simulation study that has been carried out to test the efficiency of TA-ACS for assuring routing security and reliability in a hostile DTN environment. The performance of TA-ACS's has been evaluated in terms of Message Delivery Ratio (MDR), Removed Messages Count (RMC) and Message Overhead (MO) in the presence of selfish, bad-mouthing, and ballot-stuffing attacks. The simulation-based experimental study has been carried out

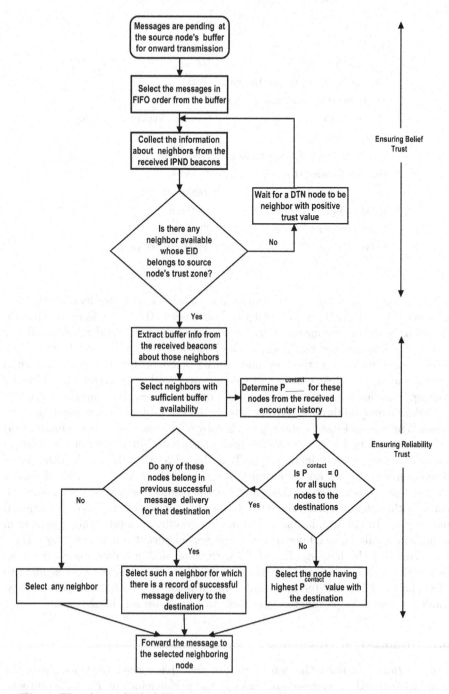

Fig. 1. Flowchart of TA-ACS for secure and reliable routing in hostile DTNs

Table 1. Parameters for simulation model

Parameters	Value
Beacon packet interval	100 ms
Message lifetime	750 s
Message retransmission timeout	1000 s
No. of message retransmissions	3
Mobility model	Random Waypoint Mobility
Velocity of the nodes	2 m/s
Maximum size of Beacon packet	2280 bytes
Message header size	28 bytes
Nodes' buffer size	1000000 bytes
Total simulation time	3600 sec
Total number of nodes	20
Network area	$[1200 \times 1200]$ m^2

with ns-3 [22] simulator and a comparative analysis with Epidemic [18], First Contact [19] and Trust based routing [14] have been studied to determine its efficiency in next-hop carrier selection for message forwarding and reliable delivery to the destination. For comparison, the Epidemic [18], and First Contact [19] have been considered as the base line routing protocols for their performance in terms of message delivery ratio and message overhead, respectively. In Epidemic routing, bundles are replicated at contact opportunities. This improves delivery probability and minimizes delivery latency at the cost of higher message overhead. Whereas, in First Contact, a single copy of the message is being maintained in the network and involves low resource utilization, but results in low delivery ratios and long delivery latency. The Trust-based routing [14] on the other hand counts on social trust and QoS trust to estimate the nodes' behavior. In order to gain good confidence in the experimental results, each simulations run ten times with different seed values to obtain mean value of the above mentioned parameters. In the simulations, every node periodically sends *beacon packets* in regular intervals for neighbor discovery. A *beacon packet* broadcasted by a DTN node contains the message IDs along with its available buffer space advertisement. The messages are fragmented into 1500 byte datagrams before sending to MAC Layer. The UDP based message transmission is used for simulation study. Table 1 depicts the parameters and their values set for all simulations.

5.1 Results and Discussion

This section examines the set of results that have been obtained from the simulation-based experiments to evaluate the performance of TA-ACS protocol. A comparative analysis with Epidemic, First Contact, and Trust-based routing is also furnished to justify its efficiency in a hostile DTN environment.

Impact of Number of Selfish Nodes: In this set of simulations, the impact of the number of selfish nodes on the performance of Epidemic, First Contact, Trust-based routing, and TA-ACS are investigated. The percentage of selfish nodes are varied from 10% to 50%.

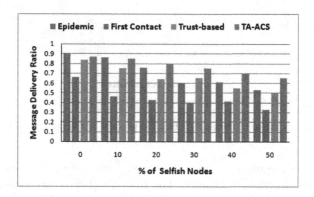

Fig. 2. Message delivery ratio vs. percentage of selfish nodes

Figure 2 depicts the message delivery ratio as a function of selfish nodes for Epidemic, First Contact, Trust-based routing, and TA-ACS in the underlying hostile DTN environment. It is calculated as the ratio between the number of messages successfully delivered to the number of messages created. In the simulation study, a decreasing trend in delivery ratio for all the protocols have been observed. This is due to the fact that, with increased number of selfish nodes, the probability of potential carriers willing to become message custodian decreases. This leads to the dropping of messages due to message TTL expiration or buffer overflow at the source DTN nodes. It is noticeable that with less number of selfish nodes (i.e, with 10%), the message delivery probability of Epidemic routing does not degrade significantly and shows some form of resiliency. This is due to its flooding characteristics that creates multiple message copies in the network. However, with further increase in selfish nodes, their is a significant degradation in message delivery ratio of Epidemic protocol. The delivery ratio of First Contact shows a steep decline since a single copy is forwarded in the network. The reasons behind the low delivery ratio of Trust-based routing with increasing number of selfish nodes are the lack of collective evidences about nodes' selfish behaviors as well as non-consideration of the probable vulnerabilities that may occur in the "store-carry-forward" paradigm of DTN message propagation scheme. The exhibited better performance of TA-ACS is due to its "custodian willingness" criteria in *belief trust* and "buffer capacity", "connectivity" in "reliability trust" computations and thus enabling nodes to select a secure forwarder in the routing path.

Figure 3 exhibits the fraction of removed message count with the variation of selfish nodes in the network. This performance metric reflects the effectiveness of the TA-ACS in carrier selection in DTN routing. The "removed message

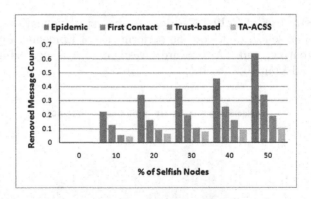

Fig. 3. Removed message count vs. percentage of selfish nodes

count" keeps the account of removed messages due to the presence of selfishness or maliciousness in nodes' behavior. The fraction of removed message count is zero in the absence of selfish nodes. The low performance of Epidemic and First Contact is due to their blind flooding and forwarding of messages in the network that causes selfish nodes to drop messages once received and thus increasing the fraction of removed message count. Again, as compared to the trust-based protocol, the TA-ACS shows better performance in terms of removed message count. This is due to the consideration of "Custodian Willingness" criteria in next hop carrier selection that avoids selfish nodes in the forwarding path. Moreover, in TA-ACS, the compatibility of the willing custodian is also judged in terms of its "buffer capacity" for accommodating incoming messages and "connectivity" to the destination node. All these considerations cause TA-ACS to perform better in presence of selfish nodes.

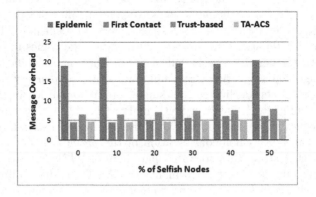

Fig. 4. Message overhead vs. percentage of selfish nodes

Figure 4 depicts the message overhead for all the protocols under consideration. In DTN based applications, message overhead is measured by the number of replicas created for each message's successful transmission to reach the destination. It has been observed that TA-ACS protocol outperforms trust-based and non trust-based protocols in terms of message overhead with increasing proportion of selfish nodes. This is justifiable by the fact that in TA-ACS, blind forwarding is avoided and a single copy of the message is forwarded based on the evaluated "belief trust" and "reliability trust" of a potential carrier. These enable the messages to traverse less number of hops resulting in fewer relays for successful delivery to the destinations.

Impact of Number of Malicious Nodes. In this set of simulations, the impact of the number of malicious nodes on the performance of Epidemic, First Contact, Trust-based routing, and TA-ACS is investigated. The percentage of malicious nodes is varied from 10% to 50%. The behavior of the malicious nodes is emulated to generate "bad-mouthing" and "ballot-stuffing" attacks.

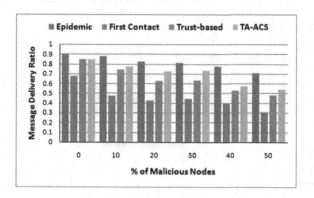

Fig. 5. Message delivery ratio vs. percentage of malicious nodes

Epidemic and First Contact protocols are popular for their better performance in terms of message delivery ratio and overhead, respectively. From the simulation results, as depicted in Figs. 5, 6, and 7, it have been observed that the performance of these protocols degrade significantly in the presence of malicious nodes whose intension is to disrupt normal routing functionality either by dropping messages or by boosting trust values of other colluding misbehaving nodes. Simultaneously, the results exhibit the facts that when compared to the Trust-based routing, the performance of TA-ACS has shown much better efficiency in terms of message delivery ratio, removed message count, and message overhead. It is justiciable because in TA-ACS, nodes' malicious activity have been quantified through collective evidences in the *belief trust* formation phase. The trust criteria "maliciousness" quantify the nodes behavioral abnormality in information exchange procedure, and "consistency" measures the disparity in self estimated trust with received recommended trust for an observed node. The disparity is the effect of "bad-mouthing" and "ballot-stuffing" attacks by the malicious nodes.

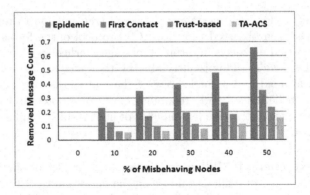

Fig. 6. Removed message count vs. percentage of malicious nodes

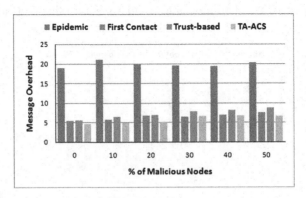

Fig. 7. Message overhead vs. percentage of malicious nodes

6   Conclusion

In this paper, a novel unified scheme called TA-ACS is proposed for ensuring routing security and reliability in hostile DTNs. The salient feature of the TA-ACS is that it not only considered nodes' behavioral status, but also examined their technical competency for being selected as a next hop message carrier in DTN routing. The TA-ACS has been evaluated and analyzed through extensive set of simulations study in presence of selfish and malicious node behaviors. Results generated from simulations verified the usability and efficiency of TA-ACS in DTN based applications viz., PSNs or MSNs, for ensuring security and reliability. The applicability of TA-ACS as a security scheme for DTN routing has advantages of less complex computational overheads, as learning of the entire network is based on locally available information and trust. Moreover, the reliability trust of each candidate node is calculated only for neighbor nodes inside the trust zone. Excellency in these qualities of TA-ACS make it a worthy secure and reliable scheme for routing in hostile DTNs.

In the future, we plan to enhance TA-ACS as a generic and dynamic trust management framework for DTN routing. Further, a selfish node could frequently switch between the role of a good and of a malicious node to minimize its efforts and maximize its score in other nodes. Such a behavior shall be scrutinized in our future work. Moreover, the process of trusted carrier selection may incur additional amount of end-to-end delay by filtering undesirable encounter opportunities (i.e., misbehaving nodes) in the forwarding path. Though the primary objective of message forwarding in a hostile DTN is for secure and reliable delivery to the destination, but minimization of delay conforms to the Quality of Service (QoS) requirements of underlying routing protocols. Thus, in future we plan to consider nodes' other technical competencies (in terms of energy, delay, link capacity) in the trust computation process of TA-ACS.

Acknowledgements. The work has been carried out as a part of the Collaborative Research Scheme awarded for the project titled "On Ensuring Reliable Communication over Mobile Social Networks (MSNs)", of Assam Science and Technology University (ASTU) under TEQIP-III program of MHRD.

References

1. Fall, K., et al.: Delay-tolerant networking architecture (2007)
2. Fall, K.: A delay-tolerant network architecture for challenged internets. In: Proceedings of the 2003 Conference on Applications, Technologies, Architectures, and Protocols for Computer Communications, pp. 27–34. ACM (2003)
3. Voyiatzis, A.: A survey of delay-and disruption-tolerant networking applications. J. Internet Eng. **5**(1), 331–344 (2012)
4. Conti, M., Giordano, S.: Mobile ad hoc networking: milestones, challenges, and new research directions. IEEE Commun. Mag. **52**(1), 85–96 (2014)
5. Fall, K., Farrell, S.: DTN: an architectural retrospective. IEEE J. Sel. Areas Commun. **26**(5), 828–836 (2008)
6. Li, Q., Cao, G.: Mitigating routing misbehavior in disruption tolerant networks. IEEE Trans. Inf. Forensics Secur. **7**(2), 664–675 (2012)
7. Lu, R., Lin, X., Zhu, H., Shen, X., Preiss, B.: Pi: a practical incentive protocol for delay tolerant networks. IEEE Trans. Wirel. Commun. **9**(4), 1483–1493 (2010)
8. Castelfranchi, C., Falcone, R.: Trust is much more than subjective probability: mental components and sources of trust. In: Proceedings of the 33rd Annual Hawaii International Conference on System Sciences, 10-pp. IEEE (2000)
9. Xu, Z., Jin, Y., Shu, W., Liu, X., Luo, J.: SReD: a secure reputation-based dynamic window scheme for disruption-tolerant networks. In: Military Communications Conference, MILCOM 2009, pp. 1–7. IEEE (2009)
10. Dini, G., Duca, A.L.: A reputation-based approach to tolerate misbehaving carriers in delay tolerant networks. In: 2010 IEEE Symposium on Computers and Communications (ISCC), pp. 772–777. IEEE (2010)
11. Ayday, E., Fekri, F.: An iterative algorithm for trust management and adversary detection for delay-tolerant networks. IEEE Trans. Mob. Comput. **11**(9), 1514–1531 (2012)
12. Li, N., Das, S.K.: A trust-based framework for data forwarding in opportunistic networks. Ad Hoc Netw. **11**(4), 1497–1509 (2013)

13. Zhu, H., Du, S., Gao, Z., Dong, M., Cao, Z.: A probabilistic misbehavior detection scheme toward efficient trust establishment in delay-tolerant networks. IEEE Trans. Parallel Distrib. Syst. **25**(1), 22–32 (2014)

14. Chen, R., Bao, F., Chang, M., Cho, J.H.: Dynamic trust management for delay tolerant networks and its application to secure routing. IEEE Trans. Parallel Distrib. Syst. **25**(5), 1200–1210 (2014)

15. Singh, A.V., Juyal, V., Saggar, R.: Trust based intelligent routing algorithm for delay tolerant network using artificial neural network. Wirel. Netw. **23**, 1–10 (2016)

16. Ellard, D., Brown, D.: DTN IP Neighbor Discovery (IPND). Internet-Draft draft-irtf-dtnrg-ipnd-01, IETF Secretariat, March 2010

17. Li, F., Wu, J., Srinivasan, A.: Thwarting blackhole attacks in disruption-tolerant networks using encounter tickets. In: INFOCOM 2009, pp. 2428–2436. IEEE (2009)

18. Vahdat, A., Becker, D., et al.: Epidemic routing for partially connected ad hoc networks. Technical report, Technical Report CS-200006, Duke University (2000)

19. Jain, S., Fall, K., Patra, R.: Routing in a delay tolerant network, vol. 34. ACM (2004)

20. Scott, K.L., Burleigh, S.: Bundle protocol specification (2007)

21. Resnick, P., Iacovou, N., Suchak, M., Bergstrom, P., Riedl, J.: GroupLens: an open architecture for collaborative filtering of netnews. In: Proceedings of the 1994 ACM Conference on Computer Supported Cooperative Work, pp. 175–186. ACM (1994)

22. NS-3 Network Simulator. https://www.nsnam.org/

SAS: Seasonality Aware Social-Based Forwarder Selection in Delay Tolerant Networks

Amrita Bose Paul[1]($\boxtimes$), Akhil GV[2], Santosh Biswas[2], Sukumar Nandi[2],
and Niladri Sett[2]

[1] Department of Computer Applications, Assam Engineering College,
Guwahati 781013, Assam, India
amritabosepaul@gmail.com
[2] Department of Computer Science and Engineering,
Indian Institute of Technology Guwahati, Guwahati 781039, Assam, India
{gv.akhil,santosh_biswas,sukumar,niladri}@iitg.ernet.in

Abstract. In social-based delay tolerant network (DTN) applications, hand-held mobile devices exchange information. The inherent social property of DTN has encouraged contemporary researchers in exploiting social metrics to devise forwarding techniques for efficient routing. This work observes evidence of seasonal behavior in contacts between node-pairs in real mobility traces, and exploits it to devise a novel seasonality aware similarity measure. We incorporate seasonality information into tie-strength, and then use it as link weight in a weighted similarity measure which we extend from Katz similarity index. We propose a Seasonality Aware Social-based (SAS) DTN forwarding technique based on the proposed similarity measure and ego-betweenness centrality. Finally we perform real trace driven simulations to show that SAS outperforms baseline social-based DTN forwarding methods significantly.

Keywords: Delay Tolerant Network · Social metrics ·
Ego-betweenness · Centrality · Social-based forwarding · Mobile Social
Networks · Tie-strength

1 Introduction

Intermittently connected Mobile Ad hoc Networks (MANETs) lack contemporaneous end-to-end routes from source to destination. Message delivery in these networks must be delay tolerant, and so these networks are often called as Delay Tolerant Networks (DTNs). DTN was originally developed for Inter Planetary Networks (IPNs), but later its applications have been realized in terrestrial mobile networks such as Mobile Social Networks (MSNs) [1], Pocket Switched Networks (PSNs) [2], Vehicular Ad hoc Networks (VANETs) [3], which are characterized by sporadic connectivity, frequent link disturbance, existence of non-contemporaneous end-to-end route, long and unpredictable communication

© Springer Nature Switzerland AG 2020
S. S. Rautaray et al. (Eds.): I4CS 2020, CCIS 1139, pp. 245–265, 2020.
https://doi.org/10.1007/978-3-030-37484-6_14

latency, etc. To deal with sporadic connectivity pattern, DTNs follow a message propagation scheme referred as *store-carry-and-forward* [4], where intermediate nodes (known as carriers) store and physically carry buffered messages until they get in contact with the destination or a suitable next-hop carrier. In this scheme, each node independently makes forwarding decisions for opportunistic message exchange between them when they are in communication range of each other. In most of the terrestrial DTN applications, the mobile nodes/devices are carried and used by people and thereby making forwarding decision based on peoples' social behavioral perspectives. So, a class of DTN forwarding, namely *social-based DTN forwarding* algorithms [5] have emerged, which exploit social network properties in DTN forwarding. Our work in this paper proposes a **S**easonality **A**ware **S**ocial-based (SAS) DTN forwarding mechanism, which capitalizes on seasonal behavior in human contacts.

Popular social-based DTN forwarding techniques [5] usually exploit three social network metrics: similarity between node-pairs [6], centrality of a node [7], and community of nodes [8]. Intuition behind use of these three metrics are: (i) similar nodes meet each other frequently, so a node similar to the destination node has better delivery probability of the message; (ii) central nodes act as hub, and are reachable to other nodes; and (iii) nodes inside a community meet frequently, so forwarding the message to a node that resides within the destination's community increases the chances of message delivery. SimBet [9] is a social-based DTN forwarding technique which has utilized similarity and centrality metric, whereas BubbleRap [10] has exploited centrality metric and community structure. Lack of infrastructure in DTN forces individual nodes to take forwarding decisions independently through message exchange. Unavailability of a centralized view of the network limits the social-based DTN forwarding techniques to use only locally calculable social network metrics. However, advanced social network metrics, such as random walk similarity measure [6], betweenness centrality measure [7], community detection algorithms [8] are global in nature, and can not be directly applied to DTN forwarding. So, approximated versions of the global metrics have been devised for forwarding in DTNs. The authors in SimBet [9] have used an approximated version of betweenness centrality called ego-betweenness centrality [11], that calculates the betweenness centrality of each node in their respective ego networks. BubbleRap [10]'s approximation of betweenness centrality has been a modified version of degree centrality and has used a distributed community detection algorithm for DTNs [12]. Further, it has been observed that, SimBet and BubbleRap dynamically calculate the social relationship between the nodes to choose the best relay node. SimBet models the relationship between the nodes as binary and does not consider the relative strength of its neighbors. To justify the reason, the authors of SimBet argue that ego betweenness has high correlation with sociocentric betweenness. However, by analyzing the different mobility traces [13,14] we found that the correlation of ego betweenness and social betweenness is not that high but correlation of ego betweenness and sociocentric betweenness of a node inside a community has very high correlation as shown in Table 1. Moreover, in their work, the small world created by the network of mobility traces also have very less diameter (<2)). Again, BubbleRap uses the concept of sociocentric betweenness centrality which requires the knowledge of the whole network, which in reality is not possible in DTN. Therefore, these issues of the existing state-of-the-art routing protocols of social-based DTNs motivate us to observe evidences of seasonal behavior in node contacts in real mobility traces and exploit it to devise a novel seasonality aware similarity measure.

Table 1. Characteristics of the mobility traces

Trace		Reality	Sassy	Cambridge
#Nodes		96	25	36
#Edges		3085	155	541
Average degree		64	12	30
Average clustering co-efficient		.816	.712	.892
Average shortest path length		1.324	1.503	1.141
Co-relation of sociocentric betweenness and ego betweenness	Whole network	.75	.88	.608
	Within community	.984	.987	.990

In our work, we model the contact history between node-pairs to formulate tie-strength which preserves seasonality of human contacts. Traditional approaches to model tie-strength [15–18] use variants of average separation duration between node-pairs. We observe strong seasonality, i.e., repetitive contact pattern in real mobility traces and exploit it to formulate tie-strength. Our model measures the tie-strength as weighted average of separation duration and a seasonality aware contact strength. Based on Katz [19] similarity index we define a weighted similarity index between two nodes. Our motivation of using Katz similarity metric has been its inherent property of giving more importance to the direct contacts over the indirect ones. By analyzing real mobility traces, we find that although ego-betweenness centrality is not a good substitute for sociocentric/global betweenness, but it can accurately approximate global betweenness within communities. Our proposed DTN forwarding technique SAS exploits the proposed weighted Katz based seasonality aware similarity measure and ego-betweenness centrality, where the similarity value effectively deals with intra-cluster forwarding and ego-betweenness drives the inter-cluster forwarding. We adapt the utility proposed in SimBet, which exploits similarity and centrality, and propose the Seasonality aware DTN forwarding algorithm SAS. Finally, we simulate our work on real mobility traces to demonstrate the effectiveness of SAS over state-of-the-art social-based DTN forwarding algorithms: SimBet and BubbleRap.

The rest of the paper has been structured as follows. Section 2 discusses related works on social-based forwarding in DTNs. The drawbacks associated with these works are listed out, which provide the motivation for the work carried out in this paper. Our proposed seasonality aware social-based forwarding in DTNs has been presented in Sect. 3. Section 4 presents the performance evaluation and analysis of the proposed social-based forwarding scheme with the benchmark SimBet [9] and BubbleRap [10] to validate its effectiveness in attaining routing objectives. Finally, in Sect. 5 we conclude our work.

2   Background and Literature Review

This section introduces the different approaches of routing techniques available in the literature of DTNs with a special focus on the social-based forwarding techniques.

The routing protocols in DTNs can be broadly classified into two categories: *flooding* and *forwarding* [20]. The protocols in the flooding family induce multiple "replicas" of each message in the network without considering the potentiality of the candidate node for being selected as a next-hop carrier [21–24]. In this routing approach, a source node tries to send all its' messages to its' neighbors if they do not have the copy of the messages. This approach does not require to store any past information about the routing or mobility of the nodes. So, flooding is the obvious choice when no information is known in advance about the movement of the nodes or about the topology of the network.

In [21], the authors have proposed "Epidemic routing" as one of the basic flooding based routing protocol in DTNs. In Epidemic, a node floods the messages to it's neighbor nodes who does not have a copy of the message. In this protocol, whenever two nodes have an encounter, they exchange their summary vector which contains the IDs of the messages they are carrying. After comparing the summary vector, each node determines the messages they are not carrying which the other nodes have and requests for those messages. Depending on this request message transfer is done between the nodes. Random pairwise exchange of messages are used to ensure eventual message delivery. This process of continuous replication flood the network with same copy of messages to guarantee maximum delivery ratio in presence of infinite storage availability for all the nodes in the network. However in reality, nodes have limited storage capacity, and a limited number of messages can be stored. Flooding the network with messages causes high overhead in term of storage and power spent on transmission and reception. This causes the degradation of network performances. In an another approach called "Two-Hop Forwarding" [25], each node is assumed to encounter every other node for some short duration of time. Within this duration, the source node replicates each message to the first encountered node and the messages are stored until they come in contact with the destination. In this protocol, routing overhead is reduced at the cost of increased message delivery latency. In addition, "Spray and Wait" [24] is a controlled flooding based routing protocol that requires no knowledge about the network. Unlike epidemic it limits the number of message copies to be forwarded in the network. The protocol works in two phases (i) *spray* and (ii) *wait*. In spray phase the source spreads $\mathcal{M}$

copies of the messages in the network. If the destination is not found in spray phase, then the relay nodes having message copies will enter into a wait phase in which they wait until the messages are delivered to the destinations directly. Relay nodes do not make any additional copies of the message, in turn reducing the resource usage.

Though, these protocols in the flooding family achieve good delivery ratio and less delivery latency, but flooding the network with duplicate messages cause high network overhead in term of storage and power spent on transmission and reception. These cause congestion leading to network performance degradation. So, another class of routing approaches called "forwarding-based" have been explored to restrict the generation of bundle replicas in the network.

The protocols in the forwarding family calculate an utility metric based on "knowledge" to qualify the candidate node as the next hop carrier on the routing path. A single copy of each message is forwarded to the qualified node. Most of these knowledge-based protocols select a suitable next-hop carrier based on contact history of potential carriers [26,27], knowledge about traffic patterns in the network [28] or on probability of encountering the destination node [29]. Furthermore, some of them have used multi-copy spraying mechanisms to improve reliability amidst intermittent connectivity [30,31].

In the basic forwarding based protocol called "First Contact" (FC) [23], the source node tries to forward the message to one of the randomly selected link among all the current contacts. The authors have tried to improve the performance of the protocol by forwarding the message in a direction closer to the intended destination node. To avoid the routing loop, a path vector has been proposed. In this scheme a single copy of each message is maintained in the network.

In an another approach, the Probabilistic Routing Protocol using History of Encounters and Transitivity (PRoPHET) [22] uses utility based replication for delivery of messages. PRoPHET uses history of encounter information to calculate the utility metric of a node. In this protocol, each source node calculates its delivery probability to every other node in the network. These probability values are updated on every contact for each known destination. The delivery probability is aged by a factor over time. It also uses, transitive relation to update the delivery predictability of a node, with whom it is not directly connected. In Rapid [32], a node calculates the utility value of each message that is present in its buffer and this utility value decides in which order it should be relayed to the next node. RAPID derives a per-packet utility function from the routing metric. At a transfer opportunity, it replicates a packet that locally results in the highest increase in utility. To calculate this utility value, it first estimates the delivery delay of the message. This estimation is based on the two or three hop's information. This limits the estimation because the destination may be present beyond two or three hops.

Recently, social-based routing is relatively a new approach and has become popular for addressing the routing problem in DTNs. It is based on the observation that in most of the terrestrial DTN applications people are carrying mobile devices (like Pocket Switched Networks, Mobile Social Networks etc.) and thereby making forwarding decision based on peoples' social behavioral perspectives. In social-based DTN applications, hand-held mobile devices exchange information. The inherent social property of DTN has encouraged contemporary researchers in exploiting social metrics to devise forwarding techniques for efficient routing. So, a class of DTN forwarding, namely *social-based DTN forwarding* algorithms [5] have emerged, which exploits social network properties in DTN forwarding. Social-based DTN forwarding has been popular in DTN specific applications like vehicular networks, mobile social networks, pocket switched networks etc. In such application domains, people carry mobile devices, whose behaviors are unpredictable from social aspects as well as from ad hoc networking aspects. Zhu et al. [5] and Wei et al. [33] have provided two recent surveys on social-based DTN forwarding techniques. "Centrality", "Similarity" and "Community" have been the most effective social network metrics used for DTN forwarding.

Authors in [34–36] explored the usefulness of community detection algorithms in DTN forwarding. The motivation of using communities has been: if the carrier encounters a node which belongs to the destination's community, the message will be delivered with high probability. The authors in [34–36] explored the possibility of community detection and interest profile based forwarding algorithms in DTNs. In these approaches, messages are forwarded to the encountered node if it belongs to the same community as the destination node or if it's interest profile matches with the destination node's interest profile. The shortcoming of these approaches is that they do not capture the dynamics of social relations among the nodes.

In an another approach, SimBet [9] has exploited ego-betweenness centrality and similarity to forward messages in DTN. Central nodes work as hubs and are reachable to all other nodes in the network, and nodes similar to the destination contacts with it frequently. However, the shortcoming of SimBet is that, the authors model the relationship between the nodes as binary and does not consider the relative strength of its neighbors.

Again, BubbleRap [10]'s approximation of betweenness centrality has been a modified version of degree centrality and it has used a distributed community detection algorithm for DTNs [12]. The proposed betweenness centrality of BubbleRap requires the knowledge of the whole network, which in reality is not possible in DTN.

Another set of social-based forwarding techniques have exploited the concept of tie-strength [37]. Few of these can be found in [15–18]. These techniques have modeled the change in contact patterns during time, and predicted strength of social relationships between node-pairs. The authors in [15–18] have failed to model the dynamic changes in contacts from human behavioral perspectives.

Therefore, these issues of the existing state-of-the-art routing protocols of social-based DTNs motivate us to observe evidences of seasonal behavior in node contacts in real mobility traces and exploit them to devise a novel seasonality aware similarity measure. Our work has incorporated seasonality behavior of human contacts into tie-strength towards DTN forwarding. To the best of our knowledge, our work is the first one to exploit seasonality behavior of human contacts in DTN forwarding.

3 Proposed Seasonality-Aware Forwarding Scheme

Here we present our Seasonality Aware Social Based DTN Forwarding (SAS), a DTN forwarding algorithm which exploits seasonal behavior of human contacts. Our proposed measures of seasonality aware "tie-strength" is detailed in Sect. 3.1. The modified version of "similarity", and "centrality" measure with incorporation of seasonal behavior of node contacts are detailed in Sects. 3.2 and 3.3, respectively. The newly formed "utility" function to determine the node's potentiality as a next-hop forwarder in DTN routing is presented in Sects. 3.4. Finally Sect. 3.5 represents the proposed seasonality aware forwarding algorithm in social-based DTNs.

We consider a category of DTN like Pocket Switched Networks [2] or Mobile Social Networks [1], which consists of cellular devices carried by human beings. They use Bluetooth interface to exchange data among themselves. Each device can act as a source, destination, or forwarder of a message. Due to mobility of these devices, a continuous source-to-destination path may not exist. These devices communicate in *opportunistic* manner during contacts, when a sender and a receiver comes into contact at a time which is unknown beforehand. During this contact, these devices make the forwarding decision of data. In DTN the network topology changes rapidly and the nodes do not have any knowledge of future connections. The inter-node contact duration is often limited. During this duration only a limited number of messages can be transferred. Also, DTN uses multihop forwarding for messages. A large number of hops increases the probability of delivery of message, but also increases the delivery cost. So it is needed to have an efficient strategy to select the best relay nodes.

Use of social network metrics have been prominent [5] in DTNs where the network is formed with hand held mobile devices carried by humans. The reason for this is that mobility in such networks is driven by the social network properties, which are less volatile than the traditional metrics. In this work, we exploit the seasonality/repetitive pattern in human contacts and have incorporated it with the other state-of-the-art social network metrics towards proposing a Seasonality Aware Social-based forwarding called SAS. Similar to SimBet [9], we select the best relay node based on a utility metric which exploits two social network metrics: centrality and similarity. We model the seasonality in human contact to propose a novel formulation for calculating tie-strength, and incorporate it as link weight into the proposed weighted similarity metric based on Katz similarity index [19]. By analyzing real mobility traces, we find that ego-betweenness [11] can be a good approximation for sociocentric betweenness [7] inside communities. We combine the proposed seasonality aware similarity and ego-betweenness in a utility function and propose the forwarding mechanism SAS.

3.1   Strength of Tie

Strength of tie [37] measures the strength of social relationship between two individuals. A simple way to measure the tie-strength may be the total number of contact or the total duration of contact. Motivation of using tie-strength in DTN forwarding has been: if a node carrying the message gets into contact with a node which is strongly connected to the destination (i.e., has met with the destination many times or for long time in the past), they may meet again and may deliver the message with high probability. Tie-strength can be regarded as a similarity measure for directly connected node-pairs. However, the destination may not be directly connected to every node the carrier meet, so multi-hop similarity measure is required. We discuss the multi-hop similarity in the next subsection.

Traditional approaches to model node-pair's tie-strength use variants of average separation duration [15–18]. In general, the average separation duration between two nodes x and y during the time interval $[0, T]$ is given as:

$$S_{avg}^{[0,T]}(x,y) = \frac{\int_{t=0}^{T} f(t)dt}{T} \qquad (1)$$

where $f(t)$ represents the estimated time remaining for the next encounter between the nodes x and y at time t. Strength of tie is usually formulated as a function which is inversely proportional to the average separation duration. This approach assumes that the node-pairs which have come into contact for longer duration in past are tied with stronger relationship, and are likely to come into contact in future.

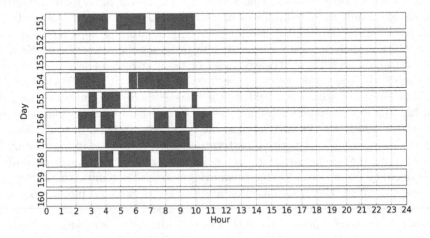

Fig. 1. Seasonality pattern in `Reality` trace

Our proposed measure of tie-strength has been encouraged by observed seasonality pattern in node-pairs' contact history. Figure 1 shows the contact pattern of two nodes in the `Reality` trace during 10 days. Each rectangle in the vertical dimension represents a day, and each day is divided into 24 parts which represent hours. The duration of a day filled with red is the contact duration between the two nodes. The figure shows that the six days which have some contacts, follow similar contact pattern. The bursts of contacts happen during the same 9 h period of these days. It might be explained as, the two persons workplace may be same and this nine hour duration might be their working hours. The days which observe no contact may be holidays, which repeat in every seven days. It is also observable that the contact pattern of the day at the top of the figure is very similar to the eighth day from top. It indicates that the contact pattern repeats every week. We exploit this seasonality pattern of human contact to measure of link strength, which is a weighted average of the traditional average separation duration and seasonality aware tie-strength. We describe below how each node calculates their tie-strength with its' neighbors. For simplicity and as per the requirement for the mobility traces in hand, we explain this method with two granularities of seasonality, daily and weekly. However, this method is trivially extendable for more levels of seasonality, such as monthly, quarterly, yearly, etc.

We divide the duration of a day into equal size time-window Δ_0, say an hour. $\Delta_1 = a \times \Delta_0 =$ duration of a day, $\Delta_2 = b \times \Delta_1 = a \times b \times \Delta_0 =$ duration of a week. Note that, in our case $a = 24$ and $b = 7$, but for maintaining generality we use the variables a and b. $f(t)$ represents the time remaining to the next encounter between two nodes (x, y) at time t. Each node x maintains a seasonality matrix $m^{(x,y)}$ for each of its contacts y, $m^{(x,y)}[i, j]$ be the elements of the seasonality matrix $m^{(x,y)}$. The dimension of $m^{(x,y)}$ is $b \times a$. When two nodes x and y come to contact for the first time, both of the nodes initialize $m^{(x,y)}$, and all of its elements are initialized as 0. The nodes keep a variable p which stores the total number of time-windows elapsed, and is initialized as 0. They also keep the variables q and s, initialized as 0, which keep track of the offset of the current time window in the seasonality matrix for row and column, respectively. The variable $\mathbb{T}$ representing non-seasonal strength of the link (x, y) is initialized as 0. After each Δ_0 amount of time, both of the nodes trigger the following steps, which update an matrix element, the variables, and calculate the tie-strength of (x, y) for the next time window.

$$m^{(x,y)}[q, s] = \frac{m^{(x,y)}[q, s] + \Delta_0 / \int_{t=p \times \Delta_0}^{p \times \Delta_0 + \Delta_0} f(t)dt}{p \times \Delta_0 + \Delta_0} \tag{2}$$

$$\mathbb{T} = \frac{p \times \Delta_0 + \Delta_0}{\mathbb{T} + \int_{t=p \times \Delta_0}^{p \times \Delta_0 + \Delta_0} f(t)dt} \tag{3}$$

where p is incremented as $p = p+1$ and the offsets of the next time window in the seasonality matrix for row and column are updated as $q = (p - p \mod (a \times b)) \mod b$ and $s = p \mod b$, respectively.

Finally, the seasonality aware tie-strength of the link (x, y) for the next time-window is calculated as the weighted average of average separation duration and seasonality components:

$$w^p(x,y) = \alpha \times m^{(x,y)}[q,s] + (1-\alpha) \times \frac{1}{\mathbb{T}} \tag{4}$$

where the parameter $0 \leq \alpha \leq 1$ regulates the weight of the seasonality aware component in the tie-strength formulation.

3.2 Similarity

The motivation of using similarity measure in DTN forwarding is that similar nodes meet frequently, and a node similar to the destination node is highly likely to deliver the message to the destination node. In SimBet, similarity between two nodes is calculated as the number of common neighbors between them. It treats direct and indirect contacts in a similar manner. We argue that the nodes which have met the destination at past, are more similar to the destination than those which are two hop away. We adopt Katz index [19] to define the similarity metric. Katz similarity index between the nodes x and y is given as:

$$Katz(x,y) := \sum_{l=1}^{\infty} \beta^l \times |paths_{x,y}^{<l>}|, \tag{5}$$

where $paths_{x,y}^{<l>}$ represents the set of all paths of length l between nodes x and y. $\beta > 0$ is a constant that regulates the amount of importance given to higher length paths. As $\beta \to 0$, Katz index starts behaving like common neighbor.

We modify Katz index to accommodate tie-strength. We consider upto 2 length paths to make it locally calculable. The Similarity measure between nodes x and y is given as:

$$Sim(x,y) = \beta \times w(x,y) + \beta^2 \times \sum_{k \in N(x) \cap N(y)} w(x,k) + w(k,y), \tag{6}$$

where $N(x)$ is the set of neighbors of a node x, and $w(x,y)$ is the weight of a link (x,y) for the current time window, given by Eq. (4).

3.3 Centrality

Centrality measures the importance/accessibility of a node in the network. Central nodes are considered as highly reachable to the other nodes in the network. Betweenness [7] is one of the widely used centrality measure used in social-based DTN forwarding techniques [5]. Nodes with high betweenness centrality fall into large number of shortest paths linking to other node-pairs in the network. Thus, these nodes act as bridges to reach to all other nodes in the networks. Betweenness Centrality is calculated as:

$$Bet_C(x) = \sum_{y \neq z \neq x, (y,z) \in \text{Nodes}} \frac{g_{y,z}(x)}{g_{y,z}} \tag{7}$$

where $Bet_C(x)$ is the global/socio centric betweenness centrality of node x, $g_{y,z}$ is the total number of geodesics (shortest paths) between nodes y and z, and $g_{y,z}(x)$ is the number of shortest paths between node y and z passing through x.

Socio centric betweenness is a global measure, and is difficult to measure in DTN forwarding because the nodes in DTN have access to the local information only. Flooding may be one solution, but it will increase the message cost exponentially. Moreover, due to sparse and dynamic nature of DTN, message may take long to reach the destination. Consequently, in DTN it is impossible to achieve consistent values of the global measures like socio centric betweenness throughout the network. SimBet [9] has capitalized the concept of Ego networks [11] in DTN forwarding, which approximates socio centric betweenness by calculating betweenness centrality locally, within the node's ego network. Ego network of a node is defined as a network which consists of the node, its neighbors, the links of the node with its neighbor, and the connections among its neighbors. The ego-betweenness of a node x is calculated as:

$$Bet_E(x) = \sum_{y \neq z \neq x, (y,z) \in N(x)} \frac{g_{y,z}(x)}{g_{y,z}} \tag{8}$$

where $Bet_E(x)$ is the ego-betweenness centrality of x, $g_{y,z}$ is the total number of geodesics (shortest paths) between nodes y and z, and $g_{y,z}(x)$ is the number of shortest paths between node y and z passing through x. $N(x)$ is the set of neighbors of x.

Marsden [38] has observed that ego-betweenness and socio centric betweenness are highly correlated in social networks. We investigate the relationship between socio centric and ego-betweenness in the real mobility traces discussed in Sect. 1. Table 1 shows that correlation between ego-betweenness and socio centric betweenness in the whole network is insignificant. However, when the network is partitioned into communities, ego-betweenness and socio centric betweenness correlate highly. So, we argue that a node with high ego-betweenness acts as a good hub inside its community, and can be useful in forwarding the message when the destination is inside its community.

3.4 Utility

A carrier having a message must choose another node to forward it, so that the message reaches the destination with high probability. When a carrier comes into contact with a node, it calculates an utility function of the node with respect to the destination. The carrier forwards the message to the node based on this utility function. Like SimBet [9], we define the utility as a combination of two utilities: similarity and centrality.

Utility of a node y (which comes into contact with the carrier x) for delivering a message to node d is calculated as:

$$Utility(y,d) = \gamma \times SimUtility(y,d) + (1 - \gamma) \times BCUtility(y) \tag{9}$$

where,

- $SimUtility(y, d) = \frac{Sim(y,d)}{Sim(x,d)+Sim(y,d)}$ is the similarity utility of the node y with the destination d with respect to the career x,
- $BCUtility(y) = \frac{Bet_E(y)}{Bet_E(x)+Bet_E(y)}$ is the betweenness utility of the node y with the destination d with respect to the career x,
- $\gamma \in [0, 1]$ is a balancing parameter, which allows for setting the relative importance of Betweenness utility and Similarity utility,
- $Sim(-, -)$ and $Bet_E(-)$ are calculated using Eqs. (6) and (8) respectively.

3.5   Forwarding Algorithm

Here we present our proposed forwarding algorithm based on ego-betweenness centrality and seasonality aware similarity index, which extends the forwarding algorithm of SimBet [9]. It evaluates a nodes' utility for being chosen as a potential forwarder. This algorithm makes no pre-assumption of global knowledge of the network, and makes the forwarding decisions on the fly based on locally exchanged information. For this to happen, on encountering a node y, node x verifies whether it is carrying any messages destined to y. If this is found to be true, then all messages destined for y are delivered. Subsequently, the encounter vectors are received from node y. The encounter vector contains information (list of contacts and tie-strength of the links with their contacts) about the nodes that each of them have encountered. This encounter information is then used to update the ego-betweenness value on node x and similarity value as described in Eqs. (8) and (6) respectively. Further, the two nodes x and y exchange a summery vector that contains a list of destination nodes for whom they are carrying messages, and their betweenness and similarity values. Thereafter, node x calculates the Utility value of its own and of node y for each destination in the received summery vector following Eq. (9). If the node y's utility is higher than x's, x forwards the message to y in greedy fashion. We summarize the algorithm as follows.

1. On encountering y, if node x has messages destined for y, it delivers them to y.
2. x receives the encounter vector of node y, which contains y's contacts and $w^p(y, k)$'s where $k \in N(y)$.
3. Node x and y exchange the summery vector information containing list of messages carried by them for each destination node.
4. For each message in the Message list calculate $Utility(x, d)$ and $Utility(y, d)$ for each destination d.
5. If $Utility(y, d) > Utility(x, d)$, node y becomes the forwarder and receives messages from x.

4   Performance Evaluation of SAS

This section detail the performance evaluation and analysis of the proposed social-based forwarding scheme (SAS) with the benchmark SimBet [9] and

BubbleRap [10] to validate its' effectiveness in attaining routing objectives. The different evaluation metrics under consideration are described in Sect. 4.1. Section 4.2 provides a brief description of the data traces used in the experiments and summarizes characteristics of the social network induced by the contacts in the mobility traces. The experimental setup used for generation of mobility traces through trace-driven test with dataset from the `Reality` [39] and `Cambridge` [40] datasets are represented in Sect. 4.3. Finally, the experimental results and their analysis are summarized in Sect. 4.4.

4.1 Routing Objective and Evaluation Metrics

Routing Objective of DTN routing protocol depends on application. Generally the objective is to increase the delivery ratio while not increasing the cost of delivery much. Generally, DTN routing protocols are evaluated based on the following metrics, which we follow in this work:

- **Delivery Ratio:** It is the ratio between the number of messages delivered and the total number of messages generated.
- **Delivery Cost:** It is the ratio between the number of message transmission required for delivery to the total number of messages delivered.
- **Average Latency:** It is the time duration between the message generation and its delivery, averaged over all messages.

4.2 Data Sets

We perform our experiments on three real mobility traces, namely `Cambridge`, `Reality` and `Sassy`. A brief description of the three traces are given next. The characteristics of the social network induced by the contacts in the mobility traces are already summarized and discussed in Table 1 of Sect. 1.

- `Cambridge`: This dataset [13] includes the traces of Bluetooth sightings by groups of users carrying iMotes for 11 number of days. The iMotes devices were distributed among the doctoral students and faculty comprising a research group at the University of Cambridge Computer Laboratory.
- `Reality`: The MIT's Reality Mining experiment [14] conducted in 2004 was aimed at studying community dynamics. The study consist of one hundred Nokia 6600 smart phones having Bluetooth network connectivity and were distributed among the students and staff at MIT. The study generated data, collected by these 100 human carried devices over the course of nine months, include call logs, Bluetooth devices in proximity (i.e. contact logs), cell tower IDs, application usage, and phone status. The study resulted in the first mobile data set with rich personal behavior and interpersonal interactions.
- `Sassy`: This dataset [41] is an outcome of the experiments carried out by a group of participants (22 undergraduate students, 3 postgraduate students, and 2 members of staff) forming a mobile sensor network at University of St Andrews. The experimental set up was made of 27 T-mote invent devices

(mobile IEEE 802.15.4 sensors) carried by human users and Linux-based base stations for bridging the 802.15.4 sensors to the wired network. The participants were asked to carry the devices whenever possible over a period of 79 days. The data set contains information about the participants' encounter records as well as their social network data generated from Facebook data.

4.3 Experiment Setup

We have used Opportunistic Networking Environment (ONE) simulator [42] for simulation purpose. It is specifically designed for evaluation of DTN routing and application protocols. We have evaluated our simulation through trace-driven test with dataset from the `Reality` [39] and `Cambridge` [40] datasets, described in Sect. 4.2. `Reality` dataset spans for about six months. During the simulations for reality datasets 1000 messages were generated during 5–6 month period by randomly choosing the source and destination nodes. `Cambridge` dataset spans for about 11 days. During the simulations with `Cambridge` dataset, 1000 messages were generated after 9–11 day period by randomly choosing the source and destination nodes. Each simulation is repeated 10 times with different random seeds, and the average evaluation results are reported. The parameters for the simulations for the datasets are summarized in Table 2.

Table 2. Parameters for simulation setup

Dataset	Reality	Cambridge
Number nodes	97	36
Transmission range	10 m	10 m
Transmission speed	250 kBps	250 kBps
Message size	10–100 kb	10–100 kb
Time To Live (TTL)	1–12 days	2 min–24 h

4.4 Results and Discussion

We compare the performance of the proposed forwarding algorithm SAS with the state-of-the-art social-based DTN forwarding algorithms: SimBet [9] and BubbleRap [10]. We vary the parameter α to tune the effect of seasonality in SAS. We set β, the parameter of the Katz similarity measure to a typical value .05 [6].

Figures 2, 3, 4, 5, 6 and 7 summarize the comparative performance of SAS with BubbleRap and SimBet for the three evaluation metrics viz., "delivery ratio", "delivery cost" and "average latency". Further, to evaluate the effects of the seasonality component on the performance of SAS, we set three different values for the parameter α (i.e., $\alpha = 0$, $\alpha = 1$, $\alpha = 0.3$) and have obtained

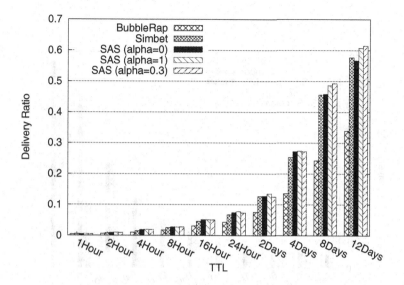

Fig. 2. Message delivery ratio Vs TTL in Reality data set

the simulation results for three different performing versions of SAS. Results for SAS (alpha = 0) measure the performance of SAS when the tie-strength does not contain the seasonality component, SAS (alpha = 1) represents SAS when the tie-strength is calculated with a high weighted value set for the seasonality component, and SAS (alpha = 0.3) represents SAS where the tie-strength is calculated with a low weighted seasonality component. Here we detail the results of these three performing versions of SAS with varying TTL values (as represented in Table 2). We also varied the utility parameter γ for SAS and SimBet, but found that $\gamma = 0.5$ gives best performance in general.

Figures 2 and 3 show that all the three different versions of SAS (i.e., SAS (alpha = 0), SAS (alpha = 1), SAS (alpha = 0.3)) outperform SimBet and BubbleRap significantly with respect to delivery ratio over the two traces (i.e., "reality" and "cambridge") and the TTL values. SAS(alpha = 0.3) outperforms SimBet by 6.50% and BubbleRap by 81.10% for TTL=12 Days in Reality trace. SAS(alpha = 0.3) outperforms SimBet by 5.41% and BubbleRap by 21.70% for TTL=12 Days in Cambridge trace. SAS (alpha = 1) always outperforms SAS (alpha = 0), which indicates the usefulness of the seasonality component of tie-strength. Again, it is also notable from Figs. 4 and 5 that all the performing versions of SAS (i.e., SAS (alpha = 0), SAS (alpha = 1), SAS (alpha = 0.3)) do not incur much delivery cost as compared to SimBet to achieve the gain in delivery ratio in Reality, and achieves better delivery cost than SimBet in Cambridge. From Figs. 6 and 7, it has been observed that for all of the forwarding techniques under consideration in the simulation study (except BubbleRap), average latency values are almost same for all the protocols.

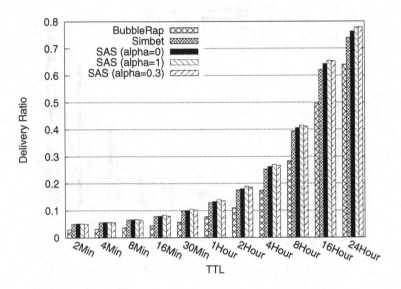

Fig. 3. Message delivery ratio Vs TTL in Cambridge data set

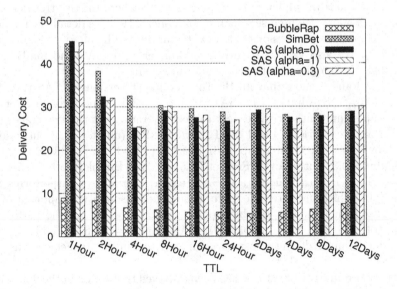

Fig. 4. Message overhead ratio Vs TTL in Reality data set

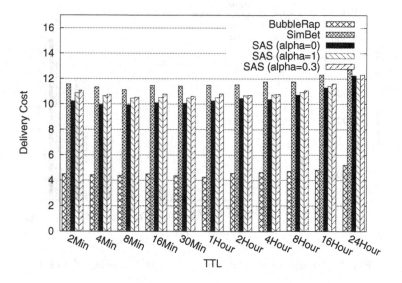

Fig. 5. Message overhead ratio Vs TTL in Cambridge data set

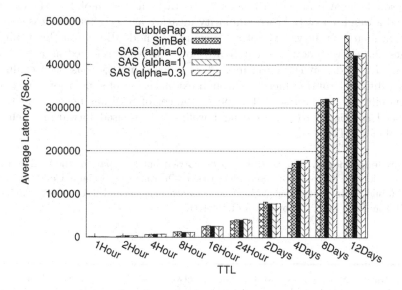

Fig. 6. Message average latency Vs TTL in Reality data set

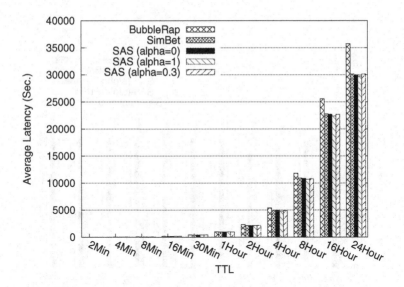

Fig. 7. Message average latency Vs TTL in Cambridge data set

5 Conclusion

This work has proposed SAS, a novel seasonality aware adaptive forwarding technique in social DTNs. The work is based on the observation of existence of seasonal behavioral pattern in node contacts in real mobility traces. SAS invoked a weighted Katz based similarity measure and ego-betweenness centrality to evaluate a utility value of an encountered node. Based on this utility, it decides the competency of a candidate node for being selected as a next hop message forwarder in DTN routing. The proposed method has been evaluated against different routing metrics through extensive set of simulation study with real mobility trace data sets. The performances of SAS has been found to get enhanced compared to the existing baseline social-based forwarding schemes available for DTNs.

Acknowledgements. The work has been carried out as a part of the Collaborative Research Scheme awarded for the project titled "On Ensuring Reliable Communication over Mobile Social Networks (MSNs)", of Assam Science and Technology University (ASTU) under TEQIP III program of MHRD.

References

1. Vastardis, N., Yang, K.: Mobile social networks: architectures, social properties, and key research challenges. IEEE Commun. Surv. Tutorials **15**(3), 1355–1371 (2013)
2. Hui, P., Chaintreau, A., Scott, J., Gass, R., Crowcroft, J., Diot, C.: Pocket switched networks and human mobility in conference environments. In: Proceedings of the

ACM SIGCOMM Workshop on Delay-tolerant Networking, pp. 244–251. ACM (2005)

3. Pereira, P.R., Casaca, A., Rodrigues, J.J., Soares, V.N., Triay, J., Cervelló-Pastor, C.: From delay-tolerant networks to vehicular delay-tolerant networks. IEEE Commun. Surv. Tutorials **14**(4), 1166–1182 (2012)

4. Conti, M., Giordano, S.: Mobile ad hoc networking: milestones, challenges, and new research directions. IEEE Commun. Mag. **52**(1), 85–96 (2014)

5. Zhu, Y., Xu, B., Shi, X., Wang, Y.: A survey of social-based routing in delay tolerant networks: positive and negative social effects. IEEE Commun. Surv. Tutorials **15**(1), 387–401 (2013)

6. Liben-Nowell, D., Kleinberg, J.: The link-prediction problem for social networks. In: Proceedings of the Conference on Information and Knowledge Management (CIKM 2003), pp. 556–559 (2003)

7. Freeman, L.C.: Centrality in social networks conceptual clarification. Soc. Netw. **1**(3), 215–239 (1978)

8. Fortunato, S.: Community detection in graphs. Phys. Rep. **486**(3), 75–174 (2010)

9. Daly, E.M., Haahr, M.: Social network analysis for routing in disconnected delay-tolerant MANETs. In: Proceedings of the 8th ACM International Symposium on Mobile Ad hoc Networking and Computing, pp. 32–40. ACM (2007)

10. Hui, P., Crowcroft, J., Yoneki, E.: Bubble rap: social-based forwarding in delay-tolerant networks. IEEE Trans. Mob. Comput. **10**(11), 1576–1589 (2011)

11. Freeman, L.C.: Centered graphs and the structure of ego networks. Math. Soc. Sci. **3**(3), 291–304 (1982)

12. Hui, P., Yoneki, E., Chan, S.Y., Crowcroft, J.: Distributed community detection in delay tolerant networks. In: Proceedings of 2nd ACM/IEEE International Workshop on Mobility in the Evolving Internet Architecture. ACM (2007)

13. Scott, J., Gass, R., Crowcroft, J., Hui, P., Diot, C., Chaintreau, A.: CRAWDAD dataset cambridge/haggle (v. 2006-09-15), September 2006. http://crawdad.org/cambridge/haggle/20060915

14. Eagle, N., Pentland, A.S.: Reality mining: sensing complex social systems. Pers. Ubiquit. Comput. **10**(4), 255–268 (2006)

15. Li, F., Wu, J.: LocalCom: a community-based epidemic forwarding scheme in disruption-tolerant networks. In: International Conference on Sensor, Mesh and Ad hoc Communications and Networks, pp. 1–9. IEEE (2009)

16. Zhou, T., Choudhury, R.R., Chakrabarty, K.: Diverse routing: exploiting social behavior for routing in delay-tolerant networks. In: International Conference on Computational Science and Engineering, vol. 4, pp. 1115–1122. IEEE (2009)

17. Wei, K., Guo, S., Zeng, D., Xu, K., Li, K.: Exploiting small world properties for message forwarding in delay tolerant networks. IEEE Trans. Comput. **64**(10), 2809–2818 (2015)

18. Bulut, E., Szymanski, B.K.: Exploiting friendship relations for efficient routing in mobile social networks. IEEE Trans. Parallel Distrib. Syst. **23**(12), 2254–2265 (2012)

19. Katz, L.: A new status index derived from sociometric analysis. Psychometrika **18**(1), 39–43 (1953)

20. Jones, E.P., Ward, P.A.: Routing strategies for delay-tolerant networks. ACM Comput. Commun. Rev. (CCR) (2006)

21. Vahdat, A., Becker, D., et al.: Epidemic routing for partially connected ad hoc networks. Technical report, Technical report CS-200006, Duke University (2000)

22. Lindgren, A., Doria, A., Schelén, O.: Probabilistic routing in intermittently connected networks. ACM SIGMOBILE Mob. Comput. Commun. Rev. **7**(3), 19–20 (2003)
23. Jain, S., Fall, K., Patra, R.: Routing in a delay tolerant network, vol. 34. ACM (2004)
24. Spyropoulos, T., Psounis, K., Raghavendra, C.S.: Spray and wait: an efficient routing scheme for intermittently connected mobile networks. In: Proceedings of the ACM SIGCOMM Workshop on Delay-tolerant Networking, pp. 252–259. ACM (2005)
25. Grossglauser, M., Tse, D.: Mobility increases the capacity of ad-hoc wireless networks. In: Proceedings of the INFOCOM, vol. 3, pp. 1360–1369. IEEE (2001)
26. Ciobanu, R.I., Reina, D., Dobre, C., Toral, S., Johnson, P.: JDER: a history-based forwarding scheme for delay tolerant networks using Jaccard distance and encountered ration. J. Netw. Comput. Appl. **40**, 279–291 (2014)
27. Ayub, Q., Rashid, S., Zahid, M.S.M., Abdullah, A.H.: Contact quality based forwarding strategy for delay tolerant network. J. Netw. Comput. Appl. **39**, 302–309 (2014)
28. Shin, K., Kim, K., Kim, S.: Traffic management strategy for delay-tolerant networks. J. Netw. Comput. Appl. **35**(6), 1762–1770 (2012)
29. Yuan, Q., Cardei, I., Wu, J.: An efficient prediction-based routing in disruption-tolerant networks. IEEE Trans. Parallel Distrib. Syst. **23**(1), 19–31 (2012)
30. Bulut, E., Wang, Z., Szymanski, B.K.: Cost-effective multiperiod spraying for routing in delay-tolerant networks. IEEE/ACM Trans. Netw. (TON) **18**(5), 1530–1543 (2010)
31. Niu, J., Wang, D., Atiquzzaman, M.: Copy limited flooding over opportunistic networks. J. Netw. Comput. Appl. **58**, 94–107 (2015)
32. Balasubramanian, A., Levine, B., Venkataramani, A.: DTN routing as a resource allocation problem. ACM SIGCOMM Comput. Commun. Rev. **37**(4), 373–384 (2007)
33. Wei, K., Liang, X., Xu, K.: A survey of social-aware routing protocols in delay tolerant networks: applications, taxonomy and design-related issues. IEEE Commun. Surv. Tutorials **16**(1), 556–578 (2014)
34. Hui, P., Crowcroft, J.: How small labels create big improvements. In: Proceedings of the International Conference on Pervasive Computing and Communications Workshops, pp. 65–70. IEEE (2007)
35. Wu, J., Wang, Y.: Social feature-based multi-path routing in delay tolerant networks. In: Proceedings of the INFOCOM, pp. 1368–1376. IEEE (2012)
36. Mei, A., Morabito, G., Santi, P., Stefa, J.: Social-aware stateless forwarding in pocket switched networks. In: Proceedings of the INFOCOM, pp. 251–255. IEEE (2011)
37. Granovetter, M.S.: The strength of weak ties. Am. J. Sociol. **78**(6), 1360–1380 (1973)
38. Marsden, P.V.: Egocentric and sociocentric measures of network centrality. Soc. Netw. **24**(4), 407–422 (2002)
39. Eagle, N., Pentland, A.S., Lazer, D.: Inferring friendship network structure by using mobile phone data. Natl. Acad. Sci. **106**(36), 15274–15278 (2009)
40. Scott, J., Gass, R., Crowcroft, J., Hui, P., Diot, C., Chaintreau, A.: Crawdad dataset Cambridge/haggle (v. 2006-09-15). CRAWDAD: Wireless Network data archive (2006)

41. Bigwood, G., Henderson, T., Rehunathan, D., Bateman, M., Bhatti, S.: CRAW-DAD dataset st_andrews/sassy (v. 2011–06-03), June 2011. http://crawdad.org/st_andrews/sassy/20110603/mobile
42. Keränen, A., Ott, J., Kärkkäinen, T.: The ONE simulator for DTN protocol evaluation. In: Proceedings of the 2nd International Conference on Simulation Tools and Techniques, (Institute for Computer Sciences, Social-Informatics and Telecommunications Engineering) (2009)

DAMW: Double Auction Multi-winner Framework for Spectrum Allocation in Cognitive Radio Networks

Monisha Devi$^{(\boxtimes)}$, Nityananda Sarma, and Sanjib K. Deka

Department of Computer Science and Engineering, Tezpur University,
Tezpur 784028, Assam, India
mnshdevi@gmail.com, {nitya,sdeka}@tezu.ernet.in

Abstract. Under-utilization of wireless spectrum by the licensed owners creates spectrum holes which can be opportunistically exploited by secondary users (SUs). By incorporating dynamic spectrum access techniques, Cognitive Radio (CR) emerges as a novel technology which facilitates redistribution of the spectrum holes dynamically. In this context, this paper proposes a double auction framework for CR networks which addresses the channel allocation problem to boost the spectrum utilization efficiency. Multi-winner allocation relates to the condition where a common channel can be utilized by multiple non-interfering SUs which induces spectrum reuse. However, a single SU obtains at most one channel. To avoid disturbances during data transmission, availability time of a channel plays a key role. In this paper, bid submission from SUs rely on channel availability time, and to lease the idle channels, licensed users specify certain ask values. The proposed double auction mechanism develops winner determination and pricing strategies which are proved to be truthful and significantly improves the usage of the radio spectrum. Network simulations validate the improved performance of the proposed auction model compared to the McAfee auction.

Keywords: Cognitive radio · Dynamic spectrum access · Double auction · Spectrum opportunities · Secondary user · Primary user

1 Introduction

Ongoing growth in the telecommunication sector drastically increases the demand for radio spectrum. Simultaneously on the other side, Federal Communications Commission (FCC) [1] declares that chunks of licensed spectrum distributed amongst the legitimate owners are left unused in different geographical locations as well as at different times. Hence, both the under-utilization and over-utilization problems collectively results in an inefficient utilization of the radio spectrum. To address this imbalance in the use of radio resource, a novel technology called Cognitive Radio (CR) [2,3] was introduced which functions

© Springer Nature Switzerland AG 2020
S. S. Rautaray et al. (Eds.): I4CS 2020, CCIS 1139, pp. 266–281, 2020.
https://doi.org/10.1007/978-3-030-37484-6_15

using the concept of dynamic spectrum access (DSA) [4,5]. CR enables opportunistic spectrum access among the unlicensed users (or secondary users) where it initially senses for the vacant licensed bands (channels), and without causing harmful interference to the licensed users (or primary users), vacant channels are exploited dynamically. Spectrum allocation [2,6] is a key feature in CR which designs allocation mechanisms for fair and efficient distribution of the unused channels. Different allocation models [7,8] have been deployed with certain predefined network constraints to achieve some suitable allocation strategy. One of the familiar method for redistribution of the spectrum is to use auction as the allocation model.

Auction [9] is the process of leasing certain items by the sellers on receiving appropriate bids from the buyers. It provides a fair and effective allocation where there is an equal possibility of every bidder to win. Auction formulation for a CR network (CRN) takes the secondary users (SUs) as bidders (or buyers) who are willing to obtain the auctioned item, that is, the idle channels which remain unused by the primary users (PUs). Two different auction scenarios can be formulated, viz., single-sided auction and double-sided auction. In a single-sided auction [10–12], it is the auctioneer who sells the item without the participation of the sellers. As such, no financial profit is earned by the sellers of the items. But, a more practical scenario is where along with bidders, sellers also compete amongst them to sell their resources. This defines a double-sided auction where buyers submit bid values, sellers submit ask values and the auctioneer decides the clearing price based on the received bids and asks. Also, sellers take the opportunity of obtaining some monetary gain. To design a double-sided auction in CRN, PUs behave as sellers and the primary owner (primary base station) act as the auctioneer. Market manipulation is a common problem in any auction model. This requires designing of a truthful auction mechanism where utility of the bidder (or the seller) cannot improve on submitting an untruthful bid value (or ask value). This appears to be one of the challenging problems in developing the auction model. Another challenging problem can be to incorporate spectrum reusability in the model. Since spectrum is different from conventional auctioned items, so, non-interfering SUs can be allowed to simultaneously access a common channel which thereby helps to enhance the overall spectrum utilization. In CRN, whenever a PU wants to return back to its channel, the SU who has been utilizing the channel for its data transmission has to vacant the channel. Such a situation may interrupt SU's transmission. So, there arises the need of channel availability time. If an SU gets a channel such that its channel availability time is less than the time duration for which the SU requires the channel, then transmission of the SU gets disturbed. Existing research works on double auction have not considered the channel availability time in their models. Therefore, this appears to be an important concern for future works concentrating on spectrum allocation in CRN. Another concern can be a situation where an SU cannot sense all the channels available for auction. This results in dynamics in spectrum opportunities (SOPs) in the network which needs to be tackled during channel allocation. Spectrum trading in 5G network [13] uses auction to rationalize the allocation process. 5G integrated with CR network can help to achieve higher capacity along with flexibility in its usage. Hence, motivated by these observations, this paper develops a double auction framework which facilitates multi-winner allocation.

In this paper, we propose a Double Auction Multi-Winner (DAMW) framework which achieves effective allocation of the radio spectrum in CRN. Multi-winner characteristic allows one channel to be assigned to more than one non-interfering SUs which in turn increases spectrum utilization and seller's revenue. However, since each SU can acquire only a single channel, so availability time of the auctioned channels should be studied before deciding the valuation of the channels. In the seller side, every PU plans to lease more than one channel if available, and accordingly determines the ask values. Subsequently, SUs in the buyer side offer appropriate bid values to get hold of the channel required for their transmission. Finally, the auctioneer figures out the winner determination and pricing rules for channel allocation. DAMW proves to be truthful to both SUs and PUs and its evaluation depicts the performance improvement when compared with the general McAfee auction.

The rest of the paper is organized as follows. Section 2 carries out a brief study on double-sided auction-based approaches in CRN. Section 3 discusses the proposed DAMW model which includes the system model, the auction mechanism and the auction properties. Performance evaluation is described in Sect. 4. Finally, Sect. 5 concludes the paper.

2 Related Works

Double-sided auction has been applied by the researchers in CRN to achieve different network objectives. PUs possessing the vacant channels pursue to earn some financial profit by leasing the channels amongst SUs who are competing to get a channel. In [14], authors propose the McAfee auction which is considered to be the primary double-auction model for single-channel allocation. Zhou et al. designed TRUST in [15] which is the first truthful double auction with spectrum reuse. Every SU's bid specifies the value for the channel and the demand showing number of channels required by the SU. On the other side, a PU auctions only a single unused channel by submitting its ask value. TRUST determines the winning buyers and sellers and the payment strategy by extending the McAfee auction. Another double auction mechanism enabling spectrum reuse is discussed in [16], where a bid-dependent algorithm results in the formation of non-conflicting buyer groups. Each PU can sell more than one channel with single-channel allocation amongst the SUs. To guarantee a strategyproof mechanism, bid-independent payment applies to both sellers and buyers. TAHES in [17] allows both buyers and sellers to compete amongst themselves by formulating a single-round multi-item double auction. In this approach, each SU is constrained to use a single channel and every PU can auction only one channel from its pool of unused channels. TAHES ensures truthfulness and enables spatial heterogeneity in the designed model. In [18], the double auction mechanism aims at profit maximization. But in CRN, we mainly concentrate on enhancing the spectrum utilization across the network. Authors in [18] allow a channel to be used by multiple users where the interference relationship between the users is modeled using Signal to Interference plus Noise Ratio (SINR) constraints. Dong et al. in [19] proposed a spectrum allocation approach where both buyer side and seller side are decoupled and winner determination is performed separately. Sub graphs are constructed in the buyer side whose results are merged and subsequently in the seller side, every seller leases a single channel. An auction model where PUs share the auctioned channels along with SUs is formulated in [20]. Using the concept of interference temperature, transmission of SUs, who are assigned a channel, is kept below a threshold value so that the PU owing the channel can use it without interfering with the SUs. Every PU auctions a single channel while incorporating spectrum reusability in the model. In [21], TAMES designed an auction mechanism which supports spectrum heterogeneity across the network. Bid-dependent buyer groups formulated in TAMES enabled spectrum reuse while achieving the economic properties for the auction model. Similarly, PreDA in [22] takes into account the SINR values to build the preference list according to which SUs submit bids for the channels auctioned by the PUs. Virtual group formation algorithm formulates spectrum reuse which allows one channel to be assigned to all members of a particular group.

Although auction-based models have been applied in many spectrum allocation problems in CRN, but they have not tackled certain network issues arising in CRN. Dynamics in SOPs and variation in availability time of the channels are two important CR network challenges. Existing double-auction models have not addressed any of the two challenge. In this paper, we restrict each SU to obtain a single channel and this necessitates every SU to obtain the availability time of the channels offered for auction. Also, due to different SU capabilities [23], the set of unused channels may differ in different SUs. DAMW encompasses the network concerns of CRN and aims to achieve an enhanced spectrum utilization efficiency in the network.

3   Double Auction for Spectrum Allocation

This section discusses the proposed DAMW mechanism by elaborately describing the system model, the double auction mechanism consisting of three different algorithms for bidder group formation, group bid computation and winner determination and the auction properties.

3.1   System Model

We consider a cognitive radio network where N number of SUs (bidders), $\mathcal{N} = \{1, 2, 3, ..., N\}$, compete for the spectrum which is offered for auction by M number of PUs (sellers), $\mathcal{M} = \{1, 2, 3, ..., M\}$ of the primary network. The responsibility of the auctioneer is taken by the primary owner (PO) who decides a clearing price to determine the winner SUs and PUs. Each PU can sell more than one channel left unused. As such, if k_q represents the number of channels temporarily available for use from PU q, then total number of channels available for the auction process are $K_{(c)} = \sum_{q=1}^{M} k_q$. So, the set of channels, $\mathcal{K}$, can be shown as follows.

$$\mathcal{K} = \{\underbrace{1, ..., k_1}_{1^{st}\ \text{PU}}, \underbrace{(k_1 + 1), ..., (k_1 + k_2)}_{2^{nd}\ \text{PU}}, ..., \underbrace{((k_1 + ... + k_{M-1}) + 1), ..., (k_1 + ... + k_M)}_{M^{th}\ \text{PU}}$$

We assume that $N > K_{(c)}$. Interference between two SUs arise if they are within the interference range of each other. To show interfering SUs, a conflict graph can be used where vertices are the SUs and an edge exists between two vertices if the SUs corresponding to the vertices interfere. Moreover, to represent the channel set available to an SU, a channel availability matrix, $X = \{x_{ij} | x_{ij} \in \{0, 1\}\}_{N \times K_{(c)}}$, is maintained. When SU i senses a channel $j \in \mathcal{K}$, then $x_{ij} = 1$ implying that SU i can look to access the channel j. Otherwise, $x_{ij} = 0$ if channel j is inaccessible to SU i. In this auction model, all the $K_{(c)}$ channels are considered to be homogeneous in their quality. This allows an SU to submit a similar bid value for all its available channels. Bid submission from an SU also depends on the channel availability time and channel requirement time. Taking $T_{A(j)}$ as the availability time of channel j and $T_{R(ij)}$ as the channel requirement time of SU i over channel j, SU i decides a valuation for the channel j only if $T_{A(j)}$ is greater than $T_{R(ij)}$. Every SU computes $T_{A(j)}$ during its sensing phase [24]. For a channel j, $T_{A(j)}$ is approximately same for all the SUs to which channel j is available. Thereafter, an SU i computes its $T_{R(ij)}$ for channel j by considering its transmission time and propagation delay. Now, on starting the auction, a PU decides a valuation for its idle channels. Valuation from a PU q, given as $v_q^{(s)}$, will be same for all the k_q channels since they are homogeneous. To compete amongst the PUs in the network, the PU q will submit its ask value, $b_q^{(s)}$, to the auctioneer as shown in Eq. 1.

$$b_q^{(s)} = v_q^{(s)}, \forall q \in \mathcal{M} \tag{1}$$

On receiving the ask values at PO, an ask vector, $B^{(s)}$, gets formed as follows:

$$B^{(s)} = \{\underbrace{b_1^{(s)}, ..., b_1^{(s)}}_{k_1}, ..., \underbrace{b_q^{(s)}, ..., b_q^{(s)}}_{k_q}, ..., \underbrace{b_M^{(s)}, ..., b_M^{(s)}}_{k_M}\}$$

Correspondingly, each SU i decides a valuation, $v_{ji}^{(b)}$, for the channel $j \in \mathcal{K}$ available at the SU. And the bid submitted by SU i for channel j, $b_{ji}^{(b)}$, to the PO is shown in Eq. 2.

$$b_{ji}^{(b)} = \begin{cases} v_{ji}^{(b)} & \text{if } (x_{ij} = 1) \wedge (T_{A(j)} \geq T_{R(ij)}) \\ 0 & \text{otherwise} \end{cases} \tag{2}$$

This constructs a bid vector, $B_j^{(b)}$, for the channel j where $B_j^{(b)} = \{b_{j1}^{(b)}, b_{j2}^{(b)}, ..., b_{jN}^{(b)}\}$. Similarly, for all available channels, we get $B_1^{(b)}$, $B_2^{(b)}$, ...,

$B_{K_{(c)}}^{(b)}$. Once the bids and asks are collected at the PO, it executes its winner determination strategy to find the winning SUs and PUs. Thereafter, the pricing strategy computes the clearing prices for both SUs and PUs. On wining a channel, an SU i pays a price, $p_i^{(b)}$, to the auctioneer. All the payments gathered from the SUs are stored in a bidder payment vector, $P^{(b)} = \{p_1^{(b)}, p_2^{(b)}, ..., p_N^{(b)}\}$. Then, to show the winning SUs, we organize them in an allocation matrix, $A = \{a_{ij} | a_{ij} \in \{0,1\}\}_{N \times K_{(c)}}$, where $a_{ij} = 1$ if channel j is leased to SU i. Otherwise, $a_{ij} = 0$, is SU i remains unallocated. From the allocation constraint, this model considers that one channel can be assigned to more than one noninterfering SUs at a time, but one SU can acquire at most one channel at a time. Hence, matrix A is subjected to the condition, $\sum_{j=1}^{M} a_{ij} \leq 1, \forall i \in \mathcal{N}$. Utility of SU i, $u_i^{(b)}$, on obtaining a channel j takes the valuation of the SU, $v_{ji}^{(b)}$, minus his payment on winning the channel, $p_i^{(b)}$, as shown in Eq. 3.

$$u_i^{(b)} = \begin{cases} v_{ji}^{(b)} - p_i^{(b)} & \text{if } a_{ij} = 1 \\ 0 & \text{otherwise} \end{cases} \tag{3}$$

Subsequently on the seller side, every PU q maintains a winner vector, W_q, to hold the number of winning SUs for each channel of PU q. $W_q = \{w_{q1}, ..., w_{qj}, ..., w_{qk_q}\}$, where $w_{qj} = m$ ($0 \leq m \leq N$) implies that the jth channel of PU q is assigned to m number of non-interfering SUs. Thereafter, to get the number of channels assigned from PU q, given as $\mathcal{C}_q$, we take the count of non-zero entries in W_q. To represent the payment earned by a PU q, a seller payment vector, $P_q^{(s)}$, is formed at each PU. $P_q^{(s)} = \{p_{q1}^{(s)}, ..., p_{qj}^{(s)}, ..., p_{qk_q}^{(s)}\}$, where $p_{qj}^{(s)}$ is the payment collected from the jth channel of PU q when the channel is assigned to m number of SUs as per $w_{qj} = m$. Accordingly, the utility of PU q, $u_q^{(s)}$, is the total payment earned by selling his channels minus his aggregated valuation for the assigned channels, as shown in Eq. 4.

$$u_q^{(s)} = \begin{cases} \sum_{j=1}^{k_q} p_{qj}^{(s)} - v_q^{(s)}.\mathcal{C}_q & \text{if } \sum_{j=1}^{k_q} w_{qj} \neq 0 \\ 0 & \text{otherwise} \end{cases} \tag{4}$$

Figure 1 shows a diagrammatic representation of the proposed DAMW model.

3.2 Auction Mechanism

The DAMW framework designed for spectrum allocation in CRN consists of three different phases to complete the allocation process and together facilitates truthfulness and individual rationality on both buyer side and seller side.

In the first phase, a bidder group formation algorithm (Algorithm 1) is developed to form groups of non-interfering SUs. $G = \{g_1, g_2, ..., g_Z\}$ represents the set of bidder groups where Z is the total number of groups formed. Every member in a group g_h can be assigned a common channel which enables spectrum reuse in the network. Initially, the conflict graph constructed based on the physical distance between SUs is taken as input for the Algorithm 1. Taking every

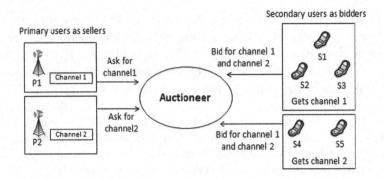

Fig. 1. Diagrammatic representation of DAMW model in CRN

SU one-by-one, a set $\mathcal{L} \subseteq \mathcal{N}$ is created everytime by considering the interference relationship of the SUs included in $\mathcal{L}$. Thereafter, the set $\mathcal{L}$ is included in G if a similar set of SUs does not exist in G. The bidder group formation algorithm is bid-independent and is carried out once during the auction process.

The next phase is to determine a bid value for each group which is further used in the winner determination process. On auctioning a channel $j \in \mathcal{K}$ in Algorithm 2, every group in G computes a group bid. We take a group g_h and look into its members in the group. If there exists any SU i such that, channel j is unavailable at SU i, then SU i is removed from g_h. Also, if $T_{A(j)}$ is less than $T_{R(ij)}$, SU i is removed from g_h. While restricting to the allocation constraint, if we find that SU i has already acquired a channel, we remove SU i from g_h. Then, for the remaining SUs present in g_h, the group bid, λ_h, is obtained and the SU with minimum bid in g_h is removed to form the group g'_h. This is performed to guarantee a truthful auction process in the model. If more than one minimum bid appears in a group, one of the bid is picked randomly. Likewise, on performing these operations for all groups in G, we get the group set G'_j for channel j which will be used in the next phase.

Finally, to decide the winners, PO executes the winner determination algorithm (Algorithm 3). On auctioning a channel j, we obtain the set G'_j using Algorithm 2 and gather the group bid for each group of G'_j in Δ_j. The group bids in Δ_j are sorted in descending order to get Δ'_j where $\mathrm{TOP}(\Delta'_j)$ implies the highest group bid. Now, if PU q owns the channel j and $b_q^{(s)} \leq \mathrm{TOP}(\Delta'_j)$, then the group of SUs having the group bid $\mathrm{TOP}(\Delta'_j)$ are assigned the channel j. Similarly, this process is repeated for all the channels.

On completing the allocation process, winner SUs pay a price to the auctioneer and winner PUs earn a benefit from the auctioneer. When a group g'_h wins a channel j, it pays the group bid, λ_h, to the PO. As such, for each SU $i \in g'_h$, payment of SU i, $p_i^{(b)}$, is shown in Eq. 5.

$$p_i^{(b)} = \min\{b_{jy}^{(b)} | y \in g_h\} \tag{5}$$

Algorithm 1. Bidder Group Formation Algorithm

Input: Conflict graph constructed based on interference distance of SUs
Output: Bidder group set $G = \{g_1, g_2, ..., g_Z\}$ where Z is number of groups formed
1: $G = \phi$
2: **for** $i \leftarrow 1$ **to** N **do**
3:    $\mathcal{L} = \phi$
4:    Get the SU i node in the graph and insert i into $\mathcal{L}$
5:    **for** $k \leftarrow 1$ **to** N **do**
6:       **if** $k \neq i$, **then**
7:          **if** k is not a neighbor of i, **then**
8:             **if** $\nexists y \in \mathcal{L}$, $y \neq i$, s.t. y is a neighbor of k, **then**
9:                Insert k into $\mathcal{L}$
10:            **else**
11:               $k = k + 1$
12:            **end if**
13:         **end if**
14:      **end if**
15:   **end for**
16:   **if** $\nexists g_h \in G$ s.t., $\mathcal{L} = g_h$, **then**
17:      Insert group $\mathcal{L}$ into G
18:   **else**
19:      Group $\mathcal{L}$ not included in G
20:   **end if**
21: **end for**

For the seller side, a PU q on selling his j^{th} channel to a group g'_h gets a payment which is equal to the group bid. That is, $p_{qj}^{(s)} = \lambda_h$. Hence, the proposed double auction model DAMW presents a spectrum allocation mechanism by incorporating different CR network constraints which can achieve an improve spectrum utilization along with spectrum reuse across the network.

3.3 Auction Properties

To avoid any kind of market manipulation, DAMW needs to satisfy two economic properties, viz. individual rationality and truthfulness.

Definition 1. *Individual Rationality: A double auction is individually rational if every winning bidder (SU) pays a price which is less than its valuation and every winning seller (PU) earns a price which is greater than its valuation. This implies that both the bidder and seller retains a non-negative utility.*

Definition 2. *Truthfulness: A double auction is truthful if no bidder (SU) or seller (PU) can improve its utility by submitting an untruthful bid value or ask value, no matter how other players bid in the game.*

Theorem 1. *DAMW is individually rational.*

Algorithm 2. Group Bid Computation Algorithm

Input: Bidder group set G on auctioning channel j
Output: Group bid, λ_h, for each group g_h and modified group set G'_j for channel j

1: **for** $h \leftarrow 1$ **to** Z **do**
2:    **for** $d \leftarrow 1$ **to** $|g_h|$ **do**
3:       Take SU $k = g_h\{d\}$
4:       **if** $(b_{jk}^{(b)} = 0) \vee (\sum_{j=1}^{M} a_{kj} = 1)$, **then**
5:          Remove SU k from g_h
6:       **end if**
7:    **end for**
8:    Group bid, $\lambda_h = \min\{b_{jy}^{(b)} | y \in g_h\}.(|g_h| - 1)$
9:    $g'_h = g_h - \{y\}$ where SU y is the minimum bid SU in g_h
10:   **if** g'_h is not empty, **then**
11:      Insert g'_h having group bid λ_h into $G'j$
12:   **end if**
13: **end for**

Proof. According to the definition of individual rationality, an SU i and a PU q should attain an utility $u_i^{(b)} \geq 0$ and $u_q^{(s)} \geq 0$ respectively.

As per the pricing strategy (Eq. 5), a winner SU i belonging to a group g'_h pays a price which is the bid value of an SU y who submitted the lowest bid in the group g_h and is removed from g_h. Every SU in the group g'_h (g'_h is obtained by removing SU y from g_h) has a valuation which is greater than or equal to the valuation of SU y. As such, SU $i \in g'_h$ on winning a channel j pays $p_i^b \leq v_{ji}^{(b)}$ which in turn results in a non-negative utility $u_i^{(b)} \geq 0$ (Eq. 3).

A PU q on selling its channel j ($1 \leq j \leq k_q$) to a group g'_h earns a payment equal to the group bid of g'_h. According to Algorithm 3, a PU leases its channel only when the group bid is greater than or equal to the ask value of the PU. As such, for PU q, payment earned $p_{qj}^{(s)} \geq v_q^{(s)}$. This is performed for every assigned channel of PU q which therefore gives the utility $u_q^{(s)} \geq 0$. ∎

Lemma 1. *On submitting a bid value $b_{ji}^{(b)}$, if SU i wins the channel j, then SU i also wins the channel when it bids $b_{ji}'^{(b)} > b_{ji}^{(b)}$.*

Proof. When an SU $i \in g'_h$ wins a channel j, it depends on the group bid which is the bid value of the lowest bidding SU y in g_h. Also SU y is removed from g_h and it cannot win the channel j. As such, even on submitting a bid value $b_{ji}'^{(b)} > b_{ji}^{(b)}$, SU i wins channel j since group bid remains unaffected. ∎

Lemma 2. *On submitting an ask value $b_q^{(s)}$, if PU q wins and sells a channel, then PU q also wins and sells the channel when it submits $b_q'^{(s)} < b_q^{(s)}$.*

Proof. With an ask value $b_q^{(s)}$, PU q sells a channel when the winning group has a group bid greater than or equal to $b_q^{(s)}$. So, on submitting an ask value $b_q'^{(s)} < b_q^{(s)}$, PU q still can sell the channel. ∎

Algorithm 3. Winner Determination Algorithm

Input: Bidder group set G

Output: Allocation matrix A and winner vector, W_q, of PU q, $\forall q \in \mathcal{M}$

1: $A = \{0\}_{N \times M}$ and $W_q = \{0\}_{1 \times k_q}$, $\forall q \in \mathcal{M}$
2: **for** $j \leftarrow 1$ **to** $K_{(c)}$ **do**
3:     *Group Bid Computation()* for channel j gives $G'_j = \{g'_1, g'_2, ..., g'_{Z'}\}$ where $Z' \leq Z$
        and the group bids stored in $\Delta_j = \{\lambda_1, \lambda_2, ..., \lambda_{Z'}\}$
4:     Sort Δ_j in descending order and store in Δ'_j
5:     **if** $b_q^{(s)} \leq TOP(\Delta'_j)$, where j^{th} channel in $\mathcal{K}$ comes from PU q, **then**
6:         $\forall i \in g'_h$, s.t. $\lambda_h = TOP(\Delta'_j)$, channel j is assigned to SU i. $a_{ij} = 1$ and
            $w_{qy} = |g'_h|$ where j^{th} channel in $\mathcal{K}$ is the yth channel of PU q
7:     **else**
8:         Channel j remains unallocated
9:     **end if**
10: **end for**

Theorem 2. *DAMW is truthful.*

Proof. Proof for truthfulness is carried out separately for both buyer side and seller side. In the buyer side, let $u_i^{(b)}$ and $u_i'^{(b)}$ be the utility obtained on bidding $v_{ji}^{(b)}$ and $b_{ji}^{(b)} \neq v_{ji}^{(b)}$ respectively by an SU i for channel j. An auction is truthful is $u_i^{(b)} \geq u_i'^{(b)}$.

Case I: $b_{ji}^{(b)} > v_{ji}^{(b)}$

(1) When SU i loses by bidding both $v_{ji}^{(b)}$ and $b_{ji}^{(b)}$, then according to Eq. 3, $u_i^{(b)} = u_i'^{(b)} = 0$.

(2) When SU i loses by bidding $v_{ji}^{(b)}$ but wins when it bids $b_{ji}^{(b)}$, then $u_i^{(b)} = 0$. SU i loses the game when it is the lowest bid SU in the winning group and it gets eliminated from the group. On bidding $b_{ji}^{(b)} > v_{ji}^{(b)}$, SU i wins when $b_{ji}^{(b)}$ is greater than or equal to the second lowest bid in the group. This implies that the payment $p_i'^{(b)}$ for $b_{ji}^{(b)}$ is the second lowest bid. So, $p_i'^{(b)} \geq v_{ji}^{(b)}$ which gives $u_i'^{(b)} \leq 0$.

(3) When SU i loses by bidding $b_{ji}^{(b)}$ but wins when it bids $v_{ji}^{(b)}$, then this cannot hold as per Lemma 1.

(4) When SU i wins by bidding both $v_{ji}^{(b)}$ and $b_{ji}^{(b)}$, then $u_i^{(b)} = u_i'^{(b)}$. This is because, on winning the channel, price paid is the lowest bid value from the group which is independent of any wining SU's bid value. As such, if $p_i^{(b)}$ and $p_i'^{(b)}$ are payment for $v_{ji}^{(b)}$ and $b_{ji}^{(b)}$ respectively, then $p_i'^{(b)} = p_i^{(b)}$ which implies $u_i'^{(b)} = u_i^{(b)}$.

Case II: $b_{ji}^{(b)} < v_{ji}^{(b)}$

(1) When SU i loses by bidding both $v_{ji}^{(b)}$ and $b_{ji}^{(b)}$, then, $u_i^{(b)} = u_i'^{(b)} = 0$.

(2) When SU i loses by bidding $v_{ji}^{(b)}$ but wins when it bids $b_{ji}^{(b)}$, then this cannot hold as per Lemma 1.

(3) When SU i wins by bidding $v_{ji}^{(b)}$ but loses when it bids $b_{ji}^{(b)}$, then $u_i'^{(b)} = 0$. However, on winning with $v_{ji}^{(b)}$, we obtain utility $u_i^{(b)} \geq 0$ as per Theorem 1.

(4) When SU i wins by bidding both $v_{ji}^{(b)}$ and $b_{ji}^{(b)}$, then $u_i^{(b)} = u_i'^{(b)}$. Similar reason as stated in Case I.

In the seller side, let $u_q^{(s)}$ and $u_q'^{(s)}$ be the utility obtained by a PU q on submitting its ask $v_q^{(s)}$ and $b_q^{(s)} \neq v_q^{(s)}$ respectively for its channel j ($1 \leq j \leq k_q$). We take $\mathcal{C}_q = 1$ for the utility. An auction is truthful is $u_q^{(s)} \geq u_q'^{(s)}$.

Case I: $b_q^{(s)} > v_q^{(s)}$

(1) When PU q cannot sell the channel by submitting both the ask values $v_q^{(s)}$ and $b_q^{(s)}$, then according to Eq. 4, $u_q^{(s)} = u_q'^{(s)} = 0$.

(2) When PU q wins by submitting the ask $b_q^{(s)}$ but loses when it submits $v_q^{(s)}$, then this cannot hold as per Lemma 2.

(3) When PU q wins by submitting the ask $v_q^{(s)}$ but loses when it submits $b_q^{(s)}$, then $u_q'^{(s)} = 0$. However, on winning with $v_q^{(s)}$, we obtain utility $u_q^{(s)} \geq 0$ as per Theorem 1.

(4) When PU q wins by submitting both the ask values $v_q^{(s)}$ and $b_q^{(s)}$, then $u_q^{(s)} = u_q'^{(s)}$. This is because, the payment earned by PU q is the group bid of the winner group. As such, payment is independent of the ask value and $p_{qj}^{(s)} = p_{qj}'^{(s)}$ where $p_{qj}^{(s)}$ and $p_{qj}'^{(s)}$ are payments for $v_q^{(s)}$ and $b_q^{(s)}$ respectively. Hence, $u_q^{(s)} = u_q'^{(s)}$.

Case II: $b_q^{(s)} < v_q^{(s)}$

(1) When PU q cannot sell the channel by submitting both the ask values $v_q^{(s)}$ and $b_q^{(s)}$, then $u_q^{(s)} = u_q'^{(s)} = 0$.

(2) When PU q wins by submitting the ask $b_q^{(s)}$ but loses when it submits $v_q^{(s)}$, then $u_q^{(s)} = 0$. On submitting $v_q^{(s)}$ PU q loses when the highest group bid is less than $v_q^{(s)}$. Now, for $b_q^{(s)}$ to win, $b_q^{(s)}$ should be less than or equal to the group bid. So, the payment $p_{qj}'^{(s)}$ for the ask $b_q^{(s)}$ is the winning group bid and $p_{qj}'^{(s)} < v_q^{(s)}$ which gives $u_q'^{(s)} < 0$.

(3) When PU q wins by submitting the ask $v_q^{(s)}$ but loses when it submits $b_q^{(s)}$, then this cannot hold as per Lemma 2.

(4) When PU q wins by submitting both the ask values $v_q^{(s)}$ and $b_q^{(s)}$, then $u_q^{(s)} = u_q'^{(s)}$. Similar reason as stated in Case I.

Therefore, this proves that an untruthful bid value or ask value cannot improve the utility of the bidder or the seller. ∎

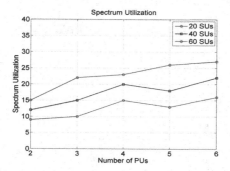

Fig. 2. Spectrum utilization of different sets of SUs when number of PUs are varied

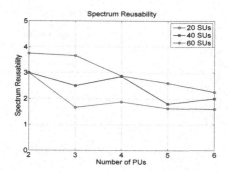

Fig. 3. Spectrum reusability of different sets of SUs when number of PUs are varied

4 Performance Evaluation

In this section, we study the network simulations to show the performance of DAMW in a CR environment. PUs and SUs acting as seller and buyer respectively are randomly distributed in an area of size 600 m × 600 m. Multiple channels can be available at every PU depending upon their usage. Here, it considers that every PU wants to auction 2 channels each. To facilitate spectrum reuse, interference among SUs is shaped by taking the physical distance between the SUs. MATLAB based simulation evaluates the proposed model and all the results obtained are averaged over 500 rounds. The performance metrics considered for the evaluation process are spectrum utilization, spectrum reusability and channel allocation ratio as discussed below.

Spectrum utilization: It is the number of SUs who won the channels offered for auction. Given as, $\sum_{q=1}^{M} \sum_{j=1}^{k_j} w_{qj}$

Spectrum reusability: It is the ratio of number of winner SUs to the number of allocated channels. Given as, $\frac{\sum_{q=1}^{M} \sum_{j=1}^{k_j} w_{qj}}{\sum_{q=1}^{M} \mathcal{C}_q}$

Channel allocation ratio: It is the ratio of number of channels assigned to the SUs to the total number of channels given away by the PUs. Given as, $\frac{\sum_{q=1}^{M} \mathcal{C}_q}{K_{(c)}}$

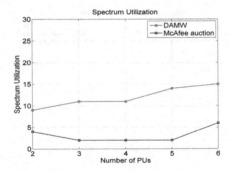

Fig. 4. Spectrum utilization of DAMW and McAfee with respect to number of PUs

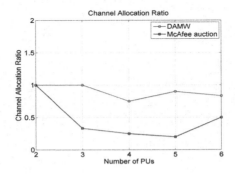

Fig. 5. Channel allocation ratio of DAMW and McAfee with respect to number of PUs

In Figs. 2 and 3, the network scenario consist of three sets of SUs where the number of SUs is varied as 20, 40 and 60 respectively. Likewise, the number of PUs vary from 2 to 6, where it is considered that each PU holds 2 channels to lease. From Fig. 2, it can be observed that with the increase in number of PUs for an SU set, spectrum utilization mostly increases since more channels are offered amongst the SUs. But, depending on the CR network constraints, if channels remain unassigned, then even on increasing the count of channels, the spectrum utilization may not show a rise. Similarly, on increasing the number of SUs for a PU set, we can obtain an improved spectrum utilization. Since this model allows spectrum reuse, so with increase in SUs, more number of SUs are capable of acquiring a channel to carry out their transmission. This in turn helps to make a good use of the unused radio spectrum. In Fig. 3, reusability of the spectrum is depicted with changing number of SUs for different PU sets. With increase in number of channels (i.e. the PUs) for an SU set, the number of winning SUs may show a moderate increase due to network constraints. This can result in a reduced spectrum utilization. But, with increase in number of SUs for a PU set, the utilization increases.

In Figs. 4 and 5, DAMW is compared with the general McAfee auction [14] when number of PUs are varied from 2 to 6 keeping number of SUs fixed at 40.

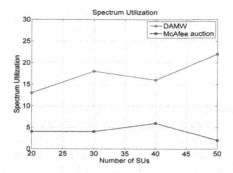

Fig. 6. Spectrum utilization of DAMW and McAfee with respect to number of SUs

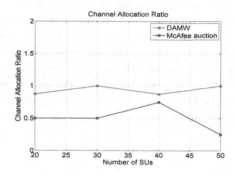

Fig. 7. Channel allocation ratio of DAMW and McAfee with respect to number of SUs

In McAfee auction, it allows a single channel allocation by sorting the ask values in ascending order and bid values in descending order to reach a point where from it decides the winning sellers and buyers. All channels may not get allocated even when the network constraints are not incorporated. Figure 4 shows the spectrum utilization for both the models where a significant increase can be seen in DAMW. This is because DAMW allows spectrum reuse where multiple non-interfering channels can get a common channel. However, with increase in number of PUs (which increases the number of channels), the performance shows a moderate increase in the value which implies that due to network constraints SUs remain unassigned to the channels. In Fig. 5, channel allocation ratio shows the fraction of allocated channels out of the channels offered for auction. A reduced allocation ratio in McAfee auction depicts the scenario where many channels are left unassigned. In comparison, DAMW proffers an improved allocation ratio which in turn effects the spectrum utilization. Similarly in Figs. 6 and 7, DAMW is compared with the general McAfee auction when number of SUs are varied from 20 to 50 keeping number of PUs fixed at 4. Here also, we can observe that DAMW gives a better performance than McAfee which accounts to the similar reasons as stated above.

Hence, the proposed double auction mechanism significantly improves the spectrum utilization in the CR network.

5   Conclusion

In this paper, we propose DAMW, a double auction framework for spectrum allocation in CRN, which supports spectrum reusability amongst non-interfering SUs. DAMW achieves individual rationality and truthfulness in the proposed model to refrain from any kind of market manipulation which may degrade the utility of SUs and PUs. More importantly, DAMW incorporates different issues arising in a CR network, viz., dynamics in SOPs and variation in availability time of the unused channels, and accordingly plans the bid submission process from SUs. A three phase procedure builds the non-interfering bidder groups, determines the bid value from each group and finally allocates the spectrum following the allocation constraint. Experimental results obtained through network simulation specify that DAMW outperforms as a spectrum allocation model by offering an improved spectrum utilization compared to the general McAfee auction. In our future work, we plan to work on heterogeneous channel condition for a similar network scenario.

References

1. FCC: ET Docket No 03–322 Notice of Proposed Rule Making and Order (2003)
2. Akyildiz, I.F., Lee, W.-Y., Vuran, M.C., Mohanty, S.: Next generation/dynamic spectrum access/cognitive radio wireless networks: a survey. Comput. Netw. J. **50**(13), 2127–2159 (2006)
3. Xing, X., Jing, T., Cheng, W., Huo, Y., Cheng, X.: Spectrum prediction in cognitive radio networks. IEEE Wirel. Commun. **20**(2), 90–96 (2013)
4. Zhao, Q., Sadler, B.M.: A survey of dynamic spectrum access. IEEE Sig. Process. Mag. **24**(3), 79–89 (2007)
5. Song, M., Xin, C., Zhao, Y., Cheng, X.: Dynamic spectrum access: from cognitive radio to network radio. IEEE Wirel. Commun. **19**(1), 23–29 (2012)
6. Devi, M., Sarma, N., Deka, S.K.: Allocation and access mechanisms for spectrum sharing in CRNs - a brief review. In: Proceedings of IEEE International Conference on Accessibility to Digital World (ICADW). IEEE (2016)
7. Ahmed, E., Gani, A., Abolfazli, S., Yao, L.J., Khan, S.U.: Channel assignment algorithms in cognitive radio networks: taxonomy, open issues, and challenges. IEEE Commun. Surv. Tutorials **18**, 795–823 (2016)
8. Tragos, E.Z., Zeadally, S., Fragkiadakis, A.G., Siris, V.A.: Spectrum assignment in cognitive radio networks: a comprehensive survey. IEEE Commun. Surv. Tutorials **15**, 1108–1135 (2013)
9. Parsons, S., Rodriguez-Aguilar, J.A., Klein, M.: Auctions and bidding: a guide for computer scientists. ACM Comput. Surv. **43**, 1–66 (2011)
10. Wang, X., Li, Z., Xu, P., Xu, Y., Gao, X., Chen, H.-H.: Spectrum sharing in cognitive radio networks-an auction based approach. IEEE Trans. Syst. Man Cybern. **40**, 587–596 (2010)

11. Kash, I.A., Murthy, R., Parkes, D.C.: Enabling spectrum sharing in secondary market auctions. IEEE Trans. Mob. Comput. **13**, 556–568 (2014)
12. Devi, M., Sarma, N., Deka, S.K., Chauhan, P.: Sequential bidding auction mechanism for spectrum sharing in cognitive radio networks. In: Proceedings of International Conference on Advanced Networks and Telecommunication Systems (IEEE ANTS). IEEE (2017)
13. Hu, F., Chen, B., Zhu, K.: Full spectrum sharing in cognitive radio networks toward 5G: a survey. IEEE Access **6**, 15754–15776 (2018)
14. McAfee, R.P.: A dominant strategy double auction. J. Econ. Theory **56**(2), 434–450 (1992)
15. Zhou, X., Zheng, H.: TRUST: a general framework for truthful double spectrum auctions. In: Proceedings of IEEE INFOCOM 2009, pp. 999–1007. IEEE (2009)
16. Sun, Y.-E., et al.: STRUCTURE: a strategyproof double auction for heterogeneous secondary spectrum markets. In: Wang, G., Zomaya, A., Perez, G.M., Li, K. (eds.) ICA3PP 2015. LNCS, vol. 9531, pp. 427–441. Springer, Cham (2015). https://doi.org/10.1007/978-3-319-27140-8_30
17. Feng, X., Chen, Y., Zhang, J., Zhang, Q.: TAHES: a truthful double auction mechanism for heterogeneous spectrum. IEEE Trans. Wirel. Commun. **11**(11), 4038–4047 (2012)
18. Zhai, X., Zhou, T., Zhu, C., Chen, B., Fang, W., Zhu, K.: Truthful double auction for joint internet of energy and profit optimization in cognitive radio networks. IEEE Access **6**, 23180–23190 (2018)
19. Dong, W., Rallapalli, S., Qiu, L., Ramakrishnan, K.K., Zhang, Y.: Double auctions for dynamic spectrum allocation. IEEE/ACM Trans. Netw. **24**, 2485–2497 (2016)
20. Zhang, X., Yang, D., Xue, G., Yu, R., Tang, J.: Transmitting and sharing: a truthful double auction for cognitive radio networks. In: Proceedings of IEEE ICC. IEEE (2018)
21. Chen, Y., Zhang, J., Wu, K., Zhang, Q.: TAMES: a truthful double auction for multi-demand heterogeneous spectrums. IEEE Trans. Parallel Distrib. Syst. **25**(11), 3012–3024 (2014)
22. Khairullah, E.F., Chatterjee, M.: PreDA: preference-based double auction for spectrum allocation in heterogeneous DSA networks. Comput. Commun. **133**, 41–50 (2019)
23. Xiang, J., Zhang, Y., Skeie, T.: Medium access control protocols in cognitive radio networks. Wirel. Commun. Mob. Comput. 1–18 (2009)
24. Kim, H., Shin, K.G.: Efficient discovery of spectrum opportunities with MAC-layer sensing in cognitive radio networks. IEEE Trans. Mob. Comput. **7**, 533–545 (2008)

Data Analytics and e-Governance

Social Inclusion and e-Governance: A Case Study in Alirajpur District

Kollapalli Ramesh Babu[1]([⊠]), A. B. Sagar[2], and Preeti Kothari[2]

[1] Vidya Jyothi Institute of Technology,
Aziz Nagar, Hyderabad, Telengana, India
krameshbabucse@vjit.ac.in
[2] National Informatics Center, New Delhi, India
sagar.phdcs@gmail.com, dpkothari@gmail.com

Abstract. There are several reasons for social and economic exclusion of citizens, and digital divide is one of the most important one. Digital divide is a social issue which denotes the varying amount of information between those who have access to the Internet (especially broadband access) and those who do not have access. Broadly speaking, the difference is not necessarily determined by the access to the Internet, but by access to ICT (Information and Communications Technologies) and to Media that the different segments of society can use. It describes a gap in terms of access to and usage of ICT. It was traditionally considered to be a question of having or not having access, but with a global mobile phone penetration of over 95%, it is becoming a relative inequality between those who have more and less bandwidth and more or less skills. In this modern world marked by a growing need for ICT skills at all levels, there is an increased need to bridge the digital divide. ICT is so tightly woven into the fabric of society today that its deprivation can rightly be considered one of twentieth century social deprivations, such as low income, unemployment, poor education, ill health and social isolation. To consider ICT deprivation as somehow less important underestimates the pace, depth and scale of technological change, and overlooks the way that different disadvantages can combine to deepen exclusion. One of the most challenging tasks being faced by India is digital divide. This paper presents an approach which has been followed by district administration in the district of Alirajpur, Madhya Pradesh, India. The significance of Alirajpur district is that it is the least literate district in the whole country. Average literacy rate of Alirajpur in 2011 is 36% compared to 31% of 2001 [1, 2]. It can be safely inferred that if positive results can be obtained in Alirajpur district, then it is very likely that better results can be obtained in any other district of the country.

Keywords: Social inclusion · Digital divide · Rural e-Governance

1 Introduction

The digital divide, or the digital split, is a social issue referring to the differing amount of information between those who have access to the ICT (Information and Communications Technologies) and those who do not have access [3–5, 13]. The digital divide

© Springer Nature Switzerland AG 2020
S. S. Rautaray et al. (Eds.): I4CS 2020, CCIS 1139, pp. 285–294, 2020.
https://doi.org/10.1007/978-3-030-37484-6_16

is based on insufficient policy regimes, illiteracy, and inefficiency in the provision of telecommunication network and service lack of locality created content and uneven ability to derive economic and social benefits from information intensive activities. To address this issue of digital divide, a systematic approach broadly attacking all these issues is required [6]. Many studies have proved the correlation between the digital divide and socio-economic growth. Fong identified that developing countries need to consider the adoption and application of ICTs for economic development [7, 14]. Although ICTs are necessary for socio- economic progress in developing countries, they are not sufficient. Therefore, access to ICTs cannot be a solution to poverty on itself, but can at best be adopted as a tool in poverty reduction initiatives [8]. ICT is a part of a much broader effort to reach general development and poverty alleviation goals. To this end, countries need to start incorporating ICT as a tool to achieve poverty alleviation by conceiving new applications and new digital inclusion models that can use the growing ICT [9, 14].

Digital divide is one of the significant reasons for uneven distribution of resources to the citizens. The 2014 United Nations E-Government Survey, which has tracked development since 2003, also highlighted that digital divides are "inextricably linked to social equity in today's information world" [10]. Equity is achieved when all the eligible communities of the country benefit from the welfare schemes of the government. In most of the developing countries, people living in rural areas and remote locations and communities that have lower literacy rates are deprived of the welfare schemes of the government as their geographical locations and lack of awareness stand as a major impediment [11].

At the same time, it must be considered that if ICT can create inclusiveness, it also can create the growing of inequalities worldwide, making even harder for people living in poverty to develop [12]. Administration must include strategies that can stimulate development for those who are excluded, the ones that live in extreme poverty [13]. So the challenge is to understand how the people marginalized from ICT can be included so that digital divide may be reduced.

The district administration has used two methods to counter this issue of digital divide in the Alirajpur District of Madhya Pradesh, India. In order to discuss these ideas, this paper is organized into six sections. After the introduction, Sect. 2 describes the research problem. Section 3 describes the methodology. Section 4 shows the implementation details.

The Sect. 5 discusses results obtained. Finally, Sect. 6 concludes and points at further investigations.

2 Research Problem

Alirajpur district community, being the lowest in average literacy rate in India, is faced with the problem of exclusion due to the digital divide. Bridging digital divide has become increasingly important to create an inclusive governance and to reap the social and economic benefits thereof. Due to lower literacy rate and differences among cultural and social groups, the implementation of inclusive programs is very challenging.

Hence the research problem is to study practical methods to make Alirajpur community more inclusive by reducing the digital divide.

3 Methodology and Results

As online interactions have rapidly become the main channel of communication, the district administration has implemented two online projects for improving the inclusiveness in the district. One is "Inclusion Drive" and the other is "JanShruti". There are several schemes and projects of the government of which many are unknown to the public. And to those that are socially backward or excluded, these schemes and projects are quite inaccessible. Inclusion Drive is an initiative which aims to include the socially and economically excluded communities into the various schemes and projects of the government. The district administration has set up computer centers known as 'hot bazaars' in the blocks of the district. Each week, on a specific day, data entry operators are made available for the public to register their grievances in JanShruti or register themselves into any scheme or project through Inclusion Drive.

Figure 1 shows the Inclusion Model followed by the Alirajpur district administration.

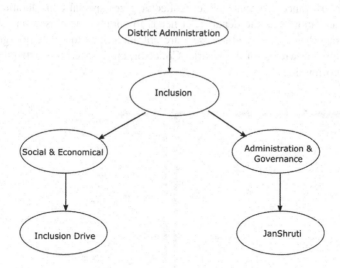

Fig. 1. Inclusion Model

3.1 JanShruti

JanShruti is a web portal for citizens of the district to communicate all their grievances to the district administration. Citizens can directly take up matters regarding pendency of their grievances directly with the district administration. Each grievance can be marked to a specific department and its specific scheme or project, and it will reach the concerned official of that department. SMS is also integrated into the application so that as soon as a grievance is registered or disposed, the involved parties are immediately updated. This quickness in registration has encouraged several people to use JanShruti for contacting the administration regarding implementation of various schemes and projects of the government. At the time of writing of this paper, the page has been accessed more than 60,000 times.

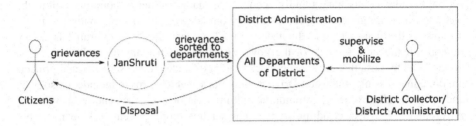

Fig. 2. JanShruti work flow

Every Monday, the District Collector conducts a meeting with all the department heads of the district. In that meeting the status of the registered grievances are personally verified for each department (Fig. 2). JanShruti highlights the oldest and unaddressed grievances so that District Collector gives special consideration to these complaints and mobilizes the department heads to address them as soon as possible. The department heads or any other users are not authorized to delete any grievances

without the knowledge of the District Collector, and hence no registered grievance could ever go missing.

सभी विभाग वार रिपोर्ट

Department ID	Department Name	Total	Complaints	Demands
0		14	1	12
1	नवोदय विद्यालय अलीराजपुर	1	0	0
2	भारतीय डाक	1	1	0
3	गृह	2	0	1
4	राजस्व	3183	565	937
5	जिला आबकारी विभाग	1	1	0
6	श्रम विभाग	15	11	0
9	वन	39	7	31
10	वाणिज्य एवं उद्योग	113	23	89
11	खनिज संसाधन	1	0	0
12	ऊर्जा विभाग	243	55	45
13	कृषि	866	4	862
14	सहकारिता	26	18	5
15	लोक निर्माण कार्य	15	4	2
16	स्कूल शिक्षा	103	15	54
17	पंचायत एवं ग्रामीण विकास	7251	133	6875
18	योजना आर्थिक एवं सांख्यिकी	2	0	0
19	पब्लिक रिलेशन विभाग	1	0	0
20	जनजाति कल्याण विभाग	5	2	0
22	खाद्य एवं नागरिक आपूर्ति	189	5	10
23	जल संसाधन विभाग	9	1	5
24	लोक स्वास्थ्य यांत्रिकी	1257	54	631
25	पशुपालन	382	0	363
26	मत्स्य पालन	1	0	1
27	उच्च शिक्षा	9	1	1
28	सूचना प्रौद्योगिकी	10	2	7
29	शहरी कल्याण (अलीराजपुर)	24	5	0
30	महिला एवं बाल विकास	155	15	93
31	तकनीकी शिक्षा एवं कौशल विकास	2	1	1
32	उद्यानिकी विभाग	19	2	5
34	पंजीयन एवं मुद्रांक	1	0	1
35	केन्द्रीय सार्वजनिक उद्यम	1	1	0
36	बैंक	37	5	13
37	सामाजिक न्याय	1172	336	836
38	भारत निर्वाचन	2	1	0
40	स्वास्थ्य विभाग	55	19	16
42	प्रधान मंत्री ग्राम सड़क योजना	33	1	31
43	पुलिस विभाग	6	4	1
44	शहरी कल्याण (जोबट)	48	11	4
45	शिक्षा केंद्र	1	1	0

Total : 15095

Fig. 3. JanShruti grievances report: department-wise

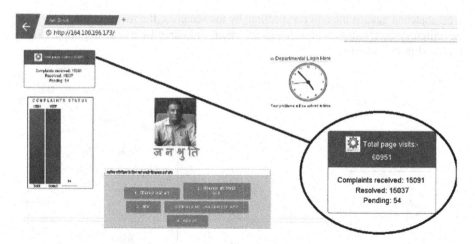

Fig. 4. JanShruti website

Figure 3 shows the summary report of the grievances received by various depart-ments. Figure 4 shows the dashboard of JanShruti. As of date of writing of this paper, there are a total of 15,091 grievances received, and 15,031 resolved and 54 pending. This implies a disposal of 99.64% of the grievances. This kind of high redress rate has encouraged the public to access the administration for various services. The District Collector would also verify the disposed grievances to ensure that fake disposals are not made by the respective departments. This ensured departments disposing the grievances genuinely. On the other hand in the public, it created a trust on the district administration and generated much interest as the public grievances were well addressed and resolved in time by the district administration. The areas from which more public grievances are being registered are identified. More number of registra-tions implied several things. Firstly, it implied that people are trusting the system and are willing to approach the administration through JanShruti. Secondly, it revealed the poor performance of some of the departments in their services to the citizens. The areas from which lesser registrations occurred implied that either the communities in those areas were excluded or the citizens in those areas are unaware of JanShruti. To combat unawareness, more publicity was given in those areas and to increase inclusiveness in those areas, the next project Inclusion Drive was brought in. The areas which were excluded were made the chief targets for Inclusion Drive.

3.2 Inclusion Drive

Government has several schemes for the welfare of the citizens. Each scheme has some eligibility criteria. Citizens qualify for a scheme when eligibility possessed by them matches the eligibility required by the scheme. In Inclusion Drive approach a super set of all the schemes of the government being implemented in the district is created and all the eligibility criteria of all the schemes were listed out. Eligibility criteria are obtained from the citizens of the district through online registration. These criteria of the citizens were matched against the criteria specified by the schemes. If a match is found between the criteria possessed by a person and the criteria required by a scheme, the person is included in the scheme.

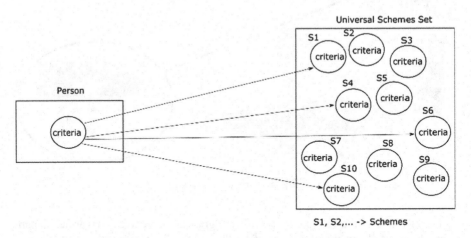

Fig. 5. Person's eligibility criteria matching with eligibility criteria required by various schemes

Figure 5 shows the mapping of a person to different schemes. Though every person possessed some criteria, their matching to the eligibility required by the scheme varied. These eligibility criteria of a citizen sometimes fully matched with the criteria required by a scheme and sometimes partially matched and sometimes did not match at all. Citizens whose criteria fully matched a scheme or schemes were given identification numbers and were included in the e-governance. This process has been very effective and fast. Figure 6 shows the result of Inclusion Drive in one month.

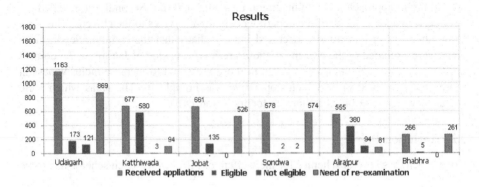

Fig. 6. One month results of Inclusion Drive

3.2.1   Calculation of Inclusiveness

For the inclusion to be complete, each region in the district is to be included in the e-governance. Higher inclusion or stronger inclusion meant that each person is part of at least one or more schemes or projects of the government. This required the calculation of inclusiveness of each region of the district. Hence a method has been devised to calculate the inclusiveness. If inclusiveness is denoted by I, then complete inclusiveness (i.e. I = 100) is said to be achieved when $R_D = N_D$ where R_D denotes the set of people that were included in schemes (e-governed) in district D, and N_D denotes total population of district D. That is, all the population in the district is included when each and every citizen in the district is registered to at least one scheme of the government. A region in the district is called a black hole if there are zero people registered for any scheme. To achieve complete inclusiveness of the district it is necessary to see that there are no black hole regions in the district. If n is the number of regions in the district, and R_{Bi} denotes population included in the region B_i, and N_{Bi} denotes total population of the region B_i, then inclusiveness (I) of district D is calculated as follows:

$$I_D = \sum_{i=1}^{n} \frac{R_{Bi}}{N_{Bi}} * 100 \qquad (1)$$

Therefore, if a region has zero population that is included (i.e. $R_{Bi} = 0$) then, inclusiveness of that region will be zero.

$$I_{Bi} = \sum_{i=1}^{n} \frac{0}{N_{Bi}} * 100$$

$$\Rightarrow I_{Bi} = 0 \qquad (2)$$

For inclusiveness of the district D to be complete i.e. I D = 100, inclusiveness of all the regions of the district should be complete i.e. I $_{Bi}$ = 100 $\forall$ i $\in$ D. If a person P k is included in one or more schemes, then the Order of Inclusiveness of that person ($O(P_k)$) is 1 or more respectively. And if he is not included in any scheme, then it is zero i.e. $O(P_k) = 0$. Order of Inclusiveness of a district ($O(I)_D$) is calculated by taking the average of the Order of Inclusiveness of the each person in the district i.e.

$$O(I)_D = \sum_{i=1}^{N_D} \frac{O(Pn)}{N_D} \qquad (3)$$

where P $_n$ is a person in the district and N_D is the total population of the district. So, if O (I) $_D$ = 3, it implies that on average, every person in the district 'D' is included in at least three schemes of the government. This way it is possible to identify highly inclusive regions and also poorly inclusive regions. A study has been suggested for those regions that were poorly inclusive to identify the reasons for such poor inclusion and also to find measures to be implemented for improving the inclusiveness.

4   Analysis, Results, Challenges and Significance of the Study

During the implementation of the two projects JanShruti and Inclusion Drive, it is evident that literacy plays an important role in the exclusion. Those who are not literate are mostly excluded socially and economically. To motivate them and include them it is first necessary to create a trust in the administration. Soon after the trust has formed in the public, the excluded community started approaching the administration and showed interest in being included into various schemes and projects of the government. Some of the complaints registered in JanShruti were about Inclusion Drive. Several citizens have reported that their villages were not included in any government schemes. This allowed the district administration to spot excluded areas and implement Inclusion Drive in those areas.

In Inclusion Drive registration, the applicants are needed to back up their claims with proper documentation. The documents provided in support of the claims of the applicants were to be verified for their authenticity by the district administration. And after verification, in a span of one month, Inclusion Drive has added 1,275 excluded citizens into government schemes and 2,405 citizens were under consideration as their document verification is under process. Implementation of these two projects have faced several challenges. ICT infrastructure in rural India is very poor. Some district headquarters even do not have Internet connection. Connectivity has been a major problem during the implementation of the projects. There is also a scarcity of sufficient trained IT professionals to install and maintain hardware, software and networks. Since literacy is less and most of the computer related tutorials, discussions, and other materials are in English, translating the content into regional language has become an overhead for the administration. Financial challenges were faced as the implementation required capital for investment in infrastructure and sustainability of projects. The excluded tend to have more limited access to more sophisticated technical devices and services. They have simple, non-Internet enabled mobiles, and, if they do have Internet access, are more likely to use least expensive plans of data access. Furthermore, there is low use and lesser interest to use online government services. As online government initiatives are not reaching the most excluded, policies to support inclusion can make a difference to engagement with ICT. Improving other factors, such as employment and rural access may also help in this cause. When home access to ICT is provided to younger generation, programmes also reached out to parents. This is not just about access. Government-related programmes on the Internet to increase electronic access to services are undertaken mostly by more sophisticated ICT users.

Administration understood that the excluded people who could benefit most by accessing their services will be the least likely to (be able to) use electronic means. This emphasized the need to provide alternative ways of accessing services; mediated access to online services through data entry operator provided by the administration. Students who secured higher percentage in higher secondary school in every block were given free laptops by the district administration. This increased the ease of access to the

Internet and computer to those that are neighbors to these students. To combat the relevancy barrier, the district administration has also raised awareness among the public by posting advertisements in the newspapers, television, running awareness campaigns and collaborating with local organizations. The district administration has also organized several community training programs where they taught basic computer knowledge, accessing the Internet and making use of JanShruti and Digital

Inclusion web portals. JanShruti has been taken to the next level by creating an Android app of JanShruti. Thus creative methods were employed for increasing community engagement. The results obtained in JanShruti and Inclusion Drive showed that the administration's approach is right.

5   Conclusion and Future Study

The general implications of this study with special relevance to social inclusion are increase in digital access and use, skills and confidence, motivation. Economically – employment and education. Health - healthy lifestyle, communicating and connecting, access to government's health services, democratic and civil participation. This is to be regarded only as a prototype and a pilot project. It needs to be more developed, tested, refined, shared and embedded.

References

1. http://www.census2011.co.in/census/district/332-alirajpur.html. Accessed 01 Sept 2016
2. Compaine, B.M.: The digital Divide: Facing a Crisis or Creating a Myth?. MIT Press, Cambridge (2001). http://www.indiamapia.com/Alirajpur.html. Accessed 01 Sept 2016
3. Norris, P.: Digital Divide: Civic Engagement, Information Poverty, and the Internet Worldwide. Cambridge University Press, Cambridge (2001)
4. Tsatsou, P.: Digital divides revisited: what is new about divides and their research? Med. Cult. Soc. **33**(2), 317 (2011). https://doi.org/10.1177/0163443710393865. http://mcs. sagepub.com/content/33/2/317. Accessed 18 Sept 2016
5. Wolf, L.: what is digital divide? p. 8, July–Sept 2002. (www.techknowlogia.org)
6. Fong, M.W.L.: Digital divide: the case of developing countries. Issues Inf. Sci. Inf. Technol. **6**(2), 471–478 (2009)
7. Leye, V.: Information and communication technologies for development: a critical perspective. Glob. Govern. **15**(1), 29–35 (2009)
8. Hewitt de Alcantara, C.: The Development Divide in a Digital Age. An Issues Paper. Technology, Business and Society Programme Paper Number 4. Geneva: United Nations Research Institute for Social Development, August (2001). http://www.unrisd.org/UNRISD/ website/document.nsf/ab82a6805797760f80256b4f005da1ab/19b0b342a4f1cf5. Accessed 30 May 2008
9. UNITED NATIONS E-GOVERNMENT SURVEY, pp. 124–140, 14 Sept 2016. https:// publicadministration.un.org/egovkb/portals/egovkb/documents/un/2014-survey/chapter6.pdf. (2014)
10. Harris, R.: A Framework for Poverty Alleviation with ICTs (2002). http://www. communities.org.ru/ci-text/harris.doc. Accessed 14 Sept 2016
11. Mansell, R.: Information and communication technologies for development: assessing the potential and the risks. Telecommun. Policy **23**(1), 35–50 (1999). https://doi.org/10.1016/ S0308-5961(98)00074-3

12. Castells, M.: Information Technology, Globalization and Social Development (1999). http://goo.gl/PFdx3A. Accessed 20 Feb 2015
13. United Nations. Transforming our World: The 2030 Agenda for Sustainable Development. 24 November 2015. https://sustainabledevelopment.un.org/post2015/transformingourworld
14. Mossberger, K., Mary, K.M.C.J.T., Tolbert, C.J., Stansbury, M.: Virtual Inequality: Beyond the Digital Divide. Georgetown University Press, Washington, D.C. (2003)

Designing a Blockchain Based Framework for IoT Data Trade

Pranav Kumar Singh[1,2]([⊠]), Roshan Singh[2], Sunit Kumar Nandi[2,3], and Sukumar Nandi[2]

[1] Department of CSE, Central Institute of Technology Kokrajhar, Kokrajhar 783370, Assam, India
snghpranav@gmail.com
[2] Department of CSE, Indian Institute of Technology Guwahati, Guwahati 781039, Assam, India
roshansingh3000@gmail.com, sunitnandi834@gmail.com, sukumar@iitg.ac.in
[3] Department of CSE, National Institute of Technology, Yupia 791112, Arunachal Pradesh, India

Abstract. With its application ranging from smart homes and wearables to smart vehicles and smart cities, Internet of Things(IoT) devices have become an integral part of our lives. These devices are enabled with sensing and networking facilities and generate an enormous amount of data, which can be highly valuable for various stakeholders of the system. Enabling the regulated exchange of IoT generated data can enhance the overall efficiency of the IoT based eco-system. However, the current state of the art data exchange frameworks is highly centralized, making it prone to a single point of failure and security breaches. Moreover, the cloud-based systems lack transparency and provide the owners of the IoT devices limited control over the data being exchanged, thus raising the privacy concerns of an individual. Also, the device owners, most of the time, are deprived of receiving proper incentives in exchange for their shared data. Blockchain Technology, with its inherent characteristics of being transparent, decentralized, always available along with smart contracts, can be one of the potential solutions for the problems mentioned above. In this work, we propose, analyze, and discuss a blockchain-based decentralized framework for IoT data trade.

1 Introduction

In recent years, we have seen a massive proliferation in the number of IoT devices around us. This rapid increase has occurred due to the shift in lifestyle and evolution of traditional cities to smart cities. It is expected that there will be around 50–100 billion communication and networking devices connected to the internet by 2020. These devices range from small and lightweight wearable devices such as a smartwatch to a smart oven in the smart homes. Irrespective of their physical size and weight, these devices are equipped with sensing, communication, and to some extent, processing capabilities. Most of the time, these devices are

© Springer Nature Switzerland AG 2020
S. S. Rautaray et al. (Eds.): I4CS 2020, CCIS 1139, pp. 295–308, 2020.
https://doi.org/10.1007/978-3-030-37484-6_17

lightweight and compact with power constraints. In the last few years, advancements in the sensor industry have led to the availability of minute and high-performance sensing devices. Major IoT deployments work on the principle of Sense, Process, and Act. The sensed data from the IoT at source is sent for processing at a centralized cloud, upon processing the decision is made, and the device is instructed for executing further actions. The state of the art architecture for IoT operation is client server-based, where an IoT device pushes the sensed data to a centralized server. The further processing of the sensed data is carried out in a cloud environment [1]. The cloud service provider is responsible for analyzing the received data to gain inner insights. With this current client-server based architecture, the provenance of user data becomes a problematic task. Such architecture makes user data to rely entirely upon the hands of the service providers, assuming them to be trustworthy, which often does not turn to be true. Such blind faith in the cloud service providers upon the user data has resulted in some of the severe data breach incidents such as Facebook-Cambridge Analytica [6] privacy breach. Also, there exists a large community of producers and consumers for data generated by IoT. Such as an auto-manufacturer might be interested to know the pollutant emission from vehicles owned by their customers. However, until now, there has not been any trusted and common platform made available to these stakeholders to market the data. It is thus required to have a transparent, unbiased framework for IoT data trade. Monetising the IoT generated data will not only enhance the quality of data received, but at the same time, will also motivate the data producers to generate high-quality data.

It turns out that decentralized technologies such as blockchain can help address some of these challenges [15]. Blockchain has recently got attention as a potential contender for enhancing IoT security [4,5]. Countering the above challenges, we in this work propose a blockchain-based framework for data trade in IoT. We propose to use a public blockchain for maintaining a shared and transparent ledger among the stakeholders allowing both the consumers and the producers of the data to allow data trade in a transparent and much more effective manner. With the notion of smart contracts [17] deployed using the blockchain, we make the trade automated and eliminate any scope of cheating among the trading parties.

Our key contributions in this paper are as follows:

- We present and contextualize the state-of-the-art IoT data trading architecture.
- By explaining the basic distinctions between IoT data trading and IoT services, we discuss the shortcomings of the existing architecture.
- We propose the system design of a blockchain-based approach for IoT data trading.

As this is an ongoing effort, we are focusing primarily on its design architecture so far.

2   State-of-the-Art Architecture

We review the state of the art architecture for IoT solutions in this section. The centralized and cloud-based approach has become the standard practice along which most IoT related services are often built. However, this trend can not be considered as the best approach for a long-term strategy, even though it offers several benefits to the users and service providers.

In the last few years, we have seen how IoT has become a solution to a wide range of problems. It has become parts of our body (smart wearables), entered into our homes (smart homes), vehicles, our societies, cities, transportation, logistics, health sectors, education, industry, etc. and can be termed as the Internet of EveryThing. And EveryThing is now being driven by the data, which plays a vital role. IoT driven solutions are providing convenience to the users, minimizing costs, reducing waste of resources, maximizing efficiency, productivity, and profit, and also helping the environment.

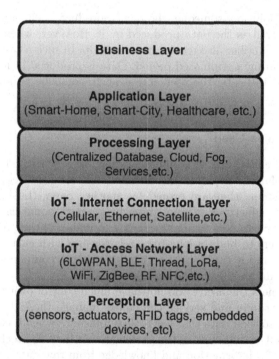

Fig. 1. Six layer architecture of IoT

Figure 1 illustrates the six-layer architecture of the IoT-based solutions [14]. The lowest layer is the perception layer, which is also called a physical layer with sensors for detecting and collecting environmental data and actuators to control the environment. The devices can be of a different type at this layer, developed in different companies. For example, smart home having smart appliances of a different make. The sensor data transfer from the perception layer to the processing layer and vice versa is done through the transport layer (a combination of access and Internet connection layer) using wired or wireless connectivity options. The processing layer, which works as a middleware layer, stores analyzes, and processes big data that comes from the lower layer. It can handle and provide the lower layers with a variety of services. It uses numerous techniques such as cloud computing, database, and big data processing. The application layer provides application-specific services to the end-user – for example, smart homes, smart health, smart city, etc. depending on IoT solution deployments. The business layer, which is an important layer, manages the entire IoT solution, including apps, services, business and profit models, and privacy. Now the question comes how these data are being used in the state-of-the-art architecture of various IoT-based solutions?

2.1   Who Owns the Data?

In an IoT-based solution, someone who buys a product, then they are the owner of the device as well as the data produced by it. However, when the product is on rent, then the supplier also retains its ownership. In such a case, the customer owns the data during a stipulated period. Data is produced in IoT architecture based on actions taken by the user and as such, could be regarded as his/her property [13].

2.2   How Data Is Used?

From the IoT architecture, it is apparent that data generated (at perception layer) by IoT solutions deployed at customer ends are collected, analyzed, and processed at systems that are owned by another party (business layer). For example, the manufacturer of appliances in a smart home can use the data generated by the customers to analyze the performance of the product. This can help manufacturers to build a long-term relationship with customers through a service contract, and it can also help them to enhance component and product design based on data analysis and reports.

The data owners themselves do not have much control over their data. The product manufacturers and service companies manage these data. The owners only have access to their data that has little significance when it comes to the discovery of knowledge, and most of the owners do not have the technical expertise to fetch meaningful information and knowledge from raw data [10].

2.3   Existing Approach

There is no such standard approach available for IoT data trading, and some of the options available for data trading are mobile app-based survey questionnaires. The survey-based models are not suitable for a complex IoT ecosystem, and we need to have some simplified and automated approach that can serve the purpose of IoT data trade. Sensing as a service [12] is one of the emerging technologies and envisioned as a business model that can facilitate the trading of IoT data between data owners and data consumers. This proposed business model consists of four conceptual layers: 1. Sensors (personal, private, and public organizations and commercial) and sensor owners. 2. Sensor publishers (detect sensors, communicate and get permission from owners to publish in the cloud). 3. Extended service providers (Embedding the intelligence to the service model). 4. Sensor data consumers (business organizations, governments, academic institutions, scientific research communities, etc.). The authors described how the model could be used to extract the hidden knowledge through data analysis and can be used to monetize in domains like smart home, smart city, supply chain, industry, health care, etc.

3 Problems with Present System

The data from IoT solutions contain a substantial quantity of knowledge which can be used to enhance our comforts, and reduce waste through effective resource consumption [11]. It should not only help manufacturers to gain profits but also customers to monetize it and help in getting better services at a low cost. As already mentioned by the authors [11] that the current IoT ecosystem is unfair and inefficient. With the present system of data trade, it is challenging for the users (product buyers) to get control over their data and monetize it. The reasons are lack of proper security and privacy mechanisms, no transparency, no mechanisms to deal with heterogeneity, scalability issues, and issues related to reliability and trust. Blockchain has been considered as one of the potential solutions to address these challenges. It has the capability to implement data trades, rewards and incentive systems, security, and privacy features, remove the need for trust and reputations in the IoT ecosystem. It can allow all parties to make the profit in a transparent, secure, and reliable manner.

4 Related Work

There are very few works available in the literature where blockchain has been proposed to implement data trade. Those works are summarized as follows: In [9], the authors discussed how sensing-as-a-service can be implemented using bitcoin and explained the method of exchanging data for earning money through Bitcoin. In the same line of thought, the authors [3], have implemented a bitcoin-based fair protocol for data trading. On top of the widely adopted IoT brokered data infrastructure, the authors [7] used evolving blockchain technologies to build an architecture, which is decentralized and open for IoT traffic metering and contract compliance. In [18], the authors proposed LRCoin, which is again a bitcoin-based approach to implement data trade in IoT. However, the authors claim that their approach, which uses a signature algorithm, is leakage-resilient.

We can see that there are very few contributions dedicated to incentive-based data trade in IoT that uses blockchain. These studies focus only on using bitcoin for data trading and how to make it secure. Contributing to the research direction, we in this work aim to harness the potential of blockchain technology along with the capabilities of the smart contracts for automated decision making for IoT data trade.

5 Background Details of Blockchain

Blockchain technology has recently gained extensive attention among the academia as well as industry with Bitcoin [8] being the first successful application of the technology. Blockchain consists of a sequence of timestamped blocks where each block is linked with its previous one with a cryptographic hash. A block in the blockchain contains the number of transactions executed by the users in the blockchain network. Fundamentally, a blockchain can be visualized as a single linked list that facilitates to traverse the chain from the current block to the first block or the genesis block in the chain. The blocks in the blockchain are added onto the chain by the maintainers of the blockchain. The maintainers, also known as the miners, need to participate in the mining procedure. Blockchain has established itself as one of the possible contenders for security applications as the addition of each block in the blockchain requires to solve a complex cryptographic computationally expensive puzzle during the block mining [16]. The miner who solves the block first and gets it verified by a majority of the other maintainers is allowed to append his block onto the chain. The other maintainer nodes check the solution for the puzzle solved by the miner, popularly termed as verifying the proof-of-work for the block. This mining procedure ensures that an adversary is not able to make any changes to the data onto the blockchain once it is committed. It requires an adversary to have control of at least 51% of the computation power of the blockchain network, which practically seems to be not possible. Some of the inherent capabilities of blockchain are:

- Censorship Resistance: Blockchain breaks the restrictions of borders and censorship of contents and applications by utilizing an underlying P2P network for communication.
- High Availability: As the same copy of data is replicated among several nodes in the network. Failure of a single node in the network won't affect the availability of the data.
- Non-Repudiable and Immutable: Data once committed onto the blockchain cannot be reverted. Thus, eliminating any attempt of an adversary to make changes to the data on the blockchain.
- Decentralized: Because of the computationally expensive Proof-of-Work mechanism. It is not possible for a single blockchain maintainer to control the entire blockchain.

Blockchain 1.0 was the first application of the technology. It was use-case specific mostly in the crypto-currency domain. The bitcoin blockchain is a live example of Blockchain 1.0. Blockchain 2.0 extends the capabilities of the previous version of the blockchain. The 2.0 allows operation and business logic to be deployed onto the blockchain in the form of computer code for decentralized and un-forgeable business contracts removing the need for intermediaries. These computer codes, also known as smart contracts, lies on the blockchain with as address and are publicly verifiable. The smart contract governs the business proceedings on the blockchain. Each business record onto the blockchain is modified via the smart contract. A transaction modifying the state of the blockchain is executed by all the computers maintaining the smart contacts.

6   Proposed Approach

Our proposed system model contains two types of entities:

(a) Producers: The producers are one who produces the data. A producer can be a human using the device to generate data, or it can be an IoT device generating data from its environment.
Secondly,

(b) Consumers: Similar to the producers, the consumers can be humans, such as one who wants to get the information from one's vehicle and an IoT device interested in getting the data to perform its further operations.

Each device on the network is identified by its blockchain address. Consequently, each human, either the producer or the consumer, is also identified by their respective addresses. The ownership of a device is mapped to its owner via the *Device Management SC*. The blockchain holds three types of smart contracts:

- *Device Management SC:* A smart contract deployed on the blockchain by the manufacturer of the device specifying the type, public key of the device, age, and the ownership of the device. The smart contract also specifies the Cloud Service Provider (CSP) having the processing rights on the data generated by the device along with the terms and conditions of the data use. The owner of the device is authorized to select its CSP.
- *Access Control SC:* A smart contract deployed by the device owner specifying the access rights to the data generated by the device stored in the cloud managed by the corresponding CSP. It is responsible for deciding which consumer can have access to the data and for what period of time. The smart contract also specifies the price at which the producer is willing to sell its data. The cloud system considers this smart contract while granting data access to a requester.
- *IncentiveSC and ReputationSC:* The producer of the data is required to be incentivized by the consumer to provide the consumer with its data. The incentives can be given to the producers in terms of increased incentive score and reputation value. An increased incentive score will let the producer make more money. The incentive score can be easily converted to the coin or token value supported by the blockchain such as ether from Ethereum [2]. Whereas an increased reputation score will let the producer attract more consumers, thus increasing its overall market value.

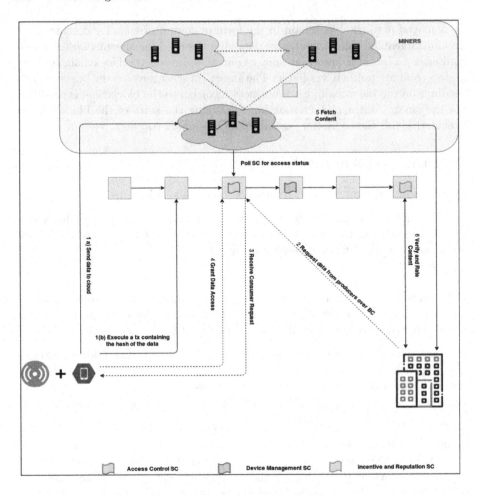

Fig. 2. Proposed system model

The system model for our proposed approach is depicted as in Fig. 2. An IoT device periodically sends its sensed data to its associated cloud service provider for analytical purposes, as specified in the smart contract. A device willing to sell its produced data marks itself as interested in the smart contract for selling the data with the selling rate per unit time. The smart contract maintains a list of prospective sellers willing to sell their data. A consumer can check the smart contract for finding a suitable seller of the data of its interest. The consumer request the producer for granting access to the data by accepting the terms and conditions for use and paying the price for the data for the stipulated period of time.

Our framework can be easily envisioned with a use case:

This festive season Riya brought a new smartphone. The smartphone manufacturer transfers the ownership of the smartphone to Riya on the blockchain via the smart contract. While configuring her phone for the first time, she sets up data access permissions to the number of applications running on her system.

Riya finds out that her smartphone is enabled with several sensing capabilities; she wants to make money out of it. She connects her smartphone to the blockchain network and selects Mist Cloud Services as the CSP for managing the sensor data of her device. Riya makes to sell the data generated from the air humidity sensor of her smartphone by making herself interested in selling the data on the blockchain with the rate at which she is willing to sell the data. Senss, a sensing company, finds out Riya's sensor data on sale. The company specifies the duration of time for which it requires the data to be brought, accept the terms of use of the data, and buys the data by paying the requisite amount via the smart contract. Mist Cloud Services, the CSP for Riya's smartphone, sees the transaction made by Senss and provides it the required data upon successful transaction. Senss, after data usages, gives a rating to the received data specifying the quality of data generated by Riya's smartphone. As Riya's smartphone is new and an advanced one, the data generated by the phone is much accurate and of good quality, which has bagged Riya good incentives and a higher reputation in the data trade market.

6.1 Data Access Control

The producer polls the *Access Control SC* for deciding whether to grant access to a requesting consumer or not. The cloud service provider also monitors the smart contract deployed on the blockchain and consults the smart contract before delivering the requested data to the consumer. Once a producer has granted access to the consumer, the data is made available for use to the consumer. Algorithm 1 shows the pseudocode of our access control smart contract.

Algorithm 1. *Access Control SC*

Input:
 1: *C:* Consumer Device
 2: *P:* Producer Device
 3: *reqData:* Data request made by C to P
 4: *t:* Duration of time for which C needs *reqData*
 5: *charge:* rate per unit time of P
Output: *accessGranted or accessDenied*
 6: **if** $msg.sender == P$ **then**   ▷ If called by P
 7:     **procedure** ACCESS CONTROL($C, P, t, charge$)
 8:         $price \leftarrow t * charge$ ▷ Amount to be paid by C
 9:         **if** $paid(C, price)$ **then**   ▷ Payment made by C
10:             IncentiveSC($P, price$);   ▷ Update incentive score of P
11:             **return** $accessGranted(t)$ ▷ Access granted to *reqData* for t period
12:         **else**
13:             **return** $accessDenied$
14:         **end if**
15:     **end procedure**
16: **end if**

6.2   Reputation and Incentives

A producer earns incentives each time it sells its data to a consumer. The *IncentiveSC* smart contract maintains the incentive score earned by each producer. A producer can use the earned incentives to avail certain services available in the ecosystem. Upon data use, a consumer may want to give feedback on the data being received from the producer. The feedback can be given in terms of rating. The *ReputationSC* smart contract maintains the reputation score of each producer. The pseudocode for *ReputationSC* and *IncentiveSC* are defined in Algorithms 2 and 3 respectively. A high rating received from a consumer will make a producer highly trustable by increasing its reputation score in the market, thus increasing its market value for data sales. Similarly, poor rating received from a consumer will negatively affect the reputation score of the producer and thus make the selling price of its data go down. A device can be profiled based upon the feedback received from its consumer also some of the factors that are considered while profiling or updating the reputation score of the device in our system are (i) data trading history of the device i.e., the number of times the producer device has participated in data trading (ii) age and (iii) the configuration score of the device. The configuration score of the device is obtained by analyzing the data in the *Device Management SC* against the device. A device having higher measuring precision will be having a higher configuration score.

Algorithm 2. *Reputation SC*

Input:
1: *C:* Consumer Device
2: *P:* Producer Device
3: *rating:* Reputation rating feedback from C to P for received data
Output: Updated Reputation score of P
4: *getAge(device):* Return the Age of the device.
5: *getConf(device):* Return the configuraton score of the device.
6: *getSharingHistory(device):* Return the data sharing history of device.
7: **if** $msg.sender == C$ **then**   ▷ If called by C
8:     $age \leftarrow getAge(P)$;   ▷ Age of P
9:     $conf \leftarrow getConf(P)$;   ▷ Configuration Score of P
10:     $history \leftarrow getSharingHistory(P)$;   ▷ Data Sharing history of P
11:     **procedure** REPUTATION UPDATE($C, P, rating, age, conf, history$)
12:         $repScore \leftarrow calculate(rating, age, conf, history)$ ▷ Calculate Score
13:         $P.reputation \leftarrow P.reputation + repScore$ ▷ Update Reputation of P
14:     **end procedure**
15: **end if**

Algorithm 3. *Incentive SC*

Input:
 1: *C:* Consumer Device
 2: *P:* Producer Device
Output: Updated Incentive score of P
 3: *price:* Amount paid by C to P
 4: **if** $msg.sender == P$ **then**   ▷ If called by P
 5:     **procedure** INCENTIVE SC$(P, price)$
 6:         $P.amount \leftarrow P.amount + price$ ▷ Increase incentive score of P
 7:     **end procedure**
 8: **end if**

6.3   Security Analysis

We consider those entities as an adversary, which makes deliberate attempts to gain knowledge about the ongoing communication between the consumers and the producers by either actively or passively listening to the communication channel. The framework provides a secure data exchange between the producer and the consumer with the notion of Public Key Infrastructure (PKI). Every transaction in the blockchain is itself digitally signed with the private key of the executor. A producer, while sending data to its Cloud Service Provider (CSP), also executes a blockchain transaction containing the hash of the data sent to the CSP. This information is used by the consumer for cross-checking the received data at a later point in time. Considering, a producer executing a transaction against its sensed data, D pushed to its CSP as:

$$tx = [(Encrypt(Producer_{PrivateKey}, Hash(D)))]||Producer_{PublicKey} \qquad (1)$$

$$Hash(D) = [(Decrypt(Producer_{PublicKey}, tx)] \qquad (2)$$

Each miner node in the network receiving the tx validates the authenticity of the received data by checking it against its signature with the provided public key of the producer, as shown in Eq. 2. The CSP, before sending the data to the consumer granted access by the producer, encrypts the data with the public key of the consumer and attaches the tx for verification purpose (3). The public key information is made publically available by the consumer via the *Device Management SC* smart contract. Upon receiving the data, the consumer decrypts it back using its secure private key (4) to get the sent data and verifies the hash of the decrypted data (5) with the hash stored on the blockchain obtained from received tx(2).

$$D1 = [(Encrypt(Consumer_{PublicKey}, D))]||tx \qquad (3)$$

$$D2 = (Decrypt(Consumer_{PrivateKey}, D1)) \qquad (4)$$

$$Hash1 = Hash(D2) \qquad (5)$$

If the hash matches with the hash stored on the blockchain i.e., Eq. 5 equals Eq. 2, then the data is considered to be unaltered and from the desired producer and is thus accepted by the consumer. This ensures that only the legitimate receiver of the data can have access to the data. Thus, making it difficult for an adversary to make sense out of the data in transit.

7 Discussion

The responsibility of maintaining the blockchain network lies with the Cloud Service Providers (CSPs), where a community of different CSPs participates in the mining procedure to maintain the blockchain. CSPs generally have high computational resources available, making it feasible for them to execute mining operations. The security of the maintained blockchain network relies on the fact that at any time, not more than 50% of the CSPs get compromised or form collusion against a benign CSP. The transactions from an IoT device are recorded as executed from their fixed length address, which is pseudo-anonymous. Although these addresses don't give much information by themselves, however, an adversary can obtain a significant amount of information by linking the transactions executed from the same address, such as which producer often does business with the said consumer, thus raising privacy concerns of a user or a device. Enhancing the un-linkability of the transactions in the network for improving user privacy can be one of the potential research directions in the domain.

8 Conclusion

In this work, we proposed a blockchain-based framework for secure IoT data trade. The framework provides the data producer much more control over its generated data. By introducing a public blockchain in our framework, we increased the transparency and the availability of the system during the data trade and eliminated the non-repudiation among the participating entities. By virtue of a public blockchain incorporated in the system, anyone is capable of verifying the transactions on the chain; thus a CSP of a producer cannot exercise his monopoly by denying data access to a consumer that has been granted access from the corresponding data producer. Also, it restricts the CSP of a device not to utilize the device data without proper consent of the device owner. As the terms of use contract are made via a smart contract, the data misuses can be easily detected and proved. At the same time, the framework also provides a common and trustable marketplace for IoT data trade among the potential un-trusted parties. By incentivizing the producers for their contribution to data sharing and managing their reputation scores, the framework not only motivates more producers for data generation and sharing but at the same time, also provides the consumer better options for data sources.

In our upcoming work, we aim to implement and test our proposed framework with a testbed setup.

References

1. Aazam, M., Khan, I., Alsaffar, A.A., Huh, E.N.: Cloud of things: integrating Internet of Things and cloud computing and the issues involved. In: Proceedings of 2014 11th International Bhurban Conference on Applied Sciences & Technology (IBCAST) Islamabad, Pakistan, 14th–18th January 2014, pp. 414–419. IEEE (2014)
2. Buterin, V., et al.: A next-generation smart contract and decentralized application platform. White Paper **3**, 37 (2014)
3. Delgado-Segura, S., Pérez-Solà, C., Navarro-Arribas, G., Herrera-Joancomartí, J.: A fair protocol for data trading based on bitcoin transactions. Future Gener. Comput. Syst. (2017)
4. Dorri, A., Kanhere, S.S., Jurdak, R., Gauravaram, P.: Blockchain for IoT security and privacy: the case study of a smart home. In: 2017 IEEE International Conference on Pervasive Computing and Communications Workshops (PerCom Workshops), pp. 618–623. IEEE (2017)
5. Huh, S., Cho, S., Kim, S.: Managing IoT devices using blockchain platform. In: 2017 19th International Conference on Advanced Communication Technology (ICACT), pp. 464–467. IEEE (2017)
6. Isaak, J., Hanna, M.J.: User data privacy: Facebook, Cambridge analytica, and privacy protection. Computer **51**(8), 56–59 (2018)
7. Missier, P., Bajoudah, S., Capossele, A., Gaglione, A., Nati, M.: Mind my value: a decentralized infrastructure for fair and trusted IoT data trading. In: Proceedings of the Seventh International Conference on the Internet of Things, p. 15. ACM (2017)
8. Nakamoto, S., et al.: Bitcoin: a peer-to-peer electronic cash system (2008)
9. Noyen, K., Volland, D., Wörner, D., Fleisch, E.: When money learns to fly: Towards sensing as a service applications using bitcoin. arXiv preprint arXiv:1409.5841 (2014)
10. Perera, C.: Sensing as a service (s2aas): buying and selling IoT data. arXiv preprint arXiv:1702.02380 (2017)
11. Perera, C., Barhamgi, M., De, S., Baarslag, T., Vecchio, M., Choo, K.K.R.: Designing the sensing as a service ecosystem for the Internet of Things. IEEE IoT Magazine **1**(2), 18–23 (2018)
12. Perera, C., Zaslavsky, A., Christen, P., Georgakopoulos, D.: Sensing as a service model for smart cities supported by Internet of Things. Trans. Emerging Telecommun. Technol. **25**(1), 81–93 (2014)
13. Saarikko, T., Westergren, U.H., Blomquist, T.: The Internet of Things: are you ready for what's coming? Bus. Horiz. **60**(5), 667–676 (2017)
14. Sethi, P., Sarangi, S.R.: Internet of Things: architectures, protocols, and applications. J. Electr. Comput. Eng. **2017** (2017)
15. Singh, P.K., Singh, R., Nandi, S.K., Nandi, S.: Managing smart home appliances with proof of authority and blockchain. In: Lüke, K.-H., Eichler, G., Erfurth, C., Fahrnberger, G. (eds.) I4CS 2019. CCIS, vol. 1041, pp. 221–232. Springer, Cham (2019). https://doi.org/10.1007/978-3-030-22482-0_16

16. Singh, P.K., Singh, R., Nandi, S.K., Nandi, S.: Smart Contract Based Decentralized Parking Management in ITS. In: Lüke, K.-H., Eichler, G., Erfurth, C., Fahrnberger, G. (eds.) I4CS 2019. CCIS, vol. 1041, pp. 66–77. Springer, Cham (2019). https://doi.org/10.1007/978-3-030-22482-0_6
17. Szabo, N.: Formalizing and securing relationships on public networks. First Monday **2**(9) (1997)
18. Yu, Y., et al.: LRCoin: leakage-resilient cryptocurrency based on bitcoin for data trading in IoT. IEEE IoT J. (2018)

A Simulation Model for Quality Assurance of e-Governance Projects

Pabitrananda Patnaik[1]([⊠]), Subhashree Pattnaik[2], and Pratibha Singh[1]

[1] National Informatics Centre, Unit – 4, Bhubaneswar, Odisha, India
{p.patnaik,pratibhasingh}@nic.in
[2] Capital Institute of Management and Science, Bhubaneswar, Odisha, India
spattnaikl2@gmail.com

Abstract. The use of e-Governance applications for the wellbeing of citizens are increasing day to day. The Government is trying to bring accuracy, availability and transparency in the system for providing services to the public at low cost. Thus the Government to Government (G2G), Government to Citizens (G2C), Government to Business (G2B) and Government to Employees (G2E) services are strengthened with use of Information and Communication Technology (ICT). Digital India Programme was formulated by Government of India for delivering effective e-Governance services in the country. Still, the sustainability, security, availability and reliability of government services is a question to-day. Many e-Governance applications are failing and some others are partially successful. Even successful e-Governance applications need improvements in service delivery, interoperability and longevity. The hassle free integration of different applications is yet to be achieved. The applications working in silo increases redundancy and result in wastage of resources. For optimal usage of resources and provisioning of services to the right person at right time, standardisation of e-Governance services is essential. Lot of standards for quality control and quality assurance are already available in different service areas including ICT. Besides international standards in Software Engineering, the Government of India emphasizes on e-Governance standards, interoperability framework, quality assurance framework, metadata & data standards and other areas to reduce failure and improvising the channels of service delivery to the public. The participation of users in governance is also encouraged to improve the quality of service. This paper focuses on provisioning a Simulation model for effective measurement of sector wise quality as well as the total quality assurance of the e-Governance projects. For an e-Governance application, in addition to software quality, the process quality, data quality and managerial quality sectors are also need to be taken care of for better result. The Simulation model will help in measuring the quality more accurately with qualitative and quantitative parameters and establish the relationship among different quality sectors of an e-Governance application. Consequently, it would be helpful in reducing the failure of e-Governance projects and create confidence in the stakeholders' mind.

Keywords: e-Governance · Quality · Quality assurance · Simulation

© Springer Nature Switzerland AG 2020
S. S. Rautaray et al. (Eds.): I4CS 2020, CCIS 1139, pp. 309–325, 2020.
https://doi.org/10.1007/978-3-030-37484-6_18

1 Introduction

According to **Dr. APJ Abdul Kalam**, former *President of India*, e-Governance means, "A transparent smart system with seamless access, secure and authentic flow of information, crossing the interdepartmental barrier, and providing a fair and unbiased service to the citizen" [33].

In India, the e-Governance services were initiated during late 60 s and early 70 s. Initially, importance was given on computerizing applications in the areas such as economic planning, national census, elections, tax collections and defence services. In 1976, National Informatics Centre (NIC) was established. Since then it has emerged as a pioneer of e-Governance applications in the country. In 1987, the networking system "NICNET" linked all the Ministries/Departments of Central Government, 36 State Governments and Union Territories and about 688 + District Administrations. The computerization support at district level made it stronger to provide informatics culture at the grass root level. During last thirty years, NIC has implemented many network based application software. During 1980s, the focus was on Management Information System (MIS) and Decision Support System (DSS). Gradually in 90 s and thereafter, the focus is on state-of-the-art technologies and application systems [20, 21].

Now, the uses of e-Governance applications are more. The securities, quality of service, availability and reliability have become the prime focus for sustainable e-Governance. The metadata, data standards, inter-operability framework, quality assurance framework etc. are being given emphasis in government sectors. The Digital India Programme is set up for better implementation of ICT in governance [5, 8].

1.1 Quality Assurance Model

Government of India focuses on developing a standard for e-Governance applications which has led to the National e-Governance Programme (NeGP). A Quality Assurance Framework is designed which emphasizes on accessibility, efficiency, reliability, transparency and economy of service. The basic objective is to provide service to the common men at their door step and making e-Governance applications inter operable [4].

Different software quality models like Capability Maturity Model (CMM), Software Process Improvement and Capability determination (SPICE), International Organization for Standardization (ISO 9001), Projects in Controlled Environment (PRINC2) and Six Sigma etc. are being used in software engineering practices [25, 32].

In software Engineering, many standards and models are in use for quality [15, 19]. Though Software Development Life Cycle follows standards, those standards are not sufficient for e-Governance applications. Many software industries and organizations follow Quality Management System, Total Quality Management, ISO certification and others; all these involve maintaining lot of documents. In practice, measuring the quality so achieved is not visible. It serves the purpose of certification only, and does not carry any meaning for the user department. Users expect secured and error free outputs. Consequently, working for quality is felt like an extra burden to the development team.

Further, the characteristics, dimensions, stake holders and other qualitative and quantitative parameters of e-Governance applications are different from other software projects in industries and institutions [1, 2].

e-Governance is a field, in which people are part of the government machinery. The involvement of people with process improves the success of e-governance projects [11, 17].

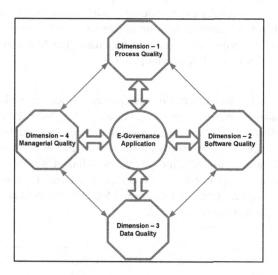

Fig. 1. Quality assurance model

The above mentioned model in Fig. 1 has 4 dimensions [27, 28].

- *Dimension – 1* **(Process quality)** The detailed process has to be defined. The analysis, logic development, implementation strategy, maintenance strategy and all other process related activities are to be defined very clearly. At this stage *Analyst* is involved to define the complete process. Necessary Business Process Reengineering is also done at this stage. The Business Process Re-engineering in government is known as Government Process Re-engineering (GPR). Many reforms, rule amendments, form and format modifications are done in government departments.
- *Dimension – 2* **(Software quality)** Here the actual software is developed, tested and put in use. The *Developers* are associated with this stage and they may develop in any platform according to the requirement, but, they must have the required skill to develop error free software. The software is tested thoroughly before implementation. Change management is also given importance.
- *Dimension – 3* **(Data quality)** The user needs error free results. If the software developed is a quality software and meets all the requirements, but the data is having errors then the output of the project suffers. Therefore, the supply of data by the user department should be 100% error free. Therefore, the *User* group has to be associated with the system and supply error free data as the user better understands the validity of data.

- *Dimension – 4* (**Managerial quality**) It is observed in many e-Governance applications that, the success of the project lies on the managerial capability of Project Manager as well as the User Manager. The Project Manager leads the software team and Manager from user department leads the team from user department, who is basically the middle level administrators. In spite of success in all the cases, there are many unseen or inadvertent errors and problems that may crop up during the project life cycle. At this stage, the Managerial capability to handle the situation is highly essential [22–24].

The association of Analyst with Process Quality, Developer with Software, User with Data and Manager are shown in Fig. 2. In addition to their direct responsibility, they are also associated with other areas shown in dashed lines and arrow-ended links. The Analyst is associated with process, but, at the same time, the analyst is also associated with software. Similarly, the Developer is linked with Software, but at the same time, he is also responsible for Processes and Data. In a way, the User is concerned with Managerial Quality. Likewise, a Manager remains connected with the Users, Developers, and Analysts [30, 31].

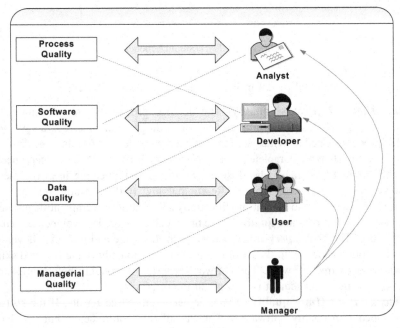

Fig. 2. [Process-Analyst]-[Software-Developer]-[Data-User]-[Managerial-Manager] model

1.2   Quality Assurance Metrics for [Process]-[Software]-[Data]-[Managerial] Model

The 4 Quality sectors are Process Quality, Software Quality, Data Quality and Managerial Quality having 9, 14, 9 and 11 parameters respectively as given in Table 1. In total, 43 metrics are there for deciding the quality achievement of an e-Governance project as furnished in Table 1 [7, 22–24].

Table 1. Quality metrics

Process Quality metrics	Software Quality metrics	Data Quality metrics	Managerial Quality metrics
(i) Requirement Analysis	(i) Correctness	(i) Accuracy	(i) Error Handling
(ii) Govt. Process Re-engineering (GPR) Required	(ii) Reliability	(ii) Completeness	(ii) Time Management
(iii) Design & Development	(iii) Efficiency	(iii) Update Status	(iii) Cost Management
(iv) Project Management Planning	(iv) Integrity	(iv) Relevance	(iv) Change Management
(v) Skill Set	(v) Usability	(v) Consistency	(v) Manpower Management
(vi) Implementation Strategy	(vi) Maintainability	(vi) Reliability	(vi) Risk Management
(vii) Maintenance Strategy	(vii) Testability	(vii) Availability	(vii) Maintenance of Team spirit
(viii) Documentation Standards	(viii) Flexibility	(viii) Presentation	(viii) Inter personal Relationship
(ix) Capacity Building	(ix) Longevity	(ix) Accessibility	(ix) Initiative
	(x) Portability		(x) Leadership
	(xi) Scalability		(xi) Ethics
	(xii) Reusability		
	(xiii) Interoperability		
	(xiv) Cyber Security Audit Compliance		

2   Simulation

Simulation theory was first introduced by John Von Neumann and Stanislaw Ulam for studying the behaviour of neutrons in nuclear shielding problem, which was too complex for mathematical analysis. With the remarkable success of this technique in the neutron problem, it became popular in business and industry [10, 26].

In general terms, simulation involves developing a model that closely imitates some real phenomenon and performing experiments with it a sufficiently large number of times, to evolve a usable deduction. The advantage of simulation is that, the real world action can be estimated before putting the decision into practice. Instead of using hunches and intuition to determine what may happen, the analyst using simulation can test and evaluate the various alternatives and select the alternative that gives favourable answer [3, 6].

Steps in Simulation

Step – 1: Definition of the problem along with the statement of objectives.
Step – 2: Collection of appropriate data and data on possible states of outcome.
Step – 3: Construction of an appropriate model for experimentation.
Step – 4: Experimentation with a large number of data, with the constructed model.
Step – 5: Interpretation of the result of simulation [29].

3   Simulation Model for Quality Analysis of e-Governance Projects

The mathematical model of Quality Analysis Simulation is provided in the figure below.

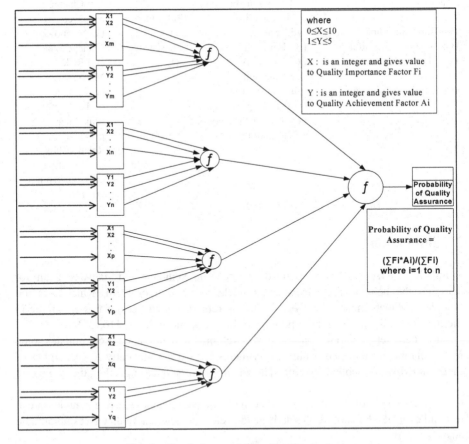

Fig. 3. Simulation model for Quality Analysis

As shown in Fig. 3, the input values for [X1, X2, ... Xm], [Y1, Y2, ..., Ym], ..., [X1, X2, ... Xr], [Y1, Y2, ... , Yr] comes from Random Number generator. The random numbers are generated for the Quality Assurance. Then with mathematical model, the Quality Achievement is calculated for the individual quality sector and the project. Here, the random numbers take the value 0 to 10 for X and 1 to 5 for Y [12, 16].

3.1 Use of Simulation for Study of Quality Assurance of e-Governance Projects

Steps for Using Quality Analysis Simulation

Step – 1: Generate 43 sets of random variables (i, j) where i is for Quality Importance and j is for Quality Achievement; $0 \leq i \leq 10$ and $1 \leq j \leq 5$.

Step – 2: The Quality Importance factor Fi takes the value from 0 to 10, on a 10 points scale and multiply by 10 to find the Quality Importance factor in percentage.

Step – 3: The Quality Achievement factor takes value from 1 to 5, where 1 – Very Low, 2 – Low, 3 – Moderate, 4 – High and 5 – Very High. The Quality Achievement percentages are 0–10%, 10–25%, 25–50%, 50–75% and 75–100% for 1, 2, 3, 4 and 5 respectively. Find the mid point of Quality Achievement Percentage i.e. Ai.

Step – 4: Find Fi * Ai for all Quality Factors.

Step – 5: Calculate $\left(\sum_{i=1}^{n} Fi * Ai\right) / \left(\sum_{i=1}^{n} Fi\right)$ for each category, such as Process Quality, Software Quality, Data Quality and Managerial Quality. Also find the Project Quality for the whole e-Governance project.

Step – 6: Draw graphs.

Step – 7: Stop Simulation.

Explanation of Quality Assurance Calculation for an e-Governance Project

Table 2. Quality importance (10 points scale, 0 to 10)

Sl. no	Quality importance	Quality importance percentage
1	1	10%
2	2	20%
3	3	30%
4	4	40%
5	5	50%
6	6	60%
7	7	70%
8	8	80%
9	9	90%
10	10	100%

Table 3. Quality achievement (5 points scale, 1 to 5)

Sl. no.	Quality achievement	Quality achievement percentage
1	Very Low	0–10%
2	Low	10–25%
3	Moderate	25–50%
4	High	50–75%
5	Very High	75–100%

Source: [25, 32]

A total of 43 metrics are defined for Quality Assurance. Each Quality area such as Process, Software, Data and Managerial is associated with a metric which may be quantitative or qualitative. The Tables 2 and 3 indicate only qualitative parameters. It focusses on quality importance and quality achievement. Quality importance refers to; what extent a particular metric is required. Whereas, Quality achievement means what percentage of quality achievement is actually felt. If it is possible to measure quantitatively then it can be used as such; otherwise, one may use the qualitative measures mentioned in Table 3.

In this study, the Quality Importance Factor (F_i) is taken on a 10-points scale (0 to 10) [25] and the Quality Achievement factor (A_i) is taken as (0–10)% - Very Low, (10–25)% - Low, (25–50)% - Moderate, (50–75)% - High, and (75–100)% - Very High [32].

The 43 factors (Quality Importance on 10 point scale, Quality Achievement on 5 points scale) belonging to Quality Metrics are generated by the Simulation Model for one e-Governance project;

These random parameters are (10,2), (10,2), (10,3), (9,2), (10,3), (10,3), (10,3), (9,1), (9,2), (10,3), (10,3), (9,2), (8,3), (10,3), (10,3), (10,3), (9,2), (9,4), (7,3), (4,1), (8,4), (8,4), (10,2), (10,4), (10,4), (10,3), (9,4), (10,3), (9,3), (8,3), (6,2), (10,2), (10,2), (9,2), (8,3), (9,2), (8,3), (10,2), (5,3), (6,2), (5,3), (7,3) and (7,3).

Calculation of Process Quality:

$(\sum_{i=1}^{n} Fi * Ai)/(\sum_{i=1}^{n} Fi)$, here n = 9.

Thus, Process Quality = (175 + 175 + 375 + 157.5 + 375 + 375 + 375 + 45 + 157.5)/(10 + 10 + 10 + 9 + 10 + 10 + 10 + 9 + 9) = 25.40%.

Similarly, the Software Quality = 36.97%, Data Quality = 42.44%, Managerial Quality = 27.02% and Project Quality = 33.25%.

The graphical representation of these qualities such as Process, Software, Data, Managerial and overall Project Quality for the e-Governance application generated by Simulation Model are shown in Fig. 4. Two graphs are drawn for better presentation of the results.

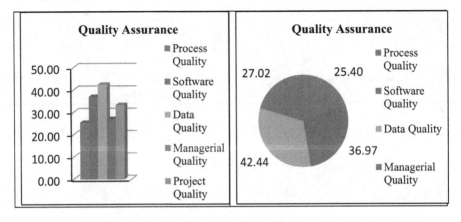

Fig. 4. Quality Assurance of an e-Governance project

3.2 Simulation Model Used for Data Analytics of e-Governance Projects

The study was done for e-Governance projects collecting data from respondents through questionnaire. But, the experiment can give more accurate result if the sample size is high. So, the Simulation Model was run to make the sample size to 404 for the study.

The frequency distribution after Simulation is given in the Tables 4 and 5 below.

Table 4. Observed frequency of simulation for risk and quality

Range	Process Quality	Software Quality	Data Quality	Managerial Quality	Quality Assurance
0–10	0	0	8	4	0
10–20	60	64	80	76	64
20–30	108	140	124	128	120
30–40	92	84	116	132	128
40–50	84	64	56	52	60
50–60	52	44	20	12	32
60–70	8	8	0	0	0
Total	404	404	404	404	404

Source: Simulation Model

The Mean Values of Quality Assurance are given in the table below.

Table 5. Mean value of the simulation

Sl. no.	Quality area	Mean value
1	Process Quality	34.56
2	Software Quality	32.21
3	Data Quality	29.99
4	Managerial Quality	30.1
5	Overall Quality Assurance	31.7

Source: Simulation Model

The larger sample size helps better for Hypothesis testing and other data analysis.

3.2.1 Testing of Hypotheses

The objective of this paper is to find the Quality Assurance and its relationship and impact on e-Governance projects. The Quality Assurance which has the sectors as Process Quality, Software Quality, Data Quality and Managerial Quality, each one has individual impact on the e-Governance applications. These are proved in the Hypothesis testing below.

Significance Level: The Significance level, also denoted as alpha or α, is the proba-bility of rejecting the null hypothesis when it is true. For example, a significance level

0.05 indicates a 5% risk of concluding that a difference exists when there is no actual difference. In entire Hypothesis testing in this chapter 5% significance level, ($\alpha = 0.05$) is taken [13, 14, 18].

Hypothesis – 1 (Chi Square Test)
    Test – 1, The Quality Assurance of a project impacts the successfulness of e-Governance Projects.
    Null Hypothesis: There is no impact of Quality Assurance of a project on successfulness of Electronic Governance applications.
    Alternate Hypothesis: There is impact of Quality Assurance of a project on successfulness of Electronic Governance applications.
    The level of significance is taken as 5%, ($\alpha = 0.05$).

Table 6. Chi Square Test - 1

Range	Observed frequency (O_i)	Expected frequency (E_i)	$(O_i - E_i)^2$	$(O_i - E_i)^2/E_i$
10.001–20	64	67.333	11.10889	0.164984
20.001–30	120	67.333	2773.813	41.19544
30.001–40	128	67.333	3680.485	54.66094
40.001–50	60	67.333	53.77289	0.798611
50.001–60	32	67.333	1248.421	18.541
Total	404	336.665		115.361

Source: Calculated from Simulation data

From the data in Table 6, the Degree of Freedom = 5 – 1 = 4.
The calculated value for
$\chi^2 = \sum(O_i - E_i)^2/E_i = 115.361$, where i = 1 to 5
The Critical value or the Tabulated value of chi-square (obtained from the tables) at level of significance 5% and degree of freedom 4 is 9.49

Conclusion of Hypothesis: Since $\chi^2_{calculated}$ value (i.e. 115.361) is greater than the $\chi^2_{tabulated}$ value (i.e. 9.49), the null hypothesis is rejected. Therefore the Quality Assurance of a project has impact on successful of electronic governance applications.

3.2.2   Use of Simulation Model to Find the Relationship Among Different Quality Sectors

Relationship Between Software Quality and Process Quality
To find the correlation between Software Quality and Process Quality, the following statistical formula for Correlation Coefficient is used.

$\overline{X}$ = (1/n) * $\sum X$ and $\overline{\overline{Y}}$ = (1/n) * $\sum Y$, where n=404

Correlation Coefficient, r(X,Y) = Cov(X,Y)/σ_X σ_Y
=[(1/n)* $\sum XY$ - $\overline{X}$ $\overline{Y}$] / $\sqrt{((1/n\sum X^2 - \overline{X}^2)(1/n\sum Y^2 - \overline{Y}^2))}$

From the simulation, the data are
$\sum X$= 13012.8 and $\overline{X}$= (1/n) * $\sum X$ = 32.2099
$\sum Y$= 13964.24 and $\overline{\overline{Y}}$ = (1/n) * $\sum Y$ = 34.56495
$\sum X^2$ = 489769.1
$\sum Y^2$ = 554324.2
$\sum XY$ = 510954.2

Thus r(X,Y) = [(1/n)* $\sum XY$ - $\overline{X}$ $\overline{Y}$] / $\sqrt{((1/n\sum X^2 - \overline{X}^2)(1/n\sum Y^2 - \overline{Y}^2))}$
=[(1/404)* 510954.2 - 32.2099 * 34.56495] / $\sqrt{((\frac{1}{404} * 489769.1 - (32.2099)^2)(\frac{1}{404} *}$
554324.2 – $(34.56495)^2)$
= **0.859846**

The Co-efficient of Correlation i.e. 0.859846 explains that, the relationship between Software Quality and Process Quality are strongly related [9, 14]. This indicates that, any discrepancy in Process Quality will affect the Software Quality.

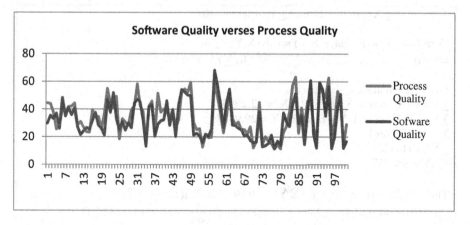

Fig. 5. Software Quality verses Process Quality

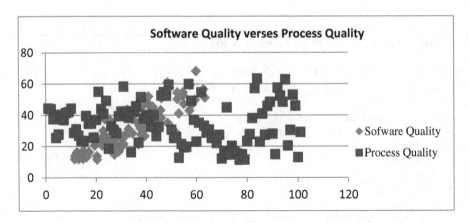

Fig. 6. Scatter diagram for Software Quality verses Process Quality

The Figs. 5 and 6 shows the association between Software Quality and Process Quality. The Correlation Coefficient of 0.859846 indicates that, these two areas are highly correlated. The line graph and scatter diagram also show the interdependency of these two components.

Relationship Between Software Quality and Data Quality

$\bar{X} = (1/n) * \sum X$ and $\bar{Y} = (1/n) * \sum Y$, where n=404

Correlation Coefficient, $r(X,Y) = Cov(X,Y)/\sigma_X \sigma_Y$
$=[(1/n)* \sum XY - \bar{X} \bar{Y}] / \sqrt{((1/n\sum X^2 - \bar{X}^2)(1/n\sum Y^2 - \bar{Y}^2))}$

From the simulation, the data are
$\sum X= 13012.8$ and $\bar{X}= (1/n) * \sum X = 32.2099$
$\sum Y= 12115.48$ and $\bar{Y} = (1/n) * \sum Y = 29.98881$
$\sum X^2 = 489769.1$
$\sum Y^2 = 414121$
$\sum XY = 440157.3$

Thus $r(X,Y) = [(1/n)* \sum XY - \bar{X} \bar{Y}] / \sqrt{((1/n\sum X^2 - \bar{X}^2)(1/n\sum Y^2 - \bar{Y}^2))}$
$=[(1/404)* 440157.3 - 32.2099 * 29.98881] / \sqrt{((\frac{1}{404} 489769.1 - (32.2099)^2)(\frac{1}{404} * 414121 - (29.98881)^2)}$
$= \mathbf{0.833447}$

The Co-efficient of Correlation i.e. **0.833447** explains that, the relationship between Software Quality and Data Quality are positively related [9, 14]. This value is lesser than the value of Software Quality with Process Quality.

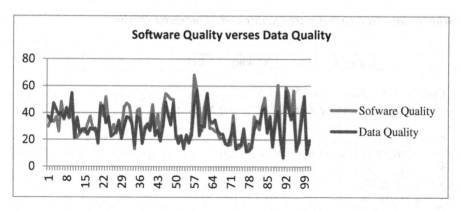

Fig. 7. Relationship between Software Quality verses Data Quality

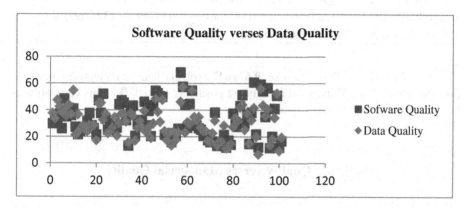

Fig. 8. Scatter diagram for Software Quality and Data Quality

The Figs. 7 and 8 indicates that, the relationship between Software Quality and Data Quality is also very strong. The Correlation co-efficient also proves it.

Relationship Between Software Quality and Managerial Quality

$\bar{X} = (1/n) * \sum X$ and $\bar{Y} = (1/n) * \sum Y$, where n=404

Correlation Coefficient, $r(X,Y) = Cov(X,Y)/\sigma_X \sigma_Y$
$=[(1/n)* \sum XY - \bar{X} \bar{Y}] / \sqrt{((1/n\sum X^2 - \bar{X}^2)(1/n\sum Y^2 - \bar{Y}^2))}$

From the simulation, the data are
$\sum X = 13012.8$ and $\bar{X} = (1/n) * \sum X = 32.2099$
$\sum Y = 12161.2$ and $\bar{Y} = (1/n) * \sum Y = 30.10198$
$\sum X^2 = 489769.1$
$\sum Y^2 = 409167.4$
$\sum XY = 426557.2$

Thus $r(X,Y) = [(1/n)* \sum XY - \bar{X} \bar{Y}] / \sqrt{((1/n\sum X^2 - \bar{X}^2)(1/n\sum Y^2 - \bar{Y}^2))}$
$=[(1/404)* 426557.2 - 32.2099 * 30.10198] / \sqrt{((\frac{1}{404} \ 489769.1 - (32.2099)^2)(\frac{1}{404}}$
$* 409167.4 - (30.10198)^2) = \mathbf{0.631642}$

The Co-efficient of Correlation i.e. **0.631642** explains that, the relationship between Software Quality and Managerial Quality are positively related. But, this correlation is not that strong like the earlier two relations.

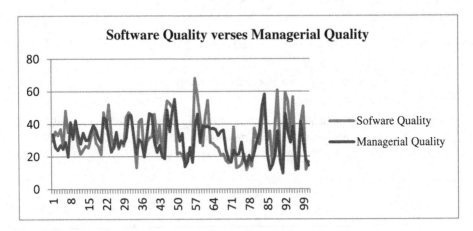

Fig. 9. Relationship between Software Quality and Managerial Quality

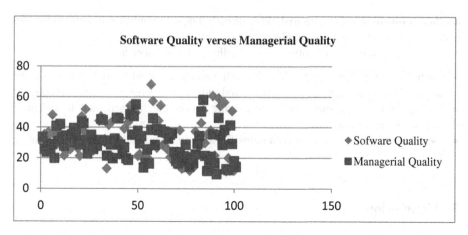

Fig. 10. Scatter diagram of Software Quality and Managerial Quality

The Figs. 9 and 10 show that, Software Quality and Managerial Quality are related. But, from the graphs, it is observed that, the relation is not that strong as it is between Software Quality & Process Quality and Software Quality & Data Quality. The Correlation Co-efficient is also **0.631642**, whereas in the earlier two cases it is more than 0.8.

4   Key Findings of the Paper

Different national and international standard bodies provide quality standards in many areas including software engineering. Some measures initiated by Government of India with respect to quality standards in e-Governance as well certain quality models in practice are discussed below.

The study shows that, Quality assurance is directly related to the success of e-Governance projects. If quality increases, then the quality of e-Governance throughput also increases.

Similarly, different components of quality assurance are also interdependent. The software quality is related to Process quality, Data quality and Managerial quality. The co-relation co-efficient calculated for Software quality to process quality, Data quality and Managerial quality are 0.859846, 0.833447 and 0.631642 respectively. This shows that, the factors are completely related to one another. The graphical representation also show the interdependency of one factor on another.

The National and international approaches require huge documentation and are quite generic in nature. As a result, many times the user is not willing to be involved in the Quality Management System of e-Governance applications. They focus on the error free output only. Rest of the things lies with the developers.

Thus, the Simulation model provides measurable quality to the user to know the percentage of quality achievement. The co-relation between one component with another is quantitatively measured. This directly helps to control the components for better result of e-Governance applications.

In addition to this, some other major findings of this paper are;

- Each quality sector can be focused individually to improve the quality of the application. This helps to examine the individual parameter for improvements.
- The qualitative and quantitative measuring scores can be accepted to calculate quality achievements.
- Generations of huge amount data helps for data analytics and to get more accurate results.

5 Conclusion

The Quality Analysis is one of the major areas in e-Governance applications. As, Information and Communication Technology grows day-to-day, the government is also dependent on this technology. The success of an e-Governance application is dependent on the process, software, data and managerial qualities. The above mentioned study proves that, the Simulation Model used in this paper is surely helpful for government data analytics. The large data helps to experiment the data more accurately. In the above study the association and relationship among Process Quality, Software Quality, Data Quality and Managerial Quality are also measured with large sample size data produced by Simulation model.

Acknowledgements. We are very much thankful to National Informatics Centre which is a pioneer organization in developing and implementing e-Governance applications in India. Further, we are thankful to Government of Odisha and Government of India for providing valuable information in the websites.

References

1. Bache, R., Müllerburg, M.: Measures of testability as a basis for quality assurance. Softw. Eng. J. **5**, 86–92 (1990)
2. Balan, S.: A composite model for software quality assurance (2003)
3. Deo, N.: System Simulation with Digital Computer. PHI, New Delhi (2011)
4. E-Governance Standards. http://egovstandards.gov.in/
5. E-Governance. http://meity.gov.in. Accessed 10 July 2017
6. Fishman, G.S.: Concepts and Methods in Discrete Event Digital Simulation. Wiley, New York (1973)
7. Gilb, T.: Software-Metrics. Stockholm, Sweden (1976)
8. Goel, B.B., Goel, P., Goel, S.: Corporate Governance: Initiative and Reforms
9. Goel, B.S.: Production and Operations Management. Pragati Prakashan, Meerut (1994)
10. Gordon, G.: System Simulation, 2nd edn, pp. 38–52. Prentice Hall of India
11. Government of Odisha. http://odisha.gov.in/
12. Gupta, P.K., Swarup, K., Mohan, M.: Operations Research, 4th Rev. edn, pp. 711–749. Sultan Chand & Sons, Delhi (1988)

13. Gupta, U.G., Clarke, R.E.: Theory and applications of the Delphi technique: a bibliography (1975–1994). Technol. Forecast. Soc. Change **53**, 185–211 (1996)
14. Gupta, S.C., Kapoor, V.K.: Fundamentals of Mathematical Statistics, 11th edn (2002)
15. Gustafson, G.G., Kerr, R.J.: Some practical experience with a software quality assurance program. Commun. ACM **25**(1), 1–9 (1982)
16. Halton, J.H.: A retrospective and prospective survey of the monte carlo method. SIAM Rev. **12**, 1–63 (1970)
17. Land Records "Bhulekh". http://bhulekh.ori.nic.in/
18. Levin, R.I.: Statistics for Management. Prentice-Hall of India, New Delhi (1986)
19. Mall, R.: Introduction to Software Engineering. http://www.scribd.com/doc/14340261/Software-Engineering-Rajib-Mall
20. National Informatics Centre. http://www.nic.in/
21. National Informatics Centre, Odisha, State Project Profile (2017)
22. Patnaik, P., Patra, M.R., Das, R.K.: Quality assurance model for e-governance projects: a case study on e-counselling. In: 6th International Conference on Theory and Practice of Electronic Governance, ICEGOV 2012, Albany, NY, USA, pp. 502–503. ACM Publication, USA (2012). https://doi.org/10.1145/2463728.2463836. ISBN 978-1-4503-1200-4
23. Patnaik, P., Patra, M.R., Panda, S.K.: Quality assurance model for Bhulekh: an e-governance application. In: International Conference on Information Technology, ICIT – 2015, 21–23 December 2015. XIMB, Bhubaneswar. IEEE XPLORE Digital Library (2015). https://doi.org/10.1109/icit.2015.40. ISBN 978-1-5090-0487-4
24. Patnaik, P., Patra, M.R., Pattnaik, S., Mohapatra, A.K.: Software quality assurance of e-governance projects: a case study of Bhulekh, Odisha. Pezottaite J. Int. J. Inf. Technol. Comput. Sci. Perspect. (2017)
25. Pressman, R.S.: Software Engineering, A Practitioner's Approach. McGraw Hill International Editions, pp. 23–30, 42–61, 95–103, 549–594 (1992)
26. Pritsker, A., Alan, B., Pegden, C.D.: Introduction to Simulation and Slam (1979)
27. Quality Assurance Metrics. http://www.eecs.qmul.ac.uk/~norman/papers/qa_metrics_article/section_2_metrics_in_qa_lifecycle1.html
28. Quality Assurance Metrics. http://www.successful-quality-assurance.com/quality-assurance-metrics.html
29. Reitman, J.: Computer Simulation Applications. Wiley, New York (1971)
30. Software Quality Attributes. http://www.qasigma.com/2008/12/how-to-calculate-software-quality-attributes.html
31. Software Quality. http://itmanagement.earthweb.com/entdev/article.php/3827841/Top-Five-Causes-of-Poor-Software-Quality.htm
32. Sommerville, I.: Software Engineering, 8th edn, pp. 28–41, 116–137, 217–231. Pearson
33. Speeches of Dr. A.P.J. Abdul Kalam, Former President of India. http://abdulkalam.nic.in. Accessed 10 July 2018

Author Index

Printed in the United States
By Bookmasters